The First World War
in British History

The First World War in British History

Edited by

Stephen Constantine
Maurice W. Kirby
Mary B. Rose

Edward Arnold
A member of the Hodder Headline Group
LONDON   NEW YORK   SYDNEY   AUCKLAND

First published in Great Britain 1995 by
Edward Arnold, a division of Hodder Headline PLC,
338 Euston Road, London NW1 3BH
175 Fifth Avenue, New York, NY 10010

Distributed exclusively in the USA by
St Martin's Press, Inc.
175 Fifth Avenue, New York, NY 10010, USA

British Library Cataloguing in Publication Data
A catalogue record for this book is available from the British Library

Library of Congress Cataloging-in-Publication Data
The First World War in British History/edited by Stephen
Constantine, Maurice W. Kirby, and Mary B. Rose.
        p.   cm.
Includes bibliographical references and index.
ISBN 0-340-64531-8.—ISBN 0-340-57053-9 (pbk.)
1. World War, 1914–1918—Great Britain—Influence. 2. Great
Britain—History—George V, 1910–1936. 3. Great Britain—
History—20th century. I. Constantine, Stephen. II. Kirby, M. W.
        III. Rose, Mary B.
                DA577.F57   1995
941.083—dc20   94-48337
                                                    CIP

ISBN 0 340 64531 8 (hb)
ISBN 0 340 57053 9 (pb)

1 2 3 4 5   95 96 97 98 99

Typeset in 10/12 pt Baskerville by
Phoenix Photosetting, Lordswood, Chatham, Kent
Printed and bound in Great Britain by J W Arrowsmith Ltd, Bristol

Contents

Contributors

Gail Braybon was a research student at the University of Sussex, was subsequently a computer programmer in Lewes, East Sussex, and is now Computer Officer for the Faculty of Art, Design and Humanities at the University of Brighton. She is the author of *Women Workers in the First World War* (1981) and (with Penny Summerfield) of *Out of the Cage: Women's Experiences in Two World Wars* (1987).

Dr Stephen Constantine is Senior Lecturer in History at the University of Lancaster, where he has been teaching since 1971. His publications include *Unemployment in Britain between the Wars* (1980), *The Making of British Colonial Development Policy 1914–1940* (1984), *Buy and Build: The Advertising Posters of the Empire Marketing Board* (1986) and *Lloyd George* (1992). He has also edited and contributed to *Emigrants and Empire: British Settlement in the Dominions between the Wars* (1990), and he is the editor (with A. O. J. Cockshut) of the bicentenary edition of Edward Gibbon's *Memoirs of My Life and Writings* (1994).

Professor John Gooch, formerly at the University of Lancaster, is now Professor of International History at the University of Leeds. He has published several works on nineteenth- and twentieth-century military history of which the most recent are *Decisive Campaigns of the Second World War* (1990) and (with Eliot A. Cohen) *Military Misfortunes: The Anatomy of Failure in War* (1990). He is chairman of the Army Records Society and joint editor of the *Journal of Strategic Studies*.

Dr Ruth Henig is Senior Lecturer in History at the University of Lancaster, where she has taught since 1968. She has also worked at Liverpool University and for the Open University, and is an awarder with the Oxford and Cambridge Schools Examination Board. She is the author of *The League of Nations* (1973) and of three Lancaster Pamphlets, *Versailles and After* (1984),

The Origins of the Second World War (1985) and *The Origins of the First World War* (1990). She is currently working on a history of Britain and the League of Nations and a modern European history textbook.

Dr Maurice W. Kirby is Reader in Economic History at the University of Lancaster. He previously taught economics and economic history at the Universities of Nottingham, Heriot-Watt and Stirling. His publications include *The British Coalmining Industry, 1870–1946* (1977), *The Decline of British Economic Power since 1870* (1981), *Men of Business and Politics* (1984) and *The Origins of Railway Enterprise: The Stockton and Darlington Railway, 1821–1863* (1993). He is currently writing an economic history of trade and industry in the United Kingdom since 1870.

Dr Rodney Lowe is Reader in Economic and Social History at the University of Bristol. He has twice been awarded the Haldane Medal by the Royal Institute of Public Administration for essays on interwar government. He is also the author of *Adjusting to Democracy* (1986) and of *The Welfare State in Britain since 1945* (1993), plus numerous other articles on related topics.

Dr Gordon Phillips is Senior Lecturer in History at the University of Lancaster where he has been teaching since 1969. His publications include *The General Strike* (1976), *The Rise of the Labour Party, 1893–1931* (1992), (with R. T. Maddock) *The Growth of the British Economy 1918–1968* (1973) and (with Noel Whiteside) *Casual Labour: The Unemployment Question in the Port Transport Industry 1880–1970* (1985). He is currently working on a history of the blind in Britain.

Professor Martin Pugh has been teaching history at the University of Newcastle upon Tyne since 1974. He is the author of *Electoral Reform in War and Peace 1906–18* (1978), *The Making of Modern British Politics 1867–1939* (1982; second edition 1993), *The Tories and the People 1880–1935* (1985), *Lloyd George* (1988), *Women and the Women's Movement in Britain 1914–1959* (1991) and *State and Society: British Political and Social History 1870–1992* (1994).

Dr Mary B. Rose is Senior Lecturer in Business History at the University of Lancaster where she has been teaching since 1978. She is the author of *The Gregs of Quarry Bank Mill: The Rise and Decline of a Family Firm 1780–1914* (1986) and of a number of articles in the general area of business history. She is also the editor of *International Competition and Strategic Response in the Textile Industries since 1870* (1991) and co-editor of *Entrepreneurship, Networks and Modern Business* (1993).

Dr Malcolm Smith is Senior Lecturer in History at St David's University College, University of Wales, Lampeter, where he has been teaching since 1974. He is the author of *British Air Strategy between the Wars* (1984), *British Politics, Society and the State since the Late Nineteenth Century* (1990) and (with

P. Miles) *Cinema, Literature and Society: Elite and Mass Culture in Interwar Britain* (1987), as well as of numerous articles on military and cultural history.

Dr Keith Vernon is a Lecturer in Social History in the School of Historical and Critical Studies at the University of Central Lancashire. He has researched and published in the area of the history of science and medicine, and he is now researching the relationship between science education and industry in the early twentieth century.

Introduction: The War, Change and Continuity

The idea that war might be the 'motor of history' is not exactly new. The organisation of states for the purposes of war may be regarded as at least one characteristic of many societies since antiquity. Moreover, the consequences for historical change of winning and losing battle have been a subject of comment by contemporary observers in all ages and cultures, and by later academic historians. The notion that triumphant as well as disastrous war could mark discontinuities in historical evolution appears to be well respected. Much writing on many periods is greatly concerned with the impact of war.

However, it has been argued that the First World War was qualitatively different from previous international conflicts in that it was the first 'total' war. The war which broke out on 28 July 1914 in the Balkans and which drew in Great Britain on 4 August developed into the first prolonged conflict between modern industrial nations. The fifty-one months that followed, it is suggested, made unprecedented demands upon the resources of the conflicting nations, largely because of the size of the armed forces involved, the weapons they employed, the duration of the conflict and to a lesser degree its geographical spread. As the scale of the war developed and the months and then years elapsed, so the needs of the armed services drew increasingly upon the human and material resources of each nation, upon the technical, organisational and political skills of governments, upon the talents and energies of administrators, labour forces and employers, and even upon those collective values and social resources which were necessary to sustain the effort and to tolerate the cost. Early in the twentieth century, it seemed, war had taken on new characteristics and exerted new demands.

Not surprisingly, contemporaries were often inclined to view the First World War as 'catastrophe'. Here was an unexpected and intolerable experience which was self-evidently destructive, of lives, of material assets, even of moral and cultural values. The First World War was an offence, a shocking affront to those sharing the liberal ethic that had interpreted European (and more generally Western) history as a progressive evolution from destructive barbarism to constructive civilisation. Many writers in the 1920s and 1930s could see only the cost of war, and they were often motivated not least to warn, in vain, against a repetition.[1]

It took perhaps a more bruised later generation after the Second World War to reinterpret the impact of total war in the light of a revitalised optimism stimulated by 1940s progressivism. 'Catastrophe', it was recognised, might sweep away the inappropriate and dysfunctional; challenge might lead to constructive response. Sociological theory recognised how other catastrophes such as natural disasters might be followed by community rebuilding on more fitting social foundations, and this theory was adapted to the notion that total war by its peculiar nature might be especially conducive to constructive consequences. In particular it was argued that certain social groups (especially manual workers and women) whose status was formerly lowly found enhanced value and greater rewards when the demands of total war called upon their participation to an unprecedented extent. Total war, it seemed, valued 'even' the services of social under-classes. As a result, it was suggested, negotiated improvements in status and rewards accrued not only for the duration of periods of total war but also – and this was crucial – with lasting benefits in post-war society either directly, for example in wider and better-paid employment, or by enhanced and better-targeted public services. The thesis obtained its most mechanistic form in the work of Andreski, who devised a 'military participation ratio' to predict the degree of reward accruing to social groups in proportion to the extent of their recruitment into the war effort.[2]

Among the early historical contributors to discussions of the impact of total war on Britain, the most signal and influential was Richard Titmuss, whose work on the official history of welfare services in the Second World War, published as *Problems of Social Policy* in 1950, led him later to write his highly influential and more general essay 'War and social policy', first delivered as a lecture in 1955 and published in his *Essays on 'the Welfare State'* in 1958.[3] These broad ideas then formed the hypothesis which has informed numerous historical works by Arthur Marwick, beginning most importantly with *The Deluge: British Society and the First World War*, first published in 1965. Marwick recognised that the study of history requires the breaking up of the past into periods, but the phases which historians adopt can affect, even distort, their perceptions and their explanations of historical change. Traditionally, historians of nineteenth-century Britain had adopted 1914 as a terminal date. However, Marwick complained that historians also tended to begin studies of

[1] *See*, for example, F. W. Hirst, 1934: *The Consequences of the War to Great Britain.* London: Humphrey Milford; alternatively, readers might recall the judgement of W. C. Sellar and R. J. Yeatman in their memorable *1066 and All That*, first published by Methuen in 1930, which concludes that as a consequence of the First World War 'America was thus clearly top nation, and History came to a .'.
[2] Stanislav Andreski, 1954: *Military Organisation and Society.* London: Routledge & Kegan Paul.
[3] Richard M. Titmuss, 1950: *Problems of Social Policy.* London: HMSO and Titmuss, 1958: *Essays on 'the Welfare State'.* London: Allen & Unwin.

twentieth-century Britain by opening their analyses in 1918. Oddly, historians of both centuries disregarded the war years. In Marwick's view, traditional periodisation therefore ignored what he argued were the formative experiences of total war. It was a theme upon which he was to elaborate in several other notable works, offering, for example, a more specific study in *Women at War, 1914–1918* (1977), a chronologically more extended one in *Britain in the Century of Total War* (1968), and an internationally comparative one in *War and Social Change in the Twentieth Century* (1974).[4]

Marwick has employed the useful notion of 'test, dissolution and transformation' to interpret the impact of total war on Britain. The effort of mobilisation and of sustaining the war economy subjected existing assets, practices and values to rigorous examination, dissolved precedents and preconceptions, and imposed innovation. Following Titmuss, some historians have argued that the war affected society most deeply by permanently increasing the involvement and controlling presence of the state in economic activities and in the provision of social welfare, feeding perhaps a 'corporate bias' which brought the state into partnership with organised industry and labour.[5] Marwick himself, however, has preferred to emphasise with reference to the First World War the more profound unguided social changes which he argues were the largely unexpected consequences of the mobilisation of labour (including womanpower), the demands placed by war upon other economic and financial resources, and the psychological stresses of the conflict, not least on the civilian population. While not denying remaining continuities, Marwick therefore generally regards the First World War as marking a discontinuity in British history. Its legacy was to affect much of the country's subsequent historical evolution – until the Second World War arrived to exert a still greater impact. This arresting interpretation has not gone unchallenged, particularly in its detailed application to specific topics such as the lasting effect of the war on the responsibilities of government, on the economy, on social structure and on the status of women.[6] However, it is no longer the case that historians can be excused from addressing the issues raised.

What the debate has helped clarify is the agenda for discussion.[7] The

[4] Arthur Marwick, 1965: *The Deluge: British Society and the First World War*. London: Macmillan; Marwick, 1977: *Women at War, 1914–18*. Glasgow: Fontana; Marwick, 1968: *Britain in the Century of Total War: War, Peace and Social Change 1900–1967*. London: The Bodley Head; Marwick, 1974: *War and Social Change in the Twentieth Century: A Comparative Study of Britain, France, Germany, Russia and the United States*. London: Macmillan. *See also* his useful introduction to his edited collection, 1988: *Total War and Social Change*. London; Macmillan and Open University course materials for 'War and Society', A301, 1973.

[5] *See* especially Keith Middlemas, 1979: *Politics in Industrial Society: The Experience of the British System since 1911*. London: Deutsch.

[6] *See*, for example, K. Burk (ed.) 1982: *War and the State: The Transformation of British Government 1914–19*. London: Allen & Unwin; Alan Milward, 1984: *The Economic Effects of the Two World Wars on Britain*, 2nd edition. London: Macmillan; Gail Braybon, 1981: *Women Workers in the First World War: The British Experience*. London: Croom Helm; Bernard Waites, 1987: *A Class Society at War: England 1914–18*. Leamington Spa: Berg.

[7] *See also* the chapters in John Turner (ed.) 1988: *Britain and the First World War*. London: Unwin Hyman; and for an excellent critical survey of the literature *see* Keith Grieves, 1990: Britain at war, 1914–1918. *The Historian* 27, 10–12.

chapters in this book are therefore intended to highlight the principal themes. They review some of the existing literature and also take forward the debate with new syntheses or interpretations. The essay by Martin Pugh examines the possible effects of the war upon British politics, considering not only the fortunes of the Liberal, Conservative and Labour Parties, but also the political system itself and the agenda of politics. The argument that the war may have permanently affected the administrative practices and responsibilities of the state is then examined by Rodney Lowe, whose brief also includes, unusually, some consideration of local government. The economic impact of the war domestically was always a concern of contemporaries, and Maurice Kirby examines both the immediate and the long-term effects of the economic mobilisation of industry and agriculture for war purposes, the state's enhanced role in that process, and the involvement of the state in labour relations. As Keith Vernon points out, the military, medical and economic demands of this war also drew upon the nation's scientific and technological resources, and how industry and the public (including the armed) services responded and with what lasting consequences form the subject of his chapter.

The social consequences of the war are examined in the next three chapters. Gordon Phillips explores its impact on population trends, on living standards, on social class and on the operations of voluntary associations. The mobilisation of women into war work was an issue of much contemporary interest and some concern, and Gail Braybon assesses the immediate and lasting consequences of 'women at war'. Social and cultural values were also challenged by the experience of total war, and Malcolm Smith explores the media through which the war was represented and its cultural legacy.

The First World War proved, of course, if it was not already clear, that Great Britain did not exist internationally in comfortable isolation, and the final set of chapters examine the immediate and lasting effects of the war on external interests. John Gooch considers what lessons for future defence were learnt by the armed services by their experiences of total war and by their involvement with continental Europe. Ruth Henig considers whether the outbreak of war, the diplomatic manoeuvres of wartime, the increasingly active involvement of the United States, and the nature of the eventual peace affected lastingly the objectives and methods of British foreign policy. The war inevitably disturbed Britain's functions within the international economy, but whether and how Britain's role and authority were transformed are considered by Mary Rose. The international economy in which Britain operated before 1914 was also in part an imperial one, and the outbreak of war drew in not just Great Britain but the British Empire: in the final chapter Stephen Constantine examines the immediate and lasting consequences for imperial policies and imperial relations.

The impact of the First World War on Britain loses none of its complexity even after the broad issue has been broken down into discrete topics for separate consideration. No one would deny that waging war from 1914 to 1918 necessarily introduced novelties: the tricky issue is to identify and assess the lasting consequences, if any, so as to be able finally to conclude whether the First World War should be regarded as marking a discontinuity in British history. It may therefore be of value to distinguish formally the various ways in which the war's impact may be conceptually approached: a concise listing of the alternatives, for subsequent reference, may assist in the reading of the following chapters (and other related literature) and in the assessment of some necessarily complex data and arguments.

1. The war might be regarded as a cataclysmic event. By this assessment, the requirements of total war were unprecedented and its consequences were lasting. The impact might be wholly negative and destructive or it might have led to positive and constructive responses, but by either judgement it enforced or made possible radical changes. The war would then be regarded as innovatory and would mark a major discontinuity in British history.
2. A milder hypothesis might still claim that the war caused change, but it would acknowledge that certain pre-war developments prefigure wartime consequences and that the true impact of the war was to accelerate, rapidly but perhaps along predictable lines, the trajectory of development.
3. By contrast, the consequences of the war might be interpreted as negative in their effects, in practice blocking lines of expected historical change or inhibiting prepared innovations.
4. On the other hand, the claim might be advanced that though the war was for its duration rich in innovation, its impact was confined largely to the months of conflict. It would follow that political, administrative, economic, social or even cultural novelties in the war years were effectively ended or reversed with the coming of peace. This would seem to turn the war into a unique event, confined in its impact to a few years and perhaps setting no precedents for later historical changes.
5. By contrast, even if it were accepted that most of the innovations demanded by war were reversed subsequently, it could be argued that knowledge of wartime practices could not be eliminated. Precedents had been established which might be employed on some later occasion when Great Britain was again subjected to stress, perhaps during the Great Depression or more obviously with the outbreak in 1939 of another total war.
6. This last comment suggests one final interpretive approach. There may be something problematic about identifying the First World War as a major turning-point in British history if the Second World War is also to be so regarded. Identifying two turning-points in close proximity may seem to debase the term. Whether it is appropriate even to describe the Second World War in such terms is, of course, another (and debated) issue,[8] but the outbreak of another total war within a generation suggests that judgements on the impact of the First World War may also gain by comparison.

[8] *See,* for example, Harold L. Smith (ed.) 1986: *War and Social Change: British Society in the Second World War.* Manchester: Manchester University Press.

It is not the intention of the editors with the schema above or of the authors in the chapters below to deny the complexity and the ambiguity of responses to the war. Indeed, in detail, the impact of an experience so multifaceted as the First World War upon a social organism so complex and plural as Great Britain invalidates simple statements. Generalisation needs to be built up by precise judgements on different elements. It may therefore help assessment to list some of the different components of British society which the war may have affected, to varying degrees.

1. It is starkly obvious that at the level of the individual the war had some shockingly cataclysmic effects. For the 723 000 British soldiers killed in the fighting (not to mention Empire contingents), plus those merchant seamen and civilians killed at sea, in air raids and in coastal bombardments by the German navy, the war marked the ultimate discontinuity in their personal history. In addition, for many individual survivors, the legacy of the war remained immediate for the rest of their lives, especially for the 1.2 million British ex-servicemen who subsequently received disability pensions but also arguably for all those who served in or with the armed forces (including medical staff). However, individual experiences become more varied and not necessarily so painful when civilian war workers are also taken into account, including many employed (though not inevitably all) in more rewarding jobs and sometimes in new places.

2. But society is made up not just of individual atoms but of families, embracing the overwhelming majority of people, and the impact of the war upon such molecules brings in different equations of loss and gain, to encompass the grieving widow and fiancée, the desolated parents, the fatherless children, those left to nurse the broken in body and mind – but also those maybe bathed in reflected glory or relishing higher family incomes owing to war-induced economic change, in the immediate or even longer term.

3. Individuals may also be collected under other generalising labels. That war experiences varied according to gender is a truism, though the predominant effect upon women has prompted extended research and, as noted, lively debate. (Curiously, the impact of the war on masculinity has been less prominently addressed.[9]) Also obvious, though less studied, are age cohorts: individual experiences and their lasting consequences inevitably varied between the young and the old.

4. Moreover, individuals and families, men and women, the young and the old, belong to and respond to a variety of other social contexts, and the war might have another impact, immediate or in the long term, upon those other units. That impact might differ from the individual's personal experience. For example, residential communities from village to city experienced war collectively, and variously. The shared losses were recorded formally in war memorials, and maybe too in a collective memory affecting

[9] Though *see* Jock Phillips, 1987: *A Man's Country? The Image of the Pakeha Male – a History.* Auckland: Penguin Books.

future actions.[10] On the other hand, war work may have been an economic stimulus locally, engendering local prosperity albeit perhaps of uncertain duration. Generalisations about the impact of the war need to take locality into account.

5. Likewise, individuals cohered in economic units, as employees or employers, operating within particular businesses, and they were variously affected, directly or not, temporarily or permanently, by the exigencies of war. The war's impact may be judged differently for such collectivities as compared with the individuals who composed them, and the dynamics of economic activity may have had a controlling influence only marginally affected by war.

6. There are, of course, other groups within society who may also have had distinctive collective experiences, such as church members, sporting clubs and cultural bodies. 'Their war' and its legacy may have a different history, also worth tracing separately.

7. Historians have, of course, addressed the impact of the war on still larger social units, however problematic the terms and fragmented the data. British society was undoubtedly inegalitarian in structure and seemingly divided by social class. Not only might the war affect different social classes in different ways and to different degrees (affecting perhaps their comparative wealth, values, status, aspirations and political power), but it follows that relations between social classes might also be disturbed. On the other hand, social classes with their accumulated practices and values may have been more resilient to shock than individuals, and inherited collective assumptions may have been a comforting resource and a drag on change in a world disturbed by war and loss.

8. Demands for change or for restoration were likely to find expression in still other large collective operations, namely through the mechanics of political parties and electoral choice, locally as well as nationally. The impact of the war on politics is a necessary part of this subject's agenda, but there may be currents of continuity or of change in politics running at variance with other social experiences. We cannot assume, at least, either that politics merely reflected war-induced social and economic change, or that politics itself determined or guided socio-economic forces.

9. Likewise, we cannot assume that continuity or change at the level of the state is a perfect reflection of socio-economic conditions. In its own terms, the effect of the war upon the state is a subject of necessary importance, but it would be rash to assume that its history, in an inegalitarian and pluralistic society, is coterminous with the history of the British people or of the impact of the First World War upon them. Moreover, it would be unwise to assume that even substantial changes in government marked discontinuities in other aspects of national experience. Not even revolution in Russia,

---

[10] Geoffrey Moorhouse, 1992: *Hell's Foundations: A Town, its Myths and Gallipoli* London: Hodder & Stoughton, argues that appalling losses in Bury subsequently affected recruiting in the Second World War.

Germany and Austria-Hungary during the war transformed all their other national characteristics, and by comparison in the British case the continuities in government through the war years are self-evident.

The above listing indicates some at least of the domestic elements which are subsumed within the term 'Great Britain'. The hierarchy presented is certainly not intended to show a rising order of importance. Rather it serves to invite a plural approach to the assessment of the war's effect: what may be true at one level may be countered by different experiences elsewhere. Nor is the listing intended to deter generalisation: rather, it merely suggests the need for a strict attention to terms when the issues of continuity and change in British history at the time of the First World War are being debated.

1

Domestic Politics

Martin Pugh

At first sight the case for regarding the First World War as a radical discontinuity in British politics seems overwhelming. Over the years, authors and publishers have underlined this view by choosing 1914, 1915 or 1918 as the starting or stopping point for their books. Contemporaries had the same instinct; by adopting phrases like 'the Great War' and 'the war to end war' they indicated that the events of 1914 marked an end and a new beginning. Well before the conclusion of hostilities, politicians frankly admitted that many of the familiar features of political life had been obliterated by the war. Certain changes, in the shape of the rise of Sinn Fein and the Labour Party, were already taken for granted. But more novel developments were widely anticipated in 1918: for example, a Women's Party stimulated by female enfranchisement, and a National or Centre Party founded on the success of Lloyd George's Coalition Government.

Although contemporary hopes and fears often failed to materialise, we are still left with evidence of the drastic impact of these years. The Liberals, dominant since 1906, became bitterly divided between Asquith and Lloyd George and ceased to be a party of government. Labour achieved a new status both by entering the cabinet in 1915 and by occupying the Opposition front bench in 1918, a position from which, despite many vicissitudes, it was not subsequently dislodged. The political battlefield became littered with casualties in the shape of wrecked careers: those of Asquith, Sir John Simon, Winston Churchill, Ramsay MacDonald and John Redmond, not to mention hundreds of lesser figures defeated at the 1918 election. Nor did political institutions escape unscathed. The normal Cabinet found itself by-passed by Lloyd George's War Cabinet of five members after December 1916. The Prime Minister's role increased greatly with the help of his personal secretariat, extra government patronage and an extended honours system. At the same time the role of the House of Commons dwindled, partly because many MPs were absent on war work, and also because of the lack of information about policy-making and the exploitation of the press by political leaders appealing to the country over the heads of the backbenchers.

Yet this impression of a radically changed political landscape requires several qualifications. Some of the shifts associated with wartime actually had their origins in earlier periods. For example, the decline of the backbencher and the aggrandisement of prime ministerial power are long-term trends which go back to the late Victorian era and have continued to the present day.[1] In this perspective the war did no more than accelerate the existing pattern.

Conspicuous discontinuities in party politics sometimes seem deceptive on closer inspection. One working-class socialist, triumphantly elected to Durham County Council just after the war, was disconcerted to find, already entrenched on the Labour bench, several of the former Liberals he had fought against in the Edwardian period.[2] The careers, even of national figures, sometimes managed to rise from the ashes: Simon, Churchill and MacDonald all enjoyed high office subsequently and under modified party labels.

Moreover, when seen in the context of the other belligerents, Britain's political system emerged relatively unscathed from war. While crowned heads were falling across Europe, King George V remained fairly secure in public affection and headed serenely towards his Silver Jubilee in 1935. Although the years from 1917 to 1920 witnessed a huge rise in strikes, the appearance of 'Soviets' and a flirtation with 'direct action' among some left-wing opponents of the Coalition Government, nothing occurred that was comparable to the revolutionary developments in Germany and France. As in 1830, 1848 and 1871, while much of Europe became engulfed in political convulsions, the British phlegmatically adjusted their parliamentary system by extending the vote to several million men and women under the Representation of the People Act, a timely consolidation of the existing system.

Clearly, first impressions do not tell us the whole story about the impact of war; it is not always easy to distinguish discontinuity from continuity in British politics. In what follows we will attempt to assess the impact of the war by reference to three distinct criteria: first, the distribution of power between political parties; second, the underlying structure of politics; and third, the effect upon the agenda of politics in Britain.

Party Politics: The Decline of the Liberal Party

Traditionally, students of high politics and political biographers have been attracted to the First World War because of the crucial struggle for power that took place within the parliamentary élite. In this perspective the argument is not so much whether the war represented a major discontinuity, but whether it was *the* key discontinuity in modern British history. One of the most readable and influential such accounts was Trevor Wilson's analysis of the dilemmas faced by the Liberal Party.[3] In this, Liberalism was graphically depicted as a

[1] Bruce Lenman, 1992: *The Eclipse of Parliament.* London: Edward Arnold.
[2] I am grateful to Norman McCord for this example.
[3] Trevor Wilson, 1966: *The Downfall of the Liberal Party, 1914–1935.* London: Collins.

healthy individual knocked down by a rampant omnibus from which he sustained major injuries and eventually expired. The idea of the war as a great tragedy for Liberalism, as indicated by the decline in the party's strength shown in Table 1.1, provides a useful organising theme for dealing with the politics of the period.

Table 1.1   The Decline in Liberal Strength

	1906	*1910* (*Jan.*)	*1910* (*Dec.*)	*1918*		*1922*	*1923*	*1924*
				(i)	(ii)			
Candidates	539	516	467	253	158	490	453	340
MPs	400	275	272	28	133	116	159	40
Vote(%)	49.0	43.2	43.8	12.1	13.5	29.1	29.6	17.6

(i) Supporters of Asquith; (ii) supporters of Lloyd George.

Since 1906 many radical Liberals had struggled to stem the drift of British foreign policy which was leading to alliance with France and Tsarist Russia, and to avert the deterioration of relations with Germany and the naval race that this entailed. In a famous polemic in 1910 Norman Angell had warned that an international war would be disastrous for the whole Cobdenite system of free trade; the economic effects of modern war would be as damaging for the victors as for the vanquished.[4] Not surprisingly, in August 1914 many Liberals regarded Britain's entry into war as a defeat for them. Even ministers like Grey and Asquith, who felt certain that it was in Britain's national interest to prevent another French defeat at the hands of Germany, were depressed at the turn of events. A few, including John Morley, John Burns and Charles Trevelyan, resigned from the Government; others, such as Sir John Simon, agonised and remained in office, but seemed unable to adjust to the new situation.

For nearly nine months Asquith's Government continued to hold office. But although it had dealt successfully with the key strategic problem – preventing the fall of Paris – it was steadily undermined by partisan attack. In the absence of any conspicuous victory on sea or land the Government inevitably lost authority. It proved only too easy for Sir John French, the Commander-in-Chief in France, to put the blame for his own lack of success on an inadequate supply of munitions from home. The clash between politicians and professionals exploded dangerously in May 1915 when Sir John Fisher resigned as First Sea Lord in protest at the way in which Churchill had bulldozed the Dardanelles campaign through the Cabinet over his own reservations. Such rows would not have proved terminal for Asquith's Liberal Government but for the looming threat of a wartime general election. The last one had been

[4] Norman Angell, 1910: *The Great Illusion.* London: Heinemann.

held in December 1910, but the Parliament Act of 1911 had shortened Parliament's life to five years; thus by the spring of 1915 time was beginning to run out.

Asquith resolved the immediate problem rather neatly by attracting the Conservative leader, Andrew Bonar Law, and his colleagues into a coalition government.[5] However, for the Liberal Party the cure proved to be much worse than the original complaint. The new coalition failed to command much loyalty in either party. The Conservatives believed their leaders had been hoodwinked by the cunning Asquith into accepting responsibility for his incompetent policies. The Liberals felt badly let down by their leaders, blamed Churchill and Lloyd George for the controversy and intrigue that had led to coalition, and feared that the war would in future be conducted by 'Prussian' methods not by liberal ones.

Above all, the coalition suffered from a succession of military setbacks over the next eighteen months: a humiliating retreat from the Dardanelles, horrendous casualties in the Somme campaign of 1916, and a growing menace to British shipping and food supplies from German submarine warfare. This culminated in December 1916, when Lloyd George, Bonar Law and others presented an ultimatum to Asquith for a reorganisation of the machinery for running the war. This initiative was partly the product of the Tory leader's perennial problem in controlling his own backbenchers, who really wanted to drive the Liberals out of office altogether. As in 1915 Law determined to frustrate them by finding a more effective approach to the war. The ultimatum also reflected the personal frustration felt by Lloyd George since he had been made Secretary of State for War. As Minister of Munitions he had succeeded triumphantly in imposing his ideas and achieving dramatic results, but as War Minister he found himself unable to make much headway against the military establishment.

In the event, Asquith decided to call the bluff of his critics by resigning. This was shrewd in the sense that the Conservative leaders remained unwilling to form a purely Conservative government because they seemed unlikely to be able to command authority with the Labour movement, whose cooperation now seemed essential to the war effort. Asquith could therefore expect to be invited to form a new coalition. But he miscalculated in the sense that he underestimated the Tories' dissatisfaction with his Government, their ambition for high office and their willingness to serve under any other prime minister who would offer them power. After some days of confabulation and consultation Lloyd George managed to patch up a majority of support in the House of Commons and accepted the royal invitation to become Prime Minister.[6]

However, although Lloyd George rapidly appeared to become the dominat-

[5] Cameron Hazelhurst, 1971: *Politicians at War*. London: Cape; Martin Pugh, 1974: Asquith, Bonar Law and the first coalition. *Historical Journal* 17, 813–36.
[6] For a good recent account of these events, *see* John Turner, 1992: *British Politics and the Great War: Coalition and Conflict 1915–1918*. New Haven, Conn.: Yale University Press, 112–51.

ing force and certainly held the premiership until 1922 as a result of his victory at the election of December 1918, he was never as secure or powerful as he appeared to be. A majority of Liberals at Westminster, and even more in the constituencies, continued to support Asquith, who remained party leader; some, even in 1916, saw Lloyd George as a traitor. Labour's membership of the coalition was essentially a matter of expediency: Lloyd George offered the Labour Party new ministries for Labour and Pensions, and a general influence over policy. When Arthur Henderson, the leading Labour parliamentarian, was effectively sacked from the War Cabinet in the summer of 1917, the party virtually withdrew from the coalition and prepared to fight an election independently. Consequently Lloyd George was critically dependent upon Bonar Law and the loyalty of the Conservative members. Yet by and large they continued to regard him as a devious radical upstart; they would put up with him only while it seemed necessary to win the war. As a result, the Prime Minister's majority was never a reliable one; its party composition was apt to fluctuate from one division to the next. Nor did Lloyd George enjoy any more immunity than Asquith to military failure and challenges from discontented generals. He nearly came to grief in the summer of 1918 when General Sir Frederick Maurice accused him of withholding troops from the Western Front; as the German offensive broke through British lines at this stage and nearly brought the war to an abrupt end, Lloyd George was clearly very vulnerable. He survived partly because the full truth about the number of troops at the front was not made known and because the Tories were loath to destroy Lloyd George if that meant restoring Asquith.

Why Did the Liberals Decline?

If the broad shift of power away from the Liberals to the benefit of the Conservatives is fairly clear, the interpretation of the effect of the war is more complicated. One important question concerns the relative significance to be given to the war. Most of the readers of Wilson's book, for example, assumed that he began in 1914 because he attributed Liberal decline primarily to the war. But when a second edition appeared Wilson went out of his way to deny this; he had simply intended to tell the story of the decline in a given period and had included the 1914–18 section only as an afterthought to the original plan. In short, Wilson did not rule out the traditional view that even in its Edwardian heyday the Liberal Party was already suffering from deep-seated problems in coming to terms with the working class and the rise of a Labour Party. Clearly, for those historians who do adopt the view that Labour was already in the process of replacing the Liberals before 1914 it follows that the significance of the war must be diminished; it might be seen as accelerating an existing pattern of change rather than initiating one. Though still important, the war would represent a less sharp discontinuity. Conversely, historians who argue that the Liberals had successfully adapted their programme to working-class politics necessarily regard the war as the key cause of the party's down-fall.[7]

A second question that arises directly out of Wilson's analysis concerns the manner in which the war made its impact on the Liberals. Broadly, there are two lines of explanation here. Wilson placed much emphasis on the destructive effect of wartime on the ideas and the creed of Liberalism. The alternative approach stresses the large element of contingency or accident at work.

Essentially the contingency thesis rests upon a number of decisions, or errors, made by the leading figures. It would, of course, be a mistake to think that the Liberals got everything wrong, and to that extent Wilson's doom-laden account misleads. Asquith scored a notable triumph in taking Britain into the war while keeping all but two minor Cabinet members behind him and while maintaining a considerable – and unexpected – degree of unity in the party and the country. The appointment of Lord Kitchener in 1914 as Secretary of State for War was a typically skilful move, and the agreement to impose a party truce in by-elections and to suspend the controversial legislation for Irish Home Rule and Welsh Church disestablishment relieved much of the pressure on the Government.

However, Asquith was sometimes too clever by half. His speedy conclusion of an agreement to replace the Liberal Government with a coalition in 1915 represented a crucial error from the party's point of view. Indeed, the news very nearly provoked a revolt by backbench MPs, and from this time onwards Asquith's authority began to slip. The coalition greatly facilitated co-operation between Lloyd George and the Conservatives over issues such as conscription, co-operation that eventually led to the split of December 1916. There has always been some dispute as to who was responsible for the split in the Liberal ranks during the war. Wilson's account is very biased against Lloyd George and clearly suffers from hindsight. Lloyd George's premiership led him to fight the 1918 election in alliance with the Conservatives, and this formalised the split in the party and reduced the Asquithian Liberals to a mere twenty-eight seats. However, Lloyd George's biographers have corrected the balance.[8] In the early years of the war, Lloyd George's conspicuous success at Munitions was an asset to the Liberals when under attack over their handling of the war. It is now clear that he did not plot to deprive Asquith of the premiership. The errors often came from Asquith himself, who neglected Bonar Law and failed to treat the Conservatives fairly in the allocation of offices; he also made a habit of embroiling Lloyd George in what looked like intractable problems – munitions, Ireland and the War Office. Moreover, it was Asquith's stubborn refusal to serve in a coalition after December 1916 that condemned the Liberal Party to division. What is beyond dispute is the damaging conse-

[7] For the former interpretation, *see* Ross McKibbin, 1974: *The Evolution of the Labour Party 1910–1924.* Oxford: Oxford University Press; for the latter, *see* Peter Clarke, 1971: *Lancashire and the New Liberalism.* Cambridge: Cambridge University Press.

[8] *See* John Grigg, 1985: *Lloyd George: From Peace to War 1912–1916.* London: Methuen; Peter Rowland, 1975: *Lloyd George.* London: Barrie & Jenkins.

quences of the 1918 election result. For not only did the Liberals cease to be one of the two main parties and thus lose their hold on government, but the election generated a bitter quarrel which kept the party divided until 1923. Even then the reunion of the two wings was only nominal. Meanwhile, the Liberals decisively lost ground in the constituencies to their Labour rivals.

Important as all this may be, it can be argued that dwindling Liberal fortunes cannot be explained entirely in terms of misjudgements, accidents and personalities. An alternative, strongly emphasised by Wilson, suggests that the ideology of Liberalism was basically unable to cope with the pressures of a mass war. If so, then the divisions within the parliamentary leadership could be seen as symptoms of the underlying dilemma rather than as the cause of decline.

How far can such a view be substantiated? It is certainly plausible that traditional elements in the popular Liberal appeal such as Nonconformity, temperance or free trade were becoming irrelevant or being discredited in this period. But the evidence is very wide-ranging and distinctly mixed. For example, free trade and cheap food continued to be an important vote winner for both the Liberals and Labour during the 1920s; it would be a mistake to assume that Labour outflanked the Liberals by a wholly novel programme. Yet it has sometimes been suggested that as the war effort required major extensions of state intervention it exposed the limitations of Liberalism and drove its spokesmen back into a negative *laissez-faire* attitude.[9] There are, however, several flaws in this claim. Before 1914 the Liberals had set the pace in moving away from Gladstonian economic and social policies; and during the war major government initiatives in housing and education were the work of Liberals. If the pressures of state interventionism had been so serious, one might have expected the Conservatives to show the strain even more than the Liberals.

On the other hand, the emphasis on the Liberal creed has more plausibility if one makes the distinction between social–economic issues and political–legal causes. Many Liberals felt profoundly unhappy about the extension of state power in the form of press censorship, the Defence of the Realm Act, military conscription, the incarceration of enemy aliens and the disenfranchisement of conscientious objectors. In so far as wartime chauvinism and emotionalism undermined respect for civil liberties it was certainly inimical to the individualist traditions of Liberalism. Several disillusioned radicals such as Charles Trevelyan and Arthur Ponsonby joined the anti-war Union of Democratic Control at an early stage in the war, but were repudiated by their local constituency parties and eventually joined the Labour Party. A serious gulf opened up between those who wished to run the war by Liberal principles and the more patriotic Liberals who were determined to take whatever steps were necessary to achieve complete victory. This spirit was epitomised by Lloyd

[9] A. J. P. Taylor was partly responsible for introducing this distinction; *see* A. J. P. Taylor, 1964: *Politics in Wartime.* London: Hamish Hamilton, 1964; for a corrective *see* E. I. David, 1970: The Liberal Party divided 1916–18. *Historical Journal* 13, 509–32.

George in his pioneering work at Munitions in 1915, his advocacy of conscription in 1916 and his insistence on landing the 'knock-out blow' on Germany rather than seeking a negotiated peace.

Yet, as G. R. Searle has pointed out, there are limitations even to these claims.[10] Wilson concentrated on the parliamentary party, and his picture of declining morale was influenced by a small number of radical members. When the focus is shifted to the country, which it has not often been, it appears that Liberals were largely willing to swallow emergency wartime measures from Asquith and remained fairly united throughout the war.[11] In this perspective the real blow suffered by the party was the election of 1918 rather than the kind of ideological crisis suggested by Wilson.

It is not possible to reach a satisfactory conclusion about this particular argument unless it is placed in the context of the other parties' wartime experiences and the development of the political debate after the war. Were the Liberals, in fact, inescapably outflanked as their opponents adapted more successfully to new issues raised by the war? To some extent all the parties were divided by the pressures of wartime. Labour, with an ideological range similar to that of the Liberals, experienced the tensions between win-the-war patriots and anti-war pacifists, though the effects on the party proved to be much less serious because the movement enjoyed alternative outlets which helped to maintain unity. The Conservatives suffered acute internal arguments, as the pressures on Bonar Law show. Issues such as protectionism and the colonies, Ireland and the strategic debate between 'westerners' and 'easterners' proved very troublesome. The Right also had to swallow a good many unpalatable measures including higher income tax, interference with private property rights, and sweeping electoral reforms. But the worst dilemma was that endured by the Irish Nationalists, who were eventually eclipsed by more radical rivals. In this context it is not clear that the Liberals were uniquely or even especially undermined by the pressures of wartime policies.

The Impact of War: The Irish, Labour and the Conservatives

Much of the discussion about the political impact of the war has focused upon the relative positions of the Liberals and Labour, the decline of the former being seen as closely bound up with the rise of the latter. But this is to miss the fundamental impact on the broad pattern of politics. This becomes clear only if one compares the Edwardian political configuration with that of the 1920s. Although the pre-1914 Government was exclusively a Liberal one, Asquith depended for his majority on the support of eighty Irish MPs and forty-two

[10] G. R. Searle, 1992: *The Liberal Party: Triumph and Disintegration, 1886–1929.* London: Macmillan, 132–6.
[11] G. L. Bernstein, 1989: Yorkshire Liberalism during the First World War. *Historical Journal* 32, 107–29.

Labour members. Since 1903 Labour and the Liberals had operated an electoral pact designed to avoid splitting the anti-Conservative vote in a limited number of constituencies. As a result the Conservatives had been defeated in three general elections, and although their share of the vote had risen to 46 per cent by 1910 they would still have had to make a net gain of around sixty seats to win a majority, a goal they appeared unlikely to achieve while the three-party radical alliance held.

The war rescued the Conservatives by decisively breaking up this alliance. The crucial step in this direction was undoubtedly the formation of the first coalition in May 1915. Asquith would have been better advised to form a coalition with Labour and the Irish; even before the war the idea of giving Labour some representation in the Cabinet had been seriously considered. But by including the Conservatives, Asquith was, in effect, turning his back on the formula that had brought success, though at the time the full significance was, no doubt, not apparent. Redmond, the Irish leader, who had given generous backing to Britain's decision to enter the war, declined to join the coalition largely because of the inclusion of Sir Edward Carson, one of the leading Unionist opponents of the Home Rule Bill. Now this legislation, which required only the royal assent in August 1914, had been suspended for the time being. A change in the composition of the Government fatally undermined the Home Rule Bill and Redmond's entire strategy.[12] He and his party had patiently played the parliamentary game on the assumption that the Liberal Government would have no option but to see the legislation through. Once Asquith had allowed the Tories into the Cabinet it became unlikely that the Bill would be resurrected; and when Lloyd George succeeded as prime minister the Conservatives exercised a virtual veto over Irish questions. This situation totally destroyed the standing of the Home Rule Party. After the Easter Rising in 1916, anti-parliamentary forces began to gain the upper hand in Ireland so that by the time of the election in 1918 Redmond's supporters were largely swept aside by the Sinn Fein candidates.

Labour's tactics were different, but the outcome for the Edwardian alliance was very similar. Once the party had joined the Government in 1915 its relationship with the Liberals began to change. For one thing, the Labour Party rightly sensed that the invitation to join reflected the enhanced status of the Labour movement. Also, it was freed from any obligation to support Asquith or the Liberal programme. This was even more true when Lloyd George took over; Labour could feel no particular loyalty to him and participated only because on balance the advantages seemed to outweigh the drawbacks. By 1917 Labour was ready to take the risk – hitherto judged too great – of abandoning electoral co-operation and fighting on a broad front. By that stage there was no prospect of the Liberals putting their Edwardian strategy back together again.

[12] J. M. McEwen, 1972: The Liberal Party and the Irish Question during the First World War. *Journal of British Studies* 12.

These developments underline a simple but easily overlooked point. Whatever conclusions are reached about the extent to which the war may have undermined the Liberals and helped Labour, there can be little doubt that the prime beneficiaries were the Conservatives. At a stroke, the Progressive Alliance that had excluded them from power had been broken up. From 1918 onwards the Labour and Liberal parties fought each other in three-cornered contests. Thus, although the Conservatives often polled only 40 per cent or less of the national vote in the 1920s, they were always the largest party in Parliament except in 1929, won comfortable majorities at every election between the wars except in 1923 and 1929, and dominated government for twenty years.

Historians have paid much less attention to the success of the Conservatives than to the problems of their rivals.[13] However, it is possible to throw some light on how the party coped with the pressures of wartime. As with the other parties, the frustration among the parliamentarians was balanced by a great deal of activity in the country. From the outbreak of war, rank-and-file Conservatives enthusiastically engaged in patriotic war work for charities and official committees. This gave the party a sense of purpose that was lacking in the Liberal ranks. At the national level the steady increase in Conservative influence had some implications for party policy. For example, in 1915 the Liberals breached free trade by imposing some special revenue-raising duties. Moreover, the gap left by the suspension of imports from Germany promoted the growth of certain infant industries. This gave fresh momentum to the case for protectionism, which had left the Conservatives rather divided in the last years of peace. They managed to commit the Lloyd George coalition to a tariff policy in the form of the Safeguarding of Industries Act of 1921. To this extent the war helped to relieve, if not entirely resolve, the party's previous dilemma over tariff reform.

On the other hand, the Tories' enthusiasm for the war effort led them into dangerous areas. The state imposed controls on private industry and farmers, rent increases were restricted, the Treasury lost control of the Budget, income tax was raised to six shillings (thirty pence) in the pound, and the huge increase in the national debt made it essential to keep postwar taxation at a much higher level than it had been even under Lloyd George's Edwardian budgets. One of the least-noticed developments of wartime was the extension of the income tax net. This was partly because the limit for tax liability was lowered from £160 to £130 annual income, and because increases in wage rates carried many people over the threshold.

Similarly, the Conservatives' success in pushing for military conscription –

---

[13] But *see* John Ramsden, 1978: *The Age of Balfour and Baldwin 1902–40*. London: Longman; J. O. Stubbs, 1975: The impact of the Great War on the Conservative Party. In G. Peele and C. Cook (eds), *The Politics of Reappraisal.* London: Macmillan, 14–38; Robert Blake, 1955: *The Unknown Prime Minister.* London: Eyre & Spottiswoode; D. Rubinstein, 1974: Henry Page-Croft and the National Party 1917–22. *Journal of Contemporary History* 9, 129–48; Turner, *British Politics*, op. cit. (note 6).

something they had shrunk from doing before 1914 – had both economic and political implications. Though they had joined Asquith's coalition they refused to rule out the possibility of a general election during wartime. Unfortunately, because of the need for twelve months' residence, many voters had lost their right to vote after moving either to take up civilian war work or to join the forces. Conservatives felt strongly that an election ought not to be held until the electoral registration system had been modified so as to allow these patriotic workers to qualify.[14] But in effect this reopened the whole question of parliamentary reform: it resulted in a sweeping set of proposals generated by the Speaker's Conference of 1916–17, which included universal adult suffrage for men, a drastic reduction in plural voting (from which the Conservatives had benefited), and the partial enfranchisement of women. Conservatives obviously had mixed feelings about all this. Some took the view that they had been hoodwinked by the radicals. Others derived comfort from the effect of wartime experience in stimulating the patriotism of the working class. Lords Salisbury and Selborne had tried to pressure Asquith into conceding the franchise for active soldiers. 'I think these men will be an immense support to us for many years to come against radical and Liberal insanity in the matter of foreign policy, navy etc.', observed Selborne.[15]

However, in the circumstances of 1918 the huge new electorate of women and young men looked volatile and unpredictable; the militant mood among the industrial labour force might easily be translated into a lurch to the left at the polls. The Tory leaders therefore concluded that the best practical means of getting through an immediate post-war election was to maintain the coalition and capitalise on Lloyd George's popularity. The result was the famous 'Coupon', a letter signed by Lloyd George and Bonar Law, and issued to 374 Conservative, 159 Liberal and 18 National Labour candidates who supported the Coalition Government. The results exceeded all expectations, for the Government received 54 per cent of the votes and 74 per cent of the seats; of 526 MPs elected as Government supporters, 383 were Conservatives, a total never previously bettered except in 1895 and 1900.

On the other hand, when politics returned to something like normality, it emerged that the Conservatives' position had been weakened by the wartime franchise reform to the extent that they commanded barely 40 per cent of the vote, which was substantially below their performance in the Edwardian elections. However, this was more than balanced by the effect of the redistribution of the constituencies in 1918. The division of many expanding suburban seats created additional middle-class constituencies in which neither Labour nor the Liberals could effectively challenge the Conservatives. As a result the party enjoyed a minimum of around 260 seats after the war. In addition, the disappearance of most of the Irish representation at Westminster enabled the

[14] Martin Pugh, 1978: *Electoral Reform in War and Peace 1906–18*. London: Routledge & Kegan Paul, 57–69; D. Close, 1977: The collapse of resistance to democracy: Conservatives, adult suffrage and second chamber reform, 1911–28. *Historical Journal* 20, 893–918.
[15] Selborne to Salisbury, 12 September 1916, Selborne Papers, vol. 6.

Conservatives to dominate the House of Commons much more easily than they had during the decades before 1914.

Working-Class Politics and the War

In some ways the controversies among the parliamentary élite have less significance than the underlying social and political constraints within which politicians operated. The conditions of the political struggle began to be altered quite early in the war by unexpected developments on the economic front. Instead of disrupting industry and creating mass unemployment as the politicians had feared, the war rapidly led to shortages of labour as key industries struggled to generate the goods demanded by an insatiable military machine. Inevitably the full employment that resulted greatly strengthened the bargaining power of the workers and produced another major advance for the trade union movement, whose membership rose from just over 4 million to 6 million between 1914 and 1918.

Not only did the organised working-class movement expand and gain in assertiveness, but there are grounds for thinking that it also became more united, in the sense that distinctions and differentials between skilled and unskilled workers diminished. All this naturally had implications for the Labour Party. One of the striking peculiarities of British society was that although it had become one of the earliest industrial and urbanised societies in the world it was not particularly quick to generate a large political party based on urban workers. Labour and all its predecessors had found it difficult to tap the resources of the organised working class for political purposes. The wartime experience clearly facilitated this objective. But it did not suddenly resolve the problem; rather it accelerated certain trends already under way before 1914. Since most of the party's membership was derived from trade union affiliations, it stood to benefit from any general expansion. As a result of the Osborne judgment of 1909, however, unions had been prevented from devoting their funds to party political purposes. In 1913 the Liberal Government changed the law so as to legalise the collection of a political levy from union members provided they first conducted a ballot on whether to establish a political fund. By 1914 most of the major unions had secured their members' approval and were thus in a position to start accumulating new funds during the course of the war.

The immediate effects of this should not be exaggerated. Many rank-and-file members had not taken part in the ballot and were reluctant to pay; some unions were slow to set up a fund and others at first declined to start financing extra candidatures.[16] However, Labour had broken through one of the chief obstacles to its growth. After the war, when full employment gave way to unem-

[16] Duncan Tanner, 1990: *Political Change and the Labour Party 1900–1918*. Cambridge: Cambridge University Press, 393–4, 401–3.

ployment and workers became aggrieved at the policies of the Coalition, they
had an obvious political outlet available. It became standard practice for aspir-
ing Labour candidates to offer the constituency for which they wished to stand
financial backing from their trade union, both on an annual basis and to cover
election expenses.

On the other hand, it would be misleading to portray Labour's breakthrough as inevitable. During 1914, 1915 and 1916 no major initiatives were
undertaken to put the party on a new footing. Only a minority of the MPs,
including Ramsay MacDonald and Philip Snowden, perceived the implications for domestic politics of Britain's entry into the war. Declining to be swallowed up in the great wave of patriotism and chauvinism, they worked for a
negotiated peace through organisations such as the Union of Democratic
Control and the Independent Labour Party. But the bulk of the Labour movement, whether in Parliament, the constituencies or the trade unions, backed
the war effort and the drive for a complete military victory over Germany.
Moreover, many members judged that the crisis offered opportunities for
Labour. Fabian Socialists realised that the need to mobilise national resources
for the war effort would tend to make 'war socialism' respectable and might
have long-term implications for the role of the state.[17] More immediately, the
authorities' anxiety to conciliate the labour force made them more than usually susceptible to pressure over food prices, rents, wages, pensions and
allowances for the families of servicemen. The War Emergency Workers'
National Committee co-ordinated campaigns on a range of topics affecting living standards and working conditions and, moreover, helped to keep the
Labour movement relatively united.

In addition, the Labour Party's status and respectability were improved
when in May 1915 Arthur Henderson joined the Cabinet in the formal role of
President of the Board of Education but effectively as adviser on industrial
relations. When Lloyd George became prime minister, the Labour MPs were
assumed to be more favourable towards Asquith, especially in view of the way
in which the new premier had promoted conscription. Yet they decided on
balance that continued participation would offer a better prospect of enhancing their ability to defend working-class interests. Labour thus operated a two-
pronged strategy: influence from within the system and extra-parliamentary
pressure.

However, one result of this approach was that it was several years before the
party showed any real sign of making a break from the Liberal electoral
alliance under whose shelter the parliamentary party had developed. Only
after Henderson's dismissal from the War Cabinet in the summer of 1917 did
Labour launch its bid for independence. This involved four major initiatives.
First, MacDonald, Henderson and Sidney Webb drafted a document on 'Peace
and War Aims', and subsequently the party adopted a new programme on
domestic politics called 'Labour and the New Social Order' which would be

---

[17] J. M. Winter, 1974: *Socialism and the Challenge of War*. London: Routledge & Kegan Paul.

the basis for an appeal to voters at the forthcoming general election. Second, in the new constitution of 1918 the party defined its basic aims in a way not previously done by including a commitment to socialism in the famous Clause Four. Many historians have minimised the importance of this step on the grounds that the socialist clause reflected the views of a handful of middle-class intellectuals, not the trade unions, and did not lead to a socialist policy for some years.[18] On the other hand, it symbolised and made overt the break with Liberalism, which was certainly reinforced by other changes at the time. Third, Labour modified the rather loose federal structure adopted in 1900. Henceforth the members of the National Executive Committee were to be chosen by the annual conference as a whole, rather than by the separate affili-ated organisations, which in effect placed control in the hands of the larger trade unions. Fourth, the party attempted to create a machine comparable to those of its rivals.[19] Hitherto, nearly all the membership had been indirect, only about 150 constituencies actually had a local Labour organisation, and in practice the party's candidates often relied on either an Independent Labour Party branch or even the Liberal Association to run their election campaigns. From 1918 the party sought to build up an individual membership – an espe-cially important route into the party for women, few of whom were likely to join via the unions. This meant establishing a Labour Party in every con-stituency and adopting a much larger number of candidates than before. As a result, whereas at the election of December 1910 the party ran only fifty-six candidates, in 1918 it was able to field 388. This obviously destroyed any pact with the Liberals and meant that Labour was making a bid to win a majority for the first time.

Franchise Reform and the Structure of Politics

In several ways the conditions were ideal for Labour's breakthrough in 1918. While the Liberals seemed divided and demoralised, the movement had gained influence and self-confidence, and the party was beginning to tap extra resources both in terms of money and personnel. But perhaps the most strik-ing structural change at this stage was the expansion of the electorate. From just under 8 million voters before the war the figure rose to 21.4 million in 1918. Several historians, including McKibbin, have argued that the franchise was indeed the crucial factor in determining the party's development.[20] In the Edwardian period only six out of every ten men enjoyed the vote, but over 95 per cent did so after 1918. If many of these were working men it seems likely

---

[18] Rodney Barker, 1976: Political myth: Ramsay MacDonald and the Labour Party. *History* 61, 46–56; McKibbin, *Evolution*, op. cit. (note 7).
[19] McKibbin, *Evolution*, op. cit. (note 7); Julia Bush, 1984: *Behind the Lines: East London Labour 1914–1919*. London: Merlin Press.
[20] H. C. Matthew, R. McKibbin and J. A. Kay, 1976: The franchise factor in the rise of the Labour Party. *English Historical Review* 91, 723–52.

that they represented a large reservoir of natural support for Labour. Was it just coincidence that when the new electorate first voted in 1918 Labour leapt ahead while the Liberals fell into a terminal decline?

However, this interpretation has been challenged in broadly two ways. The first concerns the social composition of the electorate. Tanner has shown that the pre-war system discriminated against the younger, unmarried men and those whose occupations made them mobile. Many such men failed to qualify for the householder franchise either because they lived with their fathers or because they rarely met the 12-month residence requirement; this disenfranchised middle-class men at least as much as working-class.[21] Consequently, we cannot assume that an influx of new voters necessarily gave Labour a significant advantage. In any case, 8.4 million – that is, nearly two-thirds – of the new voters in 1918 were in fact women, whose politicisation was clearly not the same as that of men.

Secondly, there is the question as to how far the actual election results from 1918 onwards bear out the view that structural change was fundamental to Labour's advance.[22] For example, in 1918 the party won sixty-one seats, which represented an advance on the highest previous total of forty-two in December 1910. Yet this was scarcely a major advance; it only appeared so in the light of the even more dismal showing of the Asquithian Liberals. Moreover, Labour's victories tended to be concentrated in the same areas as before 1914, notably coalfields; there must therefore be a strong possibility that the party would have had a similar result even if the electorate had not been changed. No doubt the share of the popular vote increased sharply from 7.2 per cent in December 1910 to 22.7 per cent, though this reflects the rise in candidatures from fifty-six to 388. Our difficulty, of course, is that we cannot easily separate the effect of the franchise from the political conditions prevailing during the Coupon Election, which favoured the Conservatives at the expense of the other parties. When the emotions aroused at the end of the war had subsided, Labour made an advance through successive elections to reach 37 per cent of the poll by 1929 when 571 seats were contested. Though an impressive record of growth, it represented a steady advance rather than one dramatic leap forward resulting from franchise reform; even in 1929 a good deal of the working-class electorate was not yet voting for Labour. John Turner has analysed the relationship between the size of the Labour vote and the increase in the electorate at the constituency level in 1918.[23] His findings suggest that the higher the proportion of new voters in a constituency the less well the party performed; this reflects the female electorate rather than the male, but it clearly undermines any assumption that franchise reform was the key factor.

---

[21] Duncan Tanner, 1983: The parliamentary electoral system, the 'fourth' Reform Act and the rise of Labour in England and Wales. *Bulletin of the Institute of Historical Research* 56, 205–19.

[22] Michael Hart, 1982: The Liberals, the war and the franchise. *English Historical Review* 97, 820–32; Martin Pugh, 1992: *The Making of Modern British Politics 1867–1939*. Oxford: Blackwell, 197–9, 252–4.

[23] Turner, *British Politics*, op. cit. (note 6), 412–17.

None of this eliminates the importance of structural changes. Electoral reform came at a stage when Labour's rival on the left was least able to respond effectively. Given the withdrawal of many Liberal candidates in 1910 and the subsequent collapse of their local organisation, Labour stepped in to fill a vacuum in many constituencies. As soon as the country began to focus on domestic politics once again, Labour began to do well, particularly in local government elections from 1919 onwards. At this level Labour offered a more constructive and distinctive programme than the Liberals. The result was a major and sustained advance in the 1920s that had the effect of driving Conservatives and Liberals into electoral pacts in many towns and cities. This reversed the pattern of Edwardian politics and helped Labour to occupy the role once filled by radical Liberalism.

Finally, it is important to note that a number of developments which had been widely feared or expected failed to materialise in spite of the sweeping changes in the British electoral system. For example, in 1918 the vote was granted to women aged over 30 years if they were local government electors or the wives of local government electors. This can be explained partly as the result of a fifty-year campaign during which some, at least, of the fears about women's enfranchisement had been allayed, and partly as by-product of the decision to grant a vote to all adult men by the Speaker's Conference of 1916–17.

But although women now comprised 40 per cent of voters there was no significant women's party. One of the reasons the politicians imposed a 30-year age requirement on women voters was their fear that the younger women would harbour feminist aspirations and might attempt to run their own candidates. In the event, the Pankhursts briefly experimented with a Women's Party in 1918 whose only object was to secure Christabel Pankhurst's election; when she was defeated in Smethwick the party promptly collapsed. The National Union of Societies for Equal Citizenship, the successor of the non-militant Edwardian suffragist organisation, supported a number of women candidates during the 1920s. But it lacked the resources to make much impact, and there were few votes in a feminist policy. In any case, most of the politically ambitious women chose to enter Parliament under the auspices of the existing political parties even if they retained connections with the women's movement. And in fact the number of female candidates rose from seventeen in 1918 to sixty-nine in 1929, of whom fourteen were elected.[24]

Nor, despite much speculation, did a new Centre Party emerge, though Lloyd George was clearly tempted to form one. He waited for too long after the 1918 election, only to be deterred in the end by reluctance among both his Liberal and his Conservative supporters. Gradually they began to be drawn back to their respective parties, and as Lloyd George's popularity with the voters waned politicians became more anxious to abandon him than to risk their future in a new party.

[24] Martin Pugh, 1992: *Women and the Women's Movement in Britain 1914–1959*. London: Macmillan, 50–6, 61–5.

The other potential development that aroused concern was the politicisation of the millions of ex-servicemen. Experience in the trenches and subsequent disillusionment with civilian life proved to be a powerful impetus to political activism for a number of young men. The careers and attitudes of several junior officers, including Sir Oswald Mosley, Anthony Eden and Harold Macmillan, were greatly influenced by the war. All the parties made attempts to pre-empt the mobilisation of ex-servicemen by creating new organisations for them: the Comrades of the Great War, the National Federation of Discharged and Demobilised Soldiers, and the National Union of Ex-Servicemen. On the whole, these organisations were not very successful or long-lived. Even the British Legion, which was designed to be non-political, recruited only one in ten of the former soldiers.[25] During the 1930s the British Union of Fascists made a certain appeal to this section of society, but there was nothing to justify the original apprehension of the conventional politicians.

Thus, in spite of the sweeping change in the composition of the electorate and the apparent radicalisation of the workers during the 1917 to 1920 period, no major threat to the British political system emerged in the aftermath of war. The key clearly lay in the Labour movement. Its leaders were the products of Gladstonian parliamentarianism: it was firmly grounded in parliamentary methods and in the pragmatism of local government. War had served to strengthen confidence in using the existing system to promote the interests of the working class rather than to generate support for its overthrow.

The Political Agenda

How far did the agenda of British politics change under the impact of war? Arthur Marwick, among others, has drawn attention to the participation of masses of the people in the war effort as a development that obliged the political élite to grant concessions in the shape of social and political reforms.[26] Certainly the war generated a considerable discussion about reconstruction, and a number of measures were enacted in 1918–19 which seemed to reflect this spirit: Addison's Housing Act, H. A. L. Fisher's Education Act, the Maternity and Child Welfare Act, the Representation of the People Act. To some extent all the parties subscribed to this programme, though the Conservatives swiftly backed away from the costly reforms in housing and education once the war was over. They were under pressure from the new electorate and the apparent rise of the Labour Party, which appeared to make a constructive social policy a political necessity. Yet this had to be set against the need to appease their middle-class supporters by bringing down income tax. In fact, the Conservatives could live with a largely hostile working class,

[25] David Englander, 1991: The National Union of Ex-Servicemen and the labour movement 1918–20. *History* 76, 24–42.
[26] Arthur Marwick, 1965: *The Deluge: British Society and the First World War.* London: The Bodley Head.

provided they did not alienate the large female element in the electorate. The female element was rather imponderable at first, but in due course all the parties reached the conclusion that the women voters should and could be treated essentially as though they were wives and mothers. One Tory summed up the implications in this way:

> *The women's vote is having a narrowing effect on politics, making them more parochial and is, at the moment, reducing them to bread and butter politics and the cost of living . . . their vote will probably be given on purely home questions . . . while Imperial and foreign issues will leave them cold.*[27]

In short, though there were potential problems with female voters, the parties felt able to deal with them. They went to some lengths to incorporate them into the formal party structures, usually by setting up separate women's branches and by giving them representation at each level, as well as holding special conferences specifically for women. By the late 1920s the Conservatives claimed a million female members and Labour about 250 000. From 1918 onwards, most candidates felt obliged to make some direct appeal to women, however brief; the specific issues commonly mentioned were widows' pensions, equal suffrage and maternity services.[28] In 1923 when the Conservatives held an election on the introduction of tariffs they attributed their losses to the reaction of housewives fearful of higher food prices. Not only did Baldwin's 1924–9 Government avoid the protectionist issue, it also took some trouble to try to outflank its rivals by enacting both widows' pensions in 1925 and equal suffrage in 1928.

However, in so far as questions of social welfare and standards of living occupied a central role in post-war politics this represented continuity with pre-war trends rather than innovation. After 1906 the Liberals had built their success on a combination of traditional causes such as free trade and popular reforms such as old age pensions. War, and the new female electorate, essentially helped to consolidate the pattern.

It is important to distinguish the intrinsic importance of the reforms from their party political implications. A particularly important example is housing. After Lloyd George's promise to build 'homes for heroes', the shortcomings of Addison's 1919 Housing Act inevitably attracted a good deal of debate throughout the 1920s. His scheme required local authorities to draw up programmes for council housing in their areas. As the great majority of families had hitherto been dependent upon private rented accommodation this had considerable implications. No major improvements had occurred before 1914; the war exacerbated shortages and led the Government to impose restrictions on rent increases. This marked the beginning of a long-term change in housing tenure in Britain away from private towards municipal housing and home ownership. It also made housing a central political issue.

[27] Malcolm Fraser to A. Chamberlain, 30 December 1921, Austen Chamberlain Papers, AC/32/4/16.
[28] Pugh, *Women*, op. cit. (note 24), 119–24.

Labour councillors showed themselves particularly keen to implement the 1919 Act, and in the process they took over the initiative from the Liberals, who were more negative, locally, and to some extent discredited, nationally, when Lloyd George's Coalition scrapped the Act in 1921. It was of more than symbolic importance that the author of the Act, Addison, subsequently left the Liberal Party and joined Labour.[29] Moreover, the principle of using state subsidies to promote the building of council houses for rent became a central part of Labour's inter-war programme. Although the Conservatives preferred to encourage private building for sale, the significant thing is that each party gave a higher priority to housing than had been the case before 1914. Indeed, the issue has remained a key item in the political struggle ever since.

In fact, housing was only one of the areas in which Labour successfully took over the leadership of Edwardian progressivism after the war. Former Liberals such as Trevelyan, Ponsonby and Wedgwood Benn justified their shift of allegiance by arguing that Labour was the best vehicle for all kinds of social reforms. But it was also an upholder of the traditional Liberal causes: free trade, temperance and land reform, for example. No doubt several of the issues that had once been central to popular Liberalism lost their significance, though this too proved advantageous for Labour. For example, Nonconformist issues dwindled rapidly once the Welsh Church had been disestablished in 1920. In the process most working-class Nonconformists moved across to the Labour Party. Similarly, the demise of the Irish Question left voters of Irish origin, who had once been a key element in Liberal majorities in urban constituencies, slightly adrift. But the local leaders of their community soon became absorbed into the Labour organisation, giving the party thereby a pronounced Catholic character in Clydeside, Merseyside and Yorkshire.

Not the least important element of continuity between pre-war and postwar politics was national defence and foreign policy. In 1914 Ramsay MacDonald's courageous stand had condemned him to the political wilderness; and like all the other critics of the war he suffered a heavy defeat in 1918. But the cooperation between him and the disillusioned Liberals Trevelyan, Ponsonby and E. D. Morel presaged a broader shift.[30] For some years before 1914 a number of radicals had regarded the arms race and the diplomatic manoeuvres with France and Russia as a betrayal of the Gladstonian tradition. In the aftermath of war there was a widespread support for disarmament, the appeasement of German grievances and the use of the League of Nations to resolve international disputes. Neither Lloyd George nor Asquith was particularly well placed to give a lead to this sentiment. Lloyd George conducted his diplomacy in an old-fashioned, if unconventional, way with little regard for the League of Nations, which he saw merely as a concession to President Woodrow Wilson. By contrast, MacDonald as Foreign Secretary in 1924 and Henderson as

[29] Jane Morgan and Kenneth Morgan, 1980: *Portrait of a Progressive*. Oxford: Clarendon Press.
[30] M. Swartz, 1971: *The Union of Democratic Control in British Politics during the First World War*. Oxford: Clarendon Press; C. A. Cline, 1963: *Recruits to Labour*. Syracuse, NY: Syracuse University Press.

chairman of the Geneva Disarmament Convention enjoyed impressive Liberal credentials. With such leaders, the Labour Party was able to reflect the widespread concern about disarmament and the maintenance of peace during the 1920s, while the Liberal leaders seemed tarnished by association with past policies.

Conclusions

Perhaps surprisingly, then, the war does not seem to have had a very radical effect on the agenda of politics. It kept the role of the state, welfare and living standards to the forefront and raised the profile of housing, one or two women's issues and defence. But one's impression is of continuity with Edwardian politics. The change consisted in Labour's capacity to seize the initiative in most aspects of radicalism, and in the Liberals' tendency to be edged towards the centre-right of the spectrum. Labour had not yet completely inherited the mantle of Edwardian progressivism; but a second world war would complete the process.

Despite the immense cost and the strain of over four years of war, the institutions and values of the British parliamentary system survived intact and continued to command broad support in the country. The fact that Britain emerged victorious no doubt facilitated this outcome. But the decision to incorporate millions of men and women into the political system pre-dated military victory; this thus represented a calculated risk – or an expression of confidence – on the part of the existing political élite. Their judgement appears broadly justified by the continuity of practice after 1918, and by the capacity of British politics to withstand the challenges posed by mass unemployment and by fascism during the 1920s and 1930s, challenges to which various Continental states succumbed.

2

Government

Rodney Lowe

The size, cost and responsibility of government exploded in Britain, as in the rest of the Western world, during the first half of the twentieth century. The main trends are summarised in Tables 2.1 and 2.2. Between 1901 and 1951 the number of government employees rose tenfold or, in relative terms, from 3 per cent to 23 per cent of the total labour force. Public expenditure increased fourfold in real terms or from 15 per cent to 35 per cent of GDP. Simultaneously, to finance such expansion, the basic rate of income tax rose from 5p to 45p in the pound and total tax revenue became the equivalent of 33 per cent, not 8 per cent, of GDP. Nineteenth-century *laissez-faire*, in other words, was decisively laid to rest during these years. Government became the predominant influence in Britain's labour and financial markets; contact between it and ordinary citizens became routine rather than exceptional; and direct taxation bit deeply into individuals' pockets. In return, the assumption became widespread that government – as opposed to the market and voluntary associations – was responsible for the delivery of certain 'social rights', such as the right to employment and to social security.

What role did the First World War play in this remarkable transformation? Superficially it would appear very little for, as Table 2.1 reveals, the two periods of major physical expansion for government were those before 1914 and after 1939. Between 1891 and 1911 the numbers employed in local government almost quadrupled, while those in central government more than doubled. Even more remarkably, between 1939 and 1951 the combined increase at local and central level was double the total increase in all public employment over the preceding century.[1] Such expansion clearly reflected a revolution in government responsibilities. Before 1914, local government became the foremost agency for combating the social consequences of urbanisation. Then, when its resources had proved to be insufficient, central government acknowledged – during the so-called period of Liberal reforms – its

[1] R. Parry, 1980: *UK Public Employment*. Glasgow: Strathclyde University, CSPP paper 62, 7.

Table 2.1   Public Employment in Britain 1891–1951

	Central government (000s)	Local government (000s)	Public corporations (000s)	Total (000s)	Percentage of labour force
1891	110	175	–	285	1.9
1901	160	375	–	535	3.2
1911	271	660	–	931	5.0
1921	508	976	–	1484	7.6
1931	441	1263	–	1704	8.0
1938	581	1273	–	1854	8.2
1951	1601	1431	2354	5415	23.3

Adapted from R. Parry, 1980: *UK Public Employment*. Glasgow: Strathclyde University, CSPP paper 62, Table 1. Employment in the armed forces is excluded.

responsibility for issues such as unemployment and poverty in old age. Expansion after 1939 marked both a culmination of this trend towards a 'welfare state' and also, through nationalisation and the commitment to maintain a 'high and stable level of employment', an acceptance of the need for direct government intervention in the economy.

In contrast, the impact of the First World War has appeared to many historians as slight. The war certainly saw the creation of an unprecedented number of new ministries of both a temporary nature (most notably the Ministries of Munitions and Reconstruction) and a permanent nature (such as the Ministries of Labour, Health and Transport). It also provoked a ferment of ideas, and spawned numerous reports on the radical restructuring and responsibilities of both central and local government. However, what were the practical long-term consequences? The really lasting legacy of the war for government, so it has been argued, was rather – at the centre at least – the reputation for inefficiency and corruption acquired in particular after 1916 under the premiership of Lloyd George. This discredited it in the eyes of many as a vehicle for peacetime reform. It also disillusioned dynamic young civil servants such as Keynes and Beveridge, upon whose ideas and expertise the post-1945 welfare state was to be constructed. They duly left Whitehall. Consequently, under the reinforced control of the Treasury, the physical growth of public employment was relatively slight during the inter-war years and government appeared little affected by the social revolution that was occurring around it. As the classic social history of the war has concluded: 'while society had changed, the state had not'.[2]

Other historians, and especially those concerned with Britain's relative economic decline, have gone further and depicted the impact of the war on central government not merely as insignificant but as counter-revolutionary.[3] Many of the wartime proposals for reform had been based, after all, on the practical

[2] A. Marwick, 1965: *The Deluge: British Society and the First World War*. Harmondsworth: Penguin Books, 334.

[3] J. Turner, 1992: *British Politics and the Great War*. New Haven, Conn.: Yale University Press, 2.

experience of leading Edwardian civil servants; and they had been identified by one percipient French commentator as 'secret dictators' within Whitehall willing and able to make Britain 'bureaucratic' in the conventional Continental sense.[4] The war may therefore be seen as having provided a golden opportunity for the creation of a 'developmental state' which, by rising above vested interest, could alone have provided the incisive expert lead necessary for the removal of the structural and institutional impediments to economic growth. Because of wartime corruption and inefficiency, however, this golden opportunity was lost.

So negative a view of the impact of the First World War on government is not, however, universally held. It has been challenged on three major grounds. First, as a result of the war – or at least in reaction to it – the machinery of government was radically overhauled. Within Whitehall, for example, a Cabinet Secretariat was established in 1916 – remarkably, for the first time – to record and circulate ministerial decisions. The debilitating effect for good government of previous practice was well illustrated by Beveridge's confession over the implementation of a major piece of earlier wartime legislation:

> *There being no secretary to the Cabinet then, and no minutes kept, the only way was to ask the Prime Minister and another member of the Cabinet. To make sure, we asked three separate ministers what had been decided and we received three different answers. . . . We chose the answer that seemed to us the most desirable in the national interest.*[5]

Immediately after the war, the home civil service was also rationalised and given a common career structure, while the retention of new specialist departments (such as the Ministries of Labour and of Health) streamlined administration in policy areas given greater prominence by the increased democratisation of politics. As a direct consequence of wartime planning, the formal relationship between central and local government was also clarified by the 1929 Local Government Act. The cumulative importance of these changes was that the anachronistic nature and essential amateurism of the nineteenth century were swept aside and a 'twentieth-century revolution in government' effected. Government now had, at a central and local level, an administrative structure capable of serving a modern, industrial society.[6]

Second, as Table 2.2 illustrates, the greatest permanent increase in government expenditure as a percentage of GDP (from 12.7 per cent in 1911 to 28.6 per cent in 1938) occurred after the war. This, it has been argued, was a result of the exceptional 'displacement effect' of the war, whereby conventional wisdom about the 'proper' level of public expenditure and taxation was overturned.[7] By 1918, for example, public expenditure had reached the

[4] E. Halévy, 1961: *The Rule of Democracy*. London: Ernest Benn, 265.
[5] Lord Beveridge, 1953: *Power and Influence*. London: Hodder & Stoughton, 133–4.
[6] R. Lowe, 1986: *Adjusting to Democracy*. Oxford: Clarendon Press, 43–52.
[7] A. T. Peacock and J. Wiseman, 1967: *The Growth of Public Expenditure in the United Kingdom*. London: Allen & Unwin, 24–8; J. Cronin, 1991: *The Politics of State Expansion*. London: Routledge, 65–7.

Table 2.2   Total Government Expenditure 1900–50

	Expenditure at constant (1900) prices[a] (£ m)	Expenditure as a percentage of GDP[b]			Taxes as percentage of GDP[c]	
		All (%)	Central govt (%)	Local govt (%)	All (%)	Central govt (%)
1900	281	14.9	9.7	5.2	7.9	5.5
1913	289	12.7	7.0	5.7	8.8[d]	6.6[d]
1920	565	27.4	21.9	5.5	20.1	18.1
1924	505	23.8	16.0	7.8	18.4[d]	15.4[d]
1938	851	28.6	19.0	9.6	17.6[d]	14.4[d]
1950	1195	35.1	26.9	8.2	33.2	30.7

[a] Figures from A. T. Peacock and J. Wiseman, 1987: *The Growth of Public Expenditure in the United Kingdom.* London: Allen & Unwin, 164.
[b] Figures from P. Flora, 1983: *State, Economy and Society*, vol. 1. Basingstoke: Macmillan, 440–1.
[c] Figures from Flora, *State, Economy and Society*, vol. 1, op. cit., 262–8.
[d] Figures for 1910, 1921 and 1940 respectively.

unprecedented height of 48 per cent of GDP and the basic rate of income tax 30p in the pound. Whatever the short-term reaction, there could never be – especially after the extension of the franchise in 1918 – a return to 'pre-war normalcy'. Thus the war lifted the rigid fiscal constraints which, whatever the rhetoric, had held back the expansion of the Edwardian state. Moreover, it was not just on the financing but on the actual nature of policy that the war had a decisive effect because, in the emergency of war and wartime reconstruction, choices had to be made from the wide range of pre-war options. As one historian of housing policy has perceptively noted: 'what the war did was convert one strand in the pre-war debate into the dominant policy, which was pursued during the period of reconstruction to the exclusion of all other possibilities considered before the war.'[8]

The third major change which has been associated with the war concerns the nature of the policy decisions taken and the attitude towards government which they reflected. The prevailing assumption in Britain before 1914, in contrast to much European thought, had been that government represented neither a country's corporate identity nor an innovative force. According to Jose Harris:

> The corporate life of society was seen as expressed through the voluntary association and the local community, rather than the persona of the state ... More extensive government was widely viewed as not merely undesirable but unnecessary, in the sense that most of the functions performed by government in other societies were in Britain performed by coteries of citizens governing themselves.[9]

[8] M. Daunton, 1987: *A Property-owning Democracy?* London: Faber & Faber, 39.
[9] J. Harris, 1990: Society and the State in twentieth-century Britain. In F. M. L. Thompson (ed.), *The Cambridge Social History of Britain*, vol. 3. Cambridge: Cambridge University Press, 67–8. This chapter, together with the one by Thane cited in note 14, provides the best recent overview of the evolution of government between the 1870s and the 1930s.

Thus whatever the premonitions of a few exceptional Edwardian civil servants and its rationality in hindsight for certain historians, the political, industrial and above all cultural traditions and values simply did not exist on which permanently to found a developmental state during or immediately after the First World War. Nevertheless, in social policy at least, the war did mark a significant if subtle shift in the relationship between central government and both voluntary associations and the local community.

This shift was in part the result of a pragmatic acknowledgement, based on pre-war experience, that the nature and size of many social problems were so great that government alone had the resources to resolve them. Such pragmatism was to be reinforced during the inter-war years by the extent of social need arising from economic depression. However, it was during the war itself that the key decision was taken in major areas of policy that government should not subsidise other agencies traditionally responsible for the provision of essential services. Rather it should provide the services directly itself. Thus, whereas in Continental countries – with their centralist traditions – State intervention was restricted in the inter-war years to the subsidisation of housing associations and private insurance schemes, ironically it was in Britain – with its voluntarist tradition – that government itself came to provide council housing and unemployment benefit.

This move towards greater centralisation had major long-term consequences and helps to place in perspective the allegedly 'revolutionary' change in the role of government during the Second World War – be that change judged by the exceptional extent of mobilisation (in comparison to that seen in other countries), its public acceptability (in marked contrast to the experience of the First World War) or the exceptional centralisation of the postwar welfare state (especially in relation to the National Health Service and social insurance). It may be not to the unique circumstances of 1939–46 that attention should be turned for an explanation, but rather to the nature of policy options taken between 1914 and 1918, their later administrative rationalisation and their pragmatic acceptance both inside and outside government. The Second World War, in this view, merely reaped what the First World War had sown.

The principal purpose of this chapter is therefore to examine the three competing views of the impact of the First World War on government that have commonly been expressed by historians. Was it insignificant, counter-revolutionary or revolutionary? This begs the more traditional question of whether the war was the initiator, the catalyst or merely the occasion for such changes that did take place. It also begs the more fundamental question of whether any changes in government during, or as a result of, the war should be related to a wider crisis in the British State between 1880 and 1930 or to the creation of an 'extended state'.[10] The 'state' is rather an awkward subject in

[10] M. Langan and B. Schwarz (eds), 1985: *Crises in the British State 1880–1930*. London: Hutchinson; K. Middlemas, 1979: *Politics in Industrial Society*. London: Deutsch.

Britain, as opposed to Continental Europe, because of the different political traditions already identified; and it has often been used in historical analysis interchangeably with 'government' – sometimes, it would appear, simply to avoid the need to support theoretical assertion with empirical evidence. Certainly those who have conscientiously sought to identify the evidence which would support the claim that the state after 1880 was the vehicle for the reimposition of middle-class values ('the renegotiation of hegemonic values') have tended to be frustrated by the contradictions displayed by its component parts.[11] Equally, what would appear most significant about the attempts during the war to extend the conventional boundaries of government through the incorporation of other institutions, such as employers' organisations and trade unions, is their ultimate failure. Even Keith Middlemas, the leading proponent of corporatism, has acknowledged in his later work that its British variant ('corporate bias') was not 'the dominant trend' in inter-war politics and that organised labour, far from being a 'governing institution', remained 'on the margin of power'.[12] While keeping in mind these wider perspectives, therefore, this chapter will concentrate specifically on organisational change and the evolving attitude towards government which it represented.

The War and Central Government

The permanent impact of the First World War upon central government can best be judged if the exceptional disruption of war, and the immediate reaction to it, is discounted and a balanced comparison drawn between government's pre-war and postwar role. To achieve this, organisational changes will first be placed in the broad context of what was expected of government both inside and outside Whitehall; and they will then be illustrated by developments in one of the most sensitive areas of policy during the pre-war Liberal reforms and the postwar depression: the regulation of the labour market.

Before 1914 central government lacked corporate unity. This was reflected in part by the lack of a Cabinet Secretariat, and thus of a formal administrative link between the highest policy-making body and the departments expected to implement its decisions. It was also reflected by the semi-autonomous nature of many administrative departments. Regular attempts had been made since the 1850s to foster greater unity. Gladstone, for example, had sought in his annual budget to lay down the moral principles upon which all government expenditure should be based, and the 1855 Northcote–Trevelyan Report had sought to standardise recruitment, promotion and administrative practice throughout the civil service. Some progress had duly been made towards these

[11] Langan and Schwarz, *Crises*, op. cit. (note 10), ch. 5.
[12] K. Middlemas, 1986: *Power, Competition and the State*. Basingstoke: Macmillan, vol. 1, p. 6. For a fuller discussion of corporatism, *see* the following chapter. For its rebuttal, *see* Lowe, *Adjusting to Democracy*, op. cit. (note 6), 246–7 and Turner, *British Politics*, op. cit. (note 3), 336.

ends. In 1870, for instance, the Treasury was given formal responsibility to co-ordinate and control the finance and establishments of other departments; all recruitment was based on competitive examination; and transferability between departments of junior (Second Division) clerks became increasingly possible. However, in 1914 the most senior appointments within each depart-ment were still technically within the gift of ministers, and the transfer of higher-grade (First Division) staff between departments was extremely rare. This absence of effective 'Treasury control' was once again criticised in 1914, by the MacDonnell Commission on the Civil Service, as extremely wasteful of both money and manpower.[13] Interdepartmental jealousies prevented the rationalisation of administrative responsibilities and able staff, denied the opportunity for promotion within their own department, became frustrated and disillusioned.

There were many reasons for this continuing lack of corporate unity. One was simply the institutional jealousy of departments, such as the Home Office and the Foreign Office, which had traditionally been the equal of the Treasury. Two more justifiable reasons were the method and underlying ratio-nale of 'Treasury control' as it developed after 1870. The Treasury itself was handicapped in two particular ways. It was not given the authority to check the cost-effectiveness of existing departmental expenditure, only that of demands for additional money; and it was repeatedly denied political guidance on the critical issue of how to distinguish between the financial and political implica-tions of a new policy – the two being inextricably linked with the effectiveness of policy normally dependent upon adequate funding. The consequences were serious. On the one hand, the Treasury could effect economies only by opposing policy innovation. Thus, of necessity, it developed a ritual of delay and obfuscation both to test the will of spending departments and to discour-age unnecessary claims. On the other hand, friction between it and the spend-ing departments was inevitable once there was a breakdown in the consensus in favour of the policy of 'positive retrenchment' adumbrated in Gladstone's budgets – the assumption that government should provide the minimum framework within which private citizens would be able, and obliged, to exer-cise the maximum of independence and responsibility.[14]

By the turn of the century, this consensus had indeed broken down as a greater awareness of widespread poverty, Britain's declining international competitive-ness and the growing power of labour inspired cross-party support for a pro-gramme of 'National Efficiency'. The 'minimum' degree of state intervention needed to maximise individual initiative was redefined and a more active role for government demanded. To all this, however, the Treasury was inherently opposed upon political as well as administrative grounds. With some justifica-tion, therefore, Treasury control could be depicted by its opponents as

[13] H. Roseveare, 1969: *The Treasury*. London: Allen Lane, 242–3.
[14] P. Thane: Government and society in England and Wales, 1750–1914. In F. M. L. Thompson, *Cambridge Social History*, op. cit. (note 9), vol. 3, p. 27.

unconducive not only to good interdepartmental relations but also to good government.

The war brought to an abrupt halt further attempts to extend Treasury control and indeed undermined the economic premise and administrative practices upon which it had been developed. Gladstonian faith in minimum government was destroyed by the inability of the market to respond to wartime need. The economic role of government had to expand (*see* Chapter 3), and this in turn required rapid administrative innovation. Twelve new ministries were created, some 160 new boards or commissions established and over half a million extra civil servants employed. Most dramatically of all, out of a twenty-man Army Contracts Department there developed a full-blown Ministry of Munitions which by 1918 was employing 650 000 officials and had been responsible for the expenditure of £2000m.[15]

With such extensive improvisation, the Treasury's traditional delaying tactics quickly became redundant and it became clearly impossible for it – with a mere thirty-eight administrative officials (themselves with enlarged financial responsibilities) – to maintain any detailed control over public expenditure. Indeed, it was expressly prevented by statute from interfering with the size or organisation of many new ministries. Even where it was not, it was confronted by ministers who, freed from traditional party political and Cabinet responsibilities, often took a close personal interest in their administrative fiefdoms more in keeping with political practice in the United States than in pre-war Britain.[16] In addition, although it continued to supervise the expenditure of public money abroad, the Treasury also lost effective control over the terms of domestic contracts and capital expenditure.

In place of the traditional concept of Treasury control, two alternative visions of postwar government were advanced. Both embraced the concept of a more active or 'developmental' state. The first was most clearly expressed in the report of the Haldane Committee on the Machinery of Government in 1918 – one of the plethora of committees set up by Lloyd George early in 1917 to 'think the unthinkable' and brought in July 1917 under the umbrella of the newly created Ministry of Reconstruction. The initial call for such a committee had been made by the Treasury in an attempt to forestall 'waste', but its membership (which included the fiercely independent Sir Robert Morant and Beatrice Webb) was very different from that which the Treasury would have chosen. Consequently its Report, although fully recognising the chaos into which government had been reduced by traditional jealousies and wartime

[15] S. Pollard, 1983: *The Development of the British Economy*. London: Arnold, 21. The purely temporary ministries were: War Trade and Munitions (1915); Blockade, Food, Shipping, Air and National Service (1916); Reconstruction (1917); Information (1918). The permanent ones were Pensions, Labour, and Scientific and Industrial Research (1916) to be supplemented by Health and Transport in 1919. The fullest study of the war's administrative impact is K. Burk (ed.), 1982: *War and the State*. London: Allen & Unwin.
[16] Roseveare, *The Treasury*, op. cit. (note 13), 243.

intervention, was based on the broad assumptions of those Edwardian civil servants who had led the battle against the Treasury.[17]

It made three major recommendations. First, to minimise administrative friction, departmental responsibilities should be placed on a clear functional basis (such as production, employment and health). Second, all officials should recognise the 'duty of investigation and thought as preliminary to action'. Not only did this mean the development of a separate Research Ministry out of the germ of the Department of Scientific and Industrial Research (founded in 1916) but also it entailed the creation of research departments in each ministry. Finally, the power of the Treasury, it was agreed, should be strengthened. 'The interests of the tax-payer', the Report accepted, 'cannot be left to the Spending Departments', and so the Chancellor of the Exchequer, unlike any other European finance minister, should retain overall responsibility for the control of public expenditure. Economy could be guaranteed only if 'the Minister responsible for the raising of revenue ... had a predominant voice in deciding the amount'. The Treasury should also be assisted by strong finance officers in each ministry, to ensure the continuing cost-effectiveness of policy, and should itself develop an establishments department to disseminate good business practice throughout the civil service.

There were, however, strict conditions attached. There must be no return to Treasury control as traditionally practised. 'The success of a system of control', the Report warned, 'which is, in theory at least, so comprehensive, so rigid and so minute, must depend on the manner in which it is applied.' The economic rationale and administrative practices of Treasury control had, therefore, to be transformed. 'The obligation upon Spending Departments to formulate a full and reasoned statement of their proposals must be recognised as placing upon the Treasury a corresponding obligation not to assume a negative attitude in the first instance towards suggestions for improving the quality of a service and the efficiency of the staff which administers it.'

The second, alternative, vision of postwar government was advanced by business and, in particular, the Federation of British Industries after its foundation in 1916.[18] In order to maximise national efficiency, it was argued, government should give industry more active support, be it through a more aggressive trade policy (especially against protectionist rivals), the restriction of domestic competition (to ensure economies of scale, profitability and hence long-term investment) or a more generous welfare policy (to minimise industrial unrest and maximise productivity). Government, and in particular a new Ministry of Industry, should be closely advised by representatives of industry, and statutory power should be devolved to representative bodies of employers and workers in order to ensure the effective 'self-government' of each industry. The self-

[17] P. B. Johnson, 1968: *Land Fit for Heroes*. Chicago: University of Chicago Press, 43–4; Ministry of Reconstruction, 1918: *Report of the Machinery of Government Committee*, Cd. 9230. The succeeding quotes are from pp. 6, 18, 19, 20.
[18] S. Blank, 1973: *Industry and Government in Britain*. Farnborough: Saxon House, 11–21; Turner, *British Politics*, op. cit. (note 3), 336–53.

government thereby achieved, however, was to be very different from that envisaged by Gladstone. The free market, and in particular free trade, would no longer be the guarantor of economic efficiency and enterprise; and statutory power would be devolved from disinterested government to unelected vested interests. This was recognised, and opposed, by the Haldane report, which noted:

> *The argument for an all-embracing and independent Ministry of Industry . . . is not that of Individualism versus Collectivism; nor has it any relation to Laissez-Faire versus Government Control. There is no suggestion that the individual workman or employer should be free to do as he likes. What is aimed at is that the control and regulation which become necessary should be exercised . . . not by a Ministry which would be . . . able to safeguard the interests of the community as a whole but by the influence of dominant corporate bodies representing either employers or workmen.*[19]

The two alternative visions of postwar government, therefore, seriously diverged over the question of the distribution of power. Should government ultimately control industry, or industry control government? Any attempt to establish a developmental state was doomed to failure unless this fundamental political question was resolved.

As Prime Minister, Lloyd George favoured the concept, and in particular the corporatist concept, of a developmental state. During the war he appointed businessmen and trade unionists as ministers, temporary officials and advisers to departments in which they had a vested interest. After the war he continued to appoint businessmen-ministers and sanctioned significant administrative developments such as the extension of the Department of Overseas Trade (to promote British exports) and the creation of a Ministry of Transport (to co-ordinate transport policy so as to reduce industrial costs and promote social welfare). The high point of such developments was reached in February 1919 when the Cabinet was presented with an explicit choice between more interventionist government and a return to orthodox economic policy.[20] It chose the former, and a month later Britain formally left the gold standard.

By August 1919, however, the tide had begun to turn and the Treasury had launched its campaign to restore financial orthodoxy, which – as the Treasury but not necessarily the Cabinet wanted – was to culminate in 1925 with sterling's return to the gold standard at pre-war parity. There were two major reasons other than the Treasury's sheer determination for this *volte face*. First, the Coalition lacked the organisation, Lloyd George the time and his businessmen-ministers the skill to consolidate support, both within and outside Westminster, for interventionist government. Secondly, businessmen – freed from fierce competition by the war exhaustion of their Continental trading

[19] Ministry of Reconstruction, *Report*, op. cit. (note 19), 46.
[20] Public Record Office, CAB 24/75/GT 6880. The best history of the Lloyd George Coalition is K. O. Morgan, 1979: *Consensus and Disunity*. Oxford: Clarendon Press.

rivals – grew increasingly concerned about the immediate threat to their vested interests posed by collectivist government (especially after it had become apparent that their version of collectivism differed from that of officials) and inflation (which they blamed on excessive public expenditure). Once these concerns had been transmitted to Conservative backbenchers, the Treasury had the basis of parliamentary support it needed to exploit the steady flow of reports on the financial extravagance and corruption of big government during the war.

Central to the campaign to restore pre-war orthodoxy were the reports of the 1922 Committee on National Expenditure – ironically chaired by Sir Eric Geddes, one of Lloyd George's leading businessmen-ministers and the creator of the Ministry of Transport (the abolition of which was included in the £87m package of cuts recommended by the Committee). By 1922, Geddes had become convinced that effective interventionist government could not be achieved and that there should therefore be an immediate restoration of conditions favourable to the workings of a market economy. Half-way measures were futile. His reports, like the Treasury, accordingly made constant references to a return to pre-war normalcy, and 'implicit in these repeated comparisons . . . was an assumption that in most respects the scope and character of the pre-war state were adequate to the nation's needs'.[21]

Not only was financial orthodoxy restored between 1919 and 1925 but also the traditional mechanisms of Treasury control. Indeed, they were strengthened. In 1919 the Treasury was reorganised and enlarged, and its permanent secretary formally confirmed as head of the civil service. Its financial authority was strengthened by the confirmation of all permanent secretaries as accounting officers for their departments (to ensure their personal commitment to economy), the appointment in all departments of strong finance officers (to ensure continuing cost-effectiveness) and, above all, the ruling in 1924 that the Treasury should vet all memoranda proposing increases in expenditure before their submission to Cabinet. Similarly, its administrative authority was consolidated by the appointment of establishment officers in all departments, the standardised regrading of all officials (to facilitate transferability throughout the service) and, most importantly, the agreement in 1920 that the head of the civil service should advise the prime minister on the filling of the top four posts in each department. At last, and as a direct result of the war, the long-frustrated ambition

[21] K. Grieves, 1989: *Sir Eric Geddes*. Manchester: Manchester University Press, 101–7; A. McDonald, 1989: The Geddes Committee and the formulation of public expenditure policy. *Historical Journal* 32, 664. Treasury officials were motivated not just by Gladstonian principles and economic orthodoxy but by narrow departmental interests. Just as high-spending politicians could be reined back by an annually balanced budget, so sterling could be more easily defended and the national debt serviced if public expenditure was low and debt repayment – rather than social expenditure – given first claim on tax revenues. The national debt had leapt during the war from some £650 million to almost £8000 million and not suprisingly greatly exercised the Treasury. For the rationale behind Treasury thinking, *see* especially P. Clarke, 1988: *The Keynesian Revolution in the Making*. Oxford: Clarendon Press, ch. 2.

to create a professional, united service, first voiced by the Northcote–
Trevelyan Report, had been realised.

Would, however, the warnings of the Haldane Committee be heeded? At
first, it seemed as though they would. The first head of the civil service was Sir
Warren Fisher, a young and energetic admirer of Lloyd George, who was
appointed from outside the Treasury and was one of its foremost critics.[22]
Fisher had risen rapidly, under Lloyd George's patronage, in the National
Health Commission and the Inland Revenue. He was zealously committed to
the creation of a unified service, freed from wartime corruption and motivated by an *esprit de corps* based on a commitment to public service. His zeal and
hostility to traditional Treasury negativism were well illustrated by his advocacy
before the 1929–31 Tomlin Commission on the Civil Service of the recruitment of Treasury officials from other departments and not straight from university. 'If you do that', he complained, 'they then get to work and take their
little pens in their infant hands and they write away criticism of every sort and
kind, very clever ones no doubt, but there is no training for constructive
work.'[23]

The tragedy was, however, that in the breaking down of barriers within the
civil service and the building up of a new professionalism, the Treasury under
Fisher erected new barriers between the service and the rest of society, and
became dismissive of views other than its own. Thus, for example, when the
Royal Institute of Public Administration was established in 1922 under the
patronage of Lord Haldane to promote good management, it was rebuffed on
the somewhat contestable grounds that 'for the most part civil servants had no
concern with Administration'.[24] Recruitment to the administrative class
became even more exclusive, with an increase from 80 per cent to 89 per cent
of successful candidates from Oxbridge, despite the greater democratisation
of society and the greater specialism of other universities (particularly
London) in the social sciences. It was a strange paradox, as one professor of
political science noted, that 'a group of subjects which should, if anything, be
specially encouraged [were] specially rebuffed'.[25] New policies to resolve
intractable problems, such as Lloyd George's 1929 Keynesian programme *We
Can Conquer Unemployment*, were also summarily dismissed. Keynes lived, so
one senior Treasury official sarcastically remarked,

> *in a little economic world of his own up at Cambridge and he is pleased to consider
> the group of theorists up there as representing the sole exponents of 'modern eco-
> nomic thought'. In fact the rest of the universe treats their theories with much*

[22] E. O'Halpin, 1982: *Sir Warren Fisher*. Cambridge: Cambridge University Press.
[23] Quoted in Roseveare, *The Treasury*, op. cit. (note 13), 253.
[24] R. Nottage and F. Stack, 1972: The Royal Institute of Public Administration, 1922–39. *Public
Administration* 50, 284.
[25] E. Barker, 1937: The Home Civil Service. In W. A. Robson (ed.), *The British Civil Servant*.
London: Allen & Unwin, 37.

scepticism and their general acceptance is in reverse ratio to the dogmatism with which they are expressed.[26]

It was, in other words, under reinforced Treasury control, and again as a direct result of the war, that the 'traditional' gulf between insiders and outsiders in British government and the 'traditional' obsession of British officials with secrecy were invented.

Such attitudes inevitably had a major impact on the internal management of the civil service. Establishment and finance officers duly attempted to re-create each department in the Treasury's image. Intelligence and statistics departments, expanded during the war in response to the Haldane Report, were severely pruned. So too were all other wartime developments designed to improve the regulatory, let alone the interventionist, role of government – with the overall result that by 1924 the civil service was cut by one-quarter from its peak of just over 400 000 employees in 1918. Establishments policy, as before the war, was also used to check and even reverse policy initiatives, in accordance with Fisher's early realisation that the 'big money' was 'in policy'.[27]

Most important of all, however, Fisher sought to use his powers of patronage to reverse totally the pre-war convention that all senior posts should be filled by internal promotion. The cult of the generalist was thereby more firmly entrenched. 'Permanent secretaries', he insisted for example, 'are not experts. Let us guard ourselves against the idea that the permanent head of a department should be an expert; he [*sic*] should be nothing of the kind.'[28] Such strongly held views were insidious because no young, ambitious civil servant could fail to notice that the way to preferment did not lie in the advocacy of unorthodox financial proposals or indeed the development of specialist expertise. To compound matters, the Treasury also did not – as the Haldane Report had insisted – respond to greater unity within the civil service by lifting its traditional delaying tactics or its instinctive negativism. It was little wonder, therefore, that those who wished to see a quicker resolution of Britain's underlying economic and social problems grew increasingly frustrated by the performance of inter-war government. As Keynes (admittedly no unbiased observer) summarised developments since the war in 1939:

> *The civil service is ruled today by the Treasury school, trained by tradition and experience and native skill to every form of intelligent obstruction ... we have experienced in the 20 years since the war two occasions of terrific retrenchment and axing of constructive schemes [1922 and 1931]. This has not only been a crushing discouragement for all who are capable of constructive projects, but it has*

[26] Public Record Office, T 161/303/S40504/04: minute by Sir F. Leith-Ross.
[27] Public Record Office, T 171/170: Fisher to Lloyd George, 3 September 1919.
[28] Quoted in G. K. Fry, 1969: *Statesmen in Disguise*. London: Macmillan, 57–8. For an excellent critique of the Treasury's attitude towards women, *see* M. Zimmeck, 1984: Strategies and stratagems for the employment of women in the civil service, 1919–1939. *Historical Journal* 27, 901–24.

inevitably led to the survival of those to whom negative measures are natural and sympathetic.[29]

Of the three possible options for the development of government available in 1919, therefore, postwar politicians ultimately chose not to construct a 'developmental' state but to restore, and indeed to reinforce, traditional Treasury control. This might appear to confirm the reputation of the war as a conservative – if not a counter-revolutionary – force, for traditional Treasury control had already been exposed in Edwardian England as inimical to good government. Such an impression, however, would be misleading because – whatever its impact on the machinery of government – the war fundamentally altered the conditions within which government had to work. This was most apparent from the significant increase in public expenditure, which, despite the strenuous efforts of the Treasury in the 1920s, could not be reduced to the levels of pre-war normalcy and indeed began inexorably to rise again in the 1930s (*see* Table 2.2). High wartime rates had transformed taxpayers' perception of what government might require of them, just as the introduction of universal suffrage in 1918 had transformed the electorate's perception of what was required of government.

During the emergency of war, the relationship between government and traditional relief agencies also permanently changed. This was reflected not just in the adoption of more centralist policies (such as unemployment insurance and council housing) but also in the very outlook of the two predominant charitable bodies before and after the war: the fiercely independent Charity Organisation Society and the more accommodating National Council of Social Service – the latter established, significantly with government support, in 1919.[30]

In principle both the Charity Organisation Society and the National Council of Social Service adhered to an 'idealist' philosophy with its concept of 'active citizenship', that state intervention was acceptable so long as it did not demoralise taxpayers (by substituting the passive payment of taxes for an active involvement in social policy) and recipients (by substituting automatic rights for self-help).[31] In practice, however, this philosophy was applied very

[29] *New Statesman*, 28 January 1939.

[30] For the foundation of the National Council of Social Service, *see* M. Brasnett, 1969: *Voluntary Social Action*. London: NCSS, ch. 2.

[31] J. Harris, 1992: Political thought and the Welfare State, 1870–1940. *Past and Present* 135, 116–41. The acceptance of greater centralisation in housing and unemployment insurance requires further research. It would appear to have been the result of a strange mixture of trust and mistrust. In housing at least, manual workers – in contrast to their German counterparts – would seem to have trusted the impartiality of government, and especially local government, but mistrusted middle-class philanthropic organisations. The Treasury, on the other hand, feared the misuse of public money by outside bodies. In relation to the entrusting of the administration of unemployment insurance to employers and trade unions, for example, it became evident that the real stumbling-block was its doubt over 'whether an industry should be allowed to set up a sort of *imperium in imperio* with compulsory powers conferred by the State, and a state contribution, but without . . . the measure of state control which would ordinarily be a concomitant of those privileges.' Public Record Office, PIN 7/13, memo by T. W. Phillips.

differently. After 1919 it was fully accepted that the State should satisfy minimum needs while charities pioneered remedies for newly identified social problems (for which, if successful, the State might later assume responsibility). In the depression of the 1930s a similar constructive relationship between government and private institutions also became acceptable in economic policy either through overt State intervention or covert 'industrial diplomacy'.[32] That it did become acceptable was also directly due to the impact of war. Reinforced Treasury control may have discouraged the expertise required for incisive economic leadership but at least, in relation to the ill-organised and often aggressive bureaucracy of Edwardian Britain, it did develop a rational framework for such intervention as was publicly required, free from corruption and (despite the insinuation of contemporary lawyers and later neo-liberals) from any lust for self-aggrandisement.[33] The corollary was that, when an even more urgent need for State intervention arose after 1939, the groundwork had been laid to make it both efficient and publicly acceptable.

The paradoxical impact of the war on the organisation of government and the role expected of it can be well illustrated by the increasing regulation of the labour market. The major pre-war advances were the inauguration in 1896 of a conciliation service, the establishment in 1909 of employment exchanges and trade boards (to impose minimum wages in low-paid industries) and the introduction in 1911 of unemployment insurance. Each eroded the Gladstonian definition of minimal government because, although the underlying objective remained the maximisation of market efficiency and individual self-help (unemployment insurance, after all, being little more than enforced thrift), the presumption was that direct government action was needed to achieve these ends. Significantly, each service was also the responsibility of the Board of Trade, one of the leading opponents of pre-war Treasury control, whose administrative practices defied the principles of the Northcote–Trevelyan Report and represented a throwback to the days of Chadwick, which the Report was expressly designed to end. To maintain its expansion, for example, mature experts (at an average age of 42) were recruited and given the maximum possible freedom to use statistical and other research to identify problems within the labour market and propose solutions.[34] To gain necessary expertise and the acceptance of trade unions, a 'corporatist' strategy was also employed. To man the employment exchanges, for instance, a selection committee was appointed which included the president of the Trades Union Congress (David Shackleton), and over a hundred trade unionists were appointed.

[32] Lowe, *Adjusting to Democracy*, op. cit. (note 6), ch. 6; R. Lowe and R. Roberts, 1987: Sir Horace Wilson, 1900–1935. *Historical Journal* 30, 655–60.
[33] In particular, Lord Hewart, 1929: *The New Despotism.* London: Ernest Benn; W. A. Niskanen, 1973: *Bureaucracy: Servant or Master?* London: Institute of Economic Affairs.
[34] R. Davidson and R. Lowe, 1981: Bureaucracy and innovation in British welfare policy 1870–1945. In W. J. Mommsen (ed.), *The Emergence of the Welfare State in Britain and Germany.* London: Croom Helm, 264–77.

The Board, however, made enemies not just of the Treasury but also of employers (who feared an erosion of their managerial prerogatives) and, more importantly, of trade unionists (who conversely feared that state action would undermine their collective strength and independence, thereby creating a 'servile' state along Bismarckian lines). Consequently, during the war, opposition to its policies mounted not only on emergency issues, such as the ban on strikes enacted under the 1915 Munitions of War Act, but also on reconstruction policy, such as the extension of unemployment insurance to munitions workers in anticipation of heavy unemployment during demobilisation.[35] To counter such non-compliance, Lloyd George characteristically chose to adopt a corporatist strategy. The responsibilities of the Board were divided and a Ministry of Labour created in December 1916 with a trade unionist as minister and Shackleton as permanent secretary.

The Ministry was not an immediate success. Trade union suspicion of government was so great that it could not be allayed by such a token measure. With no clear definition of its administrative responsibilities – particularly in relation to manpower and industrial relations – it also clashed bitterly with rival departments such as the Ministry of National Service and the Ministry of Munitions.[36] The Ministry became, in other words, a prime example of the political 'corruption', extravagance and inefficiency of wartime government. Nevertheless, its creation did mark one significant change in policy: the permanent substitution of the paternalistic tradition of the Board in which 'you govern labour for the good of labour, on behalf of labour, but keep labour at a distance' by a policy designed to maximise the independent self-government of industry. As a senior Ministry official responsible for reconstruction (an Old Etonian) explained in January 1918:

> *It is the strong belief of the Department that the great problems of industrial reorganisation which were looming ahead before the War and which have now been brought definitely to the front by war conditions, can only be successfully solved by a policy of decentralisation. It is clear that no system of bureaucratic control of industry is ever likely to succeed in this country. There are two reasons for this:*
> *(a) that state interference is foreign to the whole temper and outlook of English people, who have always been bred in the belief that they are competent to manage their own affairs, and*
> *(b) that no system of centralised administration is likely to produce such good results as a system by which people concerned are themselves interested in the working out of their problems and the success of the scheme adopted to solve them.*[37]

[35] J. Hinton, 1973: *The First Shop Stewards' Movement*. London: Allen & Unwin, ch. 1; N. Whiteside, 1980: Welfare legislation and the unions during the First World War. *Historical Journal* 23, 857–74.

[36] R. Lowe, The Ministry of Labour. In Burk, *War and the State*, op. cit. (note 16), 111–19.

[37] *Parliamentary Debates* (Commons), 5th ser., xcv, 596, 28 June 1917; Public Record Office, Lab 2/454/ML2574/8, memorandum by H. B. Butler.

This policy in itself did not mean a reversion to the Gladstonian definition of minimal government because, as the Ministry recognised, there was a need actively to build up organisations that could effectively achieve 'home rule for industry'. Thus the creation of Whitley Councils was championed to provide a forum for independent self-government; trade board legislation was extended from low-paid to poorly organised industries to give workers an additional reason for joining, and thus strengthening, trade unions; the number of conciliation officials was increased so that they could follow up disputes and assist in the permanent improvement of negotiating practices; and a National Industrial Conference was called in February 1919 to establish common ground between employers and trade unionists upon which government, if necessary, could legislate.[38] Wartime innovation, in other words, did not alter the extent but only the nature of government intervention. It also left open, however, fundamental questions about the distribution of power. Did, for example, a policy of 'home rule for industry' guarantee the workforce a genuine share of industrial control or merely the right to be consulted by management? Could – and should – government give statutory force to an industrial agreement if it contradicted its perception of the consumers' or the broader public interest?

Such questions were never to be directly answered because, as a perceived example of wartime extravagance (with a staff in 1919 of over 26000) and a proponent of interventionist government (albeit to reinforce industry's self-sufficiency), the Ministry of Labour became a prime target of postwar Treasury retrenchment. Its continued existence was challenged by the 1922 Geddes Report and not confirmed until 1924. The recruitment of mature experts was forbidden and its Intelligence and Statistics Department emasculated, as was the department responsible for the promotion of Whitley Councils. Most significantly, the Treasury's administrative powers were used to challenge and reverse agreed government policy in relation to trade boards and the conciliation service. Both were deemed not only to incur 'unnecessary' public expenditure but also, by establishing minimum wages and encouraging trade unions to resist wage cuts, to interfere with the natural workings of the market and hence economic recovery.[39] By the mid-1920s, therefore, the Treasury appeared to have successfully reversed the pre-war trend towards active intervention in the labour market.

However, the Ministry of Labour survived and thereby provided a prime example of the new political constraints under which the postwar Treasury had to work. A return to pre-war normalcy was simply not possible. Moreover, the Ministry, with its extensive responsibilities for the relief of unemployment, quickly came to epitomise the positive virtues of the postwar civil service. Its officials designed and largely manned the Unemployment Assistance Board,

[38] Lowe, *Adjusting to Democracy*, op. cit. (note 6), 87–105.
[39] R. Lowe, 1978: The erosion of State intervention in Britain, 1917–24. *Economic History Review* 31, 270–86.

which centralised the payment of relief to the uninsured after 1934 and provided the model for the postwar National Assistance Board and the
Supplementary Benefits Commission. They also designed and largely manned
the Special Areas Commissions, which after 1932, and especially after 1937,
developed most of the policy initiatives that came to be incorporated into postwar regional policy. In short, they successfully pioneered a middle way
between the perceived aggression of the pre-war Board of Trade and the traditional negativism of the Treasury. As one official summarised this essentially
constructive, if modest, compromise role: 'it is for us alleged bureaucrats who
are supposed to be depressing private initiative to encourage it, and to dis-
courage people from unduly relying on bureaucrats'.[40]

The War and Local Government

The impact of the First World War on local government – so far as it has been
acknowledged by historians – has conventionally been portrayed as slight. The
immediate shock was to the structure and role of central government. There
was no such shock to local government and thus, with the exception of housing, no major discontinuity to compare with that before the First World War
(with, as has been seen, its quadrupling in size) and immediately after the
Second World War (with the loss through nationalisation of such major
responsibilities as hospitals, electricity and gas). The inter-war period, as
exemplified by the 1929 Local Government Act, was one of consolidation in
the face of economic and social pressures that had been building up before
1914. Consequently, such impact as the war had was essentially indirect: the
intensification of pre-war pressures and a transformation of the social and
political context in which they had to be resolved. How accurate is this conventional picture?

   In 1914 local government faced two major organisational problems. The
first was the continued existence of the boards of poor law guardians – the last
surviving example of the Victorian expedient of creating specially elected bodies to implement a single policy. Both the majority and minority reports of the
1905–9 Royal Commission on the Poor Law had agreed that they should be
absorbed into the all-purpose county councils and county boroughs established in 1888; but they had disagreed over the precise details and so no break-
up of the poor law had occurred. The war injected a new sense of urgency.
Within the Ministry of Reconstruction a committee on local government was
established with Sir Donald Maclean as chairman, and under Beatrice Webb's
driving leadership it produced a unanimous report by December 1917.[41] It re-
emphasised the need for the boards to be abolished. It also resolved earlier
disagreements by recommending that their special facilities (such as hos-

[40] Quoted in Lowe, *Adjusting to Democracy*, op. cit. (note 6), 75.
[41] Johnson, *Land Fit for Heroes*, op. cit. (note 18), 80–5; Cd. 8917 (1918).

pitals) should, where appropriate, be integrated with other local authority services, while the destitute should continue to be relieved separately, according to the principle of less eligibility, by a public assistance committee of the relevant local authority. This report provided the rock by which a return to pre-war normalcy was prevented, and the 1929 Local Government Act duly implemented its proposals – although, in certain districts, the forces of conservatism were so strong that existing poor law guardians were simply re-elected *en bloc* to the public assistance committees and resisted all attempts to integrate their facilities with the counties' specialist services.[42] Historians' attention is too often fixed on the small number of boards and guardians, such as that of Poplar, which exceeded their statutory powers. There were far more boards that equally broke the law by failing to fulfil them.

The second organisational problem was the size of, and relationship between, the various units of local government: county councils (with their secondary tier of non-county boroughs, and urban and district councils) and county boroughs. Historic boundaries were being made increasingly redundant by the movement of people from city centres into suburbs and the surrounding countryside (due to improved transport) and the technical need to plan certain services (such as roads, sewerage and the supply of gas and electricity) on an ever-widening scale. However, the weight of history – and in particular the jealous independence of many towns – was against rationalisation. In 1888 an attempt had been made to extend county councils over the whole of England and Wales, with only ten major cities remaining fully independent: to act otherwise, it was argued, would undermine the whole economic and social coherence of each region. In fact the exact opposite happened. At the height of municipal enterprise (especially in relation to profit-making services such as gas and electricity), the initiative lay with urban government and it accordingly grew at the expense of the county. Between 1888 and 1926, the original sixty-one county boroughs took over an additional 250 000 acres and 1.7 million people from the counties, while twenty-three non-county boroughs achieved independence and annexed a further 100 000 acres and 1.3 million people.[43]

Increased mobility and technical improvements during the war threatened to expand urban government still further. This expansion, however, was effectively halted by central government. Increased powers were given to the county councils (especially supervisory powers over their secondary tier), and after 1926 the mechanism for boundary changes was made increasingly difficult. The war was thus the occasion on which a halt was brought to a spontaneous process of urban expansion which many later reformers, including Bevan in 1949 and the Redcliffe-Maud Royal Commission on Local Government in 1969, considered to be the best way in which local government

[42] J. P. Bradbury, 1990: The 1929 Local Government Act. Unpublished Ph.D. thesis, University of Bristol, 203–4. Much of the succeeding section is based on this thesis.
[43] J. Owen, 1989: Defending the county. *Local Government Studies*, 15, 52.

could evolve.[44] Why did this happen? Successive governments' underlying rationale was almost certainly administrative: the need for larger administrative units (perceived in 1888) and concern over how the rump left by the advance of urban government could be governed. There was, however, undoubtedly an additional conservative motive which the war had done little to dispel and may even have strengthened. This was a political desire to defend rural against urban culture and, more narrowly, to counterbalance potential Labour Party voters in the towns with traditional Liberal or Conservative voters in the countryside.[45]

Before 1914, local government had also faced two major financial problems: the insufficiency of local sources of finance to meet the escalating cost of new services, and the need to redistribute resources from rich to poor authorities. Both problems appeared intractable. In the first case, increased taxation was inevitably opposed by those who would have to pay (as demonstrated by the 'ratepayers' revolt' in Edwardian England), while further subsidies from Whitehall would upset the delicate balance between local and central government. The widespread wish was not only for local government but for local self-government so that, by 1914, central grants still covered only 15 per cent of local expenditure.[46] In the second case, any redistribution of resources would have antagonised the richer authorities which dominated the representative institutions (the County Councils Association and the Association of Municipal Corporations) upon which central government was in turn dependent for the implementation of policy. A partial solution, advanced hesitantly by the minority report of the 1901 Royal Commission on Local Taxation and more confidently by the Treasury's Kempe Committee (which reported just before the outbreak of war in 1914) was for central government to allocate money to local authorities in a block grant calculated on a needs-based formula. This was the solution adopted by the 1929 Local Government Act, at least in relation to health expenditure; and it provided an important precedent for the future financial relationship between central and local government.[47]

Although welcomed by local authorities because it relieved them of detailed inspection by Whitehall, the block grant was not, however, unreservedly 'progressive'. Indeed, in many ways it represented a triumph for the increased power of the post-war Treasury and for the richer authorities. Within the department responsible for the 1929 legislation (the Ministry of Health) it was, for instance, the finance officer who, in the debate opened up by the Maclean Report, pressed hard for the reform because it placed a definite ceil-

[44] Public Record Office, CAB 134/170, memorandum by Ministry of Health 29 April 1949; the majority report of the Royal Commission on Local Government in England, Cmnd. 4040 (1969).
[45] Owen, Defending the county, op. cit. (note 46).
[46] A. Offer, 1981: *Property and Politics.* Cambridge: Cambridge University Press; J. H. Warren, 1950: Local government. In Sir G. Campion *et al.*, *British Government since 1918*. London: Allen & Unwin, 194.
[47] Cd. 638 (1901); Cd. 7315 (1914).

ing on Treasury commitments. In contrast, those officials concerned with the promotion of health policy fought for the retention of percentage grants (whereby central government was committed to pay a fixed percentage of all local expenditure) because local government was thereby given an incentive to expand services, such as the antenatal and child welfare clinics inaugurated during the war. In negotiations with the CCA and AMC over the 1929 Act the redistributive element within the block grant was also seriously eroded so that it had little immediate beneficial effect.[48] Consequently, such financial rationalisation as was achieved in the aftermath of the war was contained within a tight conservative framework. Moreover, it is significant that the war provoked no investigation of additional sources of local finance (such as a local income tax or the taxation of site values, both of which had been suggested before 1914). Local self-government was to be sustained but clearly not strengthened.

The conventional picture of the impact of the First World War on local government is, therefore, largely justified. The war injected a new sense of urgency into reform and forced choices to be made from the variety of policy options debated before 1914. The war itself, however, generated no new ideas, and the options chosen – in particular the halting of urban expansion and the introduction of the block grant – reinforced the traditional balance between central and local government and between rich and poor authorities. Local self-government was respected but not reinforced, and so it was denied the organisational and financial strength it needed to respond not only to the major challenge of the inter-war period (unemployment relief) but also after 1939 to the emergency of war.[49] The major impact of the First World War was, therefore, not direct but indirect: its influence upon the social and political context in which local government had to operate and in which its limitations became slowly exposed. Among the most important changes here were the withdrawal of the traditional landed élite following either the loss or the diversification of its economic resources; the incursion of party politics, especially into urban government, as a consequence of the enlarged electorate; and the increasing professionalism and bureaucratisation of local officials as a result of enhanced public expectations and the desire for a greater uniformity of services.[50]

Conclusions

One of the most important effects of the First World War, so it has been recently argued, was to turn a minority demand for a developmental State into

[48] Bradbury, Local Government Act, op. cit. (note 45), 213–29.
[49] R. Middleton, 1983: The Treasury and public investment: a perspective on inter-war economic management. *Public Administration* 61, 351–70.
[50] D. Cannadine, 1990: *The Decline and Fall of the British Aristocracy*. New Haven, Conn: Yale University Press, ch. 4; W. Holtby, *South Riding*. London: Collins, 1936; J. M. Lee, 1963: *Social Leaders and Public Persons*. Oxford: Clarendon Press.

an 'ideological and political movement centred on the Coalition and then to pack it with the seeds of its own destruction.'[51] In the short term, the rapid abandonment of many wartime innovations was indeed remarkable and, to this extent, the war can be portrayed as a lost opportunity for the modernisation of British government. However, in a longer-term perspective stretching from the 1870s to the 1930s and embracing the political culture underpinning both central and local government, the war can be seen as the occasion that forced choices to be made from a wide range of options long debated but largely evaded during late Victorian and Edwardian Britain. The structure of both central and local government was at last rationalised and made responsive to new political demands arising from the greatly increased electorate.

However, rationalisation was effected within a strictly conservative framework. Treasury control, which had been successfully resisted since 1855, was fully implemented and, moreover, implemented in such a way that the civil service adopted an exclusive, secretive and generalist ethos. Similarly, the reinforcement of county councils and the restriction of financial innovation to the block grant impaired the ability of local government to adapt to changing circumstances by halting the historic expansion of urban government and placing a clear ceiling on the financial resources of local authorities.

The impact of the First World War on government may, therefore, reasonably be described as conservative if not actually counter-revolutionary. Certainly it had none of the dramatic effect on government that it had in other combatant nations such as Germany and Russia. However, as was constantly remarked at the time, there were two methods of making a revolution – the Russian and the British method; and the more subtle ways in which government, above all at a central level, was permanently changed as a result of the war should not be underplayed. These included the acceptance by taxpayers of a far higher rate of taxation and the acknowledgement by previous proponents of voluntary action of the need for greater centralisation. The war also made the expansion of central government ultimately more acceptable, as was illustrated by the evolving regulation of the labour market, by the substitution of the aggressive, paternalistic bureaucracy of Edwardian Britain for a more pragmatic and politically sensitive civil service. As with all 'revolutions', there was an immediate reaction and an attempt to restore the past – in this case the restoration of pre-war normalcy in the 1920s. This proved to be impossible, and so a new equilibrium was established in the 1930s. It was upon this equilibrium, rather than upon any unique event during the Second World War, that the major organisational changes in both central and local government after 1945 were essentially based.

---

[51] Turner, *British Politics*, op. cit. (note 3), 445.

3

Industry, Agriculture and Trade Unions

Maurice W. Kirby

The secular impact of the First World War on Britain's industrial economy is exceedingly difficult to determine. On the one hand it can be argued that the logistic needs of the war, capped by the expansionary effects of a short but intense postwar boom, boosted the fortunes of old-established staple trades such as coal-mining, shipbuilding and heavy engineering to the detriment of structural change and economic modernisation. Structural rigidities had been present in the pre-war economy, as reflected in the slow growth of sectors such as advanced chemicals, electrical products and light engineering in general. Such industries were the 'wave of the future', but Britain's lop-sided or 'over-committed' industrial structure, reinforced by the war and subsequent boom, arguably precluded their rapid development. It is an equally credible view, however, that the First World War marked a major discontinuity in British industrial development in the sense that it paved the way for product and process innovations which were profoundly beneficial for long-run economic progress. On this interpretation the impetus to industrial modernisation unleashed by the logistic needs of the war redounded to the peacetime competitive advantage of industry by helping to resolve the pre-war problem of structural stagnation.

The impact of the war on the agricultural sector is rather less contentious. It is generally agreed that in impoverishing landowners the conflict hastened the pre-war trend towards the break-up of agricultural estates, while the war-induced subsidisation of cereal producers disappeared in the wake of financial retrenchment after 1919. But if continuity rather than discontinuity marked agriculture's inter-war experience, any commentary on the legacy of the war must allow for the fact that it bequeathed major lessons of policy which were rapidly relearned when the international situation deteriorated in the later 1930s.

The contradictory themes of continuity and discontinuity applicable to the industrial sector are also writ large in analysing the development of labour relations after 1914. At one level the war can be perceived as marking the decisive breakthrough to the national recognition and complementary wage bargaining so desired by leading elements within the trade union movement before 1914. That this was achieved as a result of government intervention in the context of an expanding war economy is commonplace in the literature. It is important to note that it was also facilitated in some measure by the formation of employers' associations at the trade and federal levels. Taken together, these trends towards co-operation have been viewed by some historians as consistent with an emerging corporatism, or corporate bias, in the British political system, whereby state policy is formulated within a network of interlocking public and private bureaucracies.

Yet the moves towards centripetalism in labour relations, apparently confirmed by the war, were arguably retarded, even reversed, after 1920 in the face of economic recession and a reversion to the confrontational stance between workers and employers typical of the pre-war period. According to this perspective the labour relations environment of the inter-war years, far from reflecting the spirit of wartime co-operation between capital and labour, was conditioned by the free play of market forces as self-interested intransigence gained the upper hand. Such circumstances were hardly conducive to corporatist notions of government.

In order to analyse further the central issues of continuity and discontinuity the first substantive section of this chapter provides an account of industrial and agricultural development, including labour relations, in the context of the expanded wartime state. The following section then considers the postwar experience of the economy in the light of wartime developments. The final section provides a brief overview of the war's secular legacy for Britain's economic development.

The War Economy

The extent to which the First World War imparted a modernising impetus to British industry can be discussed most appropriately by reference to the role of the state. The first total war gave rise to logistic demands of unprecedented magnitude. In this respect, the expansion of munitions output at the behest of government had immediate and direct effects on a wide spectrum of industrial sectors, from coal-mining and iron and steel to advanced chemicals and light engineering. Government intervention, moreover, was sufficiently sophisticated to move beyond acceptance of the status quo in industrial structure and organisation. Military requirements for advanced technical equipment necessitated the founding of new production facilities, and there was an unprecedented concern to maximise physical output by reference to efficiency criteria. After 1915 the Government assumed wholesale powers in the industrial field and used its status as a monopsonist to secure logistic requirements in terms of volume and the efficiency of production.

A further element in the evolution of the war economy was a growing preoccupation at official level with the quality and extent of labour relations. Industrial disputes had been rife in the immediate pre-war period, with a particular focus on the labour-intensive staple trades. Wartime production schedules, however, placed a new premium on the maintenance of industrial harmony and this went hand in hand with the inauguration of efficiency-enhancing workshop procedures. In all of these respects – industrial diversification, the boost to productivity and improved labour relations – there is a case for claiming that governmental agencies fulfilled a critical role in improving the condition of the industrial economy. High-throughput mass production techniques had made little headway in British manufacturing before 1914, and the industrial structure as a whole failed to reflect the diversification into modern sectors which had been achieved in Germany and the United States. Wartime developments, however, remedied these deficiencies in ways that redounded to the peacetime competitive advantage of industry. Judged in an optimistic light, therefore, the war economy can be viewed as a significant discontinuity in Britain's industrial experience.

At the outset of the war the immediate reaction of government to the acquisition of logistical supplies was to rely on private enterprise and the laws of supply and demand. In retrospect such complacency appears astonishing, if not reprehensible. However, as has so often been emphasised, the general expectation in August 1914 was that the war would be of short duration and would therefore 'bear some reasonable relation to the historical past'.[1] Hence, the need for State intervention could be confined to a few specific areas, such as the foreign exchanges and the requisition of transport and war supplies. In short, 'the economic organisation which [had] served so well for a century of peace' could be relied upon to secure effective resource allocation.[2] These attitudes, prevalent at the highest levels of government, were soon undermined as Britain's preponderant military commitment moved far beyond a strategy of naval blockade to encompass the recruitment of a mass army to fight a major European land war. The lesson that the state would have to play a far more active role in the economy was learnt first in the munitions industries, where the 'Great Shell Scandal' of 1915, arising from the scarcity of ordnance at the front, revealed the limitations of the existing controls administered by a Cabinet committee. The Ministry of Munitions was established in June 1915, headed by Lloyd George, and the Munitions of War Act, which reached the statute book two months after his appointment, marked the beginnings of 'a considerable extension of the Government's powers of economic control' over large sections of industry.[3]

In analysing the wartime record of the Ministry of Munitions, Wrigley has concluded that it was 'an innovatory department' receptive to new ideas and a

[1] E. M. H. Lloyd, 1924: *Experiments in State Control.* Oxford: Clarendon Press, 23.
[2] E. V. Morgan, 1952: *Studies in British Financial Policy, 1914–25.* London: Macmillan, 37.
[3] Sidney Pollard, 1992: *The Development of the British Economy, 1914–1990.* London: Edward Arnold, 44–5.

vital force in securing the nation's logistic supplies.[4] This judgement, based on a consensual view of the Ministry's achievements, is validated by the considerable upsurge in armaments production after 1915. The Ministry not only provided financial subsidies to engineering firms to expand productive capacity, but also established state-owned munitions factories and shipyards equipped with electric power and best-practice production techniques. In the latter context, standardisation and mass production were encouraged by the introduction of automatic and semi-automatic machinery in engineering establishments and, in the case of iron and steel, the spread of the arc furnace. Contracting firms, moreover, were encouraged to amalgamate their interests and to engage in concerted research and development programmes. Scale economies were also underwritten by a trend toward engineering specialisation coupled with improvements in managerial organisation and procedures. In both respects the Ministry used its leverage as a powerful monopsonist to secure the spread of best-practice techniques in areas such as cost accounting and labour management. Time-and-motion studies were implemented extensively, especially in controlled establishments, while welfare provision, focusing on the 'health and comfort' of employees, many of them female, received the attention of the Ministry's Welfare and Health Section.

In observing that the Ministry of Munitions combined 'paternalistic altruism' with 'tough efficiency', Wrigley concluded that it

> *seems to have purveyed the scientific management of Taylor and his disciples, to have gone for the combination of high output and relatively high pay, sweeping aside impediments be they trade union safeguards or old management practices. The Ministry pressed on those factories under its control the latest ideas in technology and management and attempted to bring the policies of the least efficient into line with those of the best.*[5]

The reference to 'trade union safeguards' is a reminder that the Munitions of War Act, the penal clauses of which came into force in July 1915, provided for the suspension of trade union rules in the munitions industries for the remainder of the war. Thus, in the name of labour dilution, women were permitted to operate automatic machinery, semi-skilled workers could carry out operations normally undertaken by skilled mechanics, and the work of skilled men could be subdivided and simplified. Strikes on war-related work were declared illegal, while compulsory arbitration was to be invoked in all labour disputes.[6]

The elimination of innumerable restrictive practices was an essential complement to technical and managerial reorganisation in facilitating the expan-

[4] C. J. Wrigley, 1982: The Ministry of Munitions: An innovatory department. In Kathleen Burk (ed.), *War and the State: The Transformation of British Government, 1914–1919*. London: George Allen & Unwin, 32–56; R. J. Q. Adams, 1978: *Arms and the Wizard: Lloyd George and the Ministry of Munitions, 1915–1916*. London: Cassell.
[5] Wrigley, Ministry of Munitions, op. cit. (note 4), 51.
[6] S. J. Hurwitz, 1968: *State Intervention in Great Britain: A Study of Economic Control and Social Response 1914–19*. London: Frank Cass, 89.

sion of munitions output. It also made a vital contribution to the achievement of higher levels of productivity. Indeed, it was the efficiency-enhancing aspects of the war economy that were seized upon by the Ministry of Reconstruction, established in August 1917, as the critical element in rebuilding 'the national life on a better and more durable foundation' once the war had ended. Although the new Ministry's remit embraced social reconstruction in conformity with Lloyd George's undertaking to create a 'land fit for heroes', its economic aims were equally far-reaching in that it wished to see the improvements in business organisation and industrial efficiency achieved in the munitions industries perpetuated into the peacetime economy. The principal consideration in this respect was to secure the competitive advantage of British industry in the expectation that the pre-war export penetration of British markets by German industry would be resumed.[7] At the time of the Ministry's formation this prospect appeared all the more likely in view of the distinct possibility that the war would end in a stalemate peace, leaving the sinews of German economic power intact.

For the Ministry, the key to successful social and economic reconstruction lay in enhanced co-operation between workers and employers. The war had wrought considerable changes in the labour relations environment and these had led to the dawning realisation that 'Increased output and improved conditions are two sides of the same shield.'[8] Reconstruction was therefore dependent on the maintenance of confidence between capital and labour and the laying down of sectional interests. As early as 1916 a Committee on Relations between Employers and Employed had been established under the chairmanship of John Wheatley 'To make and consider suggestions for securing a permanent improvement between employers and workmen'.[9] The outcome of the committee's deliberations was the establishment of Joint Industrial Councils in industries as diverse as motor vehicles, chemicals, bobbins and pottery.[10] By 1918 twenty-six councils were in existence with fourteen more at the stage of draft constitutions. Embraced enthusiastically by trade unions in unskilled trades and in those industries with little tradition of collective bargaining, the co-operative Whitley philosophy elicited an equivalent response from employers' groups, notably among those that took a less than sanguine view of British industry's postwar market prospects in the face of renewed German and American competition.

A key development in this respect was the foundation in 1916 of the

---

[7] Maurice Kirby and Mary B. Rose, 1991: Productivity and competitive failure: British government policy and industry, 1914–19. In Geoffrey Jones and M. W. Kirby (eds), *Competitiveness and the State: Government and Business in Twentieth Century Britain*. Manchester: Manchester University Press, 25.

[8] Ministry of Reconstruction, 1918: *Problems of Reconstruction*. Pamphlet 1, *The Aims of Reconstruction*. London: Ministry of Reconstruction, 5.

[9] Ibid.

[10] Ibid., 8. For a detailed study of Whitleyism, *see* Rodger Charles, 1973: *The Development of Industrial Relations in Britain, 1911–1939: Studies in the Evolution of Collective Bargaining at a National and Industry Level*. London: Hutchinson, 77–226.

Federation of British Industries under the guiding hand of the arch-productioneer and trade warrior, Dudley Docker. An ardent supporter of industrial modernisation buttressed by tariff protection, Docker also played important roles in precipitating the foundation of the Ministry of Reconstruction and in launching the Joint Industrial Councils in 1917.[11]

Thus, the state's approach to both the evolution of the war economy and economic reconstruction was characterised by a new level of consultation with employers and unions, supplemented by a growing concern with issues of industrial efficiency. Such centripetal tendencies were evident on many planes, not least in terms of the participation of businessmen and trade unionists in the direction of the war economy. For Wrigley, the most striking innovation in the creation of the Ministry of Munitions was the recruitment of active business leaders as senior administrators.[12] As Lloyd George claimed subsequently in his *War Memoirs*, 'The Ministry of Munitions was from first to last a business-man organisation. Its most distinctive feature was the appointment I made of successful businessmen to the chief executive posts.'[13] Over ninety businessmen were recruited during the first three months of the Ministry's existence. Prominent among them was Sir Eric Geddes, chief manager of the North Eastern Railway, who owed his reputation as 'the leading hustler' in munitions supply

> to his remarkable efforts at improving machine gun output [and] reorganising the administration of Woolwich and implementing the National Factories scheme. He undertook detailed surveys, delivered data, prioritised needs and established production schedules. He advanced the view that statistics represented the knowledge of a problem and without data, the wasteful use of resources easily occurred.[14]

Geddes' effective dynamism was, however, exceptional. Indeed, the Parliamentary Secretary to the Ministry, Christopher Addison, complained frequently about 'big businessmen' who guarded their departmental boundaries jealously and found it difficult to 'play the game'.[15] It is also important to note that the extent of labour dilution was more apparent than real. Experience in the west of Scotland, for example, indicates that official claims in the summer of 1916 that dilution in the engineering and shipbuilding industries had been implemented extensively were little more than an attempt to boost public morale. In a case-study of the Clydeside shipbuilding industry, Alastair Reid has demonstrated that dilution – as defined by the Ministry of Munitions in favour of female employees – was slight.[16] Of the 14 000 women

[11] R. P. T. Davenport-Hines, 1984: *Dudley Docker: The Life and Times of a Trade Warrior.* Cambridge: Cambridge University Press, 4, 99–100, 116.

[12] Wrigley, Ministry of Munitions, op. cit. (note 4), 40.

[13] David Lloyd George, 1938: *War Memoirs*, vol. 1. London: Odhams, 147.

[14] K. Grieves, 1989: *Sir Eric Geddes: Business and Government in War and Peace.* Manchester: Manchester University Press, 26.

[15] Christopher Addison, diary entry, 8 July 1915. Cited in K. Grieves, 1989: Improvising the British war effort: Eric Geddes and Lloyd George, 1915–18. *War and Society* 7, 43.

[16] Alastair Reid, 1985: Dilution, trade unionism and the state in Britain during the First World War. In Steven Tolliday and Jonathan Zeitlin (eds), *Shopfloor Bargaining and the State: Historical and Comparative Perspectives.* Cambridge: Cambridge University Press, 46–74.

recruited to war work on Clydeside in the first half of 1916, only 1000 were placed in shipyards. The reasons, applicable to other heavy industrial sectors, are not far to seek. Conditions in the yards were especially dangerous to new-comers on account of open bulkheads and high scaffolding. Opportunities to employ women in self-contained gangs to avoid sexual incidents were extremely limited, and it is significant in this respect that most female recruits were directed to marine engineering shops engaged in repetitive production of 'light and simple components'. In addition, employers had their own ulter-ior motives in resisting dilution. Initially prevalent among merchant ship-builders, the desire to retain as much skilled male labour as possible spread even to the Admiralty. Moreover, as Reid points out, in the context of a tight labour market the skilled unions, such as the Boilermakers' Society, were able to capitalise on their employers' resistance to female dilution by increasing their control both over conditions of work and the employment of unskilled male labour.

While the shipbuilding industry provides an essential counter to the image of an efficiency-enhancing war economy this should not detract from the sheer magnitude of the productive achievements of the Ministry of Munitions. Despite Addison's reservations, the evidence suggests that Lloyd George's recruitment of active businessmen paid dividends in improving productive organisation in the munitions industries. In July 1916, at the time of Lloyd George's departure from the Ministry of Munitions, three weeks' production of 18-pounder ammunition was equivalent to total output in the first year of the war.[17] In the period from August 1914 to June 1915, the army received 1105 artillery pieces, 94 of them in the 'heavy' category. The equivalent figures for the first year of the ministry's existence were 5006 and 894 respectively. In the same period grenade output increased spectacularly from 68 000 to 27 million, trench mortars from 312 to 4279 and machine-guns from 1486 to 17 679.[18] These increases were entirely dependent on the innovation of high-throughput mass production technology.

Equally significant was the mounting involvement of leading trade unionists in the conduct of the war economy. In munitions, their participation in the National Advisory Committee was the critical element in the reorganisation of work schedules and the removal of restrictive practices. In coal-mining, union officials enjoyed full representation on the advisory board to the official Coal Controller, while the creation of pit committees at the most important col-lieries served to enhance the miners' role in the management of the industry.[19] That said, the overall impact of the war on trade union structures was inher-ently ambiguous. Centralising tendencies, as reflected in the growing status of national leaders, were certainly present, while the formation of national employers' associations was complemented by the movement towards

[17] Adams, *Arms and the Wizard*, op. cit. (note 4), p. 244.
[18] Lloyd George, *War Memoirs*, op. cit. (note 13), 389–90.
[19] M. W. Kirby, 1977: *The British Coal Mining Industry, 1870–1946: A Political and Economic History.* London: Macmillan, 31–2.

amalgamation and the formation of federations among trade unions. Motivated in part by wartime changes in labour markets in relation to the level of production and dilution, these developments also reflected the centralising strategies of union leaders. The latter were prompted by the desire both to exert control over local memberships and to secure more effective relationships with employers' organisations and government.

In contradistinction to these trends in favour of national collective bargaining was the growth of shopfloor collective action at the behest of increasingly influential shop stewards. As Richard Hyman has emphasised, the First World War 'transformed the role of the steward' in industrial relations: 'If one consequence of war conditions was to force collective bargaining from the district up to national level, a converse effect was to drive the struggle for job control down to the workplace.'[20] This was the direct product of the erosion of traditional work practices in the face of dilution, the general speeding up of work, and the spread of payments by results. As Hyman points out, shop stewards did have a role to play in the peaceful resolution of localised disputes. In this respect it is a notable fact that the number of strikes fell more sharply after 1914 than after 1939. Yet in popular demonology stewards have traditionally been viewed as subversive elements in capitalist society, not least on account of their commitment to workers' control. While the bulk of shop steward activity was routine and tedious, the very fact of localised bargaining, often in the face of official union ignorance or indifference to specific grievances, 'created a natural receptivity to radical conceptions of industrial relations'.[21] In so far as shop steward activity was strongest among skilled workers most threatened by the exigencies of wartime production, it is readily understandable why those in favour of craft sectionalism should often have been led by revolutionary socialists opposed in principle to worker élites. However, as Hyman concludes,

> *the unity of seeming opposites was facilitated by the duality of notions of workers' control: appealing simultaneously to the pre-capitalist self-determination of the independent journeyman, and the post-capitalist and collective direction of the totality of economic relations.*[22]

It is thus hardly surprising that employers and national trade union bureaucracies should have sought to curb, if not to control, shop steward activity. Excellent examples of this are provided by nationally negotiated agreements in engineering in 1917 and 1919 which defined stewards' responsibilities narrowly, and the proposed works committees recommended in the Whitley Reports, which if established on a firm basis would have the effect of undermining shop steward authority.

The rise of a shop stewards' 'movement' committed to decentralised labour relations and with little interest in the Whitleyite philosophy of industrial

[20] Richard Hyman, 1987: Rank-and-file movements and workplace organisation, 1914–39. In C. J. Wrigley (ed.), *A History of British Industrial Relations.* Vol. 2, *1914–1939.* Brighton: Harvester, 132.
[21] Ibid., 134.
[22] Ibid., 135.

partnership was not the only factor that conflicted with the Government's ideal of national co-operation between capital and labour as the cornerstone of reconstruction. The Ministry of Labour, for example, newly formed in 1916, believed that Whitleyism was fatally flawed, if only because the craft-based unions feared that industrial partnership would lead to combinations between semi-skilled workers and employers, to the detriment of their privileged position in the hierarchy of industrial relations.[23]

Above all, Whitleyism was regarded with deep suspicion and scepticism by key sections of employers and workers.[24] In the former case the centre of opposition lay in the hard-line Engineering Employers' Federation (EEF). Its secretary was Sir Allan Smith, a prominent recruit as a man of business to the Ministry of Munitions. As an apparent advocate of industrial consensus, Smith was, initially, a supporter of Whitleyism. By the end of the war, however, his true feelings had emerged. Far from espousing co-operation with labour, he began to refer habitually to trade unions as 'the enemy', and, as 'an expert in procrastination', his 'icy cold speeches' were enough to 'freeze to death any progress his members might feel'.[25] Complementing the engineering employers in its preference for a strategy of confrontation on pre-war lines was that 'weapon of unpredictable power', the Triple Industrial Alliance, formed in 1913 and composed of the Miners' Federation of Great Britain (MFGB), the National Union of Railwaymen (NUR) and the Transport Workers' Federation (TWF). In 1919 the NUR's *Railway Review* stated that no 'useful purpose is served by collusion with the employer through the Government to preserve the existing order of society.'[26] Such sentiments struck at the very roots of reconstruction, but the most uncompromising rejection of industrial consensus was to be found within the coal industry. In the three decades before 1914, two mutually incompatible views of the industry had emerged, with the miners favouring national wage settlements while colliery owners remained committed to the industry's decentralised wage structure. The state-controlled national profits pool during the First World War drove the two sides further apart.[27] As William Brace, the Welsh miners' leader, stated in 1919, 'the war has driven us at least twenty-five years in advance of where we were in thought in 1914. The young men have thought deeply and, indeed, they are educated.'[28] Thus, the belief that wartime state controls had enhanced their position irreversibly helps to explain the apparent audacity of the miners' postwar programme, published as a series of demands in January 1919. In addition to a 30 per cent increase in gross wages (exclusive of wartime increases) and a six-hour day, it included a demand for the nationalisation of mines that

[23] Rodney Lowe, 1986: *Adjusting to Democracy: The Role of the Ministry of Labour in British Politics, 1916–1939.* Oxford: Clarendon Press, 92.
[24] Alan Fox, 1985: *History and Heritage: The Social Origins of the British Industrial Relations System.* London: George Allen & Unwin, 296.
[25] Walter Citrine, 1964: *Men and Work: An Autobiography.* London: Hutchinson, 247.
[26] NUR, *Railway Review*, 27 June 1919.
[27] Kirby, *The British Coal Mining Industry* op. cit. (note 19), 24–48.
[28] Public Record Office (PRO), CAB 24/90, 9 October 1919.

contained the stipulation that there should be 'joint control by the workmen and the State' – clearly a reflection of the miners' participation in the wartime control apparatus. In combining political with economic demands the MFGB had moved far beyond any notion of an industrial consensus based on a partnership between labour and capital.

In analysing the impact of the war economy on labour relations in British industry it is apparent that it acted simultaneously as an accelerator of pre-war trends and as a catalyst of change. For workers in general the circumstances of war confirmed the status of trade unions as legitimate bargaining agents in conformity with pre-war programmes of advancement. This was reflected in the rising trend of total union membership, from 4 135 000 in 1913 to 6 533 000 in 1918 with a further surge to 8 347 000 in 1920. Moreover, for specific groups in strongly organised trades, the war economy gave every appearance of validating radical programmes inherited from the years of peace. As indicated, this was exemplified in the miners' reaction to the wartime control system, which provided a major impetus to the campaign for public ownership of the coal-mining industry inaugurated in the 1890s. Although mining trade unionists participated in the wartime control apparatus this should not be taken as evidence of consensual co-operation with employers and the state. On the contrary, the miners and their allies in the NUR and TWF were determined to maintain their distance from Whitleyism in so far as it stood in the way of radical changes in industrial organisation in general and labour relations in particular. As a catalyst of change in labour relations the war economy provoked conflicting tendencies: centripetalism on the one hand, as reflected in union mergers, the growing status of official union leaders, and the spread of national agreements; and on the other, decentralisation focusing on shopfloor bargaining and the related role of shop stewards. In overall terms, the war tended to enhance the status of the semi-skilled at the expense of the skilled and, via Whitleyism, inaugurated effective collective bargaining in a number of trades ranging from electricity and water supply, to paper making, silk, quarrying and cement.[29]

For the structure and organisation of British industry the war economy provided a major discontinuity with previous experience. Its most extreme manifestation has been well described by Sidney Pollard:

> *Some industries had hardly existed at all in this country before the war and had to be established in war-time to maintain supplies formerly drawn from Germany. They included the making of scientific instruments, of ball bearings, of chemical and laboratory glassware, of tungsten and of chemical products including benzol, toluol and ammonia liquor. Others, again, had been in infancy in 1914 and grew to manhood only because of military demands, the most important being the aircraft industry.[30]*

---

[29] C. J. Wrigley, The trade unions between the wars. In Wrigley, *British Industrial Relations*, op. cit. (note 20), 87.

[30] Pollard, *The Development of the British Economy*, op. cit. (note 3), 20.

As an appropriate guide to structural trends in the economy some of the employment statistics in Table 3.1, relating to the trans-war period, may be cited. Employment in vehicles, for example, rose from 197 000 in 1911 to 357 000 in 1921; in electrical apparatus from 80 000 to 166 000; in chemicals, paint and oils from 133 000 to 198 000; and from 24 000 to 46 000 in rubber

Table 3.1   Industrial Distribution of Population, Great Britain

| Industry | Number of persons engaged, including those out of work (in thousands) | | | | |
| | England and Wales | | | Scotland | |
	1911	1921	1931	1921	1931
Expanding					
Building, decorating and contracting	861	758	1 048	68	102
Woodworking, furniture, etc.	242	228	302	42	45
Bricks, pottery and glass	171	177	214	12	15
Vehicles	197	357	382	18	20
Rubber	24	46	54	8	10
Road transport	291	297	456	38	53
Electrical apparatus	80	166	286	10	10
Silk	32	33	70	1	2
Hosiery	59	80	110	15	22
Food, drink, tobacco	486	541	717	82	93
Paper making, printing, etc.	285	340	425	46	52
Chemicals, paint, oils	133	198	211	18	21
Gas, water, electricity	109	163	228	16	17
Local government	489	689	911	84	108
Personal service (hotels, restaurants, domestic)	2452	2025	2406	200	223
Contracting					
Agriculture	1230	1124	1018	183	177
Coal-mining	971	1133	1030	163	133
Iron and steel	166	239	198	51	37
Engineering and shipbuilding	637	887	761	245	171
Cotton	628	596	571	25	20
Wool and worsted	233	237	228	22	20
Flax, hemp and jute	30	27	24	59	54
Lace	44	24	16	3	3
Railways	455	549	496	73	60
Water transport	284	330	310	41	50
All industries	16 284	17 178	18 853	2191	2221

Source: G. A. Jones and A. G. Pool, 1940: *A Hundred Years of Economic Development in Great Britain, 1840–1940*. London: Duckworth, 280.

manufacture. Although numbers employed in these expanding sectors continued to increase to 1931, it is significant that the greatest proportionate surge in employment occurred across the trans-war period.

The ability to give birth to technically advanced industries under the duress of war is, for Pollard, a prime indication of the latent flexibility and innovatory capacity of the British industrial economy, fully in accord with his recent reassessment of Britain's economic performance in the later Victorian and Edwardian periods.[31] In rejecting the fundamental tenet of the 'declinist' tradition in British economic history – that the ultimate causes of economic failure after 1945 can be traced back to the actions of economic decision-makers before 1914 – Pollard has drawn attention, *inter alia*, to the ongoing process of structural change in the economy after 1870. Thus, by the outset of war Britain possessed an extremely diversified business structure embracing not only the conventional staple industries of coal-mining, cotton textiles, iron and steel, and heavy engineering, but also sophisticated business services which in their international guise played a critical role in stabilising the external account. On this basis alone, the pre-war economy was 'fundamentally sound', but what was especially encouraging was the emergence of 'mass production industries and commodities of a new type, most of them pioneered in Britain and catering for the higher available incomes, especially for the working and lower middle-classes.'[32] These included soap, chocolates, tobacco, newspapers, pharmaceuticals and drugs, and ready-made clothing and footwear.

That said, Pollard is at pains to emphasise the discontinuous effects of the war on those industries of direct relevance to munitions output. Citing R. H. Tawney's view that the war economy 'stimulated organisation, advertised rationalisation' and broke down 'trade jealousies and secrecies', especially in the engineering sector, Pollard concludes that it bequeathed 'new methods such as automatic welding, or the use of limit gauges by unskilled labour, as well as new techniques of management.'[33] Lack of standardisation and craft specialisation had been rife in peacetime, and it is reasonable to presume that the experience of war production established valuable precedents for the future. It is important to remember, however, that the revolution in munitions supply was heavily dependent on centralised programmes of rationalisation, and still more on the abandonment of pre-war restrictive labour practices. The first total war had inevitably placed an overwhelming emphasis on maximising physical production and, equally important, greater efficiency in the use of scarce resources. It had also elevated productioneers such as Dudley Docker to positions of influence both in the worlds of industry and in Whitehall.

In the light of all these factors a number of questions can be posed which are of central relevance to the issue of the secular impact of the war on British industry. If it is reasonable to conclude that the war economy was bound to

[31] Sidney Pollard, 1989: *Britain's Prime and Britain's Decline: The British Economy 1870–1914*. London: Edward Arnold.

[32] Ibid., 269.

[33] Pollard, *The Development of the British Economy*, op. cit. (note 3), 20.

result in some benefits to structural and productive efficiency of a long-term nature, it is also legitimate to argue that the extent of these benefits would be dependent in some measure on the manner in which the conflict was terminated. Assuming away the counterfactual scenario of military defeat, two outcomes remain as worthy of consideration. The first concerns the view, widespread in 1916–17, that the war would result in a stalemate peace with no clear victor, the economic implication being that the conflict would continue by other means, focusing on a trade war. The resumption in these circumstances of the pre-war export penetration by German industry, strongly organised in cartels, and with the advantage of a protected home market, would pose a major threat to British industry. It was thus the prospect of commercial annihilation that provided productioneers and other reconstructionists with their strongest argument for measures of corporatist reform aimed at industrial modernisation.[34] If, however, the end of the war marked a clear Allied victory, paving the way for a peace settlement that circumscribed the material and commercial base of German industry, the case for capitalising on war-induced productive achievements would be severely undermined.

A further issue of relevance to both of these possible outcomes relates to the aspirations of labour. In so far as the war economy owed its success to the laying down of restrictive practices and to an unprecedented degree of co-operation between labour and capital, it is strikingly obvious that the best chance of sustaining these efficiency-enhancing developments depended on the continuation of the 'expanded state'. One critical factor, so far unmentioned, is that under the terms of the Treasury Agreement of 1915 the trade unions had agreed to lay down restrictive practices for the duration of the war only, while the government in its turn 'had pledged [itself] up to the hilt to restore the pre-war conditions'.[35] Official prevarication would be likely to provoke considerable labour unrest, especially in a postwar context of demobilisation.

There remains to be considered in this section the immediate impact of the war on agriculture. At first glance it might be thought that a country which had sacrificed its agriculture on the altar of free trade following the symbolic repeal of the Corn Laws in 1846 would be desperately anxious to protect and encourage its home agriculturists in time of war. It is certainly the case that 'Other nations tended to see British reliance on imports as a potential weakness in time of war',[36] a predictable judgement, perhaps, in view of the fact that, in 1914, 80 per cent of cereals consumed domestically were imported from abroad, 40 per cent of meat and 75 per cent of fruit. It is salutary to note, therefore, that during the first two years of the war, despite loss of productive factors and the adverse effects of inflation, few direct measures were taken to reorganise domestic agriculture. In one sense this is not surprising. A country

[34] Kirby and Rose, Productivity, op. cit. (note 7), 24. Wartime debates on post-war economic policy are summarised expertly by John Turner, 1992: *British Politics and the Great War: Coalition and Conflict 1915–1918*. New Haven and London: Yale University Press, 336–53.

[35] Hansard, *House of Lords Debates*, vol. 907, col. 1923, 7 November 1917.

[36] P. E. Dewey, 1989: *British Agriculture in the First World War*. London: Routledge, 4.

whose military strategy was based upon a sea blockade of the enemy was unlikely to view itself as a potential victim of hostile naval action on a scale substantial enough to threaten food imports.

Complacency concerning munitions supply may have been undermined in 1915: in foodstuffs the recognition of crisis came in the following year in the wake of a poor North American grain harvest and the onset of submarine warfare in the Atlantic. It was in the second half of the war, therefore, that an emergency programme of expanded food production was instituted. It came to fruition in 1918 when 3 million acres more than in 1916 were ploughed up. As a result, compared with average annual harvest production in 1904–13, wheat production was raised from 1.56 to 2.58 million tons, oats from 3.04 to 4.46 million, barley from 1.52 to 1.56 million and potatoes from 16.59 to 19.22 million tons. At the same time, the area devoted to grassland fell by 3.5 million acres, while the domestic output of milk was cut back.[37] Accompanying these changes were official efforts, via the Food Production Department of the Board of Agriculture, to secure effective allocation of scarce resources, as well as the dissemination of technical knowledge and farm mechanisation. Complementing the compulsory ploughing strategy of 1917–18 was the guarantee of minimum prices for wheat, oats and potatoes for a period of six years under the Corn Production Act of 1917.

While it appears that structural change in agriculture in the final year of the war was substantial, a recent and authoritative survey by P. E. Dewey has concluded that 'the most striking feature of wartime agriculture was its stability', as evidenced by the minor fall in real agricultural output after 1914 in conjunction with 'the comparatively slight fall in food production to 1916, and the more or less equally slight recovery to 1918'.[38] In terms of production, therefore, the discontinuity attributable to the war was manifest chiefly in the structural changes induced by official policy after 1917. In this latter respect the subsidisation of agriculture under the Corn Production Act was also a notable departure from the inherited *laissez-faire* regime of the nineteenth century. Indeed, it provoked in agriculture the same kind of productioneering sentiment noted earlier in the case of industry. This was exemplified in the campaign for a permanent plough policy in order to diminish the peacetime volume of food imports.[39] As in the industrial setting, however, it is reasonable to conclude that the ultimate outcome of a campaign for greater self-sufficiency in food production was heavily dependent on the military fate of the warring powers.

Industry, Trade Unions and Agriculture after the War

We have seen that continuation of the impetus towards industrial modernisation, unleashed by the expanded wartime state, was crucially dependent on a

[37] T. H. Middleton, 1923: *Food Production in War*. Oxford: Clarendon Press, 112, 154, 192.
[38] Dewey, *British Agriculture*, op. cit. (note 36), 240.
[39] Ibid.

termination of hostilities which preserved Germany's economic and industrial power. But, as Peter Cline has stated graphically, 'Germany's sudden collapse in the closing months of the war removed the strongest, least vulnerable justification for the expanded state; it removed the prop which would have sustained the programme of state-initiated economic development.'[40] The Allied victory in 1918 was clearly a significant factor in undermining the credibility of productioneers such as Docker, and, while physical destruction of the German economy was minimal, the victors proceeded during the course of 1919 to impose a 'Carthaginian' peace settlement that appeared to wreak havoc on the German economy. The loss of key raw materials in Alsace-Lorraine and the surrender of colonies and of a considerable proportion of the merchant marine could be viewed as crippling blows to the material and commercial base of German industry. This was certainly the view of J. M. Keynes and it takes no account of the reparations settlement imposed on the defeated powers to the detriment of their external and internal financial stability.[41]

This is not, of course, to suggest that the German defeat was the sole cause of the demise of the expanded state. Concern at the growth of public expenditure had already been evident in 1917–18, and in the wake of the armistice the chorus of complaint about staffing levels in new ministries and the domestic spending of the War Office began to mount, reaching a peak in the summer of 1919.[42] By that time Treasury worries about the vastly increased floating debt were reinforced by the deflationary implications of the declared policy of returning to the gold standard as soon as practicably possible. The outcome of these developments was a marked determination to rein back public expenditure, a policy that reached its apotheosis in 1921–2 when substantial economies were announced. Ironically, the axe on expenditures was wielded by Sir Eric Geddes, one of the chief architects of the war economy.

If considerations of fiscal and monetary stability rendered the abandonment of economic control inevitable this was also true in an overtly ideological sense. Writing in 1943, in the midst of a war in which state controls were far more extensive and rigorously applied than in the earlier conflict, R. H. Tawney referred to the inevitability of decontrol after 1918 in view of the lack of any intellectual conversion to the merits of a greater degree of government participation in economic affairs in peacetime.[43] That Tawney regretted the abandonment of controls was understandable given his political persuasion, as was his valid observation that decontrol was against the general historical

---

[40] Peter Cline, 1982: Winding down the war economy: British plans for peacetime recovery, 1916–19. In Burk, *War and the State*, op. cit. (note 4), 159.

[41] J. M. Keynes, 1920: *The Economic Consequences of the Peace*. New York: Harcourt, Brace & Howe.

[42] *First Report from the Select Committee on National Expenditure; Second Report from the Select Committee on National Expenditure*. Parliamentary Papers, 1917–18.

[43] R. H. Tawney, 1978: The abolition of economic controls, 1918–21. In J. M. Winter (ed.), *History and Society: Essays by R. H. Tawney*. London: Routledge & Kegan Paul, 129–86.

trend towards collectivism. Yet Tawney would presumably have agreed with Ashworth that although the war economy was 'a considerable achievement and an indispensable element in military victory . . . it left Britain with an unfamiliar economic organisation devoted to unfamiliar ends'. Ashworth's conclusion, therefore, was that the 'guidance it might have to offer for the solution of newly emerging problems . . . had not been plainly demonstrated', and thus it was only to be expected that 'the majority of a weary and sickened people were willing to get rid of it entirely as soon as possible.'[44]

The reversion to a conception of the economic functions of the state rooted in pre-1914 perspectives was powerfully reinforced by immediate economic conditions in the post-armistice period. Reference has already been made to the stimulus given by the war to industrial sectors such as motor vehicles, aircraft and light engineering, industries that 'had the best selling prospects of all types of goods and for which Britain was not unfitted to supply . . . in quantity in view of the growing importance of the engineering sector in the economy.'[45] But the war had also resulted in the growth of productive capacity in traditional industries such as shipbuilding, iron and steel, and general engineering, and this war-induced expansion was further intensified during the boom conditions of 1919–20. Again, the employment statistics given in Table 3.1 are revealing, with the work-force in coal-mining increasing from 971 000 in 1911 to 1 133 000 in 1921, in iron and steel from 166 000 to 239 000, and in engineering and shipbuilding from 637 000 to 887 000. The boom, which began in April 1919, lasted for approximately one year. Its direct causes were to be found in the backlog of demand for civilian goods, the need to reconvert industrial equipment and replace that which was worn out, and the renewal, at least on a temporary basis, of former overseas trading contracts. It was also facilitated by government financial policy, which, the recommitment to the gold standard notwithstanding, was unusually lax at that time in order to ease the problem of military demobilisation against a background of politically motivated strikes in a number of key industries. Thus, it was not until April 1920 that Bank Rate was raised to the penal level of 7 per cent at the same time as the Treasury announced a deflationary budget.[46]

The importance of the postwar boom for the economy is that it had seriously adverse consequences for British industry which acted as a major offset to the favourable organisational changes produced by the war. The boom was, in fact, artificial, characterised by speculation in property and commodities. It was also an era of speculative company flotations – a financial orgy in the buying and selling of industrial concerns at vastly inflated prices, often on the basis of borrowed money from a highly liquid banking system. According to A. C. Pigou, up to £550 million of credit was made available by the banks 'for

[44] William Ashworth, 1960: *An Economic History of England, 1870–1939*. London: Methuen, 284.
[45] Ibid., 320.
[46] Susan Howson, 1975: *Domestic Monetary Management in Britain, 1919–38*. Cambridge: Cambridge University Press, 17–24.

industrial and other purposes' during the course of the boom.[47] Some of the worst excesses were to be found in the cotton textile industry: in the latter half of 1920, 109 mills with an original share capital of £4.5 million were sold for £31.7 million. The shipbuilding and iron and steel industries were similarly affected. In the former case 30 companies were floated in one month alone, with a combined capital of £4.5 million, whilst in the latter, the nine largest firms increased their capital from £20 million to £67 million during the course of the boom. Thus, the accumulated wartime profits of these industries 'were dissipated in a frivolous manner and they were left with a heavy burden of debt as a result of increased interest liabilities, the issue of bonus shares and the watering of capital.'[48]

The consequences of the boom would have been less catastrophic for British industry if the postwar decade had been characterised by buoyant demand both at home and abroad. The collapse of the boom, however, was followed by the most severe cyclical downturn in British economic history, and the recovery, when it began in 1922, was sufficiently muted for Pigou to describe the economy during the first half of the 1920s as being in 'the doldrums' in direct consequence of deflationary economic pressures at home, an uncertain international economic environment and adverse changes in the structure of world trade.[49] According to D. H. Aldcroft, the encouragement given by the war to import substitution abroad and new sources of foreign competition were less important in explaining the problems of British industry after 1920 than the adverse effects of the boom. As Aldcroft concludes:

> *There is little evidence that much of the investment and re-equipment of this period [1919–20] took place in areas of future growth potential (for example newer sectors of activity) or in modern technology. Indeed, the signs are that most of the investment went into second-hand assets and old technologies while many of the benefits of wartime rationalisation and streamlining of production methods were quietly forgotten as manufacturers and trade unions sought to return to the antiquated practices of the past.*[50]

In terms of industrial restructuring it might seem that one lasting benefit of the war economy was the direct evidence produced in favour of large-scale organisation and the associated access to scale economies, both technical and managerial. Yet the results in terms of the organisation of the peacetime economy were ambiguous. The failure of British industry to achieve scale economies on account of its heavily disintegrated structure inherited from the nineteenth century has recently come to prominence as an explanation of the country's relative economic decline after 1900.[51] That contemporaries were

[47] A. C. Pigou, 1971: *Aspects of British Economic History, 1918–1925.* London: Carr, 172.
[48] D. H. Aldcroft, 1970: *The Inter-War Economy: Britain, 1919–1939.* London: Allen & Unwin, 36.
[49] Pigou, *Aspects of British Economic History,* op. cit. (note 47), 73.
[50] D. H. Aldcroft, 1986: *The British Economy.* Vol. 1, *The Years of Turmoil: 1920–1951.* Brighton: Wheatsheaf, 7.
[51] Bernard Elbaum and William Lazonick (eds), 1986: *The Decline of the British Economy.* Oxford: Clarendon Press.

aware of this deficiency is confirmed by the reports of official committees of inquiry into the postwar commercial prospects of a number of British industries. A Board of Trade Committee on the shipping and shipbuilding industries commented in 1918:

> *Whilst individualism has been of inestimable advantage in the past, there is reason to fear that individualism by itself may fail to meet the competition in the future in Shipbuilding and Marine Engineering, as it has failed in other industries.*[52]

Such judgements were informed by an appreciation of German business organisation, where relatively large-scale firms in industries such as iron and steel and chemicals secured important advantages in overseas markets by co-operation in marketing and selling agencies. Even the coal-mining industry, the supposed bastion of die-hard individualism, responded to the mood of the times when, in 1919, the employers' Mining Association issued for private circulation to its members a plan for a nationally co-ordinated system of regional sales agencies. That nothing came of the proposed scheme can be attributed directly to the miners' campaign for public ownership, which reached its height in the deliberations of the Sankey Commission in 1919. This episode served to politicise the issue of industrial reorganisation to the extent that dispassionate consideration of proposals for industrial restructuring, especially in the context of State intervention, was virtually precluded for the whole of the 1920s, if not beyond.[53] Compulsory cartelisation, when it came in 1930, was less the product of wartime experience than of the post-1924 collapse of export markets for coal and the desire of the then Labour Government to redeem its pledge to reduce working hours in the mines.[54]

Similarly, in electricity supply, the Williamson Committee, reporting in 1918, recommended greater co-ordination in the industry in the light of wartime problems. Sixteen District Electricity Boards were proposed to take over from existing undertakings the right to control generation and transmission, but the scheme was rejected by Parliament, 'which feared the extension of state control and remained divided by interest groups representing the monopoly power of municipalities and companies.'[55] While a statutory Electricity Commission was established in 1919, its role was limited to encouraging voluntary links between companies and the negotiation of bulk supply agreements. Thus, it was not until the mid-1920s, in the wake of continuing inefficiencies and limited voluntary co-ordination, that a further official committee under the chairmanship of the Scottish industrialist, Lord Weir, was

[52] *Report of the Departmental Committee Appointed by the Board of Trade to Consider the Position of the Shipping and Shipbuilding Industry after the War.* Cd. 9062 (1918), para. 89–90, 31.
[53] Kirby, *The British Coal Mining Industry*, op. cit. (note 27), 40–1.
[54] Barry Supple, 1987: *History of the British Coal Industry*, Vol. 4, *1913–1946: The Political Economy of Decline.* Oxford: Clarendon Press, 332.
[55] Leslie Hannah, 1977: A pioneer of public enterprise: The Central Electricity Board and the National Grid, 1927–1940. In Barry Supple (ed.), *Essays in British Business History.* Oxford: Clarendon Press, 208.

established to investigate the problem of electricity supply and to make re-commendations for its improvement. Noting the limited achievements of the Electricity Commissioners, compounded by Parliament's failure to intervene decisively, the Weir Committee recommended the establishment of a statutory body to secure national co-ordination. Despite the opposition of right-wing Conservative backbenchers in Parliament, the Central Electricity Board was established in 1926 to construct and oversee the operation of a national grid of transmission lines. The legislation secured a smooth parliamentary passage because of support from the Federation of British Industries as well as the Liberal and Labour Parties, and also because it was proposed that the owner-ship of power-stations should remain in private hands, thus obviating fears of wholesale nationalisation of the industry.[56]

An unequivocal example of war-induced industrial reorganisation is pro-vided by the railways. The issue of nationalisation had been raised tentatively in Asquith's Liberal Cabinet before 1914 and, as an authoritative survey has concluded, most informed observers had come to accept before the end of the war that 'the railways could not return to the wasteful competition and dupli-cation of facilities of pre-war days' in view of the self evident benefits of state control.[57] In the event, nationalisation was rejected as an option in 1920, partly because of the budgetary implications of state purchase, but also because rail-way nationalisation would compromise Lloyd George's coalition administra-tion in its opposition to public ownership of the coal industry.

Instead, the Government used the creation of a Ministry of Transport in August 1919 as a vehicle for devising a scheme of reorganisation that would leave the industry in private hands. The task was given to Sir Eric Geddes as the first Minister of Transport, and his Railway Act passed into law in August 1921. Much modified in the parliamentary process, the legislation provided for the compulsory merger of the existing railway companies into four large groups, while the Ministry of Transport was endowed with powers to secure measures of standardisation. Whatever the merits of outright public owner-ship, the inter-war history of the railways would have been more troubled than it actually was in the absence of grouping. Although it was alleged that group-ing possessed 'the inherent diseconomies of competition without its alleged virtues' and 'the extortions of monopoly without its potential savings', the abil-ity of a disintegrated industry to cope with the turbulent economic conditions of the inter-war years would have been severely limited.[58] As it was, the merged companies managed to reduce operating expenses by approximately £29 mil-lion between 1924 and 1938 while coping simultaneously with intense com-petition from motorised road transport and sustained recession among major industrial customers.

[56] Ibid., 210–11.
[57] H. J. Dyos and D. H. Aldcroft, 1974: *British Transport: An Economic Survey from the Seventeenth Century to the Twentieth*. Harmondsworth: Penguin Books, 312.
[58] Ibid., 318.

The formation of the Central Electricity Board and the grouping of railways may be regarded legitimately as representative elements in one of the most significant developments in the inter-war period, namely the declining faith of the business community and of its political supporters in market mechanisms. This was the direct product of trade recession, high-cost under-capacity working, and the failure of the market to clear redundant capacity from the field. This was especially the case in the staple export industries, where market collapse was compounded by the burden of debt inherited from the post-war boom. In response to these difficulties the later 1920s witnessed the emergence of a 'rationalisation' movement in British business, proclaiming the virtues of mergers and 'organised competition'.[59] Although the 1920s as a whole was a merger-intensive decade, marking 'the rise of the corporate economy', it was the later part of the period that gave birth to such corporate giants as ICI and Unilever. The years after 1925 were also marked by the growth of governmental interest in industrial reorganisation and actual intervention by the Bank of England to bring it about in hard-pressed sectors such as cotton textiles and iron and steel.

The question arises as to the extent to which rationalisation owed its origins, at least in part, to the war economy. The historian of ICI, W. J. Reader, has noted that although there was 'no tincture of public ownership' in the new company, 'the public purpose was there' in so far as large-scale organisation in the chemical industry was regarded by government as an essential safeguard for the supply of strategic raw materials.[60] It is also the case that leading lights in the rationalisation movement such as Sir Harry McGowan and Lord Weir in business, and Baldwin, Runciman and Cunliffe-Lister in politics, had been actively involved in the administration of the war economy. Weir, for example, was a business recruit to the Ministry of Munitions, subsequently serving as Secretary of State for Air, and chairman of the committee that proposed the establishment of the Central Electricity Board, before being appointed to the board of ICI. Similarly, Sir Alfred Mond, the first chairman of ICI and joint managing director with McGowan, had held office as First Commissioner of Works from 1916 to 1922. As Reader concludes, all of these men 'had easy access to each other and continued the wartime habit of consultation and co-operation, thereby facilitating the growing interpenetration of government and industry'.[61]

There is merit in Reader's view that the origins of rationalisation can be traced back to the war economy, in so far as several of its leading protagonists first became alerted to the possibilities of scale economies as a result of their experience as administrators in wartime production departments. However, as indicated already, the importance of immediate circumstances and trends specific to the 1920s should not be discounted. These included critical compar-

[59] Leslie Hannah, 1983: *The Rise of the Corporate Economy*, 2nd edition, London: Methuen, 27–40.
[60] W. J. Reader, 1977: Imperial Chemical Industries and the state, 1926–1945. In Supple, *Essays in British Business History*, op. cit. (note 55), 241–2.
[61] Ibid., 241.

isons between industrial organisation in Britain and overseas competitors, notably Germany and the United States, and the impact of direct large-scale foreign investment in Britain. The weight of semi-official opinion can also be cited, well reflected in the reports of the Samuel Commission on the coal industry and of the Balfour Committee on Industry and Trade, all of which proclaimed the virtues of industrial integration as a solution to the inter-related problems of foreign competition, shifting comparative advantage and commercial depression.[62]

If the favourable legacy of the war for the organisation of industry was blighted by the effects of boom and recession, this applied with no less force to labour relations. In this respect there are two issues for consideration. The first concerns the governmental commitment, enshrined in the Treasury Agreement of 1915, to restore the peacetime trade practices 'in our work-shops, shipyards and other industries' at the end of the war. A related issue is the ultimate fate of reconstructionist hopes in so far as they were based upon continuation of the wartime co-operation between government, industry and unions.

That the relaxation of trade practices was for the duration of the war was recognised on many occasions by government spokesmen in 1917 and 1918. In the final summer of the war Sir Stephenson Kent, Director-General of Demobilisation, was appointed to chair an interdepartmental conference on the redemption of the pledge to labour, and in a report to the Ministry of Reconstruction he concluded that preparation of a draft bill was essential as a means to placate mounting labour unrest.[63] Despite a blistering attack on restoration by leading productioneers within the Government, such as Lord Weir and Sir Albert Stanley, legislation was enacted in August 1919 for the reintroduction of trade practices 'as obtained before the war'. Between 30 000 and 40 000 trade restrictions had been laid down under the Treasury Agreement: as G. D. H. Cole pointed out, the provisions of the Act were imple-mented 'rapidly and smoothly and with relatively little friction', thus suggest-ing that employers preferred 'in the face of immediate demand, to avoid trouble, to revert to old methods and to get back their former staffs, rather than engage in the hazardous enterprise' of radical workshop reorganisation to improve their competitive position in peacetime markets.[64]

That the advocates of reneging on the Government's pledge were unsuc-cessful can be ascribed to the weakness of their case. Stanley, for example, reminded his fellow ministers that redemption of the pledge would be tanta-mount to official connivance at the restriction of output, which would inevitably be 'contrasted with the repeated declarations of ministers that our only hope of economic salvation after the war is to secure the maximum of output'.[65] His colleague, Weir, was even more hostile to restoration, arguing

[62] Hannah, *The Rise of the Corporate Economy*, op. cit. (note 59), 41–53.
[63] Kirby and Rose, Productivity, op. cit. (note 7), 33.
[64] G. D. H. Cole, 1923: *Trade Unionism and Munitions*. Oxford: Clarendon Press, 124–5.
[65] Cited in Kirby and Rose, Productivity, op. cit. (note 7), 33–4.

that in view of the vital need for enhanced productive efficiency in the face of the postwar renewal of foreign and particularly American competition, restoration 'would represent the industrial suicide of Britain'.[66] In the event, these doom-laden forecasts were discounted as a result of a combination of immediate circumstances, contemporary political realities and, more especially, an alternative view of the future of the British economy grounded in the concept of industrial consensus. The Minister of Reconstruction at the time of the restoration debate was Christopher Addison, a convinced believer in Whitleyism and the creation of joint councils in industry generally. Far from accepting the productioneers' case, Addison argued that restoration was the essential precondition for industrial reconstruction:

> *The future of women in industry, the place of the semi-skilled worker, the develop-*
> *ment of improved methods, increased productivity, all depend in the last resort*
> *upon the attitudes of the trade unions of skilled workers, which will be determined*
> *by the action of the government with regard to the restoration of pre-war practices.*[67]

It was unlikely, moreover, that trade unionists would insist on literal restoration, viewing it as a bargaining counter. But undue hesitation on the part of government 'would be tantamount to throwing over the accredited leaders of the unions, who would be charged with having betrayed the men. The upshot would be the destruction of organised trade unionism and a great stimulus to the extremists'.[68]

Reinforcing Addison's views was a direct appeal to the War Cabinet from the Ministry of Labour, pointing to the uncertainty concerning restoration as a potent factor in stimulating unrest. Employers in general supported restoration as the best guarantee of isolating the unofficial far left and extremist elements within the trade unions.[69]

It is a considerable irony that the *coup de grâce* for reconstructionist hopes based upon the principle of consensus was administered by the National Industrial Conference of trade union and employers' representatives, which met under government auspices in February 1919. Summoned by Lloyd George to give form and content to the proposals for the limitation of the working week and minimum rates of pay, the detailed schemes drawn up at the conference were stillborn.[70] Although a number of minor recommendations were implemented, the Government balked at surrendering executive responsibility in peacetime to a proposed 600-strong national industrial council or parliament. It appears also that the representatives of Whitleyism in

[66] Cited in Kirby and Rose, Productivity, op. cit. (note 7), 34.
[67] PRO, RECO1/800, The Restoration of Pre-War Practices Bill, 12 October 1918.
[68] PRO, CAB 23/8, WC 491, 19 October 1918.
[69] P. B. Johnson, 1968: *Land Fit for Heroes.* Chicago: University of Chicago Press, 266.
[70] Rodney Lowe, 1978: The failure of consensus in Britain: The National Industrial Conference, 1919–21. *Historical Journal* 21, 649–75; Larry G. Gerber, 1988: Corporatism in comparative perspective: The impact of the First World War on American and British labour relations. *Business History Review* 62, 121–2.

attendance at the conference were all but ignored, as was the movement's potential role in the proposed industrial parliament. In this sense the conference was 'a political betrayal of Whitleyism' of such magnitude that its growth was permanently stunted.[71] While joint consultation became established in industries such as building, cement, printing and electricity supply, its hold elsewhere was either non-existent or tenuous. Negotiations for joint councils in leading trades such as coal-mining and engineering were terminated soon after the conference, and although Whitleyism was adopted in soap and candle manufacture, paint and varnish, heavy chemicals and electrical cable-working, 'it was soon apparent that employers had never been under any illusion as to who would effectively determine the pattern of postwar industrial relations'.[72]

It is conventional to regard the National Industrial Conference as a significant element in helping to curb the threat of labour militancy in general and 'direct action' in particular after 1918. A similar role was fulfilled by the Sankey Commission on the coal industry, established by Lloyd George in 1919 to consider the miners' postwar programme (*see above*), including the demand for nationalisation. The latter was not only the product of long-term political and social objectives, but also a reflection of the miners' keen appreciation that decontrol of the coal industry would entail the loss of war-related wage advances and a return to the pre-war structure of inter-coalfield competition.

In the event, the campaign for public ownership was unsuccessful owing to a combination of Lloyd George's political astuteness and the miners' failure to enlist the support of their Triple Alliance partners. Decontrol, when it came in 1921, did indeed lead to substantial wage reductions, although the vestiges of national wage bargaining were preserved in an agreed formula for the determination of district wage settlements.[73]

Even this was removed after the miners' defeat at the end of the prolonged lock-out of 1926. The employers' victory followed in the wake of the collapse of the General Strike. This had been called by the TUC in recognition of the moral debt owed to the miners after the earlier Triple Alliance débâcle of 1921 and of the perceived need to defend pay and conditions in the coal industry. Unionists feared that capitulation on the part of the miners would pave the way for wage reductions in other hard-pressed exporting industries. It is well known that despite impressive rank-and-file support for the strike at local level, it was called off by a TUC afraid of its political and constitutional implications and the potential loss of control to extremist elements.[74]

The defeat of organised labour in 1926 represented the final extinction of

---

[71] Lowe, The failure of consensus, op. cit. (note 70), 672–3.
[72] W. R. Garside, 1987: Management and men: aspects of British industrial relations in the inter-war period. In Supple, *Essays in British Business History*, op. cit. (note 55), 248.
[73] Kirby, *The British Coal Mining Industry*, op. cit. (note 27), 49–65.
[74] G. A. Phillips, 1976: *The General Strike*. London: Weidenfeld & Nicolson, 206–17; Margaret Morris, 1976: *The General Strike*. Harmondsworth: Penguin Books, 239–57.

the philosophy and strategy of 'direct action', which had infected elements within the labour movement at the end of the war. In particular, the miners' case for nationalisation involving workers' control was a dead letter. Although the later 1920s witnessed an attempt by corporate and progressive employers led by Sir Alfred Mond to reinvoke the spirit of wartime co-operation with labour, the resulting 'Mond–Turner talks', covering such issues as rationalisation of industry and unemployment, received a cold response from employers elsewhere, notably those representing medium-sized and smaller firms in traditional industries. This was especially the case in engineering, where the Employers' Federation, having won a significant victory over the trade unions in 1922, was determined to retain the managerial prerogatives which the Federation believed to have been eroded after 1915.[75]

In terms of numbers the peak of trade union membership was reached in 1920 at 8 347 000, double the level of 1914. Thereafter, the number fell consistently, reaching a low of 4 397 000 in 1933. In one obvious sense the decline in membership reflected the onset of trade depression in 1921, the product of changes in the structure of world trade, the growth of overseas competition and the pursuit of deflationary economic policies at home. In itself this provided those employers determined to restore the status quo in labour relations with the ideal environment in which to launch an offensive against trade unions in the form of wage reductions and harsher working conditions. Reconstructionist hopes would have been difficult enough to maintain in this climate, but they were further undermined by the action of government, beginning with the 'foiling of labour' via the Sankey Commission and National Industrial Conference of 1919, the Emergency Powers Act of 1920, and finally the political outmanoeuvring of the TUC in 1926. In the light of these developments the co-operation between capital, labour and the State in wartime was a major, but temporary, discontinuity in the record of labour relations. Certainly, it was not to be revived until the 1940s in similar circumstances of total war. The fact that elements of co-operation persisted after 1919 in industries such as iron and steel, glass, painting, and hosiery and knitwear was less the product of the war economy than of conservative leadership in the respective trade unions, as evidenced by the willingness of union leaders 'to educate their members into accepting co-operation as a norm rather than an exception'.[76]

An emphasis on the breakdown of co-operation after 1918 runs directly counter to the claim by Keith Middlemas that the war years precipitated an emergent corporatism in British society.[77] His argument is based on the concept of 'corporate bias' to distinguish it from notions of explicit power sharing between government and leading interest groups in industry. Thus the inter-

[75] Howard F. Gospel, 1992: *Markets, Firms and the Management of Labour in Modern Britain*. Cambridge: Cambridge University Press, 87–8.
[76] Garside, Management and men, op. cit. (note 72), 254.
[77] Keith Middlemas, 1979: *Politics in Industrial Society: The Experience of the British System since 1911*. London: Deutsch.

war years witnessed an ongoing process of consultation between government and trade union and employers' organisations on matters of common concern. The effect was to underwrite social and political stability in a period of exceptional economic turmoil. From the standpoint of government, the ceding of some power to 'governing institutions' was counterbalanced by the implicit commitment of these bodies to discipline their members in order to contain dissent.

The fatal flaw in this thesis is that neither employers nor trade unions were in a position to impose tripartite agreements on their members. In the case of the TUC, the formation of a General Council in 1920 did not result in co-ordinated union policies for the simple reason that 'General Council members – general secretaries or presidents of affiliated unions – were only willing to authorise enlargement of TUC authority when convinced that collective action would either enhance or protect their personal or their union's interests.'[78] Similarly, employers' interests were effectively divided according to the size of firm and industrial sector. This was well illustrated in their response to the Mond–Turner talks (*see above*). It is true that governments in the inter-war years, both Conservative and Labour, engaged in consultations with industry on a range of matters, but the motivating force was far removed from corporatism. Closer government–industry relations were more the natural product of increasing political pluralism after the extension of the franchise in 1918, together with governments' need to consult with those possessing the requisite technical knowledge to resolve or ameliorate specific industrial problems. As Rodney Lowe has concluded, appositely,

> *government policy* [between the wars] . . . *remained resolutely the decentralisation, not the centralisation of responsibility. Each industry was to be responsible for its own affairs whilst government itself stood above the fray, free to defend its perception of the 'national' interest; corporatism or 'corporate bias' had to await the Second World War when economically the two sides of industry were equally matched and, politically, the purpose of such a deal was uncontentious.*[79]

The legacy of the war for agriculture was on the whole minimal. The Corn Production Act of 1917, offering price guarantees to farmers, was followed in 1920 by an Agriculture Act that consolidated minimum prices, endowed tenants with greater security of tenure and maintained the system of wage regulation. Germany's defeat notwithstanding, the Agriculture Act was inspired in part by strategic warfare considerations. However, following the abrupt downturn in agricultural prices in 1921 financial priorities came to the fore. Thus, in the midst of accusations from farmers of a 'great betrayal', the Agriculture Act was repealed, thereby removing price guarantees as well as fixed wages.

---

[78] Fox, *History and Heritage*, op. cit. (note 24), 342.
[79] Rodney Lowe, 'The Government and industrial relations, 1919–39. In Wrigley, *British Industrial Relations*, 199.

Exposed to the full force of international competition, British agriculture reverted to its pre-war pattern. The downward trend in arable farming re-appeared at the same time as livestock, fruit and dairy production increased their respective shares of total agriculture output. But even these relatively buoy-ant sectors were eventually subject to mounting foreign competition so that by the end of the 1920s agriculture was once again a generally depressed industry.[80] When the policy of governmental neglect was reversed after 1930 with the re-introduction of agricultural subsidies and protection under the Agricultural Marketing Acts of 1931 and 1933 and the Import Duties Act of 1932, this was less the product of renewed strategic concerns than of awareness of the imme-diate and desperate plight of the farming community. Moreover, the movement towards protection was all-embracing, as was belief in the virtues of collusion.

The emphasis on continuity rather than discontinuity in agriculture's post-war experience, at least until 1930, should not deflect attention from two longer-term legacies of the war. In the first instance, the renewed wartime con-trol of agriculture, as for other industrial sectors, after 1939 owed its success, in part at least, to the administrative lessons learnt during the First World War. Secondly, because the war severely depressed real incomes from rents, it undermined the financial position of landowners. Thus, in the aftermath of the war, when land prices were high, there were strong incentives to sell, all the more so since changes in the calculation of death duties in 1917 provided an incentive to dispose of land in order to meet the cost. The bulk of the land was bought by tenants, who enjoyed their war-boosted incomes until 1921. The majority of sales thus took place in the three years after the war and the net effect, reinforced by a modest revival of sales in the mid-1920s, was to boost the proportion of owner-occupied land to 37 per cent by 1927 compared with 13 per cent in 1909. In this period between 6 and 8 million acres changed hands, representing 'a watershed in the history of land ownership and rural life'.[81]

Before concluding the chapter it is worthwhile introducing a statistical ele-ment with a view to shedding some light on the impact of the war on Britain's economic and industrial performance, with particular reference to productiv-ity movements. If the war boosted the fortunes of new capital-intensive growth sectors and bequeathed a favourable legacy of process innovations, it might reasonably be expected that the effects would be reflected in an index of over-all economic efficiency. However, in interpreting the statistical trends indi-cated in Table 3.2, it should be borne in mind that growth rates incorporate many influences, reflecting the historical past and contemporary circum-stances. Thus, in the case of column A, which measures the growth of total out-put, the figure for 1913–24 is distorted not only by the war economy, but also by the effects of boom and recession in the period 1919–21. Similarly, the figure for 1924–37 incorporates the slump of 1929–32 and the cyclical re-covery for the years 1932–7. Interpretation of the figures is made doubly diffi-

[80] Dewey, *British Agriculture*, op. cit. (note 36), 240.
[81] Ibid., 242.

Table 3.2 Annual Percentage Growth Rates of Output, Inputs and Multifactor Productivity, UK and USA, 1856–1984[a]

	A Output		B Labour inputs[b]		C Capital		D Multifactor inputs		E Multifactor productivity	
	UK	USA	UK	USA	UK	USA	UK	USA	UK	USA
1856–1973	2.2	–	0.0	–	1.9	–	0.8	–	1.4	–
1873[c]–1913	1.8	4.6	0.9	2.6	2.9	3.8	1.3	2.9	0.5	1.6
1913–1924[d]	0.1	3.2	−2.3	0.8	0.9	1.8	−1.1	1.1	1.0	2.1
1924[d]–1937	2.2	1.5	1.5	−0.4	1.8	1.0	1.5	0.0	0.7	1.5
1937–1951[e]	1.8	4.5	0.1	1.5	1.1	1.1	0.4	1.4	1.4	3.0
1951[e]–1973	2.8	3.8	−0.5	0.7	3.2	2.5	0.5	1.3	2.3	2.5
1973–1984	1.0	2.3	−1.3	1.4	2.4	2.8	−0.2	1.8	1.2	0.5

[a] For UK: total domestic economy; for USA: private domestic economy.
[b] Hours worked.
[c] For USA: average for decade 1869–78.
[d] For USA: 1923.
[e] For USA: 1948.
Source: Charles Feinstein, 1988: Economic growth since 1870: Britain's performance in international perspective. *Oxford Review of Economic Policy* 4 (1), 10.

cult by changes in economic policy, from the deflationary requirements of the gold standard in the 1920s to the removal of monetary constraints on growth in the 1930s. In this setting, therefore, it would certainly be naïve to claim that the upsurge of growth in the 1924–37 period owed anything to the beneficial economic effects of the war. Rather more revealing is column E, which provides an index of multifactor productivity growth, i.e. a measure specifically designed to compare changes in total output with average changes in inputs of labour and capital. In a comparative setting the British performance in comparison to that of the United States was mediocre for the period to 1913. In the trans-war period (1913–24) the British rate doubled before falling back in the later 1920s and 1930s to a level slightly above the average for 1873–1913.

If attention is focused on the productivity record in manufacturing industry alone, as in Table 3.3, the postwar growth surge is far more impressive, a result that appears at odds with Aldcroft's pessimistic conclusions noted above (*see* p. 67). In accounting for the trebling of the rate of productivity growth after 1924, an authoritative survey of British economic growth has concluded that one key factor was the belated adoption of earlier technological innovations as part of the ongoing 'catch-up' phenomenon in relation to the United States as the most dynamic contemporary economy. But in so far as the productivity surge represented a significant discontinuity from the early 1920s onwards it is legitimate to conclude that 'catch-up' must have been complemented by other 'domestically originating sources of improvement'.[82]

[82] R. C. O. Matthews, C. H. Feinstein and J. C. Odling-Smee, 1982: *British Economic Growth 1856–1973*. Oxford: Clarendon Press, 537.

Table 3.3   Annual Percentage Growth Rates of Multifactor Productivity in Manufacturing Industry, 1856–1973

1856–73	1873–1913	1924–37	1937–51	1951–73
0.9	0.6	1.9	0.9	2.4

Source: R. C. O. Matthews, C. H. Feinstein and J. C. Odling-Smee, 1982: *British Economic Growth 1856–1973*. Oxford: Clarendon Press, Table 17.2, p. 532.

In this respect there may be parallels with experience in the 1980s, when the dramatically improved productivity record of British industry has been ascribed in some measure to the 'cold bath' aspects of the Government's commitment to free-market forces and a high exchange rate as the process of bankruptcy eliminated relatively inefficient firms whilst others were forced to upgrade their products.[83] The economic policy environment of the 1920s, with its emphasis on monetary and fiscal restriction, conceivably produced the same results, all the more so since deflation at home was complemented by the collapse of export markets for Britain's major staple industries. To the extent that the conduct of economic policy after 1920 was a reaction to the destabilising effects of the war, at the same time as declining overseas markets were the consequence of war-induced import substitution, it is possible to argue that the discontinuity in productivity performance was the result, indirectly, of the war.

This does not, of course, discount the further possibility that not all of the technological developments induced by the war economy in favour of mass production and standardisation were lost after 1918, especially in the context of the rationalisation movement. That said, the turbulent postwar labour relations environment, following on the restoration of pre-war restrictive practices, can only have served to limit the positive effect of the war, at least until the defeat of the General Strike in 1926 ushered in a period of more quiescent labour relations. The same can be said of the postwar boom, which not only inflated the fortunes of the labour-intensive staple industries, but also placed an institutional barrier in the way of structural change. This took the form of the joint stock banks, which as creditors of a significant number of overcapitalised firms kept them afloat via mounting overdrafts, thereby impeding industrial restructuring in response to the process of liquidation and bankruptcy.

Conclusions

In terms of its immediate impact on the British industrial economy there can be no doubt that the First World War marked a profound discontinuity with previous experience. The Munitions of War Act and the Treasury Agreement

[83] N. F. R. Crafts, 1991: Economic growth. In N. F. R. Crafts and N. Woodward (eds), *The British Economy since 1945*. Oxford: Oxford University Press, 261–90.

ushered in a period of unprecedented government intervention in industry in terms of structure, organisation and tripartite relations between the state, employers and labour. Productioneers and reconstructionists hoped to see this departure from Victorian *laissez-faire* perpetuated into the peacetime economy as an integral part of economic and social reconstruction, and also as a means of combating German commercial expansion. In the event, the collapse of the Central Powers fatally weakened these hopes, leading to a decontrol movement, powerfully buttressed by economic depression, financial stringencies and renewed ideological sympathy for the free market as the arbiter of resource allocation. In the context of government–industry relations the overall conclusion of this chapter is that taking the trans-war period as a whole, from 1913 to the mid-1920s, continuity of experience was far more evident than discontinuity. It is true that towards the end of the 1920s, British industry was subject to a constellation of forces which, vacillations and ambiguities apart, was conducive to the development of an embryonic 'mixed economy' during the course of the following decade. But this movement can be explained substantially by the immediate circumstances of unprecedented economic depression at home and abroad and with little reference to wartime precedents.[84]

As for the impact of the war on the productive efficiency of British industry in peacetime, the statistical record of productivity growth is consistent with the view that the legacy of the war was positive. The growth surge from the early 1920s can certainly be interpreted as a consequence of the war economy's effect in promoting knowledge of, and investment in, best-practice techniques, as well as in stimulating the development of advanced, relatively capital-intensive high-growth sectors such as motor vehicles, electrical products and chemicals. It is also possible to argue that the war had indirect and positive effects on productivity performance via the 'cold bath' effects of induced deflation after 1919 and import substitution.

There were, however, substantial detrimental effects, notably the adverse structural effects of the post-war boom, reinforced by the resumption of the kind of labour relations conflict that had afflicted the immediate pre-war years. In this latter respect the effects of the war were ambiguous. While the official participation of trade unionists in the administration of the war economy confirmed the legitimacy of the unions as bargaining agents at the national level, the conflict also raised the profile of the shop floor in the guise of shop stewards. It is also clear that the tripartite co-operation characteristic of the war economy was a short-term phenomenon. Whitleyism may have made permanent headway in industrial sectors formerly devoid of labour organisation, but elsewhere, especially in the established staple industries, the joint control structures of wartime were transient. This was exemplified in the case of coal-mining, where the end of the war was followed by the resumption

[84] M. W. Kirby, 1987: Industrial policy. In Sean Glynn and Alan Booth (eds), *The Road to Full Employment*. London: Allen & Unwin, 125–39.

of labour relations conflict even more bitter than had occurred in the pre-war period. In this respect, one effect of the war was to boost temporarily the power and influence of those who had been at the forefront of pre-1914 programmes of advancement. However, the expectations raised by the war were deflated progressively by the onset of economic depression and large-scale unemployment after 1920, and the determination of embattled employers to reassert managerial prerogatives. In a long-term perspective the effects of the Second World War and its aftermath were far more decisive in consolidating the power of organised labour. But the disposition of political forces was fundamentally different after 1940, as were contemporary economic conditions and policy assumptions.

Only in the case of agriculture is it possible to claim that the experience of the war was wholly transient. The status of agriculture in the economy was boosted powerfully by the onset of submarine warfare after 1915 such that by the end of the war farmers were in receipt of subsidies and other forms of protection which represented a major departure from the free-market ethos of the later nineteenth century. However, the defeat of Germany and the onset of financial retrenchment after 1919 removed the rationale of agricultural support until the manifest economic distress of the farming community after 1930 prompted renewed measures of state intervention in the form of marketing schemes. That said, the full flowering of state support programmes for agriculture in peacetime had to await the aftermath of the Second World War, when a renewed appreciation of its strategic importance and the onset of acute balance of payments weakness ensured that there was no return to the *status quo ante.*

4

Science and Technology

Keith Vernon

To capture the appalling tragedy of the Western Front, John Singer Sargent in his desolate painting *Gassed*[1] depicted lines of soldiers stumbling, choked and blinded through a wasted landscape, strewn with bodies. Poison gas seems to summarise the particular horror of the First World War. An unseen and indiscriminate form of death, against which one could not fight, it deprived men of the means of life – unmanning and devoid of heroism. It was also a fundamentally scientific weapon, the product of warped inventive genius. The new artefacts of mass destruction – machine-guns, high explosive, submarines, aircraft and tanks – similarly point to a new style of technological warfare. The dehumanised, faceless killing machines and paradoxically scientific methods of wantonly dispensing death give the First World War a peculiarly scientific and technological character.[2] As national resources, including the scientific and technical, were mobilised to sustain the industrial conflict and to provide new weaponry, the war has been seen as a watershed in the recognition of science and technology. It is often suggested that before the war British industry and government neglected science and held scientists in poor regard. The early stages of the war demonstrated how far the rot had gone when shortages of chemicals, optical glass and electrical components revealed Britain's

[1] J. S. Sargent, *Gassed*, 1918–19, Imperial War Museum, London. Commissioned by the British War Memorial Committee of the Ministry of Information. R. Ormond, 1970: *John Singer Sargent: Paintings, Drawings, Watercolours*. London: Phaidon.
[2] G. Hartcup, 1988: *The War of Invention: Scientific Developments, 1914–18*. London, Brassey's Defence Publishers, 1; M. Ferro, 1973: *The Great War 1914–1918*, translated by Nicole Stone. London: Routledge & Kegan Paul, 85–97; J. Terraine, 1982: *White Heat: The New Warfare 1914–1918*. London: Book Club Associates; M. Pearton, 1982: *The Knowledgable State: Diplomacy, War and Technology since 1830*. London: Burnett Books; A. Marwick, 1991: *The Deluge: British Society and the First World War*, 2nd edition. London: Macmillan; R. M. MacLeod and K. MacLeod, 1975: War and economic development: Government and the optical glass industry in Britain, 1914–18. In J. M. Winter (ed.), *War and Economic Development*. Cambridge: Cambridge University Press, 165–203; R. MacLeod and K. MacLeod, 1977. The social relations of science and technology 1914–39. In C. Cipolla (ed.), *Fontana Economic History of Europe* Vol. 5, *The Twentieth Century*. Brighton: Harvester Press, 301–63.

perilous reliance on its chief enemy, Germany.[3] With this revelation, however, government and industry finally became aware of how important science was to national life and heeded the calls of those scientists who had long lobbied for greater investment in science and technology. The creation of the Department of Scientific and Industrial Research (DSIR) especially has been seen as a landmark in the support of scientific research, geared to industrial development.[4]

More recent work, however, indicates that there were important continuities across the war. Industry, government and the military were actively engaged in scientific and technological research from at least the turn of the century, and significant new developments were in the offing in the last years of peace.[5] Still, one can see that the First World War marked an important change in perceptions of science and saw the creation of institutional structures that had not been in place before. Most historical work on science and technology in the First World War has concentrated on the state sector, particularly the role of the DSIR. In this chapter an attempt will be made to redress the historical balance by taking a wider view, with some emphasis on the role of the Ministry of Munitions and on the technical contributions of private industry. The role of science and technology during the war in a number of areas – the armed forces, civil research and education, industry and, so far as is possible, everyday experience – will be examined. In the process, the debates on the place of the war in the history of science and technology will also be considered.

Before we begin, it may be as well to indicate what, for these purposes, con-

[3] The literature on these topics and other reasons for the wider British decline is now considerable; the following is a sampling. M. Wiener, 1985: *English Culture and the Decline of the Industrial Spirit.* London: Penguin Books; C. Barnett, 1986: *The Audit of War: The Illusion and Reality of Britain as a Great Nation.* London: Macmillan; S. Pollard, 1992: *The Development of the British Economy, 1914–1990,* 4th edition. London: Edward Arnold; D. S. Landes, 1970: *The Unbound Prometheus: Technological Change and Industrial Development in Western Europe from 1750 to the Present.* Cambridge: Cambridge University Press; D. S. L. Cardwell, 1957: *The Organisation of Science in England.* London: Heinemann; C. Russell with N. G. Coley and G. K. Roberts, 1977: *Chemists by Profession: The Origins and Rise of the Royal Institute of Chemistry.* Milton Keynes: Open University Press; H. Rose and S. Rose, 1970: *Science and society.* London: Penguin Books; D. C. Coleman and C. MacLeod, 1986: Attitudes to new techniques: British businessmen, 1800–1950. *Economic History Review* 39, 588–611; D. H. Aldcroft, 1964: The entrepreneur and the British economy, 1870–1914. *Economic History Review* 17, 113–34; S. B. Saul, 1979: Research and development in British industry from the end of the nineteenth century to the 1960s. In T. C. Smout (ed.), *The Search for Wealth and Stability: Essays in Economic and Social History presented to M. W. Flinn.* London: Macmillan, 114–38.
[4] I. Varcoe, 1970: Scientists, government and organised research: The early history of the DSIR 1914–16. *Minerva* 8, 192–217; R. M. MacLeod and E. K. Andrews, 1970: The origins of the DSIR: Reflections on ideas and men, 1915–1916. *Public Administration* 48, 23–48; I. Varcoe, 1974: *Organising for Science in Britain: A Case Study.* Oxford: Oxford University Press.
[5] By way of example, *see* R. Floud and D. McCloskey (eds), 1981: *The Economic History of Britain since 1700.* Vol. 2, *1800 to the 1970s.* Cambridge, Cambridge University Press; P. Alter, 1987: *The Reluctant Patron: Science and the State in Britain, 1850–1920.* Oxford: Berg; D. E. H. Edgerton and S. M. Horrocks, 1994: British industrial research and development before 1945. *Economic History Review* 47, 213–38; M. Sanderson, 1988: The English civic universities and the 'industrial spirit', 1870–1914. *Historical Research* 61, 90–104.

stitutes science and technology. A broad view will be taken which incorporates not only research, but also invention, innovation, development and aspects of education and training. The focus will not be on particular inventions or the discovery of new scientific knowledge, but on the organisation and institutionalisation of science. Although the extension of knowledge is what science and technology are primarily about, it is when systematic and co-ordinated means of generating new knowledge are developed that it can have most far-reaching practical consequences.[6]

We shall see that in most areas the importance of science and technology had already been recognised by the first decade of the twentieth century and that much wartime development was based on pre-war precedents. The nature and extent of the war, however, required the mobilisation and expansion of technological resources on an unprecedented scale. This gave rise to a new awareness of what part it could play in national life, leading to the large-scale organisation and planning of science and its closer integration into national institutions. By the end of the war, industry and the military were investing heavily in scientific and technological capacity. It is noticeable that in the government sector, which is the one we know most about, a pattern of research quickly emerged. In medical, agricultural and even industrial areas, programmes of fundamental research into pure science were established. This partially followed pre-war directions, but was confirmed by wartime initiatives. It is questionable though whether this style of research really contributed much to the war effort. Rather, a technically sophisticated war was waged on a massive scale primarily through the industrial innovation, adaptation and organisation co-ordinated more or less directly by the Ministry of Munitions, which drew only minimally on new fundamental scientific research. This will be another recurring theme of the chapter, and we shall consider further why this model was adopted and what the implications were for the future.

Science and the Armed Forces

The First World War saw the development and deployment of an increasingly sophisticated and technically refined weaponry, as well as the proliferation of scientific advisory and research bodies for the forces. Once the armies in the West had fought each other to a standstill, the search for novelty acquired high priority as each side sought some new device that might break the deadlock. Although military recognition of science was not unprecedented, and although it is not obvious just how important military research during the war proved to be, by its end, all the armed services had created major, permanent establishments for research and development. At first, civilian scientists were brought into military organisations, but this was fraught with difficulties.

[6] G. Meyer-Thurow, 1982: The industrialisation of invention: A case study from the German chemical industry. *Isis* 73, 363–81.

When new, permanent institutions were created, military authorities kept closer control of research.

The American Civil War had demonstrated in the mid-nineteenth century the potential of technological warfare, but the Franco-Prussian War brought home more dramatically that an army which was better organised and technically more sophisticated could easily defeat another major European power.[7] In Britain the lessons were reinforced by the experience of the Boer War, and the first decade of the twentieth century saw a considerable reorganisation and modernisation of both the army and navy, including the extension of associated research organisations. There had been a scientific advisory committee based at the Royal Arsenal, Woolwich, set up during the Crimean War, but this had been dissolved in 1891. In 1901, however, the initiatives of the Rayleigh Committee on explosives resulted in the establishment of a permanent Research Department at Woolwich. Technical expertise for the War Office was co-ordinated and strengthened in the formation of the Ordnance Board in 1907, and a separate subdivision, (A.)4, of the Department of the Master-General of Ordnance administered research and experiments.[8] The Royal Arsenal retained primary responsibility for design, testing and manufacture of armaments, but increasingly the War Office (and the Admiralty) looked to private firms to provide not only manufacturing capacity but also to do major research and development work of their own. Large firms such as Vickers, Armstrong-Whitworth, Coventry Ordnance Works and Beardmores were on the official 'army list' as bona fide suppliers and inventors of weapons.[9]

The navy too had undergone extensive reshaping, beginning somewhat earlier in the 1880s, and bringing about a remarkable transformation in the design of warships. In the 1870s, the navy was still largely equipped with wooden sailing vessels. By the early twentieth century a technological pinnacle had been reached in the Dreadnought class with their gun turrets, internal combustion engines, armour plate and enormous speed. By the outbreak of war, new technological fire control and communication by wireless telegraphy were in place. Neither the British Grand Fleet nor the German High Seas Fleet fully recognised, however, the potential vulnerability of capital ships to the threat posed by submarines. Thus, although the period preceding the war had

[7] Pearton, *The Knowledgable State*, op. cit. (note 2), 69–76; W. H. McNeill, 1983: *The Pursuit of Power: Technology, Armed Force and Society since A.D. 1000.* Oxford: Basil Blackwell, 242–53; Terraine, *White Heat*, op. cit. (note 2).

[8] Hartcup, *The War of Invention*, op. cit. (note 2), 6–10; HMSO, 1922: *History of the Ministry of Munitions*, vol. 9, part 2. London: HMSO; R. J. Q. Adams, 1978: *Arms and the Wizard: Lloyd George and the Ministry of Munitions, 1915–16.* London: Cassell.

[9] R. C. Trebilcock, 1966: A 'special relationship': government, rearmament, and the cordite firms. *Economic History Review* 19, 364–79; R. C. Trebilcock, 1969: 'Spin-Off' in British economic history: armaments and industry, 1760–1914. *Economic History Review* 22, 474–90; H. Lyon, 1977: The relationships between the Admiralty and private industry in the development of warships. In B. Ranft (ed.), *Technical Change and British Naval Policy 1860–1939.* London: Hodder & Stoughton, 37–64; Pearton, *The Knowledgable State*, op. cit. (note 2).

been one of enormous innovation, developments had been along fairly traditional tactical lines and the navy still saw its ultimate role as taking on the opposing fleet in formal combat.[10]

The other key area of military research and development was aircraft. The Wright brothers had been explicit from the start in exhibiting their machines to the military and offering to supply complete air forces. In Britain, following the Esher inquiry into the future of aerial navigation, an Advisory Committee on Aeronautics was formed in 1909.[11] Research was carried out at the National Physical Laboratory (NPL) and at the Royal Aircraft Establishment, whilst the Admiralty maintained an independent facility with the Royal Naval Air Service (RNAS). Air research was probably the most formally organised area of military research before the war; its potential for warlike purposes was well recognised even if its precise role was not clearly formulated.

By the outbreak of war, then, all arms had undergone significant reorganisation and technical development. But had tactical thinking kept pace with technological innovations? With hindsight, one can see that the American Civil War and the Russo-Japanese War had demonstrated the futility of attacking entrenched positions, defended by artillery, machine-guns and rifles, in open order. It is unlikely, however, that either the army or the navy could have fully predicted the role that weapons such as submarines or aircraft would come to play. Although the potential may have been recognised in the predictive literature of Wells and Verne, both devices were capable of very little in 1914; submarines were limited in range and aircraft limited by weight.[12] Moreover, it was established dictum that weapons development stopped during wartime; furthermore, all the experienced military tacticians across Europe envisaged a rapid war in which speed would be of the essence, putting a premium on organisation and efficiency for immediate, short-term combat. To expand inventive capacity was not therefore an anticipated wartime priority, but no one expected the sort of war that actually materialised by the end of 1914. Only when the murderous combination of long-range rifles and machine guns had proved open movements suicidal, and armies on the Western Front had sought refuge in the earth, did established thinking alter and invention become seen as the way to achieve the breakthrough.[13]

[10] McNeill, *Pursuit of Power*, op. cit. (note 7), 294–9; Pearton, *The Knowledgable State*, op. cit. (note 2) 123; Hartcup, *The War of Invention*, op. cit. (note 2), 118. For the tactical implications, *see also* B. Ranft, 1977: The protection of British seaborne trade and the development of systematic planning for war 1860–1906. In Ranft, *Technical Change and British Naval Policy*, op. cit. (note 9), 1–22; and A. Cowpe, 1977: The Royal Navy and the Whitehead torpedo. Ibid., 23–36. Both authors suggest that before the war the possibilities of submarines seemed decidedly limited.

[11] D. E. H. Edgerton, 1991: *England and the Aeroplane: an Essay on a Militant and Technological Nation.* London: Macmillan, 2–4; M. Paris, 1992: *Winged Warfare: the Literature and Theory of Aerial Warfare in Britain, 1859–1917.* Manchester: Manchester University Press, 67–8.

[12] Hartcup, *The War of Invention*, op. cit. (note 2), 145; Paris, *Winged Warfare*, op. cit. (note 11), 16–59.

[13] Hartcup, *The War of Invention*, op. cit. (note 2), 61; Terraine, *White Heat*, op. cit. (note 2).

Since the technological capabilities of existing weaponry had produced the deadlock, mobility could only be regained by achieving new levels of power and sophistication. In the first place, supremacy was sought in recourse to artillery of ever-increasing calibre in ever-increasing numbers. This, in turn, generated its own scientific problems: the supply, in hitherto unheard of quantities, of complex and often rare explosive materials. As shortages of existing supplies were tackled, more or less successfully, a number of inventions and research departments were established by the Admiralty, the War Office and the Ministry of Munitions to find the novel devices that could turn the tide of the war. Although there were problems, by the end of the war scientific research had become firmly established within military institutions.

The crucial organisation that mobilised the scientific and technological capacity on the scale required to wage the war was the Ministry of Munitions.[14] A vast and sprawling edifice, the Ministry was created in 1915 to supply stupendous quantities of munitions. To do this it came to take on responsibility for all aspects of production, from the supply of raw materials to factory layout and workers' canteens. It took over and directed huge tracts of British industry and built on its own account whole new enterprises. Almost every area of the war was affected by the Ministry's organisational and efficiency measures. Part of its work was to counteract and keep ahead of what seemed like a constant stream of German inventions. Many of the divisions catering for the different categories of munitions had research teams working on improvements of product or process, new sources of supply or novel devices. The Ministry worked with industry, as we shall see in the next section, and with the War Office. Relationships between civilians working for the Ministry and the military were always strained, particularly over armaments, which were thought by the War Office to be an exclusively military matter.[15]

Gradually, however, the Ministry acquired more and more responsibility from the War Office, including provision for research, which was confirmed in the Munitions of War Act in November 1915, although it never gained absolute authority over technical questions.[16] It quickly created an independent Munitions Inventions Department (MID), initially to sift through the thousands of suggestions for new weapons – from death rays to bad smells – submitted by the public.[17] It soon took responsibility for supervising and

[14] HMSO, 1922: *History of the Ministry of Munitions.* London: HMSO. Hereafter MM.

[15] Adams, *Arms and the Wizard*; op. cit. (note 8); C. Wrigley, 1982: The Ministry of Munitions: An innovatory department. In K. Burk (ed.), *War and the State: The Transformation of British Government, 1914–1919.* London: Allen & Unwin, 32–56. Adams is an enthusiastic supporter of the Ministry of Munitions, while Wrigley defends the War Office, although he also suggests that one of the functions of the Ministry of Munitions was as a Ministry of Science and Technology. *See also* C. Addison, 1934: *Four and a Half Years: A Personal Diary from June 1914–January 1919,* vol. 1. London: Hutchinson.

[16] MM, vol. 9, part 2, p. 45. For the Munitions of War Act, *see* R. Macleod, 1989: The 'arsenal' in the Strand: Australian chemists and the British munitions effort 1916–1919. *Annals of Science* 46, 45–67.

[17] M. Pattison, 1983: Scientists, inventors and the military in Britain, 1915–19: The Munitions Inventions Department. *Social Studies of Science* 13, 521–68.

carrying out munitions research, but continued to have problems with military authorities. Collaborative work on anti-aircraft gunnery, for example, was constantly relocated, and only late on did it get facilities for field trials. The Trench Warfare Department, however, established at Kitchener's request, recruited more military personnel and enjoyed closer relationships with those at the front line.[18] A signal success for this department was the Stokes mortar. It was a pattern of military research organisations throughout the war that they increasingly employed service officers who could better judge the potential of new devices.

The Royal Navy's Board of Invention and Research (BIR) was closely analogous to the MID, constituting in fact the prototype. It was created by the First Sea Lord and long-time supporter of science – A. J. Balfour – in early 1915, but independently of the Admiralty establishment and under the rather tetchy supervision of Fisher.[19] As in the MID, the civilian scientific staff at first spent most of their time sorting through inventions submitted by the public. They too, however, were soon put on to research work, particularly to counter the threat of submarine warfare. By 1918, ultrasonic devices to detect submarines had been developed to a high level by Rutherford and his colleagues. Relationships between these scientists and the Admiralty, though, were also strained, the former feeling that they did not get sufficient co-operation, particularly for sea trials, the latter criticising the time it took to come up with directly useful results. In 1917, the Holland Committee recommended the dissolution of the BIR and the incorporation of its work into a central Admiralty Experiments and Research Organisation with large-scale funding and closer integration of scientists and navy personnel.[20]

In September 1917, a third body, the Air Inventions Committee, was created for the air forces. Aircraft had been still quite rudimentary machines by the outbreak of war, although many fundamental problems of aeronautics had been worked out. The key issue was to develop materials and equipment that were light enough for aircraft, and a great deal of work was done on lightweight metal alloys, petrol engines and transportable wireless, as well as on synchronised gunnery and bomb-sights.[21] Control of this research was retained by the military, both at the Royal Aircraft Establishment and by the RNAS, and was geared much more specifically to the development of a fighting machine than some of the research in other military establishments seems to have been.

[18] Hartcup, *The War of Invention*, op. cit. (note 2), 61–93; MM, vol. 11, part 1.

[19] J. K. Gusewelle, 1977: Science and the Admiralty during World War One: The case of the Board of Invention and Research. In G. Jordan (ed.), *Naval Warfare in the Twentieth Century, 1900–1945*. London: Croom Helm, 105–17; R. M. MacLeod and E. K. Andrews, 1971: Scientific advice in the war at sea, 1915–17: The Board of Invention and Research. *Journal of Contemporary History* 6, 3–40. Both articles point to the strained relationships between the scientists and the Admiralty, and the Board's poor wartime record.

[20] Lyon, The Admiralty and private industry, op. cit. (note 9), 64; MacLeod and Andrews, Scientific advice in the war at sea, op. cit. (note 19).

[21] Pattison, Scientists, inventors and the military, op. cit. (note 17), 522; Hartcup, *The War of Invention*, op. cit. (note 2), 145–65; Edgerton, *England and the Aeroplane*, op. cit. (note 11), 35–7.

What, then, did all this military research, development and invention actually come up with? There were clear advances in the case of aircraft, which in the course of the war were transformed from fairly primitive contraptions into formidable weapons with enormous strategic potential. The two other inventions departments yielded rather less impressive results. To be sure, ultrasonic detection of submarines was highly developed, but prototypes were only installed on ships late in 1918. Similarly, the problems of anti-aircraft ballistics had been largely ironed out, but only by the end of the war did a reasonably effective weapon become available.

The combined efforts of research into new weapons on land and sea did not seem to alter noticeably the course of the war. With poison gas, offensive and defensive measures largely counteracted each other and tended to neutralise what was undoubtedly a particularly nasty, but only marginally effective, weapon.[22] Nor did developments in artillery, or the other main novelty of the war, the tank, achieve the hoped-for breakthrough. Hartcup cites a number of smaller-scale gains, such as the 106 fuse, direction-finding aerials, the Stokes mortar, the small box respirator, depth charges, and gun- and bomb-sights, but they appear rather feeble when compared to the lack of large-scale success.[23] Indeed, it was not scientific or technological innovations that kick-started the war into mobility again, but the extended deployment of existing weapons and the ultimate wearing down of the German military industrial economy. Convoys rather than sonar saw off the worst of the submarine threat; it was mass concentrations and co-ordination of aircraft, tanks and artillery that finally caused German resistance to crumble. Brute industrial might triumphed where scientific sophistication could not.

By the end of the war, however, the investment in military science and technology was beginning to pay dividends. As we have seen, devices for the underwater detection of submarines were being fitted to ships in 1918, and an effective anti-aircraft gun was also in the offing. Tanks, entirely the offspring of war, as well as aircraft were beginning to realise their tactical and strategic potential. The Allied offensive planned for 1919 envisaged a co-ordinated attack involving high-speed tanks, aerial bombardment and motorised infantry. The interrelationships of research, technology and military thinking had become so integrated that the type of tanks required had not even been developed at the time of the plan's formulation, but there were confident expectations that they would be.[24]

Although the different assumptions and criteria which scientists and soldiers brought to their work had made for difficult relationships, it had become clear to the armed forces that, ultimately, new scientific and technological research could be of enormous significance and could not be shelved until such time as another conflict broke out. The scientists working for the forces

[22] L. F. Haber, 1986: *The Poisonous Cloud: Chemical Warfare in the First World War*. Oxford: Clarendon Press.
[23] Hartcup, *The War of Invention*, op. cit. (note 2), 193.
[24] McNeill, *Pursuit of Power*, op. cit. (note 7), 334.

largely went back to their peacetime occupations once the war was over, but the armed services continued to keep connections with research work done in the universities.

They were not, however, going to be reliant on civilians and, by the end of the war, all three branches institutionalised research and development (R & D) where it could be more closely geared to military requirements. When the Ministry of Munitions was wound down, the War Office reclaimed its former responsibilities and established permanent centres for armaments development at Woolwich and chemical research at Porton.[25] The work of the BIR was taken over by the Admiralty Central Research Institute in which scientists and naval officers worked in closer co-operation. The RAF and the Air Ministry pushed ahead with R & D on the largest scale, carving out a distinct military and strategic identity, supported by high-level research at the Royal Aircraft Establishment and the NPL as well as at universities. Although the British armed services were considerably wound down after the war and a strong pacifist opinion helped keep arms spending lower than in other European countries, still there were more State funds given for military research than civilian; the air force getting much the largest share.[26] If science and technology had not provided the hoped-for breakthrough, still it had apparently given enough proof of its value. The war had amply demonstrated that it was not enough to fight with the weapons and tactics of the previous war. The enemy, it seemed, was continually devising new and devilish schemes that could be combated only by keeping up a constant stream of one's own innovations. Without continual novelty the country would fall behind, with potentially disastrous consequences.

In other respects, though, military inventiveness had been all too successful. Scientific and technological research was essentially devoted to finding new ways of killing people, which it achieved with diabolical effectiveness. Authors such as Fussell and Winter have attempted to assess the cultural impact of the First World War, and a significant part of this must be attributed to the technical artefacts of the war: high explosives, machine-guns, tanks, aeroplanes, and what in many ways summarises the peculiarly scientised horror of the chemists' war, namely poison gas.[27] Whilst all wars are brutalising, few can have been so dehumanising. The trenches were a result of a technical stalemate; the appalling casualties of four years of static warfare the consequence of pitting men against killing machines.

---

[25] Pattison, Scientists, inventors and the military, op. cit. (note 17), 555–8; Hartcup, *The War of Invention*, op. cit. (note 2), 193–5.

[26] Edgerton gives figures of funds spent annually on R & D for the mid-1920s as: Air Ministry £1.34 million, Admiralty £0.98 million, War Office £0.49 million, and DSIR £0.38 million. *England and the Aeroplane*, op. cit. (note 11), 35.

[27] J. M. Winter, 1988: *The Great War and the British People*. London: Macmillan; P. Fussell, 1975: *The Great War and Modern Memory*. Oxford: Oxford University Press.

Science and Industry

The issue of science and technology in the First World War largely revolves around its place in industry, for it was there that science needed to make an impact if it was to affect the course of an industrial war. There are overlaps between this section and that which follows, on science and government, because one of the chief areas of government activity was in promoting research for industry. In this section we shall concentrate on what private firms themselves were doing and consider further the role of the Ministry of Munitions in directing British industry. Much has been written concerning this topic, yet it is perhaps the area about which least is known. Reliable figures of sums invested in R & D are unavailable until about the 1930s, and evidence of what exactly firms were doing is sketchy.[28] There are also problems of definition – in deciding what counts as invention, innovation, R & D, or analysis and quality control. Some of the questions are quite intractable; how, for example, are we to measure the impact or the role of science and technology in so vast and heterogeneous an entity as British industry?

These problems, though, have not prevented numerous authors from suggesting that British industry had neglected science in the half-century before the war. At the time, lobbyists for science pointed to the superior German model of higher technical education and the Germans' employment of graduate scientists in research-based chemical and electrical industries. Germany's progress and Britain's decline, they argued, were due in no small measure to this discrepancy. Historians have pursued these themes: British firms did not employ scientists in sufficient numbers, or in requisite positions of influence, nor did they devote enough effort to R & D.[29] The structure of British industry in small-scale family firms has been blamed for the low take-up of science.[30] Indeed, the whole ethos of English culture has been criticised for being fundamentally anti-science and industry.[31]

In some respects, the outbreak of war proved the sceptics correct. The country was faced with desperate shortages of vital commodities in precisely those areas in which Germany's science-based industry excelled: organic chemicals, particularly dyestuffs, optical glass, magnetos and other electrical

[28] Edgerton and Horrocks, British industrial research, op. cit. (note 5).
[29] Landes, *The Unbound Prometheus*, op. cit. (note 3); Aldcroft, The entrepreneur and the British economy, op. cit. (note 3); Coleman and MacLeod, Attitudes to new techniques, op. cit. (note 3); Pollard, *The Development of the British Economy*, op. cit. (note 3); Saul, Research and development in British industry, op. cit. (note 3).
[30] D. C. Mowery, 1984: Firm structure, government policy, and the organization of industrial research: Great Britain and the United States, 1900–1950. *Business History Review* 58, 504–31; G. Jones, 1988: Foreign multinationals and British industry before 1945. *Economic History Review* 41, 429–53.
[31] Wiener, *English Culture and the Decline of the Industrial Spirit*, op. cit. (note 3); Barnett, *The Audit of War*, op. cit. (note 3).

equipment.[32] Britain was even reduced to buying dyestuffs from Germany, via intermediaries, to colour the uniforms of troops going to the Western Front. Here, apparently, was clear proof of the absurd neglect by British industry of scientific research and technical education.

Yet the record is not as poor as some would have us believe. Some years ago, Sanderson drew up a list of companies engaging in research from well before the war.[33] More recently, increasing evidence has been compiled on the extent of research being done by private firms.[34] These authors have shown that many of the larger firms had invested in research departments and were actively incorporating new technologies and processes. Nor were British entrepreneurs so lamentably deficient or so dully ignorant of the usefulness of research. If we consider what was achieved during the war, it becomes clear that industry was the driving force of innovation and development that allowed a technologically sophisticated war to be waged on an enormous scale. Although Britain was faced with severe shortages at the outbreak of the war, it is also the case that within two years not only had these shortages been made good (and not just with American imports), but Britain was also able to supply the Allies with much equipment as well.[35] The War Office and the Ministry of Munitions relied on private firms, particularly the 'army list' companies, to supply *matériel* and to deliver the sought-after innovations. As central research organisations such as the MID came to concentrate on more long-range research, product and process development was increasingly left to private firms; for example, while the BIR investigated principles of underwater sound detection, Marconi and the GPO did work on wireless.[36]

The Ministry of Munitions, especially, systematically mobilised the expertise of its suppliers. One of the key successes of the Trench Warfare Department, the Stokes mortar, was developed initially by W. Stokes of Ransomes & Rapier Ltd, which became a major supplier.[37] Similarly, tanks were a collaborative venture between the Admiralty, Ministry of Munitions, W. Foster & Co. and the Metropolitan Carriage Wagon and Finance Co. Ltd. A committee of Malleable Iron Founders was formed by the Ministry to promote investigation and dissemination of results between firms for production of metal for tanks.[38] To make good the deficiencies of raw materials required for explosives, the Ministry again depended on private initiative. The shortfall of acetone to make cordite was solved by a university chemist, working in association with the

[32] MacLeod and Andrews, The origins of the DSIR, op. cit. (note 4); Varcoe, *Organising for Science*, op. cit. (note 4).
[33] M. Sanderson 1972: Research and the firm in British industry, 1919–39. *Science Studies* 2, 107–51.
[34] Edgerton and Horrocks, British industrial research, op. cit. (note 5); D. E. H. Edgerton, 1987: Science and technology in British business history. *Business History* 29, 84–103. *See also* the essays in J. Liebenau (ed.), 1988: *The Challenge of New Technology: Innovation in British Business since 1850*. Aldershot: Gower.
[35] MacLeod, The 'arsenal' in the Strand, op. cit. (note 16).
[36] Hartcup, *The War of Invention*, op. cit. (note 2), 14–15.
[37] Adams, *Arms and the Wizard*, op. cit. (note 8); MM, vol. 9, part 1.
[38] MM, vol. 7, part 1; MM, vol. 12, part 3.

Clayton Aniline Co. and Synthetic Products Co.[39] The South Metropolitan Gas Co. devised a synthetic route for phenol for the Explosives Supply Department, and Brunner-Mond devised a process for the production of ammonium nitrate.[40] In gas warfare, the research departments of Castner-Kellner, Nobel's, and Chance & Hunt collaborated with universities to identify and reproduce enemy offensive weapons, while Boots of Nottingham and the Royal Army Medical Corps worked on respirators.[41] To conserve stocks of vital chemicals, the ministry asked gas and coal tar companies and colliery owners to install by-product coke ovens to recover waste products; the majority did so at their own expense and provided important stocks of toluol, benzol and phenol.[42] Steelmakers accelerated the changeover to basic furnaces which allowed the use of inferior-quality home-produced ores rather than high-grade imported ore. Open-hearth furnaces replaced Bessemer methods. Steel manufacturers collaborated with the Metallurgy Department at Sheffield University in the development and take-up of new alloys and steel of increased tensile strength.[43]

Examples could be multiplied, and the official history points to an impressive list of developments achieved during the war, not only of new products and processes but also in greater efficiency, administrative organisation and accounting, as well as greater standardisation and the spread of mass production techniques. On a day-to-day level, the Ministry encouraged decentralisation and collaboration between firms to disseminate good practice and to accelerate innovation. If a new product was required, routine practice was to send the problem out to tender and award contracts, often with financial support to the most promising submissions. If large supplies were required urgently, then standard designs were copied to a number of firms, each of which might introduce its own refinements of process, for example shell filling.[44] The Ministry of Munitions itself operated great swathes of industry, either directly or through controlled status, which provided models of rational layout, efficient management and routine innovation through factory workshops and design offices.

The development that perhaps impinged most pervasively on great numbers of people was the elaboration and adoption of methods of scientific management. Various means had been introduced before the war, but it expanded enormously during the war and was systematically developed by the Ministry of

[39] J. Reinharz, 1985: Science in the service of politics: The case of Chaim Weizmann during the First World War. *English Historical Review*, 572–603.

[40] MM, vol. 7, part 4.

[41] Haber, *The Poisonous Cloud*, op. cit. (note 22).

[42] MM, vol. 7, part 1.

[43] D. Burn, 1961: *The Economic History of Steelmaking, 1867–1939: A study in competition.* Cambridge: Cambridge University Press, 362–70; M. Sanderson, 1978: The professor as industrial consultant – Oliver Arnold. *Economic History Review* 31, 585–600.

[44] This is a recurring theme throughout the official history, e.g. vol. 9, part 1; vol. 8, part 1. The latter also contains the case of the Chilwell filling factory which devised faster ways of filling shells.

Munitions.[45] The vast quantities of materials required allowed the wider introduction of mass production techniques and standardisation of tasks and
machinery. The whole ethos of wartime industrial organisation fostered by the
Ministry of Munitions was towards greater co-ordination and efficiency, which
encompassed not only specific work tasks, but planned factory design, layout,
power supply and workshops, cost accounting, scientised management and
rationalised administration.

The ministry also extended the welfare aspects of scientific management. A
Health of Munitions Workers Committee was appointed in September 1915 to
advise on matters of hours, fatigue, health and efficiency.[46] Medical officers
were attached to factories, especially filling and poison gas factories, to regu-
late light, ventilation, feeding, time-keeping and general health. The ministry
also enforced a range of welfare provisions, particularly where women were
employed. These developments had far-reaching implications for the work
experience, potentially, of millions.[47] By 1917–18 improved welfare standards
were permeating to other trades, and the ministry liked to see itself as a
demonstration of the application of labour control – similar to scientific management, 'but avoiding the rather grotesque expedients of certain American
pioneers'.[48]

The achievements of British industry during the war, aided, abetted and frequently manipulated by the Ministry of Munitions, were little short of spectacular, actually producing the goods to fight the war. What, then, were the
longer-term results? The official history is not slow to claim the credit for modernisation of the steel industry and updating of the coal industry, as well as the
virtual creation of an organic chemical industry. Other statements have less
concrete purchase. The Ministry disseminated findings on dyes and, it
claimed, 'As a result, the value of scientific research to industry was more generally appreciated by manufacturers.'[49] Certainly there is clear evidence of an
increasing use of research by British firms. Sanderson argues that the last years
of the war and the early 1920s saw a proliferation of firm-based research, for a
variety of reasons. One is that research was a useful and publicly responsible
way of soaking up war profits, although few firms would actually admit to it.[50]
For some which were subsidiaries of international organisations, for example
Standard Telephones and Cables and the GEC laboratories, the war meant

[45] Adams, *Arms and the Wizard*, op. cit. (note 8); C. R. Littler, 1982: *The Development of the Labour Process in Capitalist Societies: a Comparative Study of the Transformation of Work Organisation in Britain, Japan, and the USA*. London: Heinemann Educational. For further discussion of scientific man-agement during the First World War, *see* Chapter 3 of the present book.
[46] MM, vol. 5, part 3.
[47] Ibid.
[48] Ibid., 176.
[49] MM, vol. 7, part 1, p. 135.
[50] Sanderson, Research and the firm, op. cit. (note 33), 115. This reason is also suggested in Saul, Research and development in British industry, op. cit. (note 3), 124.

they had to become more self-sufficient.[51] Some firms saw research as a way of developing new lines, or even of changing direction entirely, either to cater for the increasing demand expected at the end of the war or, more apprehensively, to cope with renewed competition once the protected markets of the war collapsed.[52]

The war and postwar years also introduced major organisational changes in some sectors. Mass production methods, which spread widely during the war, precluded on-the-job tinkering and required a separate research body. Increasing vertical and horizontal integration, for example in steel making or chemicals, and the emergence of massive concerns allowed the creation of larger, independent research organisations.[53] The organic chemical industry, especially, grew from a quite small, fragmented scale before the war into part of a major conglomeration of international stature in ICI in 1926, with research facilities to rival the Germans'.[54] While Britain's science-based industry possessed beforehand a not insignificant base on which to grow, still the war prompted considerable new developments and encouraged the spread of science, research and development through important sectors of industry. For many of the larger players, the war confirmed their commitment to research; for others, we can relate the expansion of firm R & D between the wars to the results of scientific and technical innovation achieved during the war, and to the encouragement of research by the government afterwards.

Science and the State

For most historians, state support for science is the key area in which the First World War marked a watershed. Through the sponsoring of new research, the co-ordination of a diverse range of activity and the promotion of science and technology to industry, primarily through the creation of the Department of Scientific and Industrial Research (DSIR), the Government finally accepted its responsibility to fund science properly, to develop a coherent science policy and thus recognise that science and scientists were crucial components of modern national life; not just in wartime, but in the development of the peacetime economy as well. As noted earlier, contemporaries and historians have long argued that the perceived decline in Britain's industrial and economic performance could be put down, partially, to its perverse neglect of science on which Germany

[51] R. Clayton and J. Algar, 1989: *The GEC Research Laboratories, 1919–1984*. London: Peter Peregrinus, 1; P. Young, 1983: *Power of Speech: A History of Standard Telephones and Cables, 1883–1983*. London: Allen & Unwin, 26.

[52] *See*, for example, W. J. Baker, 1970: *A History of the Marconi Company*. London: Methuen, 177; T. I. Williams, 1981: *A History of the British Gas Industry*. Oxford: Oxford University Press, 51–3; C. Wilson and W. Reader, 1958: *A History of D. Napier and Son, Engineers Ltd, 1808–1958*. London: Weidenfeld & Nicolson, 101–15.

[53] Mowery, Firm structure, op. cit. (note 30).

[54] W. Reader, 1970: *History of ICI*. Vol. 1, *The Forerunners, 1870–1926*. London: Oxford University Press.

above all had manifestly capitalised.[55] The German government had systematic-ally supported scientific enterprise through a strong state educational system and advanced training in the universities and technical high schools. German chemists, particularly, gained experience of research which they carried over into chemical firms that valued the contribution made by graduates. This model of state organisation of science – efficient state education and advanced research experience, fully utilised in innovative industry – had the systematic organisation that Britain apparently lacked. State education was uncoordinated and still heavily classics-based at the highest levels; industry was reactionary in its attitude to science graduates, consequently there were few of them, too often poorly regarded, ill paid and lacking career opportunities.[56]

Scientists had been pointing to these defects since the 1870s, when Germany's lead first began to appear, and a number of science lobby groups, such as the British Science Guild, the X-club and the Endowment of Research Movement, vigorously argued their case. Several historians of the British decline have largely followed the rhetoric of this science lobby and blamed successive governments for their neglect of science; but the story is in need of revision. More recent work has established that significant government sup-port was forthcoming for science in the decade or so before the war. From 1911, organised schemes of research were planned for agriculture and medi-cine, although these had barely come into operation before the start of war. However, while there were significant moves in the direction of state science, the war did see very important new initiatives and moves towards co-ordination of effort. One can also identify the emergence of a pattern for state-supported scientific research. The Development Commission of 1909, Medical Research Council of 1911 and DSIR of 1916 all focused on funda-mental research in pure science. We may question, though, whether this model was sustained because it delivered results during the war.

The British government had been providing funds for scientific investiga-tion for some time, and from the mid-nineteenth century the number of pro-jects multiplied, including the School of Mines and the Geological Survey, the Science Museum and Kew Gardens.[57] Money was made available to the Royal Society to disburse for the endowment of research.[58] From 1870, large sums

[55] Landes, *The Unbound Prometheus*, op. cit. (note 3); Aldcroft, The entrepreneur, op. cit. (note 3); Coleman and MacLeod, Attitudes to new techniques, op. cit. (note 3); Pollard, *The Development of the British Economy*, op. cit. (note 3); Saul, Research and development in British industry, op. cit. (note 3).
[56] R. MacLeod and K. MacLeod, 1979: The contradictions of professionalisation: Scientists, trade unionism and the First World War. *Social Studies of Science*, 9, 1–32; D. S. L. Cardwell, 1975: Science in World War 1. *Proceedings of the Royal Society of London*, A 342, 447–56; Hartcup, *The War of Invention*, op. cit. (note 3), 191, suggests that the problems between scientists and military men stemmed partly from the ambiguous social status of scientists.
[57] Alter, *The Reluctant Patron*, op. cit. (note 5); Cardwell, *The Organisation of Science*, op. cit. (note 3); M. Argles, 1964: *South Kensington to Robbins: An Account of English Technical and Scientific Education since 1851*. London: Longmans.
[58] R. MacLeod, 1971: The support of Victorian science: The endowment of research movement in Great Britain, 1868–1900. *Minerva* 4, 197–230.

had been expended on scientific and technical education.[59] Early in the twentieth century the National Physical Laboratory was established and funds were provided for the new provincial universities, which were closely connected with local industry.[60]

In the last few years before the war, several schemes were initiated which began a more co-ordinated and comprehensive approach to scientific research in agriculture and medicine. Under the National Insurance Act of 1911, 1*d.* per insured person was earmarked for research into tuberculosis administered by a Medical Research Committee, although work had not really begun before war broke out.[61] In 1914, the MRC took the opportunity to expand its brief considerably, taking on the role of trouble-shooting experts for medical problems, and suppliers and regulators of various vaccines for the Government. Also enacted in 1911 was the Agricultural Development and Road Improvement Act, intended to revive British agriculture after the slumps of the late nineteenth century.[62] Part of the £3 million attached to the Act was put towards agricultural research and education on projects recommended by the Development Commission, which had been established in 1909. By 1912 a full-scale programme had been worked out by A. D. Hall, director of Rothamsted, and T. H. Middleton of the Board of Agriculture, both prominent supporters of scientific research. They identified a series of problem areas in agriculture and designated for each a scientific discipline that underlay it; for example, problems of soil fertility were seen as resting in inadequate knowledge of chemistry and microbiology of the soil. Research was accordingly funded in these disciplines, most conveniently by giving money to Rothamsted Experimental Station, which had a long tradition of investigations into soil fertility. A comprehensive system of research into agricultural science was thus developed at a number of research stations.

Although British science in 1914 did enjoy a good deal of support, it might

[59] Alter, *The Reluctant Patron*, op. cit. (note 5); Cardwell, *The Organisation of Science*, op. cit. (note 3); Argles, *South Kensington to Robbins*, op. cit. (note 57); G. Roderick and M. Stephens, 1978: *Scientific and Technical Education in the Nineteenth Century*. London: Longman; P. Summerfield and E. J. Evans (eds), 1990: *Technical Education and the State since 1850: Historical and Contemporary Perspectives*. Manchester: Manchester University Press.

[60] R. Moseley, 1978: The origins and early years of the National Physical Laboratory: A chapter in the pre-history of British science policy. *Minerva* 16, 222–50; E. Hutchinson, 1968–9: Scientists and civil servants: The struggle over the National Physical Laboratory in 1918. *Minerva* 7, 373–98; M. Sanderson, 1972: *The Universities and British Industry, 1850–1970*. London: Routledge & Kegan Paul.

[61] A. Landsborough Thompson, 1973 and 1975: *Half a Century of Medical Research*. Vol. 1, *Origins and Policy of the MRC*. Vol. 2, *The programme of research*. London: HMSO; L. Bryder, 1989: 'Tuberculosis and the MRC. In J. Austoker and L. Bryder (eds), *Historical perspectives on the role of the MRC*. Oxford: Oxford University Press; J. Austoker and L. Bryder, 1989: The National Institute for Medical Research and related activities of the MRC. In ibid., 35–57.

[62] C. J. Holmes, 1988: Science and the farmer: The development of the Agricultural Advisory Service in England and Wales, 1900–1939. *Agricultural History Review* 36, 77–86; H. E. Dale, 1956: *Daniel Hall: Pioneer in Scientific Agriculture*. London: John Murray.

still be fairly argued that there was a lack of overall cohesion or organisation of science and very little perception of a science policy for identifying priorities, long- or short-term needs or aims, or a mechanism by which these could be recognised and acted on. The outbreak of hostilities did bring home a very real lack of scientific expertise and personnel, and just how much Britain had relied on its enemy for scientific products. The Government moved swiftly on the problem of chemical shortages, establishing an emergency committee of the Board of Trade under Haldane to investigate stocks and alternative sources.[63] In an unprecedented move, the Government intervened directly to co-ordinate production of organic chemicals, amalgamating several small firms to form the British Dyestuffs Corporation with substantial funds for research and promises of protective legislation. Initially, however, it seems that the Government, as in other fields of skilled occupation, made no provision for the preservation and utilisation of scientific expertise. Scientists were recruited into the forces and little recourse was made to scientific advice despite the Royal Society's offer of its services.[64] The position of science in the early stages of the war was symbolised by the fate of H. G. J. Moseley, one of the most promising physicists of his generation, who was killed in action at Gallipoli. By the time H. G. Wells had written inflammatory letters to *The Times* in June 1915, however, moves were afoot to exploit more systematically the country's scientific potential.

At first, no more than an eminent advisory committee was envisaged to promote and co-ordinate existing activity in government departments and industry. But in 1916, a new department of state was created, namely the DSIR, with a wide-ranging and expanding brief.[65] It was to co-ordinate and sponsor fundamental scientific research that would be in the national interest. It was to encourage and initiate industrial research through co-operative research associations, which were to combine academic expertise with industrial interests and study problems of concern to whole sectors of industry, for example iron and steel, food, textiles, etc. It was also to fund postgraduate research and training at universities. The DSIR's main wartime task was to co-ordinate the existing work of scientists scattered across the country so as to avoid overlap of effort.[66] It did have some immediate successes, for example optical glass and photography,[67] but we cannot really expect too much from an organisation that was only created half-way through the war. From the start, though,

[63] L. F. Haber, 1973: Government intervention at the frontiers of science: British dyestuff and synthetic organic chemicals, 1914–39. *Minerva* 11, 79–94.

[64] Cardwell, 1916: Science in World War 1, op. cit. (note 56); *Yearbook of the Royal Society of London, 1916.* London: Harrison & Sons, 173.

[65] MacLeod and Andrews, Origins of the DSIR, op. cit. (note 4); Varcoe, Scientists, government and organised research, op. cit. (note 4).

[66] *Scheme for the Organisation and Development of Scientific and Industrial Research.* Cd. 8005 (1915). London: HMSO.

[67] MacLeod and MacLeod, War and economic development, op. cit. (note 2); D. E. H. Edgerton, 1988: Industrial research in the British photographic industry, 1879–1939. In J. Liebenau (ed.), *The Challenge of New Technology: Innovation in British Business since 1850.* Aldershot: Gower, 106–34.

priorities were more long term. The emphasis was on identifying pivotal science-based industries, where the research gap with Germany most needed closing, to be ready for postwar competition.[68] Although the DSIR was clearly intended to provide for industry, it believed that the best way of doing this was to develop fundamental research on industrial problems. It recognised that, at first, it would have to move slowly and make systematic enquiries of what was required. Thus, whilst it began its work in wartime, we may see that the DSIR was intended primarily for postwar reconstruction.

Historians examining the DSIR have concentrated on the extent to which it did mark a new direction and how important it actually was in supporting science and technology, especially with respect to industry in the inter-war period. We may also consider further how much its work was influenced by its wartime origins. The DSIR was undoubtedly a response to the deficiencies dramatically revealed in the early stages of the war and was a permanent organisation geared towards industry. In this sense, the lessons of the war had been learnt, in that Germany's industrial strength was seen to have derived, to an important extent, from technical expertise and its capacity for continuous innovation. The Government now believed that research was a crucial component of economic survival, so the DSIR was to provide its services in peacetime, not just to catch up on wartime shortages. Much of its postwar work was devoted to ensuring that Britain would not again be so dependent on imports. In its attention to synthetic chemicals, coal hydrogenation and food research we can see a policy aiming towards increasing self-sufficiency.[69] The DSIR, then, can be seen as being of major importance, symbolising a new commitment of support and funds for science by the State. Over the next fifty years it was a mainstay of British science, and cannot be ignored.

How far, though, did it succeed in providing useful services to industry? This question has generally been considered with respect to its record with co-operative research associations. Some, such as Sayers and Varcoe, have tended to assume their importance; others, such as Mowery and Horrocks, have belittled their effectiveness.[70] It has been argued that the whole historiographical emphasis on the DSIR is misleading in that firm-based research was much more important.[71] The resources available to the DSIR for industrial research were certainly dwarfed by those provided by private companies, but then it was never meant to compete with, or provide for, industries doing their own

[68] *Report of the Committee of the Privy Council for Scientific and Industrial Research 1915–16.* Cd. 8336 (1916). London: HMSO.
[69] *Report of the Committee of the Privy Council for Scientific and Industrial Research 1919–20.* Cmd. 905 (1920). London: HMSO; A. N. Stranges, 1985: From Birmingham to Billingham: High pressure coal hydrogenation in Great Britain. *Technology and Culture* 26, 726–57.
[70] R. S. Sayers, 1950: The springs of technical progress in Britain, 1919–1939. *Economic Journal* 60, 275–91; I. Varcoe, 1981: Co-operative research associations in British industry, 1918–34. *Minerva* 19, 433–63; D. C. Mowery, 1986: Industrial research, 1900–1950. In B. Elbaum and W. Lazonick (eds), *The Decline of the British Economy.* Oxford: Clarendon Press; S. M. Horrocks, 1993: Consuming science: Science, technology and food in Britain 1870–1939. Ph.D. thesis, University of Manchester.
[71] Edgerton, Science and technology in British business history, op. cit. (note 34).

research. The DSIR and research associations were intended to support medium-sized firms that could not afford to do their own research, but which could donate some funds to support research of value to the sector as a whole.

This, however, was beset with problems. Aside from, but connected with, the reluctance to pool trade knowledge was the issue of the type of research done. Whilst scientists advocated long-term, fundamental research, it was also the case that government agencies could not be seen to favour one firm over any other, and thus any research done had to be general purpose, fundamental research on basic problems affecting the whole sector. This meant that industrial research stopped far short of end-products or processes of actual industrial or economic value to firms. Product development still had to be done by companies, which, if they were connected with a research association, probably could not afford to do it. DSIR-sponsored industrial research, therefore, whilst providing useful results on general industrial problems, may not have specifically aided British industry very much.

We can see similar patterns emerging for medical and agricultural research. Although scientists did important work in both areas, it is not clear how much their research contributed to the war effort. Yet, at the end of the war, both fields were endowed with significant new funds and responsibilities based on fundamental research in pure science. On the outbreak of war, W. M. Fletcher, secretary to the MRC, offered its services to the army, which proved extremely useful. It supervised vaccine production, especially for typhoid, and standardised diagnostic preparations. Almroth Wright and his St Mary's team, the foremost medical researchers of the time, decamped to Boulogne in 1914 to form a mobile bacteriology laboratory for rapid identification of infectious agents. It also carried out vital work on wound treatment and problems of tetanus and gas gangrene.[72] Despite the appalling conditions in the trenches – a haven of infection – the First World War was perhaps the first in history in which more people died of combat wounds than from sickness and disease – a result firmly accorded to medical research.

Fletcher had himself been a medical scientist, and believed that the basis of medical research should be pure science located in universities, not applied investigations of particular health problems.[73] Having proved itself during the war, on the creation of the Ministry of Health in 1919, a separate, autonomous Medical Research Council was established and closely followed Fletcher's ideal. In agriculture, as with many other products, Britain had come to rely on imported food in the years before the war and when supplies were threatened, particularly during the U-boat campaign of 1917, Britain had to turn even more to what could be produced at home. Scientists at Rothamsted and

---

[72] Medical Research Committee, 1915. *First Annual Report 1914–15*. London: HMSO; L. Bryder, 1989: Public health research and the MRC. In Austoker and Bryder, *Historical Perspectives on the Role of the MRC*. Oxford: Oxford University Press, 59–81.

[73] J. Austoker, 1989: Walter Morley Fletcher and the origins of a basic biomedical research policy. In ibid., 23–33.

Cambridge advised on crops and collaborated with colleagues from the MRC on questions of nutrition. The principal way in which food production was increased, however, was not by science but by the ploughing up of grassland for grain and potatoes.[74] Nevertheless, in the aftermath of the war, state commitment to the programme of agricultural science was reaffirmed. An extra £1 million was provided for fundamental agricultural research as part of the package offered to farmers in 1921 on the repeal of the 1920 Agriculture Act. Whether the farmers made this a proviso, as Russell suggests, however, is doubtful.[75]

Just as the Government began to look at the longer-term research requirements of industry, so did concern come to rest on the provision of suitably qualified personnel. The neglect of scientific and technical education had been as problematic and dangerous as that of research, and moves were made to promote this aspect of government responsibility. As noted above, there had been increasing funds for such education from the late nineteenth century, and in the years before the war the Board of Education began considering schemes to expand the system of secondary and technical education that had been initiated in the 1902 Act.[76] On the outbreak of war, all such plans were shelved until, under the direction of the 1916 Coalition Government, the state began to look towards postwar reconstruction. Christopher Addison devised a wide-ranging scheme for education, industrial training and research, the Thompson Committee was appointed to inquire into the place of science in the educational system, and H. A. L. Fisher, an eminent academic, replaced Henderson at the Board of Education – a symbolic substitution of expertise for political expediency.[77] The main concern was the education of adolescents, particularly to try to provide appropriate training to offset the problem of dead-end jobs. The most significant feature of Fisher's 1918 Act was the day continuation schools in which school leavers received extra education while working full time. The Act, though, was primarily a continuation of pre-war developments, based essentially on the 1902 system.[78] While the part of Addison's scheme covering industrial research was taken up by the DSIR, the Thompson Committee's recommendations, although widely read, did not have much influence until the reorganisation of the mid-1920s.

---

[74] T. H. Middleton, 1923: *Food Production in War*. Oxford: Clarendon Press.
[75] E. J. Russell, 1966: *A History of Agricultural Science in Great Britain, 1620–1954*. London: Allen & Unwin, 280.
[76] G. Sherrington, 1981: *English Education, Social Change and War 1911–20*. Manchester: Manchester University Press, 18–39; E. W. Jenkins, 1973: The Board of Education and the Reconstruction Committee 1916–18. *Journal of Educational Administration and History* 5, 42–51.
[77] Addison, *Four and a Half Years*, op. cit. (note 15), Appendix 1; *Committee to enquire into the position of natural science in the educational system of Great Britain*. Cd. 9011 (1918). London: HMSO; E. W. Jenkins, 1973: The Thompson Committee and the Board of Education 1916–22. *British Journal of Educational Studies* 21, 76–87; D. W. Dean, 1970: H. A. L. Fisher, reconstruction and the development of the 1918 Education Act. *British Journal of Educational Studies* 18, 259–76.
[78] Sherrington, *English Education*, op. cit. (note 76), 99–120; L. Andrews, 1976: *The Education Act, 1918*. London: Routledge & Kegan Paul, 77–89; Dean, Fisher, reconstruction and the 1918 Act, op. cit. (note 77).

Postwar reconstruction, of course, soon ran into considerable problems with the depression of the early 1920s and the subsequent slump, which severely restricted public spending.[79] Education was hit particularly hard as post-war estimates soared, partly to pay for better teachers' salaries, and also for the provisions of the 1918 Act.[80] With cruel timing, the day continuation schools were about to come on stream just as financial stringency was called for, and very few were actually continued with by the LEAs. Other features of the 1918 Act fell, unnoticed, by the wayside. More important developments for education came from the mid-1920s with discussions on extending provision of post-primary and secondary education for all and the recommendations of the Hadow Committee.[81] The DSIR too was caught in the swing of Geddes' axe in the early 1920s, but concerted protests halted the fall in funding and finances improved from the mid-1920s.[82] As noted earlier, funds were also forthcoming for agricultural and medical research. For education, then, the war marked less of a watershed; scientific and technical education continued to expand slowly, if more or less independently of industrial requirements. The most important changes were probably in the revised pay scales for teachers, bringing enhanced status, and new funds for the universities from the University Grants Committee.[83] As MacLeod and Andrews comment, an opportunity was missed to integrate fully education, research and industry.[84]

All the wartime developments we have considered, however, had extremely important implications for the scientific community itself. There were many more jobs for scientists both in government and industry. Before the war, scientists had experienced decidedly low status with poor pay and few career prospects.[85] The elevated perceptions of science boosted the status of the occupation, and a number of new professional organisations, for example the British Association of Chemists and the Institute of Physics, emerged to consolidate their new-found importance. There was, however, a cost to pay for enhanced status. Scientists had tried since the 1860s, in a number of ways, to justify demands for higher social and political profile.[86] National efficiency groups early in the century advocated the problem-solving capacity of scientists, whether political, social, or industrial and economic, and pressed for their inclusion in decision-making fora. Internationalists had pointed to the

[79] C. L. Mowat, 1968: *Britain between the Wars, 1918–1940.* London: Methuen, 129–32; R. Lowe, 1978: The erosion of state intervention in Britain, 1917–1924. *Economic History Review* 31, 270–86.
[80] G. Bernbaum, 1967: *Social Change and the Schools, 1918–1944.* London: Routledge & Kegan Paul, 27–30.
[81] J. Firmager, 1981: The Consultative Committee under the chairmanship of Sir Henry Hadow: The education of the adolescent. *History of Education* 10, 273–81.
[82] *Report of the Committee of Council DSIR, 1921–22.* Cmd. 1937 (1922). London: HMSO.
[83] Sherrington, *English education,* op. cit. (note 76); Sanderson, *The Universities and British Industry,* op. cit. (note 60); P. H. J. H. Gosden, 1972: *The Evolution of a Profession.* Oxford: Basil Blackwell.
[84] MacLeod and Andrews, The origins of the DSIR, op. cit. (note 4), 45.
[85] R. MacLeod and K. MacLeod, The contradictions of professionalisation, op. cit. (note 56).
[86] F. M. Turner, 1980: Public science in Britain, 1880–1919. *Isis* 71, 589–608.

transcendence of science above national boundaries, even registering their opposition to the war in its first few days.[87] Very quickly, however, the Royal Society established a war work committee and put its services at the disposal of the government.[88] Scientists were thus firmly committed to national and war-like priorities. They could no longer claim qualities of leadership, or high moral ground; they were at the service of government, to be used for whatever purposes were thought fit, and it was as servants of the state that scientists got their recognition.

Since the nineteenth century, then, governments had been providing diverse support for science and education, and just before the war had begun to organise their efforts more systematically. The creation of the DSIR, though, was a major new initiative, so marking the war as something of a water-shed. It is noticeable that a style of research had been established by the Development Commission, specifically by Hall and Middleton, of focusing on fundamental research in areas of pure science, and this was the model subse-quently adopted by medical, and scientific and industrial bodies. In medicine, Fletcher was of the same mould as Hall, and the DSIR was also run by eminent Oxbridge and London scientists. The policy of fundamental research, albeit on applicable problems, was a long-term scientific strategy, not a military one, or even, arguably, an economic one. Although to an extent forced on the DSIR, it was also seen by the research organisations as the appropriate way to provide for industry, agriculture and medicine. But just how useful was this strategy? As far as waging war was concerned, the work done by these research organisations (as well as the MID and BIR) was overshadowed by the contri-bution of the Ministry of Munitions with its much closer involvement with industry. As for the inter-war period, as noted earlier we should perhaps focus our attention more on the industrial sector to see the more important legacy of the wartime role of science and technology.

Conclusions

In all the main areas considered – the armed services, industry, civil research and education – there had been significant developments well before the war. From the turn of the century, the Admiralty and War Office had begun inves-tigations into aspects of war at sea, on land, and especially in the air. Central government had been sponsoring research into an increasingly diverse range of areas from the late nineteenth century, and major new programmes in agri-cultural and medical science were in course of development prior to the out-

[87] D. J. Kevles, 1971: Into hostile political camps: The reorganisation of international science in World War One. *Isis* 62, 47–60; D. E. H. Edgerton, 1990: Science and war. In R. C. Olby, G. N. Cantor, J. R. R. Christie and M. J. Hodge (eds): *Companion to the History of Modern Science*. London: Routledge, 934–45.
[88] Cardwell, Science in World War 1, op. cit. (note 56); *Yearbook of the Royal Society*, op. cit. (note 64).

break of war. In industry too there is evidence of substantial pre-war effort by individual firms into research and development. In this respect, then, we cannot see the war as providing recognition of science and technology for the first time. On the contrary, existing lines of work were a vitally important cushion when deficiencies in other areas were revealed.

On the other hand, the war did give rise to new levels of recognition, particularly by the state, that science and technology did, emphatically, have an important place in a modern industrial society. It needed developing and institutionalising to take its place as part of the new order of things in the postwar world. Thus we see the widespread organisation of science and technology. In the armed forces, military research was founded on a permanent basis with significant funding and staffing, which even influenced the formulation of strategic thinking, particularly for the air forces. Noticeably, the fundamental research advocated by civilian scientists during the war was supplemented by more military-directed work. Although the Second World War may have seen an even closer integration of science and the military – primarily, of course, in the atomic bomb – the precedents were set during the Great War.[89] Scientists and technologists in 1939 were mobilised quickly and automatically with the threat of war and incorporated directly into military structures where they could have direct influence on operations and even on strategic thinking. The last stages of the First World War had demonstrated the possibilities of mechanised, technological warfare, and its significance was forced home with *blitzkrieg*. The role of science and technology, though, had already been recognised and needed only to be put into operation. In the DSIR, the Government established a pattern of organisation for research in a number of areas relating to industry – through fundamental research and co-operative research associations. Whatever the actual outcomes of these initiatives, they were nevertheless highly important indicators of a new way of thinking. In the industrial sector, firms already active in R & D carried on apace, and it is clear that a number of firms did begin active work in the later stages and immediate aftermath of the war, continuing through the 1920s and 1930s.

The forms in which state civil science was organised in the latter stages of the war were remarkably consistent. Very quickly a pattern emerged, in all areas, of fundamental inquiry based on pure science. In so doing, it apparently vindicated the view, promulgated by academic scientists since the late nineteenth century, that fundamental research would ultimately lead to useful results. This direction, however, is in marked contrast to the ways in which science and technology actually proved their worth during the war. For it was the applied science, invention, innovation and, at times, outright tinkering primarily by firms working to Ministry of Munitions specifications that actually met the needs of Britain's war effort. Indeed, one may recognise two styles of

[89] Pearton, *The Knowledgable State*, op. cit. (note 2), 253; Hartcup, *The War of Invention*, op. cit. (note 2), 193–5.

government intervention on behalf of science and technology: in the Ministry of Munitions and in the DSIR. The former involved itself directly in the running and planning of industry, although leaving actual production largely in private hands; the latter adopted a distinctly more hands-off approach in which state support was not to get too close to industrial production. Moreover, the first style generated quite phenomenal immediate results, while the latter has been considered by some historians to have been disappointing in providing support to British industry. Although the interventionist Ministry of Munitions, working closely with industry, remedied the initial deficiencies of British science and produced the goods to fight the war, it was paradoxically the academics who reaped the rewards of new-found government support for science. Historians of science in concentrating on other state organisations and on academic research seem to have missed the role of the Ministry of Munitions.

On this basis, we may go on to question just how serious government intentions were for science. A hands-off policy could be interpreted as a way of not actually getting too closely involved in the problems of industry. Realistically, though, one cannot have expected the Ministry of Munitions model to have been sustained long into peacetime, although the Ministry remained in existence for a few years after the war and was seen by some as a model of how to organise industry efficiently.[90] While the rhetoric for industry pulling together in peacetime as well as war was enthusiastic, it had a hollow ring. Once the emergency had passed, it would be difficult to persuade independent private firms to collaborate to the extent they had been forced to do in the previous few years. To have maintained the Ministry of Munitions approach implied a degree of State intervention in industry unlikely in postwar Britain.[91] The coalition compromise, as in many other areas of social and economic policy, was succour from the sidelines whilst maintaining a suitably safe distance. The view advocated by the science lobby meshed perfectly with government intentions: fundamental research and pure science could be reasonably advocated as significant intervention on behalf of industry, without getting too closely involved with the running of the market. The bold responses sanctioned by war could not be sustained in the postwar world.

One may further question the government's seriousness of purpose in its moves in education. Fisher's 1918 Education Act, although ostensibly capable of fitting education and training more closely with industrial requirements, was essentially the last Act of a passing era. In keeping to the structure laid down in 1902, Fisher failed to confront the two main issues which needed to be addressed before major educational developments could proceed: the class

---

[90] Pattison, Scientists, inventors and the military, op. cit. (note 17), 553–4; Adams, *Arms and the Wizard*, op. cit. (note 8).
[91] P. Cline, 1982; Winding down the war economy: British plans for peacetime recovery, 1916–19. In Burk, *War and the State: The Transformation of British Government, 1914–1919*, op. cit. (note 15), 157–81.

basis of English education and the denominational question.[92] As long as full secondary education was denied to the majority, any form of part-time industrial training would be rejected as second best. In the initial creation of the DSIR, the opportunity was missed fully to integrate education, research and industry, although, as just noted, this outcome was always unlikely. With the postwar depressions and swingeing cuts in education and science in the wake of the Geddes Committee, it was clear that any hopes of a government-led impetus for British industry based on knowledge and expertise had been severed in the conservative backlash.

It is perhaps in other respects that we can identify a more pervasive scientific and technological legacy of the First World War. New forms of scientific management altered the lives of millions of workers. Scientised, administrative efficiency and rationalised industrial organisation created new structures of work experience. Although the change is difficult to pin down in detail, we may see in the waging of the First World War a new scientific ordering of daily life in Britain.[93] Above all, though, the Great War was a scientific and technological affair of a sort previously unencountered in British experience. Science and technology could not again be viewed as benign agents for progress. The novelty and barbarity of the new scientific weapons of mass destruction affected, directly or indirectly, almost every family in the country, leaving a deep and abiding scar on national life. The technological carnage of the Western Front altered the consciousness of a generation.

Acknowledgements

I should like to thank Joe Pope, Mike Paris and the editors for their helpful comments on earlier drafts of this chapter.

---

[92] B. Simon, 1965: *Education and the Labour Movement, 1870–1920*. London: Lawrence & Wishart, 357–60.

[93] McNeill, in *The Pursuit of Power*, op. cit. (note 7), 317–45, sees the First World War as fashioning the state into a single national firm for waging war. Cooter and Sturdy have discussed managerialism in a particular area – medicine: R. Cooter and S. Sturdy: Scientific management and the structure of the medical revolution in Britain, 1900–1939. Paper read at the Anglo-American Conference on History of Science, Technology and Medicine, Toronto, 25–28 July 1992.

5

The Social Impact

Gordon Phillips

Social change is a large and complex concept. Since it has no fixed and common meaning, we must begin with a brief, theoretical preface. For present purposes, the term will be taken to denote those changes in individual patterns of behaviour which were, from a national perspective, widespread and durable, and which served to modify social relationships. This perspective therefore takes as its focal point the actions of its human subjects, and studies these actions over some limited period of time.

But of course the actions of individual men and women were almost never the outcome of an unfettered choice. They were constrained by a multiplicity of factors, hard for the historian to disentangle. The individual actors might often perceive the nature of these constraints only partially, and be unaware of the collective social consequences of their own actions. When one hundred thousand shopkeepers raise their prices, we cease to consider them as individuals determining their own existence, and refer rather to the economic system to which they were subject and to the economic situation which propelled them. Marx's well-known dictum, that men make their own history, but under conditions not of their own choosing, expresses this idea in simple form. There is virtue in remarking, however, that these 'conditions' were not the impersonal product of an inhuman environment. They represent, for the most part, the outcomes of the accumulated actions and decisions of other human agents, whether in the immediate or the more distant past. What makes social change appear impersonal is that the people who enact it are unconnected by any personal ties, and more or less devoid of any conscious social purpose. At their most persistent and extensive, such patterns of individual behaviour are crystallised into institutions and cultures. 'Social change' is thus embodied in a vast and manifold process of human decisions and responses, choices and acceptances, enterprises and adjustments. Historians can never grasp more than a fraction of these. They must select what aspects of past behaviour seem to them most significant, and make sense of the record of others' behaviour as best they can.

This chapter will, accordingly, tell its own story about a social past, not claiming more for this account than its being a reading of the evidence of past behaviour that makes it understandable to present observers. It thus offers no more than a fragmentary view of those myriad actions and sequences of behaviour that make up the social process. It seeks to highlight the particular developments which seem most clearly located, chronologically, in the years 1914–18, and which are considered in themselves historically significant, either because of the weight of numbers involved in them, or because of the force that they exercised upon the actions and decisions of others.

The First World War may, then, be regarded as a shorthand for a universe of actions flowing from, or connected with, an international military conflict. In what follows, I shall look firstly at its impact on population trends; then at some aspect of living standards and social inequalities; and finally at the history of certain voluntary associations. In all these contexts, I shall try to draw attention to changes in culture as well as to shifts of economic and social activity. My concern on the former count will not be with changing personal attitudes to the moral questions of war – to patriotism, say, or to racial supremacy. While such a recasting of values is sometimes attributed to the emotional experience of war, it remains difficult to detect on a large scale.[1] I am more interested, accordingly, in the attitudes and ideas that shaped everyday life. These mental attributes affect the choices people make, in the realm of family, of employment and so forth. But they are not themselves chosen, being rather the outcome of a shared culture, of upbringing and of communal traditions. While people express themselves directly enough in what they consume and in the organisations that they join, their hopes, fears and preferences remain subject to cultural determinants that may be almost as stringent as the economic determinants which govern, for example, the selection of occupations in the labour market. At least, however, the possibility of personal initiative exists within the cultural arena; and the effect of the war upon social values should therefore, no matter how tentatively, be addressed.

Demographic Trends and Behaviour

The First World War caused directly the deaths of about 723 000 British servicemen, or 15 per cent of males aged between 15 and 29 in 1911. This, however, was a lower rate of deaths than experienced by the other principal European belligerents.[2] In absolute terms, it was not a large demographic loss.

[1] See, for example, J. M. Bourne, 1989: *Britain and the Great War 1914–18*. London: Edward Arnold, 233 ff. Bourne discusses the alleged erosion of 'public school' values, the decline of religious allegiance, and the relaxation of sexual discipline, all connected with the effects of war. But these changes are shown with the aid of anecdotal literary evidence, and little attempt is made to link them to any widespread discontinuities in social behaviour.
[2] J. Winter, 1986: *The Great War and the British People*. London: Macmillan, 66–76, 257.

The annual death rate in England and Wales increased by 0.1 per cent between 1911–15 and 1916–20. But population grew over the decade 1911–21 by almost 2 million, albeit this represented an annual rate of growth less than half (48.7 per cent) that of the previous ten years. The mortality of young adults made some apparent difference to the age structure of the population. The proportion of males aged 20 to 40 (in England and Wales) fell from 15.5 per cent in 1911 to 14.1 per cent in 1921. This fall cannot, however, be attributed wholly to the fatalities of war: the proportion of females in the same age group also fell, by 0.4 per cent from 17.1 to 16.7. Men over 65, on the other hand, increased as a proportion from 2.2 per cent to 2.6 per cent of the country's inhabitants. But the ratio of the elderly had been rising prior to the war, advancing from 4.7 per cent of the total population of England and Wales in 1901 to 5.1 per cent in 1911 (and it continued upwards afterwards, to reach 7.4 per cent by 1931).[3]

The devastation of war, in a purely demographic sense, was repaired without much difficulty. Birth-rates had been falling long before 1914, it is true, and they continued to decline during the war years, despite the increase in levels of illegitimacy which then occurred.[4] For a short interval, in 1918–20, fertility recovered, before resuming its downward trend. The long-term decline of the death rate was not interrupted by the war. It has been argued, with much force, that civilian health improved during 1914–18: food was more efficiently and equitably distributed among all classes; the diet of the poor may well have got better; medical and infant welfare services continued to lower infant mortality.[5] Since these benefits were enjoyed particularly by the younger age groups, they assisted the capacity of the population to replenish itself. The old fared less well, in this respect; and the influenza epidemic at the end of 1918 almost certainly moderated the relative expansion of elderly cohorts in later years.

Thus far, it would appear, the war did nothing to alter established demographic patterns and tendencies. At most it sustained and reinforced processes of change that were already in train; or if it altered them, did so only very briefly. In the case of the birth-rate, as noticed already, the war had both effects. The crude birth-rate of England and Wales (infants born as a ratio of the whole population) revived momentarily from a nadir of 17.7 in 1918 to a level of 25.5 per thousand in 1920. The peak year represented 102 offspring per thousand women at the child-bearing age (15–44), which was some 0.5 per cent higher than the rate of 1910–13. But this sudden wave of fertility was quite exceptional, so that over the next two years births fell back by nearly 20 per thousand women,[6] and the crude birth rate had sunk below its previous

[3] Figures in A. L. Bowley and M. H. Hogg, 1925: *Has Poverty Diminished?* London: P. S. King, 2; A. H. Halsey (ed.), 1972: *Trends in Modern British Society.* London: Macmillan, 33.
[4] Bourne, *Britain and the Great War 1914–18,* op. cit. (note 1), 235–6.
[5] For the marked improvement in the nourishment of schoolchildren, *see* B. Waites, 1987: *A Class Society at War: England 1914–18.* Leamington Spa: Berg, 162–4.
[6] Winter, *The Great War,* op. cit. (note 2), 252, 254.

minimum by 1927. As in the pre-war years, middle-class families were typically, though not uniformly, smaller than those of the working class. In the second quarter of 1922, Masterman remarked, the birth-rate in London varied from 28 in Shoreditch to 15 in Hampstead.[7] But the trend was similar in almost every district, for knowledge of methods of family limitation had certainly been extended by military service. The investigation later conducted by the medical demographer, Lewis-Faning, recorded 41 per cent of women married in the years 1910–19 as using contraception, where only 16 per cent had done so in the previous decade.[8]

In another respect, however, the years 1914–18 did mark a more significant and lasting break in the statistics of the Registrar-General. The previous half-century had been characterised by relatively low rates of marriage. Whether from choice or necessity, large numbers both of men and women in every age group had remained single. And in areas of middle-class residence, especially, this abstention from marriage had been widespread. In the aftermath of war, a sharp and lasting rise in the marriage rate occurred. While the excess of women in the total population was growing in these years, they were nevertheless more likely to marry. The proportion of women remaining unmarried throughout their lives had risen steadily between the 1880s and 1914, when it had reached 19 per cent. But this figure was almost halved during the inter-war years. Among males, the marriage rate (in England and Wales, including widowers and divorcees) rose from 39.2 per cent in 1901 to 45 per cent in 1921 – and continued upwards subsequently. (Among women, thanks to a higher survival rate of elderly widows, the level increased from 41.4 to 46.5 per cent.) Of every hundred males currently married at the turn of the century, a further six had found partners by the early 1920s. The age of these partners, moreover, was at least slightly younger (by some 6 months) than on the eve of war.[9] It was among the younger age groups, therefore, that the marriage rate rose fastest. Between 1911 and 1921, the proportion of unmarried women fell by 3.1 per cent among the age group 20–24, by 1.8 per cent at age 25–34, and by only 0.4 per cent between 35 and 44.[10]

Had the war itself brought about this change of behaviour? One simple explanation that is sometimes offered for the rising propensity to marry is the falling volume of overseas migration. According to this thesis, a significant proportion of young men had, prior to the war, sought advancement, temporary or permanent, in the dominions or the United States, removing themselves from the marriage market at home. The war did, of course, drastically curtail emigration, and after 1918 the flow of people overseas remained in

[7] C. F. G. Masterman, 1923: *England after War*. London: Hodder, 172 n.
[8] Cited in Winter, *The Great War*, op. cit. (note 2), 271. The percentage rose to 59 for women married in the 1920s.
[9] Winter, *The Great War*, op. cit. (note 2), 261–3; Halsey, *Trends*, op. cit. (note 4), Table 2.15.
[10] N. H. Carrier and J. R. Jeffery, 1953: *External Migration: A Study of the Available Statistics*. London: HMSO, Table viii, 105.

check. Restrictions on entry were imposed by other countries; new welfare benefits in Britain created inducements to immobility; while the falling birth-rate had a similar effect.[11] It is, however, by no means clear how large and extensive was this decline in male emigration, nor whether it can account for an increase in marriage which probably affected all social classes. Contrast, for example, the estimates of Winter and Constantine.[12] The latter points to the problem of distinguishing 'passengers' from 'migrants', and suggests that there may have been only negligible change in the volume of those leaving Britain for extra-European settlements between the decades 1901–10 and 1920–9. The decline appears large only if the exceptionally high exodus of the years 1910–13 is taken as the point of comparison. The average number of British passengers departing for extra-European destinations fell from 448 000 in 1910–13 to 277 000 in 1919–23. The *net* movement, if inward pas-sengers are subtracted from the above, was 252 000 in 1910–13 and 122 000 in 1919–23.[13] It would, of course, be necessary to apply more evidence concern-ing the composition of emigrants by sex, age and class, as well as the changing rate and character of immigration, before the potential effects of this factor upon marriage rates could be assessed. In the case of native passengers from England and Wales to the United States, the ratio of adult women to 1000 adult males was 784 in 1912–13, while to Australasia the ratio was 817, and to South Africa there was an excess of female passengers of 1014 to 1000. The proportion of women increased significantly in all these cases during the years 1920–9, to 1030, 860 and 1096 respectively.[14]

The causes of the rise in the marriage rate may thus be more elusive: the attitudes and estimations that may have made young men and women more willing to marry, and perhaps more adventurous in entering the contract. The decline in residential domestic service as a female occupation inimical to mar-riage may have had a marginal effect in this respect, if women were caused to begin the search for husbands at an earlier age. The widespread improvement of real incomes, among both male and female employees, may have made sav-ing for marriage easier.[15] (It is sometimes assumed that this consideration restrained middle-class marriages rather than working-class ones; but this seems a crude distinction.) However, it is more incalculable matters, such as the waning of parental authority over adult children, the greater readiness of both men and women to select marriage partners from a wider social or geo-graphical circle, the changing perception of the rewards of family life, even of

[11] Carrier and Jeffery, *External Migration*, op. cit. (note 10), 35–7.
[12] Winter, *The Great War*, op. cit. (note 2), 269; Stephen Constantine (ed.), *Emigrants and Empire: British Settlement in the Dominions between the Wars*. Manchester: Manchester University Press, 1.
[13] Carrier and Jeffery, *External Migration*, op. cit. (note 10), Table B1, 90.
[14] Ibid., Table H1, 102.
[15] *See* C. Stella Davies, 1963: *North Country Bred: A Working-Class Family Chronicle*. London, Routledge & Kegan Paul, 70; J. A. Banks, 1954: *Prosperity and Parenthood*. London, Routledge & Kegan Paul, especially 2–3, 27–31, 48.

the images of marriage purveyed by the ever more popular cinema, which perhaps hold the key.

We must conclude that the measurable effects of the First World War upon national demographic trends were only slight. The deaths due to military action were not so numerous as to produce significant distortions in the population structure. The psychological and moral impact of the conflict is, however, much more difficult to assess. The choices that individuals made about marriage and reproduction may have been influenced, in many subtle and elusive ways, by their circumstances and experiences during these years. We cannot pretend to know whether, in the absence of war, the rate of births or the incidence of marriage would have been different. All we can suggest is that the disturbance of prevailing tendencies – temporary in the one case, enduring in the other – suggests some increased personal awareness of the existence of choice, of the possibility that past habits and norms might be relinquished. This does not mean, of course, that decisions about marriage and childbirth were simply private and autonomous, for the myriad couples who took them were bound up in a strong and tight web of cultural controls. Yet these controls, too, could be loosened or resisted; and it is not unreasonable to think that, for a time at least, the disruptions of war lessened the hold of the community over its members, of older over younger adults, and of higher-status over lower-status groups.

Employment, Wages and Occupations

What social consequences came from the economic impact of the war? There were three principal economic mechanisms of social change: the recruitment of manpower into the armed services, leading to a severe labour shortage; the interruption of normal production and trade, coupled with the rapid increase of retail prices, which brought shifts in the pattern of consumption; and the enlarged sphere of state activity, which affected social values as well as social behaviour. The rate of unemployment, measured as a proportion of trade union members claiming benefit from their organisations, fell from 3.25 per cent in 1910–13 (itself a period of trade prosperity) to only 0.75 per cent in 1915–18.[16] The cost-of-living index more than doubled during the war years, although we shall see shortly that the pattern of price changes was quite varied. The expansion of the state took many forms. It vastly increased its own expenditure, and hence required higher taxes and higher borrowings from its subjects. It imposed extraordinary regulations and restrictions upon normal economic activity: on certain sectors of trade, prices, and consumption; on the conduct of industrial bargaining; on the movement of labour. It extended the field of public welfare services, notably to servicemen and their

[16] Department of Employment, 1971: *British Labour Statistics, 1886–1968.* London: HMSO, Table 159.

families. And it created its own manufacturing enterprises for the production of armaments.

Some of these features of a war economy disappeared quickly after 1918, but the repercussions of the war, taken as a whole, were large and lasting. The conditions of full employment and inflation which prevailed during 1919 and 1920, and of unemployment and falling prices thereafter, can alike be seen as the natural aftermath of global conflict. They arose partly from the international economic conditions that had been created by war and its diplomatic resolution, partly from the mental anxieties and expectations born of war, which influenced the decisions and behaviour of government, employers, financiers and workers thereafter.

Clearly not all these outcomes can be discussed in the present chapter. Attention will be devoted here, therefore, to the question of economic gains and losses: to identifying those elements of society that fared best and worst, in terms of the enjoyment of economic resources, during the ten years or so following 1914. If we consider these relative benefits by means of the largest economic aggregates, the national statistics on incomes collected by the Inland Revenue, we can detect a trend, though not a rapid one, towards greater equality between richer and poorer households. Some 8 per cent of total personal income in 1911 had been received by the richest class: those who, with over £5000 a year, were subject to supertax. By 1924 the equivalent group (about 25 000 in number) obtained only about 5.5 per cent.[17] Members of this affluent class were somewhat more heavily taxed, and their income from overseas investments, much reduced by the war, had not been fully replaced.

If examination is made of different types of income over the years 1911–24, it appears that both farmers and landlords in the agricultural sector suffered a sharp fall of income, relative to others. But the owners of urban property also fared badly: the share of rents in the net national income fell from 11.6 per cent in 1914 to 5.8 per cent in 1921, and recovered only modestly, to 7.9 per cent, by 1924.[18] The nature of these losses (by no means confined to the wealthy) will be considered shortly.

The share of wages, which had averaged 38.5 per cent in the years 1910–14, rose significantly to 43.5 per cent between 1921 and 1924, though drifting downwards in the later 1920s.[19] There was an even sharper increase in the incomes received in salaries. At about 21 per cent in the early 1920s, this had almost doubled since the pre-war years. Whereas the expansion of the wage

[17] A. L. Bowley and J. C. Stamp, 1927: *The National Income, 1924*. Oxford: Clarendon Press, 57–8; Masterman, *England after War*, op. cit. (note 7), 137. Bowley and Stamp (p. 59) add that 'when the full effects of taxation are taken into account the real income available for saving or expenditure in the hands of the rich is definitely less than before the war. The sum devoted to luxurious expenditure is . . . definitely less than in 1911, but it is still sufficient to bulk large in the eyes of the public, since it is concentrated in small areas, enlarged by the spending of visitors from overseas, and advertised by the newspapers.'
[18] Halsey, *Trends*, op. cit. (note 3), Table 3.2.
[19] Ibid.

constituent can reasonably be attributed to increases of pay, however, a large part of the increased salary figure reflects the relative growth in this class of the occupied population – in terms of census categories, from 1.67 million in 1911 to 2.8 million in 1921. The average income of salary earners did also rise, faster than living costs, from £128 in 1911 to £265 in 1924.[20] But it was those at the bottom of the professional hierarchy whose pay advanced most rapidly, so that a greater economic equality may have come about within this section of the middle class.[21] The average wage, by contrast, rose more slowly, from £51 in 1911 to £103 in 1924, though it is likely that hours of work fell more rapidly among wage-earners than among non-manual groups. The rise in salaries per capita was smaller, however, and that of wages slightly higher, because of the altered ratio of males to females (there being more women working in white-collar jobs after the war, and fewer in domestic service in particular).[22]

These large, national calculations therefore suggest the occurrence of a modest redistribution of income during the war decade: wages and salaries gaining at the expense of rents and, to a lesser extent, of profits. These statistics, however, are by no means precise, and they convey nothing of the detail of social experience. Nor do they tell us much about the importance of the war itself in bringing about the new allocation of means. We shall need, for this purpose, to make a closer examination of the fortunes of the largest income group: those making their livelihood by working for wages.

There is general agreement among historians that the index of average money wages rose in an accelerating curve between 1914 and 1924. But different authorities produce indexes of varying shape. The increase in average real wages, on a weekly basis, has been put as low as 5 per cent and as high as 17 per cent. The figures in Table 5.1 yield an estimate at the top end of this scale.[23] They nonetheless suggest that money wages, shown in the second column, rose much less rapidly in the early stages of the war than the cost of living, and caught up with prices only about 1919. The earnings index, in contrast, though it reveals almost the same level of improvement over the whole period from 1914 to 1924, displays no comparable falling off after 1914.

The calculation of such global indices is, however, fraught with difficulties. They can only take account of a restricted number of occupations, and are not able to assess accurately, if at all, the changing balance of higher-paid to lower-paid workers in these occupations, or the tendency of particular fields of

[20] Bowley and Stamp, *The National Income*, op. cit. (note 17), 45.
[21] Waites, *A Class Society at War*, op. cit. (note 5), 92.
[22] For estimates of average wages per household, including all earners, which were naturally a good deal higher, see Bowley and Stamp, *The National Income*, op. cit. (note 17), 57.
[23] The wage quotient is that of E. H. Phelps Brown and S. V. Hopkins, 1950: Wage rates in five countries, 1860–1939. *Oxford Economic Papers*, n.s., 2, reproduced in Halsey, *Trends*, op. cit. (note 4), 121, and calculated here with a 1914 base. The earnings index is that of C. H. Feinstein, reproduced in J. C. Dowie, 1975: 1919–20 is in need of attention. *Economic History Review* 28, 429–50. The cost-of-living index is also based on Phelps Brown and Hopkins. Significant variations are to be found in the official price indexes published by the Department of Employment, *British Labour Statistics*, op. cit. (note 16), Table 87, and by the Central Statistical Office, 1991: *Retail Prices 1914–90*. London: HMSO, Table 84.

Table 5.1   Index of Wages and Earnings, 1914–24

Year	Weekly wages	Weekly earnings	Retail prices
1914	100	100	100
1915	107.7	116	115.9
1916	117.3	132	133.1
1917	138.5	168	166.0
1918	178.8	209	189.7
1919	232.7	239	205.2
1920	311.5	275	249.1
1921	250.0	257	184.8
1922	194.2	207	167.6
1923	192.3	191	164.4
1924	196.2	194	167.6

employment to expand and contract relative to each other over time. The problem is further complicated by the fact that, at the end of the war, hours of work were almost universally shortened, usually to between 44 and 48 a week – a cut of around 13 per cent on the pre-war standard. This means that the increase in hourly wages, in the years after 1919, was far higher than that of weekly pay – perhaps even by a multiple of four, according to Dowie. Using one of several Bowley wage indexes, Dowie estimates the increase in real hourly pay between 1914 and 1924 as 47.9 per cent.[24] It is all but certain, accordingly, that the average wage rates recorded above give a false impression of the true experience of very many working people.

Much personal testimony suggests that working-class families observed a greater material comfort quite early in the war years. 'It was only through the war that we got wakened up', recalled one women textile worker from Lancashire. 'People got better wages and they started going further afield and learning things. They got better wages, see, so I think that in itself got poor people out of a rut, and it made them think more.'[25] Even more revealing is the recollection of Arthur Harding, the enterprising petty-criminal chronicler of an East End neighbourhood.[26] Of the local furniture workers, who were diverted to making packing cases for munitions, he observed:

They got much more money out of ammunition boxes than out of furniture. They didn't get conscripted. It paid the top people at Lebuse's to say that a man was a good workman and couldn't be spared. There were increased wages for those who

[24] Dowie, 1919–20, op. cit. (note 23). He argues that the rapid increase of labour costs thus imposed made a substantial contribution to the subsequent rise of unemployment and malaise.

[25] Florence Atherton of Farnworth, in Thea Thompson (ed.), 1981: *Edwardian Childhoods*. London: Routledge & Kegan Paul, 118.

[26] R. Samuel (ed.), 1981: *East End Underworld: The Life of Arthur Harding*. London: Routledge & Kegan Paul, 236.

went out to work and the widows and mothers were getting large sums of money as allowances for their boys and husbands. Before the war a mother might have had a couple of sons that never fetched a bloody penny in. Now in the army they got regular wages.

This conflict between subjective impressions and economic statistics may be explained in several ways. Since the war brought with it high and consistent employment for civilian workers (both men and women), family income was often much less irregular than in peacetime. In addition, the wage index fails adequately to reflect the benefits of job mobility. Wartime conditions created many opportunities for workers to move from poorly paid to well-paid employment. Adolescents, married and single women, and elderly men might all take advantage of the general shortage of labour, and their collective contribution to the income of a household was likely to be much enhanced. Adult men, because of the labour controls in war industries, were sometimes less free to change employers (a source of considerable resentment among skilled engineering workers), though in some cases they acquired similar rewards by taking on the responsibility of supervising unskilled and inexperienced recruits. In addition, certain groups capitalised on the chance to make higher earnings from bonuses and payments for overtime. When work was plentiful, a gap between recognised wage rates and actual earnings was liable to appear and to widen. Anxious to get the most out of their skilled men, and to appease industrial discontent, employers were, in some instances, willing to engage in shopfloor bargaining, resulting in special payments for urgent orders and for extra work. In exceptional circumstances, workers such as the coal trimmers in the docks, required to perform essential tasks at high speed, were able by 1916 to double the charges they made to some contractors, when their recognised rate of pay stood at no more than 12.5 per cent above the pre-war figure.[27]

The improvement of living standards during the postwar years of 1919–24 is statistically more clear-cut. The boom of 1919–20 saw the continuation of high employment and labour shortages. Employers in a wide range of industries and services sought to re-engage the younger male workers who had been unavailable in wartime. They were, for a time, unusually willing to make concessions to the demands of the trade unions. The latter, as Masterman suggested, were most aggressive in those industries that had been at the forefront of the war effort:

The larger movements of social unrest amongst the workers in Britain were at the beginning fomented, not by or among the men who fought abroad, but by and among the men who stayed at home. It was the great centres of home industry which were exempted from conscription who first agitated the nation with truculent

---

[27] G. A. Phillips, 1968: The National Transport Workers' Federation, 1910–27. D.Phil. thesis, University of Oxford, 215–17.

*demands for the betterment of their conditions. The railwaymen, the coal-miners,
the dock-labourers, the workers in the munitions cities such as Glasgow, were the
leaders in this revolt.*[28]

Following the wage bonanza of the postwar boom, the advent of a world-
wide depression at the end of 1920 radically changed the employment situation. Among the insured workforce, unemployment reached peaks of over 17
per cent in the worst months of 1921–2. In every trade employers demanded
pay reductions, and if necessary imposed them by rescinding agreements and
co-ordinating lock-outs. Even in these circumstances, however, the real
income of those wage-earners who remained in work suffered only a transient
fall. The slump brought with it falling prices, especially of food, and though
money wages were reduced their purchasing power still rose. From 1924 economic recovery, though very incomplete, restored some of the market power
of the organised working class.

This advance of real wages between 1914 and 1924 was not, however, by any
means uniform. Which elements of the workforce did best is, indeed, a matter
of some dispute. While historians and economists generally believe that the
largest relative gains were made by semi-skilled and unskilled labour, there is
no agreement as to the scope or speed of this trend. The reorganisation of war
work tended to create more jobs for the former, and perhaps to enhance their
value in the productive process. As for the unskilled, they were no longer in
such plentiful supply; and the wartime system of compulsory arbitration
worked perhaps especially to their advantage. Wage tribunals were apt to pay
the same advances to all workers in an industry, whatever their level of skill;
and they latterly chose to lay down national wage norms, which brought substantial rewards to workers formerly living in areas of low pay.

This narrowing of wage differentials can be assessed in two ways. First,
account can be taken of the wages of skilled and unskilled in particular industries. The results of this analysis show significant variations from one occupation to another. Although the lower-paid made relatively bigger gains during
the war years, these were halted, and sometimes reversed, during the 1920s.
The advent of economic depression seems to have enabled certain craftsmen
at least partially to restore their economic advantage over the untrained. The
wage index of different grades of building and printing labour in Edinburgh
reveals reapportionments shown in Table 5.2.

The impact of the war upon pay can also be measured by studying the occupations at the summit and the base of the wages ladder. Table 5.3 presents the
figures calculated by Routh from the official censuses of earnings in 1906 and
1924. This, unfortunately, is too long a time period by which to assess the consequences of the war, except in a very approximate fashion. Money wages
changed significantly in the pre-war years, although there is not much evidence to suggest that the parities of different occupations and strata were

---

[28] Masterman, *England After War*, op. cit. (note 7), 9.

Table 5.2 Wage Differentials in Edinburgh Trades, 1914–26

	1914	*1921*	*1926*
Building			
Skilled	100	100	100
Semi-skilled	93	130	98
Unskilled	59–73	n.a.	74
Printing			
Skilled	100	100	100
Unskilled	57	74	75

Source: J. Holford, 1988: *Reshaping Labour: Organisation, Work and Politics: Edinburgh in the Great War and After*. Beckenham: Croom Helm, 31–2.

Table 5.3 Relative Gains in Weekly or Yearly Money Wages in the UK, 1906–24

	Relative gain (%)
All manual workers	112.5
(i) Selected skilled occupations	105
Gainers	
Compositors	130
Railway loco engineers	132
Losers	
Miners	61
Engineering fitters	74
(ii) Selected semi-skilled occupations	105
Gainers	
Carters	111
Rail platelayers	167
(iii) Selected unskilled occupations	126
Gainers	
Railway porters	161
Losers	
Engineering labourers	103.5

Source: G. Routh, 1965: *Occupation and Pay in Great Britain, 1906–60*. Cambridge: Cambridge University Press, 88–98.

greatly altered. The unweighted average figures suggest that unskilled workers did secure a proportionately greater rise than higher grades, but that there was nothing to choose, on this basis, between skilled and semi-skilled. But they also point to significant variations between occupations: printing craftsmen and railway engine drivers doing well, for instance, while coal-miners fared badly. In the middle and lower hierarchy, railway platelayers and porters did well, male shop assistants and engineering labourers relatively badly.[29] If Holford's Edinburgh figures are used to examine the wages hierarchy over the shorter period of 1914 to 1924, a similar change in the occupational élite is noticeable. In Edinburgh, it was building craftsmen who were at the top of the wage hierarchy in 1914, followed by electricians and compositors. At the bottom of the ladder came unskilled brewery workers and warehouse labourers in the printing trade. A decade later, compositors had moved above all other workers, followed by bricklayers and sheet metal workers in the motor industry; while the lowest rungs were now taken by foundry labourers and unskilled rubber workers. The other climbers in this game included male shop assistants and both warehouse and general labourers; notable fallers were engineering workers, although sheet metal workers had also lost ground since the post-war boom.[30]

The evidence of wage changes has frequently been used by historians to support a thesis that connects the war with growing working-class solidarity. The economic advance of unskilled workers, it was argued, made them less obviously different from the more skilled and affluent. The spread of trade union organisation among the lower-paid, and the postwar rise of the Labour party, have been adduced as further evidence for this 'homogenisation' thesis.[31] But the argument, though attractively simple, has aroused increasing scepticism. The impact of the war on wage differentials appears more and more disparate. The picture changes from the war years to the postwar; from industry to industry; and almost certainly from one locality or region to another. We must clearly refrain from making any large generalisations about the consolidation of the wage-earning population into a more uniform class, or about the destruction of a 'labour aristocracy'.[32]

Taking the period as a whole, however, we might suggest the following rough balance sheet. The war had prejudiced the position of some skilled workers, such as those in mining and heavy engineering, chiefly by expanding their industries far beyond what was required to operate in postwar markets. In addition, it engendered mistrust and animosity between employers and cer-

---

[29] G. Routh, 1965: *Occupation and Pay in Great Britain, 1906–60.* Cambridge: Cambridge University Press, 88–98.

[30] J. Holford, 1988: *Reshaping Labour: Organisation, Work and Politics: Edinburgh in the Great War and after.* Beckenham: Croom Helm, 31–2.

[31] For versions of this argument, *see* A. Marwick, 1965: *The Deluge: British Society and the First World War.* London: Macmillan; Waites, *A Class Society at War,* op. cit. (note 5); and E. J. Hobsbawm, 1984: The making of the working class. In E. J. Hobsbawm, *Worlds of Labour.* London: Weidenfeld & Nicolson, 194–213. The last, it should be noted, does not specifically link the process of homogenisation with the effects of the war.

[32] There are, of course, other aspects to the thesis of class homogeneity. For arguments on these lines, *see* A. Reid, 1988: The impact of the First World War on British workers. In R. Wall and J. Winter (eds), *The Upheaval of War: Family, Work and Welfare in Europe, 1914–18.* Cambridge: Cambridge University Press; and M. Savage, 1987: *The Dynamics of Working-Class Politics: The Labour Movement in Preston.* Cambridge: Cambridge University Press, 41–6.

tain of the unions catering for the wage-earning élite – partly because of their contrasting views of the merits of government controls. But these conditions were almost as unfavourable to the unskilled in such trades as to the skilled, so that there was, in the end, no significant progress towards internal equality.

In other sectors, the war did assist the non-skilled workers: it expanded industries and services dependent upon the home market, thanks to the rising real incomes of this period. Employers appreciated more readily that they could pass costs on to their customers, but also recognised, in some instances, that previously ill-considered employees were capable of doing more varied and productive work. National bargaining mechanisms were also established, while the introduction of a comprehensive scheme of unemployment relief held special benefits for the lower-paid. In the docks, for instance, this welfare measure helped to curtail the competition for employment, and provided a means of supplementing irregular earnings.[33] Some at least of these benefits of wartime, however, were also enjoyed by skilled workers in sheltered industries and services.

In sum, while there is little doubt that the period ends with a higher proportion of the work-force enjoying wages close to the national mean, conspicuous groups of the high-paid and the low-paid persisted. Their identity had undergone some change, but the gap remained large.

Wealth, Poverty and the Class Hierarchy

In this section we shall look from a wider perspective at the richest and poorest strata in society, and consider more broadly the way in which the war affected their economic condition. In both cases – though more obviously in that of the well-to-do members of the landed class – we shall be observing some changes of economic behaviour as well as of economic circumstances.

The years immediately after the war saw a drastic contraction, almost a voluntary extinction, of the old landed élite. The rural social scene was transformed, and the regime of the great landed estate, previously the centrepiece of rural society, was eclipsed. A further stage was reached in the long history of the commercialisation of agriculture. This, in turn, had its consequences for the farm labourers, who had seemed to gain much from the war, in both income and social power, but lost something on each count in the early postwar period. The previous value of a landed class to them, as a paternalist guardian, should probably not be rated very highly; but where it had been significant, it was now usually withdrawn.

It is questionable how far the war, in itself, sufficed to dissolve the landed élite. The readiness of the wealthier landowners to invest outside agriculture had long been apparent. Both the depression of farming in the 1880s and

[33] G. A. Phillips and N. Whiteside, 1985: *Casual Labour: The Unemployment Question in the Port Transport Industry, 1880–1970.* Oxford: Clarendon Press, ch. 6.

1890s and rising taxes on property (especially death duties) had prompted obituary notices before the war. The hostility of a radical Liberal Government to aristocratic privilege, made plain by the constitutional attack on the House of Lords in 1911 and by the various elements of its land reform programme, had intensified the landowners' mood of pessimism. On the other hand, rents were again recovering in these years, along with agricultural profits, while the immediate threat of a political assault upon rural property remained, in fact, slight. Some instances could still be found, accordingly, of aristocratic land purchases.[34] A renegade radical landowner like Arthur Ponsonby, writing of the decline of aristocracy in 1912, could still point to the reality of aristocrats' social power, and to an apparent security of wealth which did not yet require this class to make terms with an inimical plutocracy.[35]

The war altered the situation of the landed class in three main ways. First, the demand for home-produced food raised agricultural prices and profits. Though this prosperity brought only a modest increase in landlords' rents, it helped to create a more buoyant market for land in the postwar years than for at least half a century. At the same time, landowners felt new and strong inducements to liquidate their estates. They were faced, like all property owners, with a growing tax burden, which the present and future liabilities of government seemed bound to prolong. Death duties, reaching a new peak of 40 per cent on the largest estates in 1919, became an immediate or looming menace for all landed families, but especially for those that had lost proprietors or heirs during the conflict.[36] On the other hand, the outlets for capital released by the sale of estates were increasingly extensive and attractive. The Treasury bonds and loan stock that had been issued to pay for the war, and remained on offer to meet the postwar deficits, were a safe and trouble-free option. During the postwar boom, moreover, other kinds of speculation and share-holding looked just as appealing.

The opportunity of throwing off the incubus of land was seized immediately. Between about 1918 and 1922, one-quarter of the cultivated area of Britain was sold. Masterman thought that the purchasers of land comprised three groups: wartime profiteers, tenant farmers and public authorities. It seems clear, however, that the first of these groups was involved only on a tem-

---

[34] The Duke of Bedford represents an ambiguous example: the sale of his Cambridge estate shortly before 1914 is cited by F. M. L. Thompson, 1991: English landed society in the twentieth century, part II. *Transactions of the Royal Historical Society*, 6th series, 1, 1–20; but H. H. Mann, 1904: Life in an agricultural village. *Sociological Papers*, 161–93, records his purchase of new land in Northamptonshire.

[35] Ponsonby said of the danger of this merging of aristocracy with the monied class: 'The manipulating of interests, the juggling in the money market, the mania for speculation, the creation of false money standards, the international syndicates of financial adventurers to which Governments become a prey, the control of the press, the ostentatious benevolence of millionaires and the brutalising effects of the pursuit of wealth give us a foretaste of the kind of calamity it would mean.' A. Ponsonby, 1912: *The Decline of the Aristocracy*. London: T. Fisher Unwin, 313.

[36] F. M. L. Thompson, 1990: English landed society in the twentieth century, part I. *Transactions of the Royal Historical Society*, 5th series, 40, 1–24.

porary basis, perhaps buying up some estates in order to divide and resell them. The last, too, were marginal, using limited amounts of farmland for smallholdings or for housing. In truth, the preponderant part of the agricultural land thus transferred came into the hands of former tenant farmers. They had often amassed windfalls during the war, at least if they were large operators. 'The experiment of a farmer-proprietorship', wrote Masterman, 'employing landless labourers and with no landlords above them, has never yet been tried on a large scale. It appears to be the experiment which is likely to be tried next in this country.'[37]

He was not alone in forecasting, amid the subsequent collapse of food prices, 'the death of a rural civilisation'. The phrase has a somewhat facile look. The old landed class did not suffer a uniform fate. Smaller gentry estates might be sold up, and their owners take flight to more congenial colonies, or assume the role of farmers on their own behalf. Large estates were less likely to be wholly relinquished. According to Masterman, country seats were often retained, as settings for a fashionable social intercourse, though it was probably increasingly rare for aristocrats to maintain more than one great house, still less for them to draw income principally from agricultural rents. Those who remained most heavily involved in estate management, such as the East Anglian squire described by S. L. Bensusan in 1928, were cool-headed, cost-conscious businessmen, seeking to make the most of such assets as shooting rights and forestry.[38] Just because they chose no single method of adaptation, however, the landed class ceased to be recognisable as a class: ceased, that is, to act collectively in a common interest. Their altered choice of marriage partners, their withdrawal from county politics and from other public duties, their growing detachment from such traditional satellites as the established Church alike testify to the decline of this conception of *noblesse*. Lloyd George's frenzied sale of peerages for political gain probably contributed to the devaluation of title, as well as to the eclipse of the House of Lords. If a traditional landed élite survived, separable from the commercial plutocracy, it was so limited in number as to be a negligible social force. As Thompson writes,

> *The patricians had ceased to be a ruling elite. It had happened very suddenly; it had happened because the necessities and casualties of war had magnified and accelerated the tendencies visible in the previous half century; and it had happened with the connivance of the patricians' political spokesmen . . . [in] Lloyd George's Coalition government.*[39]

If we consider the other end of the income scale, there is some reason to suppose that wartime conditions diminished the extent of social destitution

---

[37] Masterman, *England After War*, op. cit. (note 7), 41.
[38] S. L. Bensusan, 1928: *Latter Day Rural England*. London: Ernest Benn, 60.
[39] Thompson, English landed society, op. cit. (note 36). *See also* David Cannadine, 1990: *The Decline and Fall of the British Aristocracy*. New Haven and London: Yale University Press.

and distress. There was, at any rate, a sharp reduction, between 1910 and 1920, in the numbers housed in the institutions of the poor law: if the hospitalised sick are excluded, the population so maintained fell, in England and Wales, from 171 000 to 111 000.[40] Part of this reduction was, it is true, the result of the enactment of old age pensions before the war; and part, at least, arose from the high rates of mortality among the mentally ill, confined to asylums where standards of care worsened in the war years. The contraction of the workhouse population also testifies to the development in some localities of a more lenient administration, which no longer regarded outdoor relief with such disapproval. Yet the war did play its part: furnishing the elderly with greater opportunities to prolong an independent existence, and possibly enhancing the ability of children to give them support.

The war also bettered the prospects of the able-bodied poor. Above all, it had practically eliminated that class of irregular, infirm or shiftless labour which had, prior to the war, haunted the building sites, the dock gates, the lodging houses and the casual wards of every large city. Arthur Harding graphically depicted this aspect of the war's impact upon the East End of London:[41]

> *The First World War had made a great change in Bethnal Green. Before then it was practically impossible to find work but with the war every firm was getting busy and the people they said was 'unemployable' became the people to fill the jobs. Even the people round the corner in Gibraltar Buildings got jobs. People who'd been scroungers all their bloody lives. They got to Aldershot, building the army huts, and on Hounslow Heath. . . . But you couldn't go there if you were of military age – not unless a doctor certified that you were unfit.*

Whether, as Masterman believed, the unemployment of the postwar years replenished the casual labour market, it is difficult to say. But six years of full employment, of better nutrition and of a more comfortable material existence were likely to have made a significant and lasting difference. (Masterman said of his own observations of the poorest districts of south London that if the material advances of wartime had been preserved 'perhaps ... the whole future of England would have been changed and the permanently inefficient and the partially unemployable, and all that mass of low-grade life which is never quite healthy and consequently never quite happy, which now coagulates in certain congested areas in the great cities, would have been altogether broken up and have disappeared.')[42]

Some rationalisation of recruitment may also have been encouraged by the extension of legal minimum wages through the Trade Boards Act of 1919. But at the same time there had been an expansion of various forms of retailing and service employment which were still inherently unstable and might often

[40] Halsey, *Trends*, op. cit. (note 3), 383. The return also covers county lunatic asylums.
[41] Samuel, *East End Underworld*, op. cit. (note 26), 236.
[42] Masterman, *England After War*, op. cit. (note 7), 124.

be ill-rewarded, and to which the out-of-work may often have graduated. The jobs of insurance agent and street-seller, of hotel staff and bookie's runner, were undoubtedly more widespread and probably no more secure than in the past.[43]

For the social investigators of the period, however, the main contraction of poverty affected neither the old nor the casually employed. The statistical methods applied by such social inquiries focused attention elsewhere. Down to the Second World War these took as their point of departure an index of 'primary' poverty, first employed by Seebohm Rowntree in his study of York in 1899. In its original form, this standard proposed a minimum level of income below which no family could practically maintain itself in 'physical efficiency'. As a method of calculating the extent of economic want, the device was admittedly imperfect. It did, however, permit reasonably reliable estimates of changes in poverty over time, and comparisons of its incidence between localities. When, therefore, Bowley and Hogg repeated in 1923–4 the investigation of poverty in five provincial towns which they had first made on the eve of the war, they were quite confident of having established an improving trend. The amount of serious deprivation, measured against their subsistence standard, had been sharply reduced, from a mean of 12.6 per cent of the working-class population to 3.5 per cent.[44] This optimistic conclusion was assigned to two principal factors: to the higher wages enjoyed by unskilled workers in regular employment; and to the continued fall in family size. Across the five towns examined, the percentage of families with four or more dependent children fell from 11.3 to 7.8. A third and related cause of improvement was the altered structure of the households themselves, for it was the centres which had experienced the lowest reduction in family size that had recorded the greatest increase in the number of earners per family.[45]

This sanguine view of poverty requires certain qualifications. First, although there can be no assurance or precision, it seems likely that levels of primary poverty had been generally declining for much of the period since the mid-nineteenth century; the war, in this respect, once again simply accelerated a process in train. How far conditions were still improving in the 1920s, moreover, was left unclear, but surveys of London in 1928–30, and of York in 1936, suggested that this trend had not continued beyond the early 1920s.[46]

Second, Bowley and Hogg found it hard to make any firm allowance for the effects of postwar unemployment upon the incidence of poverty. If their calculations were based, not upon the 'normal' earnings of their respondents,

[43] The subject is discussed, though not with much supporting evidence, in David Vincent, 1991: *Poor Citizens.* London: Longman, 89–90. *See also* John Benson, 1983: *The Penny Capitalists.* Dublin: Gill & Macmillan.

[44] Bowley and Hogg, *Has Poverty Diminished?*, op. cit. (note 3), 18.

[45] Ibid., 9–13. The towns concerned were Bolton, whose families were relatively small before the war, and Stanley, where they remained relatively large.

[46] Colin Linsley and Christine Linsley, 1993: Booth, Rowntree and Llewellyn Smith: A reassessment of inter-war poverty. *Economic History Review* 46, 88–104.

but on the incomes actually received in the week of the investigation (curtailed by short-time working, temporary illness and unemployment), the proportion of the working-class population in poverty was measured at 6.5 per cent.

Third, there remained, as in the past, considerable local variation in the amount of distress. In the five towns surveyed by Bowley and Hogg, the ratio of people in primary poverty varied from 1.6 in a hundred in Bolton to 7.9 in Reading. While there was a general picture of progress in this respect, it was not universal: in the mining town of Stanley, the least impoverished of all these communities in 1914, conditions had not altered at all during the following decade. (The rates if current incomes are taken were 4.3 per cent (Bolton), 11.9 per cent (Reading) and 7.2 per cent (Stanley). Overcrowding was also a problem more serious in Stanley than elsewhere.)[47]

Finally, because poverty continued to fluctuate with age, the amount recorded by a photographic survey significantly understated the volume of those who suffered want at some period of their lives. The 'poverty cycle' meant, according to this study, that some one in six of children under 14 would pass through such a phase during their childhood.[48]

A problem of severe poverty, and a stratum of the very poor, could therefore certainly still be discovered in the inter-war years. Yet it is manifest that the problem had shrunk. And behind the fluctuating membership of the class can be discerned some alteration of its nature. If there had been a contraction of the great body of low-paid, unskilled labour, continually struggling for survival even in the best of times, two new elements had achieved somewhat greater prominence. One was the long-term unemployed, the victims of that structural industrial decline examined elsewhere in this volume. And as the problems of large families and low wages receded, the poor inevitably came to include a higher proportion of the elderly. The old may have managed successfully to survive outside the hated workhouse, but this did not imply that they subsisted in comfort. Pensions and poor relief alike were usually inadequate to meet their minimum needs. And demographic trends meant that they were already becoming a larger component in the population.

These generalizations apply, it must be noticed, only to the most deprived sections of society. There was, however, another development of great significance in the investigation of poverty during this period. Those who made the inquiries themselves came to question whether the merely subsistence standard by which poverty had hitherto been defined was any longer appropriate. Rowntree himself had, in 1918, offered an alternative measure, which he subsequently refined in his second survey of York in 1936. In this, he acknowledged that 'the poor' might properly be identified as those unable to afford the goods and services that the great majority of society now took for granted.

[47] Bowley and Hogg, *Has Poverty Diminished?*, op. cit. (note 3), 18.
[48] Ibid., 24–5.

By this movable gauge, the term could be applied to families which, for example, could not afford a bathroom, a newspaper, a drink, or a holiday. By this index, of course, a much larger proportion of the working class were to be found in poverty: as high as 37.1 per cent in Merseyside, and 42.9 per cent in Southampton in the 1930s.[49] In short, the principal effect of the war had been, by raising the general standard of living, vastly to alter the prevailing cultural norms by which poverty was judged in everyday life. What had formerly been a struggle for existence had now become a struggle for something less easy to quantify, but still to be highly prized: a semblance of decency and respectability.

It is easy enough to see the diminishing problem of poverty in these largely impersonal terms. Again, however, we should remember that the poor themselves had a part to play in their own fate. Before 1914, even the most sanguine of radicals had been convinced that much of the squalor of Edwardian towns was the product of a kind of apathy: sometimes feckless, sometimes stoical, but always devoid of expectation. However temporary the effects of war, they demonstrated even to many of the most casual and depressed of the working population a possibility of change that had not been apparent before. Some of that same fatalism was to revive, in the course of time, among the elderly and long-term unemployed of the depressed areas. Even for them, however, existence had perhaps a greater variety, and a greater range of possibilities, than Booth or Paterson or Masterman had encountered among the unskilled strugglers before the war. Moreover, the condition of the workless of the 1920s and 1930s had periodically given rise to direct protest, as the condition of poverty *per se* had not. It was an issue of public debate, not simply an interest of private investigators, and this in itself was communicated, in some measure, to its victims.

If the aspirations of the poor had been raised, however, this might in itself, paradoxically, lead to distress. The kind of 'secondary' poverty that resulted from the mismanagement of income rather than the lack of it certainly continued after 1918. It was probably less often the outcome of conventional excess, in drinking or gambling, than in the increased appetite for other consumables. The war and its aftermath had helped foster the habit of consumption, not just by increasing money incomes, but by the methods of salesmanship which the higher income levels encouraged. To a socialist like Leo Chiozza Money, it seemed that much of the increment to wages had been misspent:

> *Not infrequently the inhabitants of some dark tenement house in a sunless street are indebted to two, four, or even six tallymen for instalments due upon petty insurances and rubbish simulating the shape of perambulators, gramophones, wireless sets, cheap trinkets, and even Bibles. Most of the stuff thus sold . . . is worked off at extravagant prices.*[50]

[49] Linsley and Linsley, Booth, Rowntree and Llewellyn Smith, op. cit. (note 46).
[50] Leo Chiozza Money, 1933: *Product Money*. London: Methuen, 64.

The theme was later developed in a more discriminating fashion by John Hilton, whose family case studies showed the common association of economic distress (however caused) and serious indebtedness. Hilton looked at some three hundred cases, and found that between half and two-thirds of these families were repaying average debts of £5. The most common creditor, however, was the landlord, while only about one in twelve were paying off hire-purchase contracts.[51] Nevertheless, when we consider the rising consumer expenditure that characterised the postwar years, it should be remembered that this carried with it two social penalties: the heightened sense of relative deprivation of those without means, and the heightened tendency to extravagance of some of the better off.

Consumption and Housing

If there was one economic consequence of war that was almost universally perceived, it was that of price inflation. The rapid increase in the cost of a large range of goods and services followed immediately upon the declaration of hostilities, and in most instances continued throughout them. Moreover, after a brief respite in the spring and summer of 1919 the level of retail prices climbed further, and even faster, in the remainder of the postwar boom. By the end of 1920 it stood at 176 percentage points above the figures for July 1914. Prices then fell quickly during the depression, to a minimum in June 1923 still 69 points in excess of July 1914.

The figures in Table 5.4, like the wage index already discussed, give at best a very rough impression of the typical experience of consumers. The model budget used to forge the index bore an uncertain, and probably aberrant, relation to actual expenditure, as households sought for ways of economising on expensive items and replacing scarce ones. The outlays of working-class families were markedly affected by the make-up of the household, the types of shop patronised, and the access to other sources of consumables, such as food from allotments and gardens, or fuel from the workplace.[52] There is no doubt, however, that inflation was acutely felt; that it led to protests about 'profiteering' which resulted in various government measures to control prices, ration

---

[51] John Hilton, 1944: *Rich Man, Poor Man*. London: Allen & Unwin, 96–7.

[52] Holford, *Reshaping Labour*, op. cit. (note 30), 25–6 cites the cost-of-living index produced by the Edinburgh Trades Council, which recorded a marginally higher rate of inflation than that of the government during the war years, but a significantly lower one between 1918 and 1920:

	Official	Edinburgh
1914	100	100
1918	205	215
1920	269	258

Moreover, if the local budget was extended to include rent, fuel and clothing as well as food, it stood at only 234 in 1920. However, in Holford's view, the index was likely to underestimate the living costs of poorer families.

goods, and even to curtail profits; and that consumer behaviour altered under the influence of all these factors.

The pattern of consumption was subject to change both because many consumers had more money to spend, and because they made choices influenced by market conditions. As Table 5.4 shows, prices did not rise uniformly across all commodities, but responded to fluctuations of demand, to shortages and difficulties of production, and to legal interference. Food prices increased down to 1920 rather faster than the general rate of inflation, although this can be accounted for almost entirely by the Government's policy of imposing higher taxes on alcoholic drink. The cost of clothing also rose disproportionately steeply, in part because the manufacturers in this sector were left without the labour to meet normal civilian demands. Fuel and lighting, on the other hand, were obtainable at more economic tariffs. Even more striking is the index for rent and rates, which reflected the Government's desire to keep down the cost of housing. An Act of 1915 prevented any advance of the rents and mortgage payments for working-class housing above the pre-war level, and while this measure was somewhat relaxed in 1919, the rental costs of most cheaper housing remained subject to restriction throughout the inter-war years.

With few exceptions, however, though the evidence is often uncertain, pre-war trends and preferences in consumption were not much changed by inflation. As in so many instances, the war did no more than inhibit some, and thereby reinforce certain other, spending preferences. This point may be illustrated in several contexts. In the choice of diet, for instance, the war brought shortages of some imported items, notably sugar, and government subsidising or rationing of others. By the armistice, there was much less difference between the fare of rich and poor families, or at least of its nutritional value, than had been the case before 1914. The reduced amount of meat was shared more equally between all classes, and its deficiency made up by the purchase of more wholemeal bread and vegetables. Inflation, amateur gardening, official regulation and the propaganda of the Ministry of Food may therefore have done something to promote a healthier diet. The war may also, on the

Table 5.4   Official Cost-of-Living Index, 1914–24

	1914	1919	1920	1924
All items	100	225	269	181
Food	100	234	282	180
Rent, rates	100	108	142	147
Fuel, light	100	–	240	185
Clothing	100	370	405	225–230
Other items	100	200	230	180

(July 1914 = 100; other indices for December)
Based on Central Statistical Office, *Retail Prices, 1914–90*, op. cit. (note 23),Table 84.

other hand, have helped to increase the demand for those dairy products and exotic imports which had been in short supply during hostilities. According to the calculations made by Richard Stone and others, the most conspicuous increases in inter-war consumer expenditure on foods that were not explicable by price changes affected canned fruits, meat and vegetables, cream, eggs and butter, oranges and bananas.[53] The consumption of alcohol, though often thought to have been discouraged by its higher cost and by the shortening of licensing hours, in fact fell no faster than in the pre-war years. Expenditure per head on this item declined from an estimated £14.2 annually in 1900–4 to £11.05 in 1910–14, and to £8.97 in 1915–19. Expenditure declined further to £7.94 per year in 1920–4, so that the decennial rate of decline was £3.15 and £3.11 respectively. While heavy drinking, and summonses for drunkenness, were markedly curtailed as the result of the activities of the Liquor Control Board, the novel impression of national sobriety was in part created by the contrast with the increase in alcohol consumption in certain localities at the outset of the war.[54] In general, the lower income group gained relatively by the altered distribution of food in the emergency, partly because they were more willing to resort to cheap substitutes such as bacon and margarine.[55] The war did, of course, prevent or deter other kinds of luxury expenditure, such as motoring and seaborne cruises, but the check here was brief; estimated expenditure on motor cars and carriages fell from £7.2 million in 1914 to £1.4 million in 1918, but increased to no less than £27.2 million in 1919.[56] There was a marked, though short-lived, increase in the purchase of clothing with the return of peace, although the taste for more stylish dress among single girls was said to have been fostered by war-time employment. One observer claimed that 'The well-dressed girl is now a commonplace in industrial districts.'[57]

In a few instances, the impact of the war was more lasting. The official curtailment of rents, to be discussed shortly, brought about a halving of the total national rent bill between 1914 and 1919. There was a marked rise, of more than one-third from the pre-war to the postwar decade, in expenditure per capita on household goods and equipment, including furniture, and by almost a half on transport and communication. In both spheres, this growth was much more rapid than that of the pre-war years. It seems apparent that, on balance, higher living standards were reflected in a wider range of purchases,

---

[53] R. Stone and D. Rowe, 1954: *The Measurement of Consumers' Expenditure and Behaviour in the United Kingdom 1920–38*, vol. 1. Cambridge: Cambridge University Press, 340–1.

[54] Ibid., vol. 2, 126.

[55] P. E. Dewey, 1988: Nutrition and living standards in wartime Britain. In Wall and Winter, *The Upheaval of War*, op. cit. (note 32).

[56] A. R. Prest and A. A. Adams, 1954: *Consumers' Expenditure in the United Kingdom 1900–19*. Cambridge: Cambridge University Press, 135. Total expenditure on travel and transport rose from £107.1 million in 1914 to 238.3 million in 1919, having generally been held back in wartime.

[57] C. S. Peel, 1929: *How We lived Then 1914–18*. London: John Lane, 8.

rather than in increased expenditure on the basic items of food, clothing and heating. More was spent on certain household items, no doubt, because a larger number of families now managed without living-in servants, whose wages had increased rapidly since the pre-war years as the supply dwindled.[58] At the same time, the rapid spread of hire-purchase companies in the inter-war years, though deplored by Chiozza Money, facilitated the acquisition of relatively expensive and durable manufactures by a far larger body of consumers, and arose in part at least because that potential market was perceived.[59]

The supply of housing was the market most drastically and permanently diverted by the war. Here economic and political factors combined to produce a shortage of accommodation increasingly acute. Building activity, which had already been depressed in 1913, was inevitably hampered by wartime conditions; but its cessation became almost complete once the state had prohibited rent rises from 1915. This drastic measure was taken to avert working-class unrest in Glasgow and other cities, and to ensure that the families of servicemen were not threatened by eviction. Under this restraint, the private housing market was unable to respond to public demand. During the years of war, indeed, the imposition of rent regulation, while it manifestly prevented the spread of rack-renting in populous city centres, probably had few other beneficial effects. Since the real cost of rents declined steadily, it was possible in theory for working-class families to afford larger houses of better quality: but the pressure of demand upon supply probably made this sort of aspiration unattainable in practice.

Across the whole population, the level of expenditure on rent and rates (at 1938 prices) stood at £7.34 before the war, at £8 between 1915 and 1919, and at £8.31 in 1920–4. These figures, however, certainly overstate the cost of rents to wage-earning families. In Edinburgh, the Trades Council estimated that rents comprised 19.7 per cent of the minimum working-class budget in 1914, declining to 8.4 per cent by June 1920. In Warrington, a similar calculation for wage earners at the higher end of the earnings tree suggested a fall in such outlay from 14 per cent before the war to about 10 per cent in 1923. These reductions tend to confirm that better dwellings were not obtained.[60] Indeed, the spending that would otherwise have been directed towards shelter was

---

[58] Prest and Adams, *Consumers' Expenditure*, op. cit. (note 56), 175. This work estimates (p. 117) the total expenditure on servants at £79.1 million in 1914 and at £145 million in 1919. These calculations are based upon somewhat unreliable census figures, but they also reflect a nearly three-fold rise in the price of all household items.

[59] P. Johnson, 1985: *Saving and Spending: The Working-Class Economy in Britain, 1870–1939*. Oxford: Clarendon Press, 158–9.

[60] Holford, *Reshaping Labour*, op. cit. (note 30), 48; Bowley and Hogg, *Has Poverty Diminished?*, op. cit. (note 3), 7. The latter held that 'working-class families [are] too unwilling to devote an adequate part of their income to house accommodation', though they acknowledged that houses were often not available.

perhaps diverted to other items. The relatively high inflation affecting clothing and footwear, for example, may have owed something to the diminished
opportunity to move home. Moreover, stationary rents and deficient housing
made for dilapidation and overcrowding in the existing accommodation.
Small landlords had no inclination, and sometimes no means, to keep their
property in good repair. The process of deterioration that converted sound
houses into slums may well have intensified, and may also have taken some
time to reverse even when peace returned. Families on the frontier of
respectability could find themselves slipping into a lower social band.

Yet one other advantage did, perhaps, spring from the very problem of
shortage. The demand for housing, particularly in centres of war industry,
both meant a higher demand for lodgings and ensured that children, including married children, remained longer at home. The size of the household
income, and of the resources at the disposal of the housewife, correspondingly
rose. The sense of wartime well-being of women and children finds in this
hypothesis another explanation.

Overcrowding was not, of course, a problem created by the war, and in some
cities, such as London, it had been worsening prior to 1914. As the condition
grew more chronic, however, government action became more imperative.[61]
The concern of politicians to facilitate demobilisation likewise made housing
a leading item of postwar reconstruction. The first national scheme of subsidised housing was enacted in 1919. Under this measure and its successors,
some 1.1 million houses were built in Britain between the wars. During the
1920s, local authorities in Britain constructed 539 000 houses, while private
builders put up another 834 000 (a few of which were subsidised). The pace of
construction was to increase during the 1930s, so that by the end of the
period, nearly one-third of the dwellings in England and Wales had been built
since the end of the war.[62]

The large council estates that appeared during the 1920s were not entirely
without pre-war predecessors; but in scale and in design they were essentially
a novel venture. They created for their residents not just a new pattern of consumption but, arguably, a different style of life. In so far as housing conditions
had worsened during the war, the attractiveness of the newly built council
houses of the 1920s was no doubt enhanced. Wage-earners with dependent
families could readily appreciate the spaciousness of such dwellings, the provision of indoor toilets, electric lights and running water, the better washing
facilities and the attached gardens, as well as the relative absence of dirt and
pollution. Those with a sense of their own status might also welcome separation from the commingling of older, working-class quarters. High rents might
lend social prestige to the new developments. In Liverpool, for example, two
in five of the tenants of early estates were in non-manual and professional

[61] For London, *see* H. Llewellyn Smith, 1930: *The New Survey of London Life and Labour*, vol. 1.
London: P. S. King, 41.
[62] Stone and Rowe, *The Measurement of Consumers' Expenditure*, op. cit. (note 53), 200–5.

employment, although later in the decade the Council had a deliberate strategy of admitting larger families from poorer backgrounds.[63]

It must be remembered, however, that this alternative environment was offered only to a minority, and at the outset a very small one. The extent of house building after the war was subject to much local variation. The 1919 Act was suspended in 1921 with only 170 000 dwellings approved, providing at most for three-quarters of a million persons. In Edinburgh, for example, the Council did little before the late 1920s.[64] Moreover, the housing estate might be less attractive for other reasons. The suburban sites were inaccessible to many workplaces. Costs of transport were therefore superimposed upon high rents. Amenities and services were often in short supply. In some instances, notably in Bristol, the better-off members of the working class preferred to buy their own dwellings on private estates.[65] This may have reflected the larger numbers of families on modest incomes admitted to the early council houses here.

The families who moved to the new council estates of the 1920s did so largely from choice; but they entered an environment in which, in many respects, their domestic lives became more tightly restricted than they had been in the residential settlements typical of the pre-war period. Under the aegis of the local authority they did not choose their own house, still less their neighbours. They were restricted in the matter of taking lodgers, and subject to rules on the upkeep of house and garden. In these circumstances, a kind of community life developed which its members could only partially shape for themselves. The irregular layout and low-density housing characteristic of the estates certainly affected their social life, though on this it is difficult to be precise. The results of a paucity of shops, markets and public houses are more apparent: their want made this milieu quite different from that of the central districts. A similar lack of churches, public halls, schools and other institutional buildings militated against communal activity. The peripheral situation of many estates cut off their residents from the culture of the city.

It is equally likely that the selection of tenants had a disruptive effect on certain kinds of social networks. In their early phases, most housing estates were dominated by nuclear families, excluding the elderly, the unmarried and the newly married. The ties that bound parents to adult children were not easily maintained within their confines. It is possible, on the other hand, that the very similarity of family structure fostered its own kind of neighbourly relationships, centred upon growing children. And another sort of solidarity resulted from the fact of a corporate public landlord, to whose authority every family was subject. Council houses gave birth, sooner or later, to local tenants' associations, sometimes as their only voluntary organisation of any significance.

[63] Madeline McKenna, 1991: The suburbanization of the working-class population of Liverpool between the wars. *Social History* 16, 173–89.

[64] Holford, *Reshaping Labour*, op. cit. (note 30), 10–11.

[65] Adrian Franklin: Home and leisure: Changing structures of working-class consumption, 1870–1930. Paper given at the Conference of the British Sociological Association, April 1990.

Voluntary Associations and Social Values

In these changes of consumer choice, restricted as they sometimes were, we can discern signs of changing social values. Chief among these, perhaps, is that increased attachment of postwar society to the private, domestic world of the nuclear family. This process was not, of course, new: the family had long been bound up with the notion of social respectability. But it seems probable that family ties were strengthened further in the circumstances of the war period. It is not without significance that what might be seen as the pre-eminent statement of the ideal of the modern conjugal family – Marie Stopes' *Married Love* – was first published in 1918, and secured an immediate popularity.

The triumph of family values, in this form, signified the retreat of other social ideals: in some measure at least, the trenching of a private sphere upon a more social and public one. While the war had also sustained and encouraged an ethic of public service and citizenship, this proved to have less substance and staying power. It is, indeed, easy to overlook the widespread belief in the possibilities of social co-operation born of four years of conflict. According to one of many works in this genre, the war had revived a common sense of civic duty:[66]

> *The traditional demarcations of public and private life are in process of obliteration. Ideas such as coordination of effort, maximising of the national energies, the restriction of wasteful and parasitic occupations, conservation of resources and the like, which were formerly taboo in the sterile strife of parties are becoming the stock-in-trade of political discussion.*

This Utopianism was partly invested in the reconstituted Labour Party. But it readily crossed party lines, and Lloyd George coined the phrase 'malleability' to describe the flux of political relationships produced by reconstruction. This spirit of optimism was therefore channelled into various enterprises: into educational projects for adolescents and adults; into bodies promoting industrial peace and co-operation; and into numerous local 'reconstruction' committees and community associations.[67] The idealism informing this movement is perhaps best viewed as a revival of the Christian Socialism voiced in the 1860s by Charles Kingsley and in the 1880s by Canon Barnett. It looked for social salvation, less to the initiatives of what some exponents called the 'Sidney Webbical' state, and more to the diffusion throughout society of a spirit of egalitarianism, high-mindedness and self-sacrifice. The key to social progress,

[66] V. Branford and P. Geddes, 1917: *The Coming Polity: a Study in Reconstruction*. London: Williams & Norgate, 15.
[67] Among other examples of wartime programmes for education *see* J. J. Findlay (ed.), 1918: *The Young Wage Earner and the Problem of His Education*. London: Sidgwick & Jackson; and Teachers' Guild of Great Britain and Ireland, [1917?]: *Educational Reforms*. London: Teachers' Guild. For collaborative enterprises between employers and employed, *see* C. Wrigley, 1991: Trade unionists, employers and the cause of industrial unity and peace, 1916–21. In C. Wrigley and J. Shepherd (eds), *On the Move*. London: Hambledon.

from this perspective, lay in the quality of personal relationships within the community as well as the family.[68] But if the war produced a further surge of this ethical doctrine, it was to be short-lived.

It is, however, instructive to consider the postwar experience of some of the voluntary organisations that had most clearly expressed the values of social co-operation and mutuality. One element of this outlook was the doctrine of personal service which had continued to inform much pre-war philanthropy: the settlement movement, the Guilds of Help, and even the Charity Organisation Society (COS).

The effect of the war on this last body is, in some respects, particularly revealing of the manner in which such ideals were redefined and – vainly – pursued. In the past, it had always been deeply hostile to any mode of welfare that hinted at socialism, while at the same time maintaining a guiding faith in the performance of neighbourly duties by richer to poorer citizens, as the quintessence of a religious code of conduct. Superficially, its policies and functions changed very little after 1914. The distribution of its funds between different kinds of applicants was much the same in the early 1920s as it had been on the eve of the war. But the Society showed itself, in other respects, profoundly aware of living in a new and more difficult world. Here it had to confront a greatly expanded apparatus of state and public welfare; a more overt political and industrial solidarity among the working class; and at the same time a greater sense of their civic rights and status on the part of individual wage-earners and their families. In these circumstances, the directors of the COS recognised, at least in part, that a wholly voluntary mode of charitable activity could achieve little of significance; and that the kind of highly personal relationship between the benevolent and the necessitous which it had sought to foster had ceased to be viable.

On the one hand, therefore, the society accepted not just a lower level of charitable activity but a far closer relationship with the state and local government.[69] 'A voluntary society can do little by itself', the Council admitted in

[68] For one statement of this viewpoint see the remarks of the Revd A. Herbert Gray, quoted in St Philip's Settlement Education and Economics Research Society, 1919: *The Equipment of the Workers.* Sheffield: The Society, 10. 'I find many people talking as if the camaraderie of the trenches between officers and men would of necessity solve labour troubles after the War. But there is an element of pathetic delusion in that expectation. What trenchlife has proved is that when officers and men are divorced from the artificial relationship of our industrial and commercial system, they discover each other as men, and arrive at a new appreciation of each other. It has been found that they are capable of happy co-operation. But if, after the War, men are asked to accept the old relationship of commerce and industry, they will be more, and not less, likely to resent them, and to rebel. Tommy will come back having suffered untold things for his country, and he will have a sense that his country owes him more than it did in the old days. . . . They [returned soldiers] will obey less than before any authority that has not deserved and won their respect, for the iron of a mere system of discipline has bitten deep into their souls.' Chapter 1 of this work expounds on this philosophy of reconstruction.
[69] The number of applications to COS offices in the London area had fallen away markedly during the war: from an average of 17 587 during 1910–13 to 11 263 in 1914–18. At the same time, unpaid charity workers were increasingly hard to recruit: the number of COS branches in the London area fell from 42 to 32 between 1914 and 1922.

1921, '[but] it can do much by cooperating with public institutions. As an executive power the voluntary system may be considerably restricted, but in its advisory capacity it has a future of boundless usefulness.'[70] On the other hand, the COS grew increasingly concerned about its reputation for overbearing paternalism. Its sense of its own identification with a more hierarchical social order led it to discuss (if not yet to agree) a change of name in 1917: 'The Society's name is undeservedly, but none the less finally, objectionable to many people, including in a notable degree the industrial classes, and ... its sub-name [Society for the Repression of Mendicity] has a tone of patronage unsuited to modern conditions.'[71] No less significant, however, is the society's evident readiness to treat its clients with greater tact and circumspection. By the end of the 1920s it had greatly modified its earlier practice of systematic personal investigation of family circumstances. Employers and relatives, for example, were no longer consulted without the assent of the applicant; neighbours and shopkeepers were not approached at all. The privacy of the family, as well as its integrity, had become an acknowledged maxim.

A quite different embodiment of the Christian Socialist tradition, the co-operative movement, was also markedly affected by the war. The co-operatives confronted the same constituents of the new social order as the Charity Organisation Society, though clearly upon different ground. For them, the state, which down to 1914 had seemed a sympathetic onlooker upon their enterprises, was afterwards more decidedly obnoxious if not hostile. The rise of organised labour, on the other hand, came to represent a needed ally rather than, as earlier, no more than a natural friend. As for the institution of the family, this had always been, from one perspective, an object of the co-operative movement's attention and aspirations. But here the question was how far co-operation could change the nature of family, and thereby of social, life, in accordance with its own principles. In this connection, indeed, its critics had long been of the opinion that the movement was in danger of becoming merely the instrument of the material expectations of wage-earners

[70] M. Rooff, 1972: *A Hundred Years of Family Welfare.* London: Joseph, 141. A somewhat different view was expressed by the Warden of Toynbee Hall, the East London settlement, in 1915. He saw a tradition of social work being eclipsed by the growth of state welfare, which the war itself had continued: 'The ten years that preceded the War were marked by a great outburst of national legislation. The younger generation began to think on a heroic scale and were impatient of anything that seemed small and humble. ... And yet it is impossible to live in a poor district without realising all the legislation which has been passed has only touched on the fringe of the question, and that much of it has tended to be out of touch with the real needs of the people. There is a greater need than ever in social reform for mystics who can not only be practical but content to labour away at humble things'. Quoted in A. Briggs and S. Macartney, 1984: *Toynbee Hall: The First Hundred Years.* London: Routledge & Kegan Paul, 88.
[71] Rooff, *A Hundred Years of Family Welfare,* op. cit. (note 70), 121. The same standpoint was taken by a self-consciously modern charitable organisation, the National Council for Social Service, established in 1919. Its journal set in opposition the new principle of co-operation, 'the old-fashioned conception of social work as an effort to help other people': National Council for Social Service, 1919: *Social Service Review.* London: the Council, quoted in J. Morgan, 1948: The National Council for Social Service. In H. A. Mess (ed.), *Voluntary Social Services since 1918.* London: Kegan Paul, 81.

and their households, losing sight of any higher social purpose.[72] Nonetheless, down to the war the co-operatives had retained their distinctive tone and style. Their members were conscious of belonging to a movement which proclaimed and rewarded thrift, which demonstrated its solidarity and ambitions through the pomp and ritual of its gatherings, and which upheld its ideals through a variety of educational and propaganda activities. Moreover, while the movement continued to strengthen its hold upon the loyalty of its working-class customers, it could still entertain the vision of cooperators as a self-sufficient community.

The war, however, brought a sharp reversal in the movement's economic progress. Its spokesmen complained bitterly at the prejudicial effects of profits taxation, of official controls on distribution and of rationing, as well as of military conscription. Some of these complaints were no doubt justified, but the co-operatives probably suffered also from their own high price structure, their tendency to frown upon consumer credit, and perhaps even from their preponderantly male body of shareholders.

After the war, the growth of their retailing operations resumed. Membership increased rapidly, from 2.9 million in 1913 (for Great Britain and Ireland) to 4.6 million in 1923 and 6.4 million by 1930. It was now, symbolically, extended to all members of the family unit. New stores proliferated in areas hitherto neglected: London, the South, and the countryside in general.[73] But the extent of the movement's hold upon the purchasing habits of this wider clientele was much reduced. The value of its trade in proportion to its membership fell away as, partly for this reason, did its dividends. As the nature of working-class consumption diversified, the co-operatives found it more difficult to cater for the whole range of their demands. In the business territories that they now entered, they faced much greater competition from established retailers, including departmental and chain stores. To its patrons in these areas, the co-operative store was no more than another shopping outlet. And this loss of a sense of distinction was reflected in the loss or abandonment of those trappings of ceremony, conviviality and display that had previously characterised the movement's inner life.[74] The formation of a Co-operative political party in 1917 and its adhesion to the Labour side in the years immediately after the war were in this sense an admission of the loss of its separate identity and larger social prestige.[75]

In a sense, therefore, we might see the war as tending to weaken and obscure that older conception of a society elevated and improved by voluntary effort and individual spiritual enrichment. Like any such large-scale cultural change this process, of course, is impossible to locate so precisely in time. The Warden

[72] *See*, for example, Johnson, *Saving and Spending*, op. cit. (note 59), 129.
[73] H. J. Twigg, 1931: *Economic Advance of British Co-operation, 1913–31*. Manchester: Co-operative Union, 22–5.
[74] Ibid., pp. 34–5; Johnson, *Saving and Spending*, op. cit. (note 59), 139–42.
[75] Tony Adams, 1987: The formation of the Co-operative Party reconsidered. *International Review of Social History* 32, 48–68.

of Toynbee Hall, J. St G. Heath, suggested that the transition was already under way in the period of Liberal social legislation before 1914. 'The ten years that preceded the War were marked by a great outburst of national legislation. The younger generation began to think on a heroic scale and were impatient of anything that seemed small and humble.'[76] But the remarks, made at the end of 1915, and made by a pacifist, doubtless reflected a feeling that the march of state power, of national organisation and of official coercion was gathering pace. To strive for social improvement apart from the state seemed increasingly futile. Groups and associations that sought to do this, such as friendly societies, housing associations, the home colonisation movement, even the Salvation Army, lost something, more or less, of their vitality.

This conclusion may seem to conflict with the growth of the most successful of the voluntary associations of the working class: the trade unions. Their membership increased, during the war years, from 4.1 million to 6.5 million – and continued to rise down to the end of 1920, when it stood at over 8 million. This impressive expansion brought into the movement, in much larger numbers, many elements who had earlier remained aloof: not just unskilled male workers, but women and white-collar employees. In these years, trade unionism clearly exerted a stronger attraction than those other types of working-class organisation, such as co-operatives and friendly societies, that may be called 'mutualist'. And it is arguable, too, that they commanded a greater loyalty among their adherents, at least if this is measured by the solidarity of the industrial strikes of 1915–20, or later the General Strike of 1926.

The success and confidence of the trade unions may be contrasted, at this juncture, with the vicissitudes and vacillations of charities and co-operatives. The unions based their appeal on a much more materialist goal. At a time of full employment and inflation they were well placed to safeguard the living standards and fulfil the economic expectations of their members. In addition they continued to provide, in some instances, facilities for insurance akin to those provided by the friendly societies. More importantly, they appeared more capable than most voluntary associations of dealing effectively with a powerful state. During the war, they had been remarkably effective in managing, simultaneously, to co-operate with the government for the purpose of mobilising civilian labour, and protecting the interests of workers against the threat of arbitrary power or 'industrial conscription'. Their bargaining with the Government in the years of reconstruction was sometimes less profitable, but it is still reasonable to credit to their influence, in greater or lesser degree, such legislation as the Restoration of Pre-War Practices, the extension of Trade Boards and minimum wages, and the provision of comprehensive unemployment benefits.

Does the growth of trade unionism testify, however, to some shift in the values and attitudes of their recruits? It is plausible enough to suggest that their growth reflected a general rise in economic expectations. To a limited degree,

[76] Quoted by Briggs and Macartney, *Toynbee Hall*, op. cit. (note 71), 88.

the development of large union amalgamations such as the Transport and General Workers and the Amalgamated Engineers may have fostered a greater sense of affinity between different occupational groups. The increasing political prominence of the union movement on a national stage had perhaps a similar effect. But whether the unions truly represented an expression of class cohesion and solidarity is, as has already been suggested, a more doubtful matter. These organisations probably did not grow because workpeople valued their principles more highly, but because they appreciated the increased capacity of organisation to deliver benefits they had always prized: better working conditions, higher remuneration, and perhaps some added security of employment.

In this respect, the membership viewed unionism primarily in instrumental terms. On this count, moreover, they saw their industrial associations as intermediaries between themselves and those larger authorities, capital and government, that exercised an influence upon their lives otherwise uncontrolled. The rise of union membership may therefore reasonably be linked both to the economic authority of the wartime state, and to the appearance of a more elaborate system of nationwide collective bargaining in the years 1917–19. Union officials were, for example, conspicuously successful in representing their members' interests before the official munitions tribunals which administered wartime labour controls.[77] And opportunities for centralised industrial negotiations were much improved by the creation of some sixty joint industrial councils between 1917 and 1920.[78]

Seen in this light, therefore, the unions were bodies providing professional services for their members; they were no longer the kind of participating, mutualist community that had, in the past, resembled the friendly society or the local co-operative. The rapid decline of membership during the depression of the early 1920s, and the high turnover at all times, invites this judgement even if not wholly proving it. There were, of course, some wage earners who regarded unions as the means to more heroic ends of social change, and who often became involved, as a result, in unofficial bodies critical of their leadership. Their numbers may have increased by virtue of the experience of government labour policies during the war. But the purest form of union-based ideology, that of syndicalism, was created in the years immediately preceding the war, and did not flourish for long in its wake.

In sum, it is difficult to find any of the voluntary associations considered here as articulating a widespread and radical change of social consciousness. Those which attempted to express the lessons of war most clearly, like the Charity Organisation Society, were aware of their own diminishing influence. Those which commanded a greater following, like the co-operatives and the unions, were sceptical of their own ability to serve more than routine ends. It

---

[77] G. R. Rubin, 1987: *War, Law and Munitions.* Oxford: Clarendon Press.
[78] J. B. Seymour, 1932: *The Whitley Councils Scheme.* London: P. S. King; W. A. Orton, 1921: *Labour in Transition.* London: Philip Allan, 179–81.

may not be unfair to propose, accordingly, that the great days of the association as a vehicle of moral purpose were past. Those which now dominated the scene did so because of their effectiveness in meeting the specific and mundane needs of a society whose concerns were increasingly materialist and whose horizons were increasingly confined to the domestic realm. Those organisations did best, in short, which demanded least of their members, and sought least to change the mores of everyday life.

Conclusions

It is almost impossible for the historian to reach a verdict on the impact of the First World War. Its effects were manifold: sometimes short-lived and superficial, sometimes more lasting and complex. It required people to change their previous modes of behaviour in some matters, and encouraged such changes in others. It acted, therefore, both upon the context of everyday life – on what is sometimes referred to as the structure of society – and on social consciousness, the way in which people regarded their own experience. We are faced, whether we address social activity or social beliefs, with the same problems: that of identifying the nature of change with the aid of evidence that is imperfect; and that of attributing it to one or more sets of causes.

Partly because of these difficulties, it is frequently suggested that the war did little to initiate social change, but much to accelerate it. This, however, is too simple a generalisation, even with respect to the outward signs of collective behaviour. In some respects, it is true, the war seems only to have reinforced earlier trends: in the reduction of mortality and of fertility, in the changing pattern of land ownership, in the growth of trade unions. In other areas, there seems to be a more visible discontinuity in the indices of social behaviour. Real incomes, having shown little elasticity before the war, now rose much more sharply. Rates of emigration may also have been checked at this juncture, while rates of marriage were significantly accentuated. And while in most fields of public welfare there is continuity, in the field of housing a substantial new departure occurs. Yet even if we place full reliance upon the evidence for these disjunctions, we must remain doubtful as to the causal significance of the war. Real wage rates, for instance, had shown some signs of improvement before 1914, while the case for a state housing programme was widely debated. At these points too, therefore, it is possible to suggest that the war merely lent an added impetus to tendencies that were already *in potentia*.

While we cannot assess the effects of the war with any precision, however, two intuitive considerations should influence our judgement upon it. In the first place, even if we adopt the assumption that it did no more than hasten developments which would have happened without it, the pace and scope of such change are themselves significant. Rapid and spectacular social processes are more disruptive of habit, and likely to be more exciting, painful and disconcerting, than slow and piecemeal transitions. In these conditions, moreover, adaptation, on the part of existing institutions and social networks, may prove the more difficult. We have seen how extended families and neighbourhood communities were unable to cope with the large-scale movement of population from inner cities to suburban housing estates; and how certain kinds of voluntary institutions, such as friendly societies, co-operatives and charities, experienced signs of strain in face of intensifying pressures. Their problems were not dissimilar to those encountered by the Liberal Party in the political sphere – which, as Pugh has shown, perhaps made all the difference between recovery and collapse. We may see a similar disorientation, though more obscurely, in other, social institutions not discussed in this chapter: in the churches, in the alehouse, in the hiring fairs of northern England.

Secondly, we should not overlook the aspect of the war as a symbolic national drama. The conflict, and its repercussions, represented an experience more widely shared, and yet more unprecedented, than anything within the national memory. The Boer War, in contrast, had been a marginal affair; while other great national occasions, like the royal jubilees and coronations, were clearly different in kind. The conflict of 1914–18 can be presented, therefore, as a sort of rite of passage in which a whole society took part. However hard it is to define a catalogue of consequences, it remains true that 'the war' became a universal point of reference in the memories of almost all its survivors. To this in itself it is difficult to attach a specific, historical significance. If this common experience was ascribed a common meaning, however, it seems probably to have lain in the newly perceived bearing of remote political decisions and official actions upon ordinary lives. In this sense, at least, 'the state' came closer to home, intruded in the everyday, and asserted a power and importance that had not been suspected hitherto. These powers may have been, in many cases, transitory expressions of an emergency, but their brief existence was not a full measure of their impact upon public consciousness.

It is not, on the other hand, easy to detect this heightened awareness of the state in any general change of social behaviour. Bernard Waites has sought to depict the emergence, during the war, of more overt class antagonism, but the evidence for this is very ambiguous.[79] The growth of collectivist political sentiments, for example, is less apparent in 1914–18 than it was to be in 1939–45. One explanation for this, more enigmatic, movement of opinion may be the contradictory conduct of the state itself, or at least of its outward form. Wartime government had, on the one hand, been caring and benevolent towards its citizens. The rationing of food, the welfare services of the national factories, the control of rents, the severance allowances to servicemen's families had all testified to its social conscience. The constant flow of official propaganda, of course, stressed just this quality of mercy and generosity. Yet at the same time, the state required of its subjects a level of obedience, of imposed sacrifice, of subordination to bureaucratic authority, never encountered

[79] Waites, *A Class Society at War*, op. cit. (note 5), ch. 6.

before. A society that looked upon its government in this light could not perceive it as simply an instrument of welfare, still less as an expression of democratic will. If the state became more familiar, it also became more formidable.

In the aftermath of war, therefore, the greater expectations of governmental beneficence were counterbalanced by a feeling, no less strong, that the state acted according to its own, autonomous principles. In the social outlook of the postwar years we can thus detect both an increased suspicion and dislike of militarism (expressed, not least, in the decline of those paramilitary youth organisations that had flourished before 1914), and an essentially passive, undemonstrative response to the welfare legislation of the Coalition Government. The decline of mutualist association, noticed earlier, was accompanied by a decline in those pressure groups which, in the past, had objected to the contagious diseases acts or to compulsory vaccination. The war had produced a society which, if it entertained higher hopes, had less capacity to encompass them.

6

Women and the War

Gail Braybon

Women occupy a particular niche in the mythology that surrounds the First
World War. Throughout the war, newspapers were full of articles about
'women in men's jobs', accompanied by photographs of fetching young
women at work on the trams or in the factories. There were numerous discussions in the daily press, trade journals and magazines about women's changing
role in industry and the repercussions this might have for 'society'.
Commentators wondered at length whether women workers would reject
their traditional domestic role and compete with men in the market-place
once the war ended, or whether they would willingly return to their old jobs
and responsibilities. There was much talk of women's 'new-found self-confidence', and many supporters of women's suffrage claimed that the
Government would now, in the face of women's splendid wartime effort, find
it impossible to deny them the vote. The striking pictures of women in munitions, of nurses, van drivers and road sweepers, have been handed down to us,
and so too have some of the debates that surrounded them, but in an abbrevi-
ated and simplified form. In school textbooks or general history books women
war workers merit a few paragraphs. Usually we are told, briefly, that women
took over from men in industry for the duration of the war, that they did a fine
job, that they were rewarded with the vote, and that their emancipation effectively began in 1914 as a direct result of the First World War.

The reality is, as usual, more complex. Women's role in industry can be
described in great detail, given the wealth of source material available, yet the
longer-term significance of this wartime work remains a subject for debate.
The historian of this period has to consider women both as 'subjects', and as
'objects' – of pity, derision, hostility or admiration. It is therefore important to
consider not only women's experiences and their own feelings about the war,
but the perceptions of their observers and critics. These reveal much about
general views of women's capabilities and their place in society. It is often as
necessary to consider what contemporaries thought was happening to women
workers as to describe what was actually happening.

Joan Scott, in an essay which is important to anyone interested in the matter of war and gender, runs elegantly through the debates that tend to emerge the moment one mentions the question of the war's effect on women. She begins by reminding us that the major wars of the twentieth century are both said to be 'watersheds for women', and that for each claim about war's impact there is always a counter-claim. She believes that there are four 'variations on the watershed theme', and that the main areas for debate are usually:

1. whether or not the war had a profound impact on women's job opportunities and wages, and whether it affected ideas about women's domestic role;
2. whether the war had any effect on the suffrage debate;
3. the effect of the war on the women's peace movement, and the extent to which it offered a particular opportunity for women to fulfil a caring, anti-militaristic role;
4. whether the war had a short or long-term impact on women, and whether there was any permanent improvement in their status.[1]

Using this list as a starting point, historians may define themselves as optimists or pessimists within the context of each separate debate, judging the war to be either a progressive or retrogressive force, or concluding that its effect was broadly neutral. Arthur Marwick is seen as one of the leading exponents of the view of the war as a progressive force. In his writings on war and social change he has often been unreservedly positive about the effects of the First World War on women's status – though his more recent work seems to show slightly less enthusiasm. To quote his words in *The Deluge*:

> it was the war, in creating simultaneously a proliferation of Government committees and departments and a shortage of men, which brought a sudden and irreversible advance in the economic and social power of a category of women employees which extended from the sprigs of the aristocracy to daughters of the proletariat.[2]

Or, to put it another way:

> the war brought opportunity in concentrated and varied form, and from the stock of patriotic bombast paid the women a valuable bonus: men and women joined together to praise women's contribution to the war effort, bringing a confidence in their new role to women, and an acceptance of it among men, which might otherwise not have been easy to create.[3]

Of course, Marwick was by no means the first to assume that the war had a positive effect on women's role and status. This kind of interpretation of

[1] Joan Scott, 1987: Rewriting history. In M. R. Higonnet, J. Jenson, S. Michel and M. C. Weitz (eds), *Behind the Lines: Gender and the Two World Wars*. New Haven, Conn.: Yale University Press, 23–5. I should add that Scott doubts whether these four variations are worth arguing about without viewing the matter of gender and war in the wider context of both world wars, the relations between men and women, representations of gender, effects of social change, and so on.
[2] Arthur Marwick, 1965: *The Deluge*. London: Macmillan, 92.
[3] Ibid., 294.

events began as early as 1915. There were those who continued to believe that the war had 'revolutionised men's minds and their conception of the sort of work of which the ordinary everyday woman was capable',[4] or, as Mary Macarthur claimed in similar vein (significantly linking 'reality' to 'perception'):

> *Of all the changes worked by the war none has been greater than the change in the status and position of women: and yet it is not so much that woman herself has changed, as that man's conception of her has changed.*[5]

A number of more recent writers have taken up the issue of the war's wider, or longer-term, effect on women, and have made some sweepingly optimistic statements that I think are hard to justify. For example, while discussing the changing expectations of marriage amongst women teachers in the 1920s and 1930s, Dina Copelman writes:

> *'Between the wars' is a convenient and workable fiction but it has its limits. Clearly many of the changes which I discuss, and especially the revolt against Victorianism, can be found much earlier. . . . But what we look for as historians and critics when we look for change is something on a much broader scale of cultural self-consciousness which we can see as a generic shift right across society and as – eventually – the making of a new common sense. It seems that the effects of the First World War made visible and precipitated further into the mainstream of English life what might otherwise have remained eccentric, sporadic and minority protests. Thus by the 1930s it was no longer simply bohemians and suffragists who argued for equality in marriage: the idea of 'the companionate partnership' had become a matter of course.*[6]

On the other hand, many commentators, then and now, have been cynical about the praise heaped on women by the press and the wartime propaganda machine, pointing out that women were still paid less than men, that their working conditions were often appalling, that there remained many areas of work from which they were excluded completely, and that it proved impossible for women to hold on to their wartime jobs when peace returned.[7] The backlash against women working in 'men's jobs' in 1919–21 soon showed how little conceptions of women's true sphere had really changed. Indeed, how

---

[4] M. G. Fawcett, 1925: *The Women's Victory and After*, quoted in Gail Braybon, 1989: *Women workers in the First World War*. London: Routledge, 157.
[5] Mary Macarthur, 1918, in Marion Phillips (ed.), *Women and the Labour Party*. London: Pitman, quoted in Braybon, *Women Workers*, op. cit. (note 4), 157.
[6] Dina Copelman, 1986: 'A new comradeship between men and women': family, marriage, and London women teachers. In Jane Lewis (ed.), *Labour and Love*. Oxford: Basil Blackwell, 189.
[7] *See* discussions in Braybon, *Women Workers*, op. cit. (note 4), and other commentators of the time. For example: Sylvia Pankhurst, 1932: *The Home Front*. London: Hutchinson; I. O. Andrews, 1921: *The Economic Effects of World War on the Women and Children in Great Britain*. Oxford: Oxford University Press; A. W. Kirkaldy, 1917 and 1920: *Industry and Finance*. 2 vols. London: Pitman; Barbara Drake, 1917: *Women in the Engineering Trades*. London: Fabian Research Department; also *Woman Worker*, and other union journals.

could one really expect them to? Discussing the same period in France, Steven Hause writes:

> *The war probably did adjust some public attitudes, but one must also ask if this new mood was far-reaching or long-lasting. Many of the changes were temporary, enduring only as long as the unusual circumstances which produced them. It is more accurate to see the war as only one factor in a longer and slower evolution than as a momentous change. Did millions of veterans return from the front having thrown off their traditional prejudices? Could any society with deeply ingrained feelings about the nature of the family and women's position within it suddenly embrace the concept of the autonomous, emancipated woman? Is it not a more probable human reaction, after so great a tragedy, to seek to revive the status quo ante bellum . . .?*[8]

Some historians have even suggested that, far from benefiting women, the war actually set back their cause and left them economically more vulnerable than they had been before.[9] When looking at wider issues, one should also consider the issues raised by such articles as 'A soldier's heart', by Sandra M. Gilbert.[10] She suggests that the radically different experiences of women and men during the war led to a greater rift between them, and that women's very willingness to work in 'men's jobs' and their apparent enthusiasm for their wartime role caused deep-seated anti-women feeling among soldiers – as represented by such people as Sassoon, Lawrence and other writers. This is a highly pessimistic view, but there is, it seems to me, some truth in the idea that the war crystallised men's and women's roles and caused additional friction between them. I have mixed views about Gilbert's interpretations. On the one hand I would suggest that the anger she describes has as much to do with soldiers' hostility to the fat cats of civilian life – the arms manufacturers, society people, music-hall stars, and so on – as to men's attitudes to women *per se*. On the other, I believe that feelings of general hostility towards women pre-dated the war and were then encouraged by wartime circumstances. These were the feelings that any woman who stepped out of her 'normal' role was likely to encounter, as expressed by anti-suffragette commentators, for example.

In this chapter, I have chosen to look at the war's possible impact on two aspects of women's lives. I am interested, first, in the effect of the war on women's employment during 1914–18, and the extent to which it influenced women's career prospects in the 1920s. Second, I shall be looking at the wider impact of the war on women, their feelings about the conflict, and its possible

[8] Steven Hause, 1987: More Minerva than Mars: The French women's rights campaign and the First World War. In Higonnet *et al.*, *Behind the Lines: Gender and the Two World Wars*, op. cit. (note 1), 102.

[9] Deborah Thom, 1986: The bundle of sticks. In Angela John (ed.), *Unequal Opportunities*, Oxford: Basil Blackwell.

[10] Sandra M. Gilbert, 1987: A soldier's heart: Literary men, literary women and the Great War. In Higonnet, *et al.*, *Behind the Lines: Gender and the Two World Wars*, op. cit. (note 1), 197–226.

effect on relations between the sexes. I shall not discuss many of the other interesting debates about women during this period, including the question of how the war affected feminism and the granting of women's suffrage, an important issue that remains the subject of much disagreement.[11]

I should add one further word of warning. 'Women in the First World War' are often referred to as though they are a clearly defined, coherent group. It cannot be reiterated too often that the experiences of women differed dramatically between geographical areas, trades, age groups and classes. The 15-year-old Belfast flax worker who went to work at Woolwich Arsenal, the middle-aged Scottish crofter with no family at the Front, the domestic servant who took up road sweeping, the laundry worker who went into munitions – all these are 'typical' women workers of one kind or another, yet all of them had very different war experiences. They can be regarded as a group by virtue of their gender, and society's expectations of them, but the differences between them are marked. One has to generalise, and yet one generalises at one's peril, for there will always be numerous exceptions.

War and Employment: Women's Public Lives

In order to consider the impact of the war, one must begin by looking at women's employment in the years leading up to 1914. Women's work before the war was characterised by low wages and influenced by the general expectation that women would leave paid work on marriage. Low pay had been recognised as a problem by such commentators as the Webbs, Hutchins and Ramsay MacDonald, by responsible employers such as George Cadbury, and indeed by a number of government committees.[12] It was a problem, clearly, for the women themselves, who when unmarried, separated or widowed normally had a lower standard of living than men of similar age and status, but it was also perceived as being a problem for male workers. If a woman could do a job more cheaply, ran the argument, then she would inevitably be preferred by an employer if she competed directly with a man for the same job. Trade unions and employers shared many prejudices about women workers, seeing them primarily as casual labour, uninterested in long-term careers or the acquisition of 'skills' – in spite of the very real skill required in many of the standard women's trades such as embroidery, dressmaking or millinery. Employers and workmen alike tended to agree that women, because of their 'dependent'

---

[11] Martin Pugh, 1992: *Women and the Women's Movement in Britain 1914–1959.* London: Macmillan; H. Smith (ed.), 1990: *British Feminism in the Twentieth Century.* Aldershot, Edward Elgar; Johanna Alberti, 1989: *Beyond Suffrage: Feminists in War and Peace.* London: Macmillan. *See also* Arthur Marwick's introduction to the new 1991 edition of *The Deluge,* London: Macmillan.

[12] E. Cadbury and G. Shann, 1907: *Sweating.* London: Headley Bros.; E. Cadbury, M. C. Matheson and G. Shann, 1909: *Women's Work and Wages.* London: T. Fisher Unwin; S. Webb and B. Webb, 1915: *Problems in Modern Industry.* London: Bell; B. L. Hutchins, 1915: *Women in Modern Industry.* London: Bell; J. R. MacDonald, 1904: *Women in the Printing Trades.* London: King.

status, should be paid lower rates as a matter of course – unless there was any sign that women might be introduced onto 'men's work' for some reason, in which case the call from the unions was always for equal pay ('the rate for the job'), made with the confident, and usually correct, assumption that when confronted with the idea of paying women 'men's rates' employers would prefer not to recruit women at all. The prevailing belief among leaders of the craft unions at this time was that technological change would always threaten the displacement of skilled men by women machine hands, although in fact the converse was often more likely, as female hand-workers in a number of trades were replaced by male machine minders.[13]

Where changing working practices or technology threw the standard definitions of men's and women's work into the melting-pot, arguments between employers and unions flourished, but in general men's and women's work seldom overlapped, except in a few industries such as cotton weaving or tailoring. Few people challenged the prevailing idea that men should be paid a 'family wage', as the assumption remained that men would always have dependants while women would not. (This was revealed to be a fallacy by a number of writers sympathetic to women's plight, such as Hutchins, Black, Drake, Cadbury, but the evidence they brought to light did not undermine the standard view.)

Although there were considerable variations in the kind of work available,[14] domestic service was still the most common employment for women before the war.[15] Women were also employed in large numbers in dressmaking, millinery, pottery, weaving and other light industrial work in the Midlands and North. They were also, of course, nearly always responsible for all domestic work and childcare within the home, whether or not they also had paid work.

The issue of women's low pay was closely connected with arguments about the desirability of married women taking paid work. By the late nineteenth century, the general feeling (expressed by people from all classes) was that married women should not go out to work, but should confine themselves to the role of wife, mother and housekeeper, supported by a wage-earning husband. Contemporary sources reveal, however, that many working-class wives

[13] *See* many contributors to John, *Unequal opportunities*, op. cit. (note 9), especially Felicity Hunt, Opportunities lost and gained: mechanization and women's work in the London bookbinding and printing trades. Also Cynthia Cockburn, 1983: *Brothers: Male Dominance and Technical Change.* London: Pluto; Sylvia Walby, 1986: *Patriarchy at Work.* Oxford: Polity; Harriet Bradley, 1989: *Men's Work, Women's Work.* Oxford: Polity.

[14] L. Davidoff and B. Westover (eds) 1986: *Our Work, Our Lives, Our Words.* London: Macmillan; John, *Unequal Opportunities*, op. cit. (note 9); Lewis, *Labour and Love*, op. cit. (note 6); Elizabeth Roberts, 1988: *Women's Work 1840–1940.* London: Macmillan; S. Pennington and B. Westover (eds), 1989: *A Hidden Workforce: Homeworkers in England 1850–1985.* London: Macmillan; J. Sarsby, 1988: *Missuses and Mouldrunners.* London: Open University Press.

[15] Mark Ebery and Brian Preston, 1976: *Domestic service in Late Victorian and Edwardian England, 1871–1914.* Reading: University of Reading. This is an excellent pamphlet on service, with full discussion of the statistics available.

earned their own money at various stages during their lives, either from necessity (poverty due to widowhood, or the unemployment, illness or selfishness of
their husbands) or because they chose to. In some areas of the country, wives
could find work in factories and workshops without difficulty – the most
famous group of married women workers being the cotton weavers of
Lancashire. In other areas, such as mining districts, there was little work available for women, and the feeling against the idea of working wives was strong.
Nevertheless, there were hundreds of thousands of married women who took
lodgers, or did paid child-minding, cleaning or washing. In addition, the
sweated industries depended on the labour of married women and children in
their own homes. The problem with this kind of paid work was its relative invis-
ibility: unlike factory work, it did not appear in census returns, and evidence
that married women were often obliged to work to survive was ignored by
those who were determined to see women workers primarily as single girls,
working for a few years between school and marriage.[16] Surveys and interviews
by people such as Hutchins, Black and Cadbury, which gave a very clear picture of women's working lives and the problems encountered by married
women, were thus ignored. The fact that a number of women did leave paid
outside work on marriage, because they could afford to do so or because they
were forced to, was always used to justify the poor training and low wages available to women in general, and to reinforce the stereotype of the casual, temporary female worker as cited by craft unions and employers alike.

There was even less work available for middle-class women, particularly
married women, before the war. The rapid expansion in numbers of clerical
workers is often cited as an example of the expanding opportunities for
women in the white-collar trades, but most female office workers were single.
Married women employed as teachers were mostly at elementary school level.
There were very few women in the professions, and one has to bear in mind
that before 1914 many universities would not even allow women to study for
degrees.[17]

It is hard to utilise statistics when talking about this period of women's work,
as census figures certainly underestimated the amount of paid work done by
women, and other government statistics tended to concentrate on numbers of
insured workers. Women were frequently not in insured trades, and the fact
that so many moved from job to job, or did casual and part-time work, meant
that their work was not registered at all. Nevertheless, the balance of men and
women in the major industries is of interest. Table 6.1, a snapshot of the position in July 1914, shows women clustered in the clothing and textile trades,
and making inroads into some other 'lighter' factory work, such as tobacco
and printing. Their numbers in heavy industry and transport were negligible.

---

[16] *See* discussions on sweating in books listed under note 12. A number of lower-middle-class married women took in sewing, but this kind of paid work was largely hidden.

[17] Carol Dyhouse, 1981: *Girls Growing up in Late Victorian and Edwardian England.* London:
Routledge; June Purvis, 1991: *A History of Women's Education in England.* London: Open
University Press.

Table 6.1   Numbers of Women in Industrial Work in July 1914, and as a Percentage of All Workers Employed

Industries	Number of workers		Percentage
	Males	Females	women
Building	920 000	7 000	0.8
Mines and quarries	1 266 000	7 000	0.5
Metal industries	1 634 000	170 000	9.4
Chemicals	159 000	40 000	20.1
Textiles	625 000	863 000	58.0
Clothing industries	287 000	612 000	68.1
Food/drink/tobacco	360 000	196 000	35.2
Paper and printing	261 000	148 000	36.1
Wood	258 000	44 000	14.6
Other industries	393 000	89 000	22.6
Total private industry	6 163 000	2 176 000	26.1
Gas/water/electricity	63 000	1 000	1.6
Government establishments			
(dockyards, factories, arsenals)	76 000	2 000	2.6
Total government/municipal	139 000	3 000	2.2
Railways	660 000	12 000	1.8
Docks/wharves/transport under			
private ownership	444 000	5 000	1.1
Tramways under local authorities	57 000	1 000	1.7
Total transport	1 161 000	18 000	1.5

Note: workers are classified under industry, rather than occupation. Thus clerical workers appear in every industrial group. These figures are extracted from A. W. Kirkaldy, 1920: *Industry and Finance*, vol. 2. London: Pitman, but percentages have been recalculated. Over a million more women worked in non-industrial trades, including teaching, banking, agriculture, catering and the professions.

The table is based on figures given by A. W. Kirkaldy, a reliable commentator of the time, who suggested that the total number of women in employment in 1914, including white-collar work, finance and teaching, was around 3 276 000, with an additional 1 600 000 in domestic service.[18] However, even these figures underestimate the number of women in some kind of paid work for the reasons mentioned above.

The outbreak of war in 1914 threw industry into disarray, and during the first few weeks women's unemployment increased drastically.[19] However, as men volunteered in their thousands and it became apparent that the war would last for months, rather than weeks, employers were forced to consider

[18] Kirkaldy, *Industry and Finance*, op. cit. (note 7), vol. 2, section 1.
[19] For descriptions of women's work in the war industries, and their exit after the war, *see* Braybon, *Women workers*, op. cit. (note 4), and Gail Braybon and Penny Summerfield, 1987: *Out of the Cage*, London: Pandora. Classic texts remain those of Kirkaldy, Andrews and Drake, as cited in note 7.

using more women in a range of industries. Kirkaldy calculated that by April 1918 there were around 4 808 000 women in employment (an increase of over one and a half million), leaving 1 200 000 still in domestic service. Almost certainly, most of those 400 000 who left service went to work in the war industries (particularly munitions or transport), as many women were eager to escape from the low pay and poor conditions that characterised domestic work. The other 'new' workers in industry were women of a variety of ages, from school leavers to middle-aged wives – some of whom exchanged low-paid irregular work for the better wages offered in munitions, while others returned to the labour market after years at home. Postcards and personal photos of the time show a very large number of middle-aged and older women working in transport, munitions and other industrial work, in contrast to the young women in government propaganda pictures.

Very few upper-class women went into industrial work, in spite of press stories about the daughters of dukes mixing with factory girls on the workshop floor. It is clear from the descriptions of many contemporary commentators, and from oral testimony, that most munitions workers were working-class. Even the middle-class munitions worker was comparatively rare, and middle-class women certainly did not move into other industrial work of a less 'glamorous' nature.[20] It should be noted that throughout the war the press and the Government alike exaggerated the extent to which women took over men's jobs in general. For example, sets of war savings stamps and postcards showed pictures of women dentists, barbers, architects, accountants and cartographers and women in many other trades and professions that in fact remained firmly in the hands of men.[21] Although the number of women in some of the professions increased during the war, particularly in banking and the civil service, it is quite untrue to suggest that women made major inroads into all these areas in 1914–18.

Expansion in the number of female workers began quite slowly. During the first few months of war, women were to be seen as van drivers, window cleaners, sweeps and shop assistants, as they moved with ease into jobs vacated by individual men, often husbands, fathers or brothers. It was clear that many of these first substitutes were 'standing in' for the men who it was assumed would return from the Front in due course, and that they would vacate these jobs willingly when the time came. As women went on to become tram conductors, bank tellers, ticket collectors and clerks in offices and railway stations, they became suddenly visible as *workers* in a way that many people found quite startling, or even upsetting. It must be remembered that the ordinary man (of whatever class) as he travelled around by bus or train, visited the gentleman's outfitter, or called at the barber, the tobacconist, the bank or post office, was used to being surrounded by male faces. Much of women's work had been

---

[20] *See* Braybon and Summerfield, *Out of the Cage*, op. cit. (note 19), for discussions about the class of workers.
[21] The stamps are in a private collection, and are not dated.

hidden – behind the doors that led to the segregated typists' pool, the women's department of the factory, or the servants' quarters. It was this sudden 'feminisation' of the urban scene that led so many people to think that society had been 'transformed' by the influx of women into 'men's jobs', and surprised those who had no idea that women could count out money, drive a horse and cart, or lift luggage on to a trolley.

Women moved into factory, office and transport work in a more formal way from 1915 onwards. The munitions industry – made up of the chemical, metal and engineering trades – became the largest employer of women, for obvious reasons. Hundreds of thousands of women went into shells and armaments production between 1915 and 1918. To use Kirkaldy's figures again, in Table 6.1 the number of women listed under the heading 'Government establishments (dockyards, factories and arsenals)' was a mere 2000 in July 1914. In November 1918, the number was 246 000, by which time women made up 47.1 per cent of the labour force.[22] In the metal trades, which included fuse and cartridge making (already classified as 'women's work'), the number of women went up from 170 000 in 1914 to 594 000 by 1918, and the Board of Trade estimated that by 1917 40 per cent of women in these industries were 'directly replacing men'.[23]

However, their entrance into munitions and engineering was often accompanied by considerable changes in working practice, with the installation of new machines, the use of cranes, lifts and hoists, and the utilisation of male labourers, supervisors and tool setters. Employers argued, with some justification, that the work had changed completely, and that women could not be classed as fully skilled 'tradesmen', or paid 'the rate for the job', given the costs associated with extra equipment or male supervision. There is little doubt that many male workers privately agreed that women were doing modified jobs, and that they lacked the skill of the qualified engineer, but the engineering unions could not afford to admit this publicly. For a number of years before the war the Amalgamated Society of Engineers (ASE) had successfully resisted any attempts by employers to change working practices and recruit cheaper, semi-skilled, male labour. If the union allowed cheap female labour on 'men's work' for the duration of the war, it risked seeing changes in workshop practice and pay scales become permanent. The union therefore concentrated on maintaining wage rates for women on 'men's work': not for women's benefit, but for the sake of the men who would return to the industry after the war.

The whole debate about the use of less skilled labour should be seen in the context of the rights that unions were forced to forgo during the war. Emergency legislation – including the Defence of the Realm Acts and the Munitions Acts – banned the use of restrictive practices in war industries, and removed the right to strike or move freely between jobs. The Government

[22] Kirkaldy, *Industry and Finance*, op. cit. (note 7), vol. 2.
[23] Figures taken from Liz Ahrends, 1976: Women and the labour force: The London metal industry 1914–38, unpublished paper.

accepted the principle that unions required certain guarantees from the state in return, and these included a promise to allow the return of restrictive practices and an assurance that skilled work would return to the hands of 'fully skilled craftsmen' in engineering after the war.[24] In contrast, little attention was paid to the wages – let alone the future job security – of women working in the so-called 'women's trades' within munitions, such as shell filling. Here the minimum wage was set at £1 a week by the Government, now itself a major employer in state-owned factories and so-called 'controlled establishments'. (Controlled establishments were independently owned factories, run for a profit, that were temporarily managed by the Government for the duration of the war.) It is symbolic of women's appalling wages in peacetime that so many saw this as a good wage.[25]

Non-munitions industries suffered severe labour shortages during the war, and here too attitudes towards the temporary women workers remained ambiguous among both managers and unions. Like engineering employers, many manufacturers used the opportunity to experiment with changes in working practices and the use of subdivided processes. This was not new, however: the war merely enabled employers to utilise lessons already learned in other industries or countries over the preceding decade, at a time when unions could do little to protest.[26] Whether unskilled and semi-skilled male or female labour would be recruited for such work in peacetime was a matter for debate throughout industry. Yet, at the same time, many other firms recruited women only with great reluctance, and made it clear that under no circumstances would they be kept on after the war. Managers in such companies continued to complain that women were more expensive, difficult to train, unwilling to take responsibility, or simply 'unreliable'. Not even the possibility of cheaper workers and higher profits could shift ingrained assumptions about women's capabilities. There also remained many jobs from which women were totally excluded (often because of objections made by trade unions), such as underground work in coal-mines, dock work, and mule spinning in the cotton industry. In no sense could it be said that women took over from men in all areas.[27] The idea that 'the nation' welcomed women into all trades with open arms is quite untrue.

[24] For discussion on wartime legislation and the Restoration of Pre-War Practices Act 1919, *see* M. W. Kirby and M. Rose, 1991: Productivity and competitive failure: British government policy and industry, 1914–19. In G. Jones and M. W. Kirby (eds), *Competitiveness and the State.* Manchester: Manchester University Press. *See also* Shells and Fuses Agreement and the Treasury Agreement, both March 1915, and further discussion on union attitudes in Braybon, *Women Workers*, op. cit. (note 4).

[25] For discussions on pay, *see* Braybon and Summerfield, *Out of the Cage*, op. cit. (note 19), 49–51. Women on skilled or dangerous work could earn as much as £6 a week – comparable to men's pay – but this was unusual. The £1 minimum was for a 48-hour week, and later went up to 24s. (£1.20).

[26] *See* detailed discussions about changes in the use of men and women workers on different machinery in Bradley, *Men's Work, Women's Work*, op. cit. (note 13).

[27] The excuses for the exclusion of women were varied, and are discussed in more detail in Braybon, *Women Workers*, op. cit. (note 4).

Attempts were often made to compare the standard of men's and women's work, inside and outside the munitions industry, but this proved difficult given other changes in workshop practice, and the frequent subdivision of labour. Even in the transport industry (another large employer of women, where numbers increased by 555 per cent during the war[28]), where one might expect one-to-one substitution of women for men, jobs were often divided and modified. Thus women were employed as station staff or guards but not as train drivers, and there was much resentment among male railway workers when they were given the 'soft options' such as ticket collecting while men were left with the heavier work. There was therefore no general verdict on the degree of women's 'success' at performing 'men's' work. As Kirkaldy astutely pointed out, 'The opinions expressed on women who were replacing men vary so greatly that it is a temptation to state that women's success depends on the skill with which suitable women are selected and the type of management under which they are placed.'[29] It is clear that all the old assumptions about women workers – as cheap, temporary, unskilled – remained largely unchallenged, and that trade unions fought hard for the continued division of work into 'men's' and 'women's', with appropriate pay scales. Kirkaldy's dry comment sums up a complex situation, in which the needs of war came into direct conflict with deeply institutionalised sexism: 'Considering the strength of the prejudices against women's employment, it is astonishing that it became so widespread.'[30] The press, meanwhile, fanned the flames of resentment among male workers by regaling its readers with exaggerated or flippant portraits of the girls who were now 'skilled engineers' after a fortnight's training, further trivialising the whole issue with their enthusiasm for discussing women's new uniforms, or propensity for buying fur coats with their 'high' wages.[31]

The number of women workers reached its peak in 1917–18, after conscription exacerbated labour shortages. However, as soon as the war ended the numbers of female factory and transport workers began to fall rapidly. First to go were women in the munitions industries, and throughout 1919 women who had worked in other 'men's trades' were laid off in increasing numbers. Most employers seemed happy to return to the status quo: patriarchal attitudes were more powerful, it seems, than the simple pursuit of profit, as there is little doubt that women could have been kept on, at lower wages, in many of the industries they entered for the duration of the war, particularly as the guarantees offered by the Restoration of Pre-War Practices Act covered only a limited

[28] Many of these were employed as bus or tram conductors and, less commonly, drivers. In comparison, the number of women in national and local government increased by 75 per cent. Figures taken from the War Cabinet Committee Report, *Women in Industry*, Cmd. 135 and 167 (1919).

[29] Quoted in Braybon, *Women Workers*, op. cit. (note 4), 66.

[30] A. W. Kirkaldy, 1921: *British labour*. London: Isaac Pitman, quoted in Braybon, *Women Workers*, op. cit. (note 4), 67.

[31] The daily press was obsessed with women's wages throughout the war, although these were always lower than men's. The equal pay debate is discussed at length in Braybon, *Women Workers*, op. cit. (note 4).

number of trades. Even the employers who had expressed satisfaction with women's wartime work proved reluctant to keep them, fearing industrial unrest among their male workforce, and influenced by prevailing notions about the needs of the ex-serviceman. Others were certainly relieved to get rid of them, or send them back to 'women's work.'

In the months immediately following the war, the attitude in the press towards women changed radically. They were suddenly urged to 'go home', release their jobs to returning soldiers, or to get back to domestic service and the laundry trade where they were really needed. This sudden surge of press hostility is quite startling in comparison with the exaggerated praise heaped upon women in the war years. In such a climate, the thousands of women who lost their jobs received little public sympathy, and the Government, anxious about the escalating costs of out-of-work donation, and nervous about the possible social impact of thousands of disillusioned, unemployed ex-servicemen, used labour exchanges to push women into what was seen as more appropriate work.

Originally, the Government had recognised the need to add war workers to the existing National Insurance Scheme and to provide the unemployed with decent, non-means-tested benefits after the war. Rates were initially fixed at 24*s*. (£1.20) a week for men, and 20*s*. (£1) for women, with additional dependents' allowances, though these increased by 5*s*. (25p) a week just before the December 1918 election. No distinction was made between those laid off from war or civilian industries. However, by 1919 it was clear that the Government's primary concern was for the unemployed man, and it was widely assumed that women could just 'go back' to their old jobs – particularly domestic service. Regulations were changed so that it became almost impossible for women visiting labour exchanges to insist on factory or office work. Former servants with several years behind them in industry or transport now found themselves refused benefit if they turned down domestic work, no matter how bad the wages were or how inappropriate the conditions. Other women, too, who had never worked in service, were now told it was something they could easily learn, and were sent for jobs as maids or laundry workers. Appeals to the Courts of Referees were seldom successful.[32]

Women's position as workers worsened from 1921, when the depression pushed up unemployment. Predictably, in view of the prejudices displayed before and during the war, most leaders of the labour movement refused to take women's unemployment as seriously as men's. Even those who represented women, such as the National Federation of Women Workers (NFWW),

---

[32] *See* Braybon, *Women Workers*, op. cit. (note 4), for discussion of changes in press attitudes to women, and the use of labour exchanges to push them into 'women's work.' Problems for married women who were unemployed were only just beginning. Jane Lewis reveals that two and a half times as many women as men were disallowed benefit as a result of 'genuinely seeking work' requirements or the means test clause between 1924 and 1928. *See* Jane Lewis, 1983: Dealing with dependency: State practices and social realities 1870–1945. In Jane Lewis (ed.), *Women's Welfare, Women's Rights*. London: Croom Helm.

had accepted during the war the principle that men should return to their old jobs, and had supported the Restoration of Pre-War Practices Act. The Labour Party, meanwhile, was increasingly preoccupied with family poverty, and women's maternal role. Only the Communist Party made a brave attempt to do something by establishing women's sections in the unemployed movement, and enabling them to take part in the hunger marches (albeit as a separate section).[33]

Unfortunately, even in the so-called women's trades women increasingly found themselves in competition with men as unemployment rose. In the laundry industry, that bastion of female employment, 'methods were adjusted to create jobs for disabled soldiers',[34] and women woollen weavers were also displaced by men.[35] In spite of the large increase in women's unionisation between 1914 and 1918 (ably discussed by Sheila Lewenhak in her book *Women and Trade Unions*),[36] other historians have argued that the roots of women's weak industrial position lay in the war. Indeed, Deborah Thom goes so far as to claim that the war was a disaster for women workers in terms of labour organisation, and that in the 1920s they were left in a weaker bargaining position than they had been before 1914. She argues that:

> *The change in the working woman's perception of herself and her capacity to organise in defence of her interests was not fully recognised until the war but in fact that change was revealed, and diverted and delayed, by war rather than created by it. Mrs Fawcett still saw women in industry with nineteenth-century spectacles when she wrote in 1918, 'The war revolutionised the industrial position of women. It found them serfs and left them free.'*[37]

She continues:

> *In the context of trade unionism the war severely restricted the field of operations of women's unions and helped to institutionalise a position for women in trade unions that presumed their inadequacies in the labour market and in self-organization.*

Those women fortunate enough to find work in the 1920s faced the same old problems: low pay, monotony and lack of opportunities for training or responsibility. In addition, the increasing use of the marriage bar in many trades meant that any hope of a long-term career was out of the question. The ban on married women's work operated not only in a number of clerical or

---

[33] Sue Bruley, 1992: A woman's right to work?', unpublished paper, Portsmouth Polytechnic. *See also* Sue Bruley, 1986: *Leninism, Stalinism and the Women's Movement in Britain 1920–39*. New York: Garland Press; and Sue Bruley, 1993: Gender, class and party: the Communist Party and the crisis in the cotton industry in England between the two world wars. In *Women's History Review* 2 (1), 81–106.

[34] M. MacFeely, 1988: *Lady Inspectors: The Campaign for a Better Workplace 1893–1921*. Oxford: Basil Blackwell. Courses were also run to retrain women as dressmakers.

[35] John, *Unequal Opportunities*, op. cit. (note 9), 228.

[36] Sheila Lewenhak, 1977: *Women and Trade Unions*. London: Ernest Benn. The statistics are usefully summed up in an unpublished paper by Lewenhak, Women in British trade unions during two world wars. The number of women in trade unions rose from 436 679 in 1914 to 1 325 683 in 1919.

[37] Deborah Thom, The bundle of sticks, op. cit. (note 9), 281.

factory jobs but also in teaching and medicine, thus affecting middle-class women as well as working-class ones. These groups had managed to stave off attempts to ban married women's work before the war, but even elementary teachers, 75 per cent of whom were women in 1914, now found it impossible to withstand the bar. To quote Copelman:

> *The tensions inherent in their position were hard to bear in a period of direct attack upon married women's work. The teaching profession as a whole and numerous other groups stood behind the rights of married teachers, and London education authorities were reluctant to ban their work, since they never found any conclusive evidence that they were any less efficient than unmarried teachers. However, their position deteriorated in the early 20th century. The ideology of domesticity that had already held women responsible for the home therefore also triumphed at work – it was stronger than married women teachers' attempts to innovate within its confines.*[38]

A group of married women teachers in the Rhondda in 1923 even tried to fight their dismissal using the Sex Disqualification (Removal) Act, but to no avail, revealing this piece of legislation to be almost useless.[39]

The justification for sacking women, or pushing them back to traditional trades, was once again the claim that women, particularly married women, belonged in the home. This was reiterated by journalists in the daily and labour press, but was also discussed in a more ambiguous way by writers in the new women's magazines. Deirdre Beddoe concludes that the push towards domesticity was as strong in Britain as in Germany[40] – or, it could be added, in France, where disappointed feminists found themselves not only without the vote, but facing a call to the women of France to return home and repopulate the nation with sons.[41]

Although several Acts passed during the war, including the Maternity and Child Welfare Act of 1918, together brought about obligatory registration of births, the improvement of training for midwives and better local authority services for mothers and babies, there is every indication that these measures would have been taken anyway. No doubt such legislation was helped on its way by the widespread feeling that the nation's babies should be seen as a more precious asset in time of war, but the Acts were the culmination of years of campaigning and local action by medical officers to try to improve health services for small children.[42] The back-to-the-home propaganda in Britain

[38] Copelman, A new comradeship, op. cit. (note 6).
[39] Jane Lewis, 1984: *Women in England.* Brighton: Wheatsheaf.
[40] Deirdre Beddoe, 1989: *Back to Home and Duty.* London: Pandora.
[41] James MacMillan, 1981: *Housewife or Harlot.* Brighton: Harvester; Steven Hause, More Minerva than Mars, op. cit. (note 8).
[42] *See* Deborah Dwork, 1987: *War is Good for Babies and Other Young Children: A History of the Infant and Child Welfare Movement in England, 1898–1919.* London: Tavistock. In spite of its title, there is very little about the impact of the war, as most of the book is about pre-war investigations into infant health, safe milk campaigns, etc. Mysteriously, infant mortality did appear to drop during the war, but there is as yet no convincing explanation for this.

never included a strong pro-natalist element (which would have clashed with the increasingly vociferous campaign for birth control in the 1920s), but was certainly accompanied by increasing hostility or mockery towards the spinster, as both Deirdre Beddoe and Sheila Jeffreys document.[43] This was particularly ironic in view of the fact that the war had deprived many women of potential husbands.

In this context, the fragmentation of the feminist movement in the 1920s was unfortunate for working women. Once 'the vote' was won, the different suffrage organisations splintered, and there was something of a gulf between those who threw their weight behind the idea of greater protection for married women and their children (including the concept of family allowances or 'mothers' pensions') and those who sought to open up the bastions of middle-class employment and further the professional woman's career.[44] The ordinary woman worker, particularly the married working woman, had few defenders in the 1920s and 1930s. It is symbolic that one of the first pre-war women factory inspectors, Rose Squire, was moved to the Department of Demobilisation and Resettlement after the war, and had the task of persuading women to 'go back' to domestic service. She proceeded to argue that, to quote MacFeely:

> 'the national service of building and staffing homes' was a patriotic duty. Squire even seems to have convinced herself; she recalled later, 'Women and girls who had never peeled a potato were turning out excellent dinners, housemaids and parlour-maids proudly showed their skill, and several enthusiastically claimed that they had "no idea housework would be so interesting".'[45]

The irony here is that the women factory inspectors' own department was merged with the men's in 1921, and the women received lower salaries.

It is true that a new range of jobs opened up for women during the late 1920s and early 1930s in the electrical, tobacco and food processing industries – industries which often began by operating a marriage bar, but which were later obliged to drop such restrictions at peak periods. However, these jobs were mostly in the South-East, and offered few opportunities to women in the older industrial heartlands. They were also new versions of the classic women's trades, with the addition of the tension inherent in assembly line production: the jobs were low paid, 'unskilled' and monotonous.[46] In addition, the sweated trades, the standby of the poor and desperate, continued to flourish throughout the 1920s and 1930s.

Clerical and white-collar trades are often cited as an example of how

[43] Beddoe, *Back to Home and Duty*, op. cit. (note 41); Sheila Jeffreys, 1985: *The Spinster and her Enemies*. London: Pandora. *See also* the strange book by Charlotte Haldane, 1927: *Motherhood and its Enemies*. London: Bell.
[44] *See* Pugh, *Women and the Women's Movement*, op. cit. (note 11); Alberti, *Beyond Suffrage*, op. cit. (note 11); Beddoe, *Back to Home and Duty*, op. cit. (note 41), for discussion on feminism in the 1920s.
[45] MacFeely, *Lady Inspectors*, op. cit. (note 35), 150.
[46] *See* Miriam Glucksmann, 1990: *Women Assemble*. London: Routledge; and Walby, *Patriarchy at Work*, op. cit. (note 13).

women's work expanded permanently as a result of the war, and they therefore make an interesting case-study, particularly as a great deal of research has
now been done by historians into the way this range of occupations became a
bedrock of female employment in the twentieth century. Table 6.2, extracted
from Gregory Anderson's figures, shows that expansion was well underway
before the war.[47]

The clerk in the mid-nineteenth century had been a well-educated man,
with fine handwriting and good book-keeping skills, who saw his work in the
office or the bank as a long-term career, and who could confidently look forward to increasing responsibility and rising wages as he grew older. With the
expansion of the commercial world in the late nineteenth century, and the
coming of the typewriter (and later the telephone and calculating machine),
clerical work altered. Women were recruited to particular, limited areas of
work. Very few of them were employed in banking or law, while in the Post
Office, the only area of the civil service that recruited female labour in the
early years of the twentieth century, they were chiefly used as auxiliary workers. Shorthand, which was initially seen as a useful skill for both sexes, soon
became part of 'women's work' as it became associated with typing and with
lower-grade work. Women, often well-educated and keen, were under-utilised
from the beginning, being seen by their new employers as quiet, respectable,
tolerant of boredom and, above all, temporary, as it was assumed that they
would leave on marriage. Unlike men, they were not expected to want a career
in the office, and they were confined to mundane tasks and low wages: about
£1 a week was the average shortly before the war, which compared well with
pay rates in other female trades (12–14s. (60–70p) average) but badly with
men's. A very small number of women worked on more interesting, better-
paid jobs for the Bank of England (where conditions were extremely good,
offering free meals, 27 days' annual leave, and pensions), but these were in a
tiny minority.[48] Male clerical workers accepted women into the office with
reluctance, worried that they would undercut them, but the clerical unions –
unlike the craft unions – were not strong enough to keep them out altogether.
To the relief of the male workers, employers and managers were lukewarm in

Table 6.2   Number of Women in White-Collar Jobs, 1881 and 1911

Year	Commerce		Civil service	
	All workers	Women	All workers	Women
1881	208 116	7 444	42 257	4 657
1911	546 948	146 133	108 386	27 129

[47] Extracted from Gregory Anderson, 1988: The white blouse revolution. In Gregory Anderson
(ed.), *The White Blouse Revolution*. Manchester: Manchester University Press, 1–26.
[48] Suzanne Dohra, 1988: Pioneers in a deadend profession: The first women clerks in banks and
insurance companies. In ibid, 48–66.

their response to women, as this quotation from a Post Office supervisor in 1910 shows:

> *I suppose that it may fairly·be said that women do well or better than men* [on] *routine work requiring care and patience but that many of them are less adapted than are the majority of men to work of a complex nature requiring judgment and initiative.*[49]

During the war, thousands more women were recruited into office work, banks and the expanding civil service. Jane Lewis's figures show that the number of women in clerical work went up from 124 843 in 1911 to 591 741 in 1921 (46 per cent of the total clerical work-force), when numbers had already declined from their wartime peak.[50] Nevertheless, most women office workers were still seen as temporary, employed for the duration of the war only. The words of the Treasury Committee Report on Civil Service Recruitment, published in 1918, showed that their prospects were not good:

> *The Report repeated frequently that women and men were not 'interchangeable':* *'The evidence we have taken on the subject convinces us that, having regard to the existing opportunities of education and in the general mental equipment of young men and women, it would be unsafe to introduce women forthwith as interchangeable with men'.*
>
> *The Committee felt that it was generally agreed, for example, that 'women do not stand either sudden or prolonged strain so well as men'. Arguments based on sexual difference underpinned assertions that women had not performed as well as had popularly been claimed (chiefly in the press) during the War. In fact, little hard evidence was produced on this score.*[51]

Meta Zimmeck's figures on the civil service, in Table 6.3, show just how rapidly women were shed from these jobs.[52] As Zimmeck writes, after the war there were men, women and *servicemen* competing for jobs, and, ominously for women, the Interdepartmental Committee on the Employment of Disabled Men in Government Departments was set up in 1919 to help returning soldiers find work in the Civil Service. Inevitably the advantage was soon given to men in general rather than to the ex-soldier, and the committee established new rules for the hiring and firing of staff based on the candidates' perceived financial responsibilities and number of dependants. Increasingly, women had to give reasons why they should not be dismissed.[53] During the 1920s and 1930s, the scales were further weighted against women in the civil service and, if anything, the distinction between men's and women's work in the white-

---

[49] Quoted by Meta Zimmeck, in John, *Unequal Opportunities*, op. cit. (note 13), 159.
[50] Jane Lewis, 1988: Women clerical workers in the late 19th and early 20th century. In Anderson, *The White Blouse Revolution*, op. cit. (note 48), 27–47.
[51] Ibid., 39.
[52] Meta Zimmeck, 1988: Get out and get under. In ibid., 88–120.
[53] Ibid.

Table 6.3   Numbers of Women in the Civil Service, 1914–28, and their Percentage of the Total

Year	No. of women	Percentage women	No. of men
1914	59 308	21	232 112
1918	235 486	56	185 024
1919	169 869	42	237 425 (10% of whom were ex-servicemen)
1920	119 030	32	249 791
1923	76 017	25	228 494
1928	74 212	25	227 601 (65% of whom were ex-servicemen)

collar trades became more marked during the 1920s. Women sitting the competitive exams for permanent posts had to achieve higher marks than men to pass, and those who failed to achieve promotion in this way were effectively barred from any career path within the civil service. Men with fewer qualifications and poorer exam marks thus moved up the hierarchy while women were left behind. Seeking material on the difference between men's and women's standards of work during this time, Jane Lewis concludes that:

> *After the war such evidence became increasingly difficult to find, because the standard of ex-service recruits was so low. The Committee relied primarily on what they considered to be the incontrovertible fact of sexual difference.*[54]

The civil service even managed to achieve exemption from the Sex Disqualification (Removal) Act by use of an Order in Council in 1920, so ensuring that its use of the marriage bar did not fall foul of the law. Although the depression of the early 1920s and cuts in the civil service instituted by the Government as a result of the Geddes Reports in 1922 both clearly played a role in reducing the numbers of women civil servants, the axe had a greater effect on women than men, as Zimmeck's figures for 1920–3 in Table 6.3 reveal.[55] As for the higher-level posts within the civil service, those posts to which the well-educated middle-class woman might, one would think, aspire, Zimmeck writes: 'both before, during and after the First World War male mandarins had a clear policy on the employment of women – "women up to a point and men above".'[56] In general, 'the regulations ensured that they

[54] Lewis, Women clerical workers, op. cit. (note 51), 39. *See also* Teresa Davey, A sissy job for men; a nice job for girls. In Davidoff and Westover, *Our Work, Our Lives, Our Words*, op. cit. (note 14), 124–44.

[55] The Geddes Committee – full title, The Committee on Public Expenditure – was set up to report on how the Government could cut waste and save money on public expenditure. Reports were issued in 1922.

[56] Zimmeck, Get out and get under, op. cit. (note 53).

[women] left before they became too discontented, ambitious or experienced'.[57] The stick of the marriage bar was accompanied by the carrot of a 'dowry' for those who left on marriage: instead of the prospect of a pension, they departed with a cash sum. This left women civil servants themselves very ambiguous about whether wives should work, as many came to depend upon that lump sum to help them set up home when they married. As removal of the bar would have led to the scrapping of the 'dowry', some women were against allowing wives to work in the service.

It is clear from this cursory look at the white-collar trades and employment opportunities for women in general that although the war boosted women's employment – and their wages – temporarily, their standard role in the workplace was not challenged. Throughout industry, they usually found themselves confined to lower wage rates than men, and to mundane tasks. However, as soon as the wartime labour shortage was over, they had little chance of escaping from the female ghettos that continued to exist in both industrial and clerical work. In addition, the disapproval faced by married working women was as great as ever.

Public and Private: Women's Response to War

The evidence I have used so far would tend to imply that any economic gains from the war, in the form of higher wages or new job opportunities, soon slipped away. However, there are other aspects of women's lives to consider. What of women's own attitudes to their wartime work and lives? Here one enters a more speculative area, for there is far less written about this aspect of women's lives than about the work they did.

We know that many women were proud of the role they played during the war. Asked by an interviewer in the 1970s whether she had enjoyed her skilled work on howitzers at the Coventry Ordnance Factory, Isabella Clarke replied: 'Yes, every minute of it. It was a very happy time and well, everything was very happy, the atmosphere at work and with all the people you worked with.'[58] Her words were echoed by many others. This enthusiasm may seem strange. We know that many women were devastated by the deaths of male relations or friends, yet Isabella Clarke, and others like her, could genuinely say, sixty years later, that they had thoroughly enjoyed those four years of war. Women interviewed by the Imperial War Museum remembered feelings of grief or anxiety, yet nevertheless the pride in their wartime work remained.

Of course, oral evidence must be treated with care. In one sense, the women who have come forward to tell their stories have been self-selecting: those who still had painful feelings about the war, or who disliked their wartime jobs,

[57] Kay Sanderson, 'A pension to look forward to ...?': Women civil service clerks in London 1925–39. In Davidoff and Westover, *Our Work, Our Lives, Our Words*, op. cit. (note 14), p. 151.
[58] Interview by Imperial War Museum, Department of Sound Records, 000774/04.

were unlikely to have volunteered to be interviewed. Furthermore, most of those interviewed since the 1970s were very young – between the ages of 14 and 20 – during the war, and readily admitted that the more serious issues did not trouble them at the time. They were usually single and childless, and most of the money they earned they spent on themselves. They had time – if they had the energy – to go to the cinema, girls' clubs and music halls, forms of entertainment that flourished during the war. Older women, many of whom had sons or husbands fighting, have not survived to give us their views on the war, or work, through interviews. It is also true that recent calls for women to be interviewed about their war work have by definition excluded those who were not in paid work between 1914 and 1918. We therefore have very few interviews with middle- or upper-class women who may have had much to say about the war years, but have not been invited to give their opinions. This is to some extent balanced by the larger number of memoirs or novels that emerged from women of these classes in later years, but nevertheless we must accept there were many ordinary women who have never put pen to paper on the subject of the war, and whose views we shall never know.

One needs to distinguish between women's attitudes to the war itself, and their feelings about other aspects of life during wartime – particularly their work. Looking purely at the world of employment, the evidence we have suggests that many working women, of all classes, felt that the war opened out their lives. A whole new range of options was suddenly open to them, and from 1915 to 1918 it was easy to change jobs (except in the munitions industry, where a leaving certificate was required). A large number of young women took the opportunity to leave home, living in hostels or lodgings and handling their own income, while older women and married women suddenly found themselves in demand as workers. It is a cliché to claim that many women blossomed in this atmosphere, but it seems they often did. Yet it would be a mistake to assume that all women enjoyed their work during the war, even in the war industries themselves. Sweated labour was still common (and utilised by the Government in the tailoring and kitbag making industries). Many women moved from job to job seeking work that suited them better, having been worn out by the shift systems in munitions. Others suffered industrial injury or illness, while women were killed or disabled by explosions in shell-filling factories.[59]

Even those who enjoyed their jobs often felt ambiguous about aspects of their work. It was recognised by women that men were afraid that they might undercut wage rates, and broadly accepted that returning soldiers should have

---

[59] As the press was censored under the terms of DORA, the Defence of the Realm Act, little was known about such explosions except locally. The best-known disaster was at Silvertown, London, in 1917, when many women were killed, but it is impossible to say what numbers were involved. Other women suffered emotional damage. Several hundred nurses, shattered by their wartime experiences, tried to enlist on postwar training schemes for other trades, according to Rose Squire, 1927: *Thirty Years in the Public Service.* London: Nisbet, 198–9.

their jobs back. It was also noted by some women in munitions that they were directly concerned with manufacturing the tools of death, though these doubts were seldom voiced publicly. As one anonymous woman wrote at the time:

> on the whole my experience . . . in a munition factory has been a bright and happy one. Only for the fact that I am using my lifes [sic] energy to destroy human souls, gets on my nerves. Yet on the other hand I am doing what I can to bring this horrible affair to an end.[60]

This was the way munitions workers tended to view their trade: they were doing something to help the men at the Front, and prevent the Germans killing 'our boys'.

Furthermore, generally positive attitudes towards work should not be confused with women's attitudes towards the war itself, which were altogether more varied. There were jingoistic women, who were quite prepared to sacrifice their sons (or others' sons) for the nation. Clare Tylee, in *The Great War and Women's Consciousness*, describes the writings of such women, which we find disturbing now. The image of this kind of patriotic wife or mother sending her man to battle was used on recruiting posters, though as the war dragged on the necessity for conscription proved that many of the 'women of Britain' did not really say 'go' with much enthusiasm. Christabel and Emmeline Pankhurst were among those who threw themselves publicly into the recruiting effort, determined not only to persuade the Government to utilise women's labour, but to show that men and women alike could fight in their own way to defend the Empire. At the other end of the scale, there were also women who were ardent pacifists, and who worked with the Conscientious Objectors' movement.[61]

The attitudes of the majority of women to the war fell somewhere in between these two extremes. Many of those women interviewed in the 1970s confirmed that it never occurred to them to challenge the necessity for war at the time: they simply accepted that it had to be fought. Those who lost husbands or sons during the war were even less likely to criticise. It was hard to admit that their men had suffered or died for no good reason, and, given that propaganda ensured that a smokescreen of patriotism clouded the real experiences of men at the Front, it was difficult for the bereaved to speak out

---

[60] Imperial War Museum, Women's Collection, MUN 24/16. It would have been seen as unpatriotic to talk too much of this, and unfair to the men who were fighting.
[61] Claire Tylee, 1990: *The Great War and Women's Consciousness*. London: Macmillan; Anne Wiltsher, 1985: *Most Dangerous Women*. London: Pandora. Rex Pope, 1991: *War and Society in Britain 1899–1948*. London: Longman, states that of the 5.2 million men who served in the army at some time during the war, just over half were volunteers. However, most of these people volunteered in the early part of the war, and by late 1915 it was clear from the failure of the Derby Scheme, which was designed to get men to voluntarily 'attest' that they would serve if necessary, that the number of willing recruits was dropping. The Conscientious Objectors' movement was small, and linked closely with the Quakers. COs were badly treated, and risked imprisonment or enforced work in the services. *See* Keith Robbins, 1976: *The Abolition of War: The Peace Movement in Britain 1914–1919*. Cardiff: University of Wales Press.

against claims that soldiers died a 'glorious death for their country', even had they wanted to.[62] Even Vera Brittain, whose *Testament of Youth* seems to imply that as a young woman she had approached the war with a sense of foreboding, was in reality far more ambiguous about the conflict. It has been pointed out that the language of her letters and diaries was quite militaristic, and that like many others, both male and female, she yearned for the old England to be swept away and rejuvenated, or purified, by war. Tylee remarks on how she remained trapped in the idea of a lost generation, 'a great generation, marvellous in its promise',[63] yet could not grasp the implication of her brother's role in sending his troops forward with a gun at their backs (for which he received a medal), or why he found this incident so unbearably painful that he could not speak of it again. Women's poetry, gathered together in *Scars Upon My Heart*, shows the agonies women went through when trying to reconcile themselves with the death of those they loved, and how much they yearned to feel that this death had not been in vain.[64]

Could any woman really grasp what it was like to fight in that war? In her introduction to the publication of her Second World War diary, Frances Partridge, a pacifist, recognised the gulf that lay between her husband's experience of 1914–18 and her own:

> *As with others of his generation, those ghastly years of trench warfare had knocked nearly all the ambition out of him. His war experiences had moved him deeply; his memory of them was extremely vivid and he often described them to me in detail. When the Second World War began he knew what was at issue; what I knew was second-hand, but unforgettable.*[65]

She was scathing of Brittain's view of the Great War. A diary entry for 1940 reads:

> *Spent most of the morning reading Vera Brittain on Winifred Holtby – frightfully bad, but it aroused various reflections. It is the glorification of the second-rate and sentimental and reeks of femininity. . . . And it's too winsome and noble somehow. But much of that belongs to the First World War, and not to women only. (There it is in Rupert Brooke.) A musty aroma of danger glamorized and not understood by girls at home floats out of this book. Vera Brittain writes of a number of women now happily married and with children who still hark back to a khaki ghost which*

[62] One can see from interviews with women bereaved during the Falklands War that it is still hard for them to come to terms with the idea that their men might have died for a pointless cause. It is less painful to believe that the country was right to go to war.

[63] Tylee, *The Great War and Women's Consciousness*, op. cit. (note 62). As she and others point out, 'the lost generation' is implicitly male. *See also* Lynne Layton, 1987: Vera Brittain's testament(s). In Higonnet *et al.*, *Behind the Lines: Gender and the Two World Wars*, op. cit. (note 1), 70–83.

[64] Catherine Reilly, 1981. *Scars upon My Heart: Women's Poetry and Verse of the First World War*. London: Virago. *See also* Alberti, *Beyond Suffrage*, op. cit. (note 11), for material on the mixed views of feminists confronted by the war.

[65] F. Partridge, 1983: *A Pacifist's War*, London: Robin Clark, 10.

> *stands for the most acute and upsetting feelings they have ever had in their lives. Which is true I think, and the worst of it is that the ghost is often almost entirely a creature of their imagination.*[66]

Partridge's statement 'much of that belongs to the First World War' is interesting, for it reminds us that we have to see women's memories not only in the context of the influence of government propaganda, and the public justification for such a war, but also as a part of the national mourning that followed.

There was an undeniable gulf between the wartime experiences of men and women, even between the nurses who worked with the wounded and the men they cared for. While many women (and again it should be emphasised, not all) found that the war opened up new job opportunities, the men who became soldiers were withdrawn from normal society; they faced the knowledge that they had to kill, or be killed, and risk suffering and mutilation. By working in 'men's jobs' and by facilitating the steady diminution of reserved occupations, women 'released' men for battle. One has only to consider the role of women in the army to see the acute difference between the role of men and women in wartime. Members of the Women's Army Auxiliary Corps (the WAACS), working a few miles from the Front, could talk of their 'wonderful experience', and of a life full of adventure and companionship.[67] Yet their role was to 'release' men for active service by taking over safe administrative, clerical and canteen jobs behind the lines: they were resented for this by male soldiers, just as women workers on the home front were resented by men who were conscripted after 1916. In addition, the very existence of 'women in the army' roused strong reactions among both soldiers and civilians: their uniforms, and the perceived 'masculine' bearing of some of their officers, encouraged anti-suffrage feelings among civilians, according to Jenny Gould, and to suspicions of lesbianism. In reality, nothing could be more conventional than the role women were required to play in the army. There was never any suggestion of women handling weapons or fighting. They, after all, were what men were fighting *for*.[68] Clearly there was also a division between soldiers and the non-combatants of both sexes, a division that led to the hostility expressed by war poets and writers like Sassoon, with his much-quoted 'I'd like to see a Tank come down the stalls, Lurching to rag-time tunes, or "Home, sweet Home." '[69] Yet, in addition, conscripts did make the connection between the recruitment of women to 'safe' civilian or army jobs and their own call-up. This certainly led to additional tension between men and women in industry and the armed services.

I have already said that women workers were not popular in the postwar era. In the press they were accused of having profited by the war – the myth of

[66] Ibid., 26.
[67] Elizabeth Crothwaite, 'The girl behind the man behind the gun': The Women's Army Auxiliary Corps 1914–18. In Davidoff and Westover, *Our Work, Our Lives, Our Words*, op. cit. (note 14).
[68] Jenny Gould, 1987: Women's military services in First World War Britain. In M. R. Higonnet *et al.*, *Behind the Lines: Gender and the Two World Wars*, op. cit. (note 1), 114–25.
[69] Quoted and discussed by Sandra M. Gilbert, A soldier's heart. In ibid., 205

outrageously high wages was never put to rest – and they were suspected of planning to abandon their true domestic role, having tasted 'freedom'. Now that their labour was no longer required to support the war effort, they were also accused of taking men's jobs. Women workers knew themselves to be under attack from many quarters, and some were even abused in the street, as letters to the papers testify.[70]

In such an atmosphere, it is interesting to wonder how the war, and the grim mood that followed, affected the sexual/social/domestic side of relations between men and women, but this is difficult to research. We know little about how women picked up the pieces of their relationships again when husbands, sons or friends returned. Thousands of women were widowed between 1914 and 1918, yet hardly anything is written about their practical or emotional experience as recipients of State aid, or as single parents, in the 1920s and 1930s.[71] Thousands more had to cope with men who were severely physically disabled by the war, and who required long-term hospital care, special medication or artificial limbs. While over 700 000 British men were killed during the war (about 500 000 of them were under 30), a further 1.7 million were wounded. By 1919, 190 000 widows' pensions had been granted, 1.2 million men were entitled to disability pensions (40 000 of these were classed as severely disabled), and around 35 000 children lost their fathers to the war.[72] Nor were physical scars the only ones men had to bear. Even ten years later, there were still forty-eight mental hospitals devoted to the care of 65 000 men classified as shell-shocked.[73] Many women had to live with men who had been altered profoundly by their experiences, and who, by and large, found it impossible to talk about them – as some surviving men still do, seventy-five years later. If fathers and husbands had fits of despair and anger, or were woken by nightmares, women had to go on coping, making allowances for moods, and managing with a reduced family income in the case of disability. Novelists and playwrights tried to describe what happened when the soldier returned home, but literary interpretations give us very little idea of what it was like for ordinary families who had sometimes seen little of their menfolk for years, and had now to watch them adjust again to 'normal' life, and the

---

[70] There was a great deal of wartime discussion about women's future role, and some feared that once women had seen their children well cared for in nurseries (of which there were in fact very few) this would break the domestic bond and lead to irresponsible mothers.

[71] Karin Hausen, 1987: The German nation's obligation to the heroes' widows of World War I. In Higonnet *et al.*, *Behind the Lines: Gender and the Two World Wars*, op. cit. (note 1), 126–40.

[72] *See* Pope, *War and Society in Britain*, op. cit. (note 62), and J. Winter, 1985: *The Great War and the British People.* London: Macmillan.

[73] Tylee, *The Great War and Women's Consciousness*, op. cit. (note 62), 249. *See also* Eric Leed, 1979: *No Man's Land: Combat and Identity in World War I.* Cambridge: Cambridge University Press, for men's feelings about the war.

hard times of the 1920s.[74] There is even less information available on the women who had themselves been physically or emotionally injured by their own wartime work or experiences. They are, perhaps, the most forgotten of the war's casualties.

It is also difficult to measure the effect of the war on the women who might have married, and whose potential husbands died during the war. Marriage statistics in the postwar period are difficult to interpret. According to Winter, marriage rates rose in 1914–15, fell in 1916–18, rose again in 1919–20, and fell in 1921–2. He suggests that there was little increase in female celibacy.[75] On the other hand, Jane Lewis points out that the proportion of women aged 35–44 who were married dropped to a new low in the mid-1920s as a result of the war.[76] Although some women may have 'compensated' to some extent for the loss of half a million men in their twenties by taking older or younger husbands, many others lost fiancés or male friends during the war. This meant that there were thousands of women who were deprived of the chance to marry, and were instead solely dependent on their own ability to earn a decent income.

What influence did this have on the attitudes and expectations of the single women of all classes who sought careers? Were the women who supported the marriage bar most strongly in the workplace those who feared for their own future, knowing that wage levels had to support them into middle age and beyond?[77] I have no intention of claiming that these thousands of so-called 'surplus' women were in some way less fulfilled because they lacked the opportunity to marry – there was little fulfilling about the life of many working-class wives and mothers – but enforced spinsterhood must have had an impact on the numbers of women seeking work in the 1920s and 1930s, and upon women's own attitudes to careers, to men and to home.

Conclusions

There were other factors affecting women's lives during the 1920s – trends in employment, protective legislation, the provision of state benefits, education,

[74] *See* Claire Tylee's discussion of 'elegiac' novels in *The Great War and Women's Consciousness*, op. cit. (note 62). Among the most striking books were Rebecca West, *Return of the Soldier* (1918); Richard Aldington, *Death of a Hero* (1929); Edmund Blunden, *Undertones of War* (1928); and Ford Madox Ford's *Parade's End* series, published in the 1920s.

[75] Winter, *The Great War and the British People*, op. cit. (note 72).

[76] Lewis, Dealing with dependency: State practices and social realities 1870–1945. In Lewis, *Women's Welfare, Women's Rights*, op. cit. (note 33).

[77] There is very little on the particular problems of poverty among single or widowed women pensioners during the inter-war years. However, pension provision and the difficulties encountered by women in the state system have been described by Dulcie Groves. She discusses the importance of the fact that there were more single women than single men between the wars, and the increasing numbers of single women who were part of the state or occupational schemes. Dulcie Groves, 1983: Members and survivors: Women and retirement pension legislation. In ibid.

health and housing – and these are sometimes difficult to distinguish from the direct effects of the war, as legislation in these areas was to some extent also influenced by the war. Yet looking at the first few decades of the twentieth century, I am always struck by the consistency of women's role at home and work, rather than the changes – although again I must repeat that individual women's experience varied according to class, income and age. One can recognise the devastating emotional and demographic consequences of the First World War, and note the dramatic effect of war work on women's skills, self-confidence and income, yet still be aware that for millions of women life offered limited opportunities for employment, combined with low pay and household drudgery, before, during and after the war. Alison Light, in her recent book on England between the wars, gives a rather optimistic picture of 1930s women in their new homes, buying books and going to the cinema.[78] A contrasting view can be found in a book by Margery Spring Rice, published in 1939, who described the results of an inquiry into the health of working-class wives in the 1930s:

> *The cinema is very rarely mentioned, and many women say they have never been to the pictures. A few who live in the country speak of walking and gardening; others of going to chapel or church on Sundays. An overwhelming proportion say that they spend their 'leisure' in sewing and doing other household jobs, slightly different from the ordinary work of cooking and house-cleaning.*[79]

Working Class Wives, full of descriptions of women treading a narrow line between survival and abject poverty or ill-health (often both), is a useful antidote to any over-optimistic assumptions about 'women's changing role' between the wars. Let one further example suffice:

> *Mrs P of Brighton has had a very hard life. She is 46 and has had eight children and one miscarriage. Her husband is much older than herself and is unemployed and has the old-age pension. She adds, 'He is ill-tempered, and no help at all in the house, which is a great trial of patience.' Seven of her children still live at home and the youngest is 3. She pays 9/5 [9s. 5d.] rent for an old house in a condemned area with only two bedrooms. . . . She says in answer to the first question, 'Do you feel fit and well?' 'No, far from it.' She has bronchitis every winter, bad phlebitis, bad headaches, rheumatism, and two years ago had a bad attack of pneumonia. She writes, 'I feel that much of my ill-health is due to insufficient nourishment after child-birth and too short a time between confinements. I don't want to grumble, but I do wonder sometimes if things are going to get any easier.'*[80]

Mrs P. would have been 21 in 1914. What happened to her during the war is not reported. One wonders what she did in 1939, the beginning of the next 'watershed' for women.

---

[78] Alison Light, 1991: *Forever England: Femininity, Literature and Conservatism between the Wars*. London: Routledge.
[79] Margery Spring Rice, 1939: *Working Class Wives*. Harmondsworth: Penguin Books, 103.
[80] Ibid., 107–8.

7

The War and British Culture

Malcolm Smith

Introduction: Cultural Disjuncture

Even what we choose to call the conflict is significant culturally. It appears to
have been Colonel Repington, the war correspondent of the *Morning Post*, who
first coined the term 'The First World War'. This was in September 1918, a full
two months before the armistice, and an eventful twenty-one years before the
outbreak of the Second World War was to give such a title retrospective valid-
ity.[1] Actually, Repington chose the name not simply to denote that the conflict
was on a wider geographical scale than would have been suggested by 'The
European War', but also to imply that this was not necessarily *the* 'Great War'
at all, not a one-off 'war to end all wars'; rather, it was possibly only the first of
a series of apocalyptic confrontations. The new title for the conflict certainly
did not go unchallenged – 'the Great War' became the norm – but in the years
after 1918 it did gain some coinage. Repington implied not only that the scale
of the conflict had been unprecedented but also that it had opened Pandora's
box. He suggested that what had been challenged, quite fundamentally, was
the notion that civilisation and catastrophe were inimical and opposed concepts. The liberal notion of meliorism, the idea that humanity was inexorably
on the path of progress, appeared to be simply wrong. History was also wrong,
and the future, consequently, appeared disjointed and unpredictable, and
threatening.

At the end of the century, after Hamburg, Dresden, Tokyo and Hiroshima,
as well as the huge slaughter wrought in the almost continuous limited wars
fought around the globe since 1945, there is a hideous credibility in the view
that what happened between 1914 and 1918 made what followed possible.
That is simply to say that what happened first caused what happened next, of
course, and is methodologically suspect. On the other hand, the impact of
that war on the modern British memory, on modern British culture, has been

[1] C. à Court Repington, 1920: *The First World War*, vol. 1. London: Constable, 391.

primarily to fashion the twentieth century as an experience quite different from what had gone before. It is almost impossible to write more than a paragraph on the effect of the war on ways of thinking without employing apocalyptic rhetoric. This is because the war generated its own apocalyptic myth, both in Britain and elsewhere, and because that myth in itself 'is part of the fabric of our own lives'.[2] A new language, new forms of communication, had to be shaped to describe a new reality, and those new forms of communication were in turn to shape the way in which those who came after imagined not only the war itself but also the world in which they lived, the aftermath of the war. Historians tend to feel unhappy with discontinuities, and it may well be realistic to argue that many aspects of postwar life in Britain had their origins in pre-war conditions, but it would be difficult indeed to show that contemporaries felt these continuities to be more significant than what had changed. Something had happened to reality: even normality, after all, had become 'normalcy'.

It is in this sense of a fundamental disjuncture occurring during the First World War, a quite basic change in historical direction, that we may describe the period as a paradigm shift in culture. Culture means more than 'art' in this sense. It refers to a system of thinking, a 'structure of feeling' as Raymond Williams called it, which displays itself in patterned regularity across the whole range of social values of a group, a class or a nation. For Britain, at the time, the impact of the First World War may have been even greater than for other combatant nations, even though the casualties were not as great as those of France, Germany or Russia, and even though the British political system did not collapse. France, Germany and the United States had all gone through major wars, and mass participation in those wars, in the half-century before 1914, and the Russian political system had almost collapsed under the impact of the war with Japan less than ten years before. In sharp contrast, Britain's wars in the nineteenth century had been fought thousands of miles away by a small, professional army, largely ignored at home.

In the same way, the cultural legacy of the Great War has also been rather different. Although the crisis of 1940 has been a further defining point in British history, it bears no comparison with the impact of Stalinism on Russia, of Nazism on Germany, or of defeat on France in 1940. For other nations, further and worse calamities came after the Great War, whereas for Britain the 1940s could be said to have been a basically heroic experience, in some way even redeeming the disaster of 1914–18. If one had to choose two moments in twentieth-century British history that have taken on iconographic status, it would probably be 'the summer of 1914' and 'the summer of 1940', the first being the end of the old world and the second the beginning of the new; in between came the bad times.

---

[2] P. Fussell, 1970: *The Great War and Modern Memory*. London: Oxford University Press, preface.

Memorialising the Modern

The First World War has a monumental quality internationally, but it may be especially monumental in British culture because of the slightly different way it is perceived to fit into British history. This perception of history is itself, of course, part of culture. This is the point in history at which those who have come after can first begin to recognise what was happening as 'modern', and not simply because there are still survivors alive. Surely this has a great deal to do with the fact that for the first time in British history a huge mass of material has survived which allows the experience to be constantly restaged. This was the first mass literate war, the first conflict in which hundreds of thousands of soldiers were abroad, felt the need and were able to write, and those letters were kept because those receiving them understood that this conflict needed – for personal and family reasons – to be 'monumentalised'. These letters survive in families and are handed down, along with the war medals. For most families, indeed, the family archive goes back only as far as the First World War. This, in short, was the point at which history begins to mean something to most people because 'the evidence' is still there.

More demotic cultural forms emerged to ensure that the cultural legacy of the war would not simply be imposed on British people, as a series of events interpreted for them by a minority, historians, or by the mass media. The First World War was also the first great photographic war. Photographs from the Front were, of course, heavily censored but in the days before semiotics became almost instinctive they probably had the desired effect of confirming the official line on what was happening. This may well have helped to cement the divide between the home front and the fighting front, the almost impenetrable barrier of ignorance about the trench experience that affected so many soldiers on leave.

But the war period also saw a huge expansion in private photography. It is a fact the significance of which is still to be fully explored that before about 1900 only a tiny minority of adults, those whose parents had had the money to commission portraits, had any clear idea of what they had looked like as children, or what their parents looked like when they were younger, and probably only the dimmest recollection of what their grandparents had looked like at all. The development of the compact family camera, and of the relatively cheap professional photographic portrait, revolutionised family history and guaranteed a more dependable popular memory. The young soldiers posing in uniform who stare into the camera in family photograph albums are not haggard victims of shell-shock but people for whom the military experience 'is making a man of him', and who are clearly proud of 'doing their bit'. Their private experience may well have been rather different from the photographic image, but the point is that what has survived in family culture is evidence that each family had a role to play in these historic events, that there are private stories behind the official histories, the war poems and paintings. Though national culture may to some extent organise the interpretation of these photographs, so that they change their meaning over time, they also guarantee that the experience of individuals cannot simply be overruled or wiped out for their children and grandchildren, and they continue to add a poignant gut feeling to the collective memory of the war. The more brown and the more cracked by handling at family gatherings they become, the more they mean as roots of the here and now.

In the ten years after 1918 the individual and family experiences were to be collectivised in the war memorial movement. Virtually every city and town and village was to build its own memorial. Formerly, though there were many Colenso and Mafeking Streets built after the South African War, only the very largest cities and the military towns had commemorated victory and defeat in public monuments. The war memorial movement after 1918 organised private grief in national consciousness. Many of these memorials were paid for largely by wealthy local benefactors, but many were also built from widespread public subscription.

What was significant about the memorial movement was the way in which so many local memorial committees decided not to build something that might be merely useful to the community – a hall or a hospital for instance – but chose instead a strikingly uniform series of sombre Portland stone pedestals and bronze statues as sites for homage. The Royal Academy organised a War Memorial Exhibition in 1919 and many prominent Fellows (FRAs) offered their work in the catalogue. Sir Edwin Lutyens was a major figure in the movement, designing the Whitehall Cenotaph, the Manchester, Leicester and Southampton memorials and many others. There can be little doubt that one of the effects of Lutyens' and other FRAs' efforts was to popularise, if only temporarily, art forms that had previously been perceived as the domain of the élite and the private.[3] This was public and easily accessible, non-modernist art for the most part, which struck exposed and raw nerves. Lutyens captured the grand scale of the tragedy in his designs and created, in effect, a populist and nationalist art form for a nation that was awestruck by what nationalism had done but which could not, and would not, forget it. Around these impressive memorials was to be played out, year by year, a ceremony of remembrance that managed to remain ambivalent, a death cult which idealised the young 'fallen' as patriots but which also underlined the new idealism: 'Never again'. In smaller towns and villages, the memorials themselves became symbols of community, re-establishing the country churchyard as an icon of local identity, linking to that underlying pastoralism which had survived well over a century of industrialisation as a central element in national identity.

The significance of the war memorial as a national shrine may be seen in contemporary newsreel coverage of the Remembrance Day ritual. In 1936 the nation had a dead King to remember as well as the dead of the Great War. The opportunity was taken by Gaumont British to describe the new King as 'one who had shared with his generation' the test of war. The minute's silence was

[3] D. Boorman, 1988: *At the Going Down of the Sun: British War Memorials.* York: Derek Boorman.

accompanied by quick cuts from the royal family to the crowds, the national family, to country churchyards, and to a shire horse in a field as an image of the 'England' which the soldiers had died saving. The item ended with shots of politicians gathered at the ceremony and the hope that never again would the sacrifice have to be made. It was an extraordinary construction of national unity feeding on a wide range of registers of British identity, particularly pastoral images, with the Whitehall Cenotaph itself as its core.[4] It was to be a telling tribute to the strength of the war memorial as a symbol of British identity that the IRA chose to attack a memorial on Remembrance Day – in 1987, in Enniskillen – and that the attack should produce outrage in the Northern Ireland community. Like the wayside Calvary in Catholic countries, the war memorial became the touchstone of one of the things that was held in common by Britons, a shared myth of mud, poppies and puttees with which to surround the smiling young faces in family photograph albums and the letters tied in ribbon. Whatever the political differences and social frictions, Remembrance Day was for decades the moment at which people and nation fused.

Another major difference between the British cultural experience of the war and that of other combatants was that Britain's dominant mode of thinking in 1914 had been far less touched than other European countries by the strains of what came to be known as modernism. Traditional attitudes appear to have survived rather longer into the war than they did elsewhere. Apart from the Decadent movement of the 1890s, which had anyway been effectively overwhelmed by the scandal surrounding the trial of Oscar Wilde, new artistic directions were slow to materialise. Vorticism and futurism, which in their violation of traditional forms in painting and sculpture declared war on traditional realism and the romantic tradition, were to be able to respond to the demands made on communication in the next few years, but these movements had few adherents as yet in Britain. Vorticists unwittingly prophesised the scale of the conflict to come. Taking their terms from current popularisations of physics, they stressed the energy, the vortex, necessary for any act of real creation, and the violence and destructiveness that that vortex would wreak. Shortly before he died in the war, the vorticist sculptor Henri Gaudier-Brzeska wrote: 'this war is a great remedy'.[5] The Futurist Manifesto declared: 'We wish to glorify war – the only health-giver of the world – militarism, patriotism, the destructive arm of the Anarchist, the beautiful Ideas that kill, the contempt for women.'[6] These were notions that look prophetic with the benefit of hindsight, but the brutal proto-fascist implications sat uneasily in liberal Britain, even with the Irish, labour and feminist revolts of the period suggesting to some an imminent breakdown in the political order.

The Wilde scandal had tarred the very notion of artistic experiment as

[4] Gaumont British, *Armistice Day* (Visnews), November 1936.
[5] T. Materer, 1979: *Vortex: Pound, Eliot and Lewis.* Ithaca: Cornell University Press, 31.
[6] Quoted in S. Hynes, 1992: *A War Imagined: The First World War and English Culture.* London: Pimlico, 7.

perverse, even perverted. The eclecticism and cosmopolitanism of so much in modernism also branded it as foreign. Among writers, notably, the pre-1914 modernists in Britain tended to be seen as foreign – American in the case of Ezra Pound and T. S. Eliot (in so far as they were known at all), French in the case of Gaudier-Brzeska – or almost foreign, Irish in the case of James Joyce, or simply untutored in the case of D. H. Lawrence. There was no public outcry or attempt at suppression of the activities of the few modernists; they were given room to publish and to hang their paintings but were largely ignored. Pound might cry 'Make it new!' and Wyndham Lewis decried 'Rousseauisms', but the Georgian poets were still quite happy in a Keatsian universe.[7]

The British artistic establishment greeted the war almost euphorically and with a remarkable degree of unanimity. It was urged into further effort by the head of the Government's new Department of Information, Charles Masterman. The public reaction to the reporting and the proselytising of the Boer War had displayed the power of the printed word in what, since the 1870s, had become a mass literate society. 'Culture' was deemed to be at stake almost from the very beginning, explicitly opposed to '*Kultur*': the first was peaceful, persuasive and ennobling, the second bellicose, perverse and domineering.

It was important, therefore, that the artists should take up the cudgels. Along with this near-conscription of the great names of contemporary literature – Thomas Hardy, J. M. Barrie, Arnold Bennett, Henry Newbolt, Rudyard Kipling – went a much more censorious attitude towards modernism, almost as if traditionalists had been waiting for the moment that they could take the liberal gloves off and fight the modern trends. Over the next few years it became a patriotic duty to defend culture from modernism. *The Times* reviewed the exhibition by the London Group of Futurists in 1915 under the title 'Junkerism in art',[8] though in fact Germans were by no means prominent in the futurist movement, which was actually dominated by artists from Italy and France, Britain's allies.

The first spectacular example of official intervention, however, was the proscription of Lawrence's *The Rainbow* in 1915. Lawrence's association with Frieda von Richthofen cemented the suspicion in right-wing cultural circles that there was a connection between Prussianism, modernism and sexual deviance, and that modernism and sexual deviance therefore constituted virtually treacherous activities. It was commonly assumed at the time that *The Rainbow* had actually been banned under the Defence of the Realm Act rather than the Obscene Publications Act, as was in fact the case.

There was no example of cultural xenophobia more absurd or more frightening than the campaign against sexual deviance and its supposed conspiratorial alliance with artistic experimentation. A performance of Wilde's *Salome* at the end of the war prompted the most dangerous example of this, the trial

[7] Materer, *Vortex*, op. cit. (note 5), 30.
[8] *The Times*, 10 March 1915.

for libel of the MP Noel Pemberton Billing. Pemberton Billing alleged that there existed, and that some of the witnesses he called had seen, a German list of 47 000 sexual deviants in high places in Britain (including H. H. Asquith and his wife and, indeed, the trial judge himself) who could be blackmailed into helping a German victory. Farcically, Pemberton Billing was cleared of the charges against him. Later in the year, a radical publisher was successfully prosecuted under the Defence of the Realm Act for publishing *Despised and Rejected*, a novel about an artistic homosexual who is mistreated in a wartime prison when he is locked up as a conscientious objector. Though the prosecution's case was that the novel was in fact a pacifist pamphlet, the real problem with *Despised and Rejected* was that it conflated 'un-English' vices: art, homosexuality and pacifism.[9] These were 'Hunnish practices'. Thus did xenophobia work in the war to create an irrational and wholly illiberal climate of opinion in which any artistic experimentation was likely to find itself under intense scrutiny for any sexual deviation, which would be treated as objective pro-Germanism.

It would be quite unfair to blame the cultural establishment for monstrous developments such as these. The problem, however, was that in aligning themselves closely with cultural nationalism, the great names found themselves sleeping with some strange bedfellows, however unwillingly. Gilbert Murray did attack German philosophers, after all. Arthur Quiller-Couch did condemn what he called the dry historicism of German academics, and Thomas Beecham did organise concerts which excluded the German greats and which were, consequently, quite dreadful by all accounts. This was to have unfortunate repercussions when many of the younger writers and artists began to have grave doubts about the direction of the war. The cultural establishment, by its continued support for the war, began to be associated with the 'Old Men' in government. This generational dispute was also to have political implications: it became a dispute between those who had to do the fighting and those who were too old to fight but who were still powerful enough to control the war, whether politically or intellectually. Not that the younger men who both fought and attempted to communicate their experience turned in any deliberate way to modernist methods. Siegfried Sassoon and Wilfred Owen continued to think of themselves as Georgian poets, in the same school as Rupert Brooke, though their subject matter was increasingly antagonistic to anything the latter wrote.

In spite of their unwillingness to declare any modernist leanings, however, or perhaps through their ignorance of what modernism stood for, the simple fact was that the landscape and the human condition that poets like Sassoon and Owen recorded actually looked more like a vorticist painting than anything that could be taken from the realist or romantic traditions. In their war paintings Paul Nash, C. R. W. Nevinson and Wyndham Lewis, on the other hand, actually drew back from their more overtly experimental pre-war work

[9] Hynes, *A War Imagined*, op. cit. (note 6), 233.

to depict, sometimes in almost naturalistic terms, the new reality. Comparing soldiers' diaries and memoirs with Nash's 'The Menin Road' or Orpen's 'Dead Germans in a Trench', for example, it seems that painters of the Western Front were able to express the strange light and the sharp relief which that light gave to detail much better than those fuzzy contemporary photographs.

If painters appear to have felt it was unnecessary to experiment unduly with the subject of the Western Front – because reality had in effect moved to meet them – the war poets found themselves ill at ease with tradition. Though Owen frequently borrowed images from the traditional pastoral vocabulary in his later poems, it was for ironic contrast with what the Romantic tradition would have made of that image, as in 'Exposure':

> *Pale flakes with fingering stealth come feeling for our faces,*
> *We cringe in holes, back on forgotten dreams, and stare, snow-dazed*
> *Deep into grassier ditches. So we drowse, sun-dozed,*
> *Littered with blossoms trickling where the blackbird fusses.*
>   *Is it that we are dying?*[10]

Owen here does not repudiate the pastoral tradition, he merely refers to it as a kind of poignant, nostalgic irrelevancy, worrying evidence that he might be slipping into a fatal unconsciousness. Rosenberg, in 'Returning, We Hear the Larks', constructs a sense of the weird irrelevancy of a lark singing in such a landscape, such a context. Though not necessarily modernist in themselves, such references have the same ironic and sardonic inflection of post-war modernist writing, that literary traditions are there to be inverted, and that they actually make more sense if they are, as in the more complete inversion of pastoralism in Eliot's 'The Waste Land':

> *What are the roots that clutch, what branches grow*
> *Out of this stony rubbish? Son of man,*
> *You cannot say, or guess, for you know only*
> *A heap of broken images, where the sun beats,*
> *And the dead tree gives no shelter, the cricket no relief,*
> *And the dry stone no sound of water.*[11]

In this sense, the war poets and artists helped to validate a modernist way of seeing. Though rarely obscure themselves, they used those disjunctures and disorders in language and vision which were to be typical of modernists and the attempt to alienate the reader or viewer from a comfortable reading of a text. Reality is too complex to be approached directly, and crumbles as soon as you grasp it; much easier to express it in terms of what it is not, to show that the very act of communication itself is complex, many-layered and imprecise. This was a process that the war poets lived through, trying to invent a poetry which would express the breakdown of traditional forms faced with such a

[10] W. Owen, 1973: *War Poems and Others*, ed. D. Hibberd. London: Chatto & Windus, 91.
[11] T. S. Eliot, 1974: *Collected Poems*. London: Faber, 6.

catastrophe, and distanced from a home front which simply was not able to comprehend what the soldiers had experienced. Like the postwar modernists again, the work of the war poets offered no resolution, only the putting of a question: what, basically, is this all about? The war poets could not offer a resolution because the war was not yet over: they were writing *in media res*, the essential modernist predicament. The postwar modernists tended to see themselves permanently *in media res*, and – again like the war poets – as having more in common with other artists, alienated from their audience, condemned to launch 'raids on the inarticulate'.[12]

None of the front-line modernist writers of the inter-war years – Pound, Eliot, Woolf, Lawrence, Joyce – fought in the trenches, and none of the soldier-poets made it into the accepted literary canon, though they did ease the path for the new. Even the ones who survived physically seem to have been burnt-out cases. Wyndham Lewis, actually an exception to the rule of the war-fighting burnt-out case, described his generation as 'the first men of a future that has not materialized',[13] itself a typically modernist stance. Lewis felt that the vortex had finally blasted the vorticists: 'the community to which he belonged would never be the same again: and . . . all surplus vigour was being bled away and stamped out.'[14] Apart from the *cause célèbre* of Sassoon's stand on the war, his letter to *The Times* (which, anyway, had nothing to do with his poetry), the soldier poets really had very little effect during the war itself. It is a cause for gratitude that Sassoon's homosexuality did not become known during his public crisis over the war because that would surely have sunk him, given the prevailing climate of opinion.

The war poets were hardly published in the years of the conflict and, even thereafter, Rupert Brooke remained the most popular poet of the war. But they are worth more than simply a footnote in cultural history, not only because of the seriousness and heroism of what they tried to do, but also because their eventual publication in the 1920s coincided with the first big spate of post-war modernist publications. Their struggle with the imprecision of words and the complexity of communicating what they had been through lent historical validation, the *gravitas* of recent experience, to the modernists' efforts.

War and Masculinity

The target of the soldier poets was the Old Men, politicians and generals, but also, often indirectly but clearly, women. Though women may well have gained at least a degree of liberation in economic terms during the war, they still lived with the fundamental fact that they were not faced with the responsibility for the physical defence of the state: they did not have to kill or be killed

[12] T. S. Eliot, 1944: *Four Quartets*. London: Faber, 31.
[13] Hynes, *A War Imagined*, op. cit. (note 6), 464.
[14] Materer, *Vortex*, op. cit. (note 5), 32.

for their country. The war was fundamentally 'about' and 'by' men, and its long-term cultural effect has been within a discourse on masculinity. Any effect on women was indirect, a spin-off. It was in the nature of things, therefore, that women should be for the soldiers part of the home front, part of those who did not understand. Indeed, in the icon text of women's involvement in the Great War, *Testament of Youth*, written by someone at least close enough to the fighting as a nurse and as someone who lost three men, Vera Brittain admitted fully that she swallowed the official culture of the war, hook, line and sinker.[15]

Much has been written about the homo-erotic strands in war poetry and it is clearly true, however much pacifists shook their heads in disbelief at the idea after the war, that war is a kind of sport – a team game at least, an important ritual of male solidarity.[16] For the young public-school officers on the Western Front in particular, war was the ultimate test of their training in masculinity. The duration of the war, the fact that the British Army did not crack, seems to suggest that the system had worked extremely well. Even some of those who did crack under the strain – Owen and Sassoon are the best-documented examples – went back to the front even though they loathed the war, not to kill more Germans if they could help it, but to help their men. The relationship that often appears to have developed between young middle-class officers and working-class soldiers was an opportunity for the more benevolent aspects of male solidarity to work through into a redefined paternalism. The spirit of Herbert Read's 'My Company' translated into the politics of former young officers such as Attlee, Eden and Macmillan.

This is not to say that the Great War produced the first examples of the 'new man', simply to point out that it tested not just man the fighting animal but also man the social animal. By the time the Second World War arrived, moreover, the concept of cowardice had been softened by an understanding of shell-shock, based on the experience and research of the Western Front. Not quite so much was to be expected of masculinity as a whole in a future national crisis and, in this sense at least, the Great War allowed masculinity to be quietly redefined.

Yet the trench experience bequeathed to post-war culture the phenomenon of the mentally scarred veteran. Orwell wrote of spending most of the 1920s with men older than himself who had fought the war, been damaged by it, but who fascinated him: 'you felt yourself a little less than a man' for having been too young to fight, Orwell later remembered.[17] Christopher Isherwood found inter-war Britain divided not so much between the rich and the poor but between those who had fought the war and those who had not, and found himself 'obsessed by a complex of terrors and longings associated with the

[15] V. Brittain, 1933: *Testament of Youth*. London: Gollancz.
[16] *See* Fussell, *The Great War and Modern Memory*, op. cit. (note 2), ch. VIII.
[17] G. Orwell. My country right or left. In S. Orwell and I. Angus (eds), 1968: *The Collected Journals, Essays and Letters of George Orwell*, vol. 1. Harmondsworth: Penguin Books, 540.

idea "War".'[18] For Isherwood the idea of the war presented him with a test of his manhood and his sexuality. Time and again, both during the war and in its aftermath, culture comes back to the question of the relationship between war, masculine duty and sexuality at the core of a continuing discourse on art and national identity.

New and Old Patriotisms

Time and again, too, culture comes back to the question of new commitments to replace those shattered by the war. For Eliot, Waugh and Greene the move was towards Catholicism. For many younger members of this élite, socialism appeared as at least a temporary alternative. The trajectory of George Orwell's career may have been unique but in a wider sense it was typical of the search for new loyalties, now that the Old Men had made simple patriotism virtually an uninhabitable ruin. In other words, it was the need to search for such loyalties that those intellectuals had in common, not the solution they found. Through the search, moreover, fascination with 'the test' remained.

For Orwell, the near-trench experience led him to convert to socialism on the road from Mandalay to Wigan Pier, a macho, populist socialism that never really crossed the class divide. Orwell himself was aware that he always remained a gentleman slumming it and that the cockney accent he adopted on his tramping missions was easily seen through by real cockneys. The war in Spain, however, was a chance to participate in an international crusade against fascism in which accent and background were irrelevant compared to commitment; it was also a chance to expiate the guilt he said he felt at having been just too young to fight the Great War. The Spanish war seemed to him like a bad copy of the Great War, that when he finally heard guns fire in anger 'it was so different from the tremendous unbroken roar for which my senses had been straining for twenty years'.[19] Yet one senses, reading *Homage to Catalonia* and 'Looking back on the Spanish Civil War', that for the first and perhaps the only time in his life Orwell actually belonged in Spain, fighting for a cause as his public-school background had trained him to do, even if the cause itself was certainly not Empire and Country, and even if the new cause was also to be sullied by the fighting and by the politicians.

When Orwell was hounded out of Spain by the communists, the Soviet leaders were to become the equivalent of the Old Men of the trench poets. The process that had begun in the Great War – the totalitarianisation of the state – proceeded still further in Spain, setting up for Orwell the belief that Soviet Russia was essentially no different from Nazi Germany, and that Britain would itself have to become fascist if it were to take on Hitler. Yet the spirit of

[18] C. Isherwood, 1968: *Lions and Shadows*. London: Signet, 46.
[19] Quoted in P. Miles and M. Smith, 1987: *Cinema, Literature and Society between the Wars*. London: Croom Helm, 212.

the Great War remained with Orwell: 'the dead men had their revenge after all', so that when the war with Hitler finally broke out he knew he could not sabotage that effort as he had intended. His basic training in patriotism had finally triumphed now that England was once more in a mess, though there was at least a hope that the war against fascism would revolutionise Britain: a 'socialist could be built on the bones of a blimp' in a people's war.[20] Yet, for Orwell, a Labour victory at the polls might only lead to a more subtle form of totalitarianism, made even more sinister by the development of the A-bomb. Totalitarianism, it seemed, was an essential development of modern war, the core of the argument that Orwell was to develop in *Nineteen Eighty-Four*, an argument that had been brooding at the back of his mind ever since his alien-ation from imperialism in the days when the names of the dead old boys had been read out every Sunday in College Chapel.

Auden, Isherwood and Spender conjured the Old Men into a conspiracy of mythical proportions. The Mortmere fantasy, the private world into which Auden and Isherwood and their coterie could escape, elided themes of viol-ence, authority and sexuality explicitly opposed to the world of the Old Men and impenetrable in fact to virtually everyone outside the group. The rejec-tion of the pre-1914 codes that had made possible so much of the violence of the Great War proved difficult to replace, however, and as Europe proved once more threatened by conflict the Auden–Spender group lapsed into polit-ical muteness. The socialism that the 1930s poets so often proclaimed proved in most cases to be no more than skin deep, rarely surviving the decade, not so much a true commitment as a weapon in a generational dispute within a social class, rather than between classes. Auden was to christen the 1930s 'the low dis-honest decade': what he was describing, perhaps, were the frustrations and the sense of impotence of men of his background and generation who had been a little too young to fight the Great War and who had despised what the war had come to represent for them, and who could also now begin to see their early mature years as coinciding with a mere hiccup of history between two cata-strophic wars.

Victorianism was a dead system of values. It is noticeable how Lytton Strachey's *Eminent Victorians*, published in May 1918, only seventeen years after Victoria's death, seems to describe a world almost lost in the mists of history.[21] Yet there had at least been a sense of certainty about the pre-war world, even if those very certainties had contributed to the catastrophe. Compared with the overweening uncertainties, the sense of doom that pervaded inter-war cul-ture, pre-1914 was soon bathed in nostalgia. Vera Brittain, recalling a 1914 speech day at an English public school, the last before the men closest to her went off to be killed, remembered that 'roses with velvet petals shading from orange through pink to crimson foamed exuberantly over the lattice work of an old wooden trellis ... it was the one perfect summer idyll that I ever

[20] Orwell, My country right or left, op. cit. (note 17), 539.
[21] L. Strachey, 1918: *Eminent Victorians*. London: Chatto & Windus.

experienced, as well as my last care-free entertainment before the Flood.'[22] The 'summer of 1914' became a kind of tombstone of the pastoral tradition, the idea of England as Arcadia that was to be destroyed by the first of the machine wars, culturally formalised in the inversion of the pastoral tradition by the trench poets and the postwar modernists. The popularity of Rupert Brooke's poetry both during and after the war was almost solely a nostalgic reaction to the Arcadianism of Brooke's verse, a notion of England made elegaic by the knowledge that Brooke had died young. Orwell's George Bowling, returning to where he had grown up, found that a little village had turned into a town just like all the rest of the medium-sized suburbanised towns in Britain: 'Is it gone for ever? I'm not certain. But I tell you it was a good world to live in. I belong to it. So do you.' Bowling's return to his roots turns out to be a literally shattering experience as well, when the RAF drop a bomb on the town by mistake.[23] The future is dark and violent and the past is a green and peaceful land: the turning point is the Great War.

There is a basic paradox here, a rejection of the Old Men but a keen fondness for the world in which they had ruled. It was actually a paradox central to the popular appeal of the most successful politician of the postwar years, Stanley Baldwin. Baldwin looked around him in the postwar House of Commons and saw 'hard-faced men who looked as though they had done well out of the war'.[24] He rejected the pre-war Tory grandees such as Lords Birkenhead and Curzon. He also rejected the charismatic war leader Lloyd George in favour of quieter and more consensual politics. At the same time, his vision of England came straight out of Gray's 'Elegy', and he sold himself as a solid English squire, a link between the old England and the new.[25] This bridging strategy in Conservative political culture, linking tradition with modernity, was to be continued by Baldwin's Tory reform successors after the Second World War, and may have done much to cushion the shock of the new in politics and economics. Baldwin's popularity is instructive, because it reminds us that Britain survived the immediate impact of the Great War much more successfully than did the other major European belligerents. Ways of seeing the war as a massive historical discontinuity vied with other constructions which adapted traditional notions of national identity to what had happened.

The First World War and Popular Culture

Modernism was the preserve only of a few, after all, an artistic élite, alien to all but a minority. For the majority, the Great War was mediated in other ways. The mentally scarred veteran was not always the haunting victim of whom Orwell and Isherwood wrote. In popular literature, Lord Peter Wimsey did not

[22] Brittain, *Testament of Youth*, op. cit. (note 15), 90–1.
[23] G. Orwell, 1971: *Coming up for Air*. Harmondsworth: Penguin Books, 223–4. First published 1939.
[24] *See* M. Smith, 1990: *British Politics, Society and the State*. Basingstoke: Macmillan, 126–33.
[25] *See* S. Baldwin, 1938: *On England*. London: Hodder & Stoughton.

exactly dwell on his experiences. As in the case of Bulldog Drummond and Richard Hannay, the war if anything gave him added spiritual strength to set the world to rights. The 'popularity' of Siegfried Sassoon's memoirs must be set against the publishing success of Ernest Raymond's *Tell England*, the fictional story of two public-school boys who join up and go to the Dardanelles, a spiritual journey towards the supreme sacrifice at Cape Helles. There is not a hint of anti-war sentiment in the novel, which is a homo-erotic celebration of middle-class English youth.[26] The public-school story also survived in children's comics well into the post-Second World War period and was never aimed, of course, at public-school children themselves. The tradition of *Tom Brown's Schooldays* and *Stalky and Co.* easily survived the war in children's culture even if, as Orwell put it, the characters with whom lower-middle and working-class children were identifying were in fact the kind of 'monocled idiot who made good on the fields of Mons and Le Cateau'.[27] In the world of comics it was still 1910, and in the world of popular literature the sacrifice was a source of pride as well as a guarantee of maturity and moral righteousness in those who had survived the trenches.

Cinema also glided relatively happily between registering the horror of it all and celebrating the heroism and the patriotism. Cinema was not as important during this war as it was to become during Hitler's war. Nevertheless, it made a measurable impact as an area of mass entertainment for the first time in Britain between 1914 and 1918, moving from being simply a fairground attraction into being a serious medium. This period also saw the rise of the first great star of the cinema, Charlie Chaplin, whose little-man persona fitted snugly with the situation of the conscripted tommy. Not surprisingly, since Chaplin had emerged from the music hall of the Victorian and Edwardian periods, he took that tradition of humour with him to the United States, that heroism of the downtrodden that Gareth Stedman Jones has labelled 'the culture of consolation'. Stedman Jones implied that music-hall humour registered a non-combative class feeling, a 'keep-your-heads-down' stance that denoted the development of a stable class society in late Victorian Britain. In turn, the street-wise chirpy cockney sparrow could fairly easily be smartened up to become the sardonic soldier with his black humour and parody:[28]

> *Oh! the moon shone bright on Charlie Chaplin.*
> *His boots were cracking*
> *For want of blacking,*
> *And his baggy trousers needed mending*
> *Until they sent him to the Dardanelles.*

Documentary film also first made an impact during the war. *The Battle of the Somme* hardly showed that what was being depicted was actually 'the blackest

[26] E. Raymond, 1922: *Tell England.* London: Cassell.
[27] Miles and Smith, *Cinema, Literature and Society*, op. cit. (note 19), 77.
[28] G. Stedman Jones, 1974: Working class culture and working class politics. *Journal of Social History* 4, 99–115.

day in the history of the British army'. It showed, rather, cheery troops with hordes of prisoners, though at least it did show the mud and the shell-flattened landscape. It did at least dare to show an apparent death in action as well: ironically, however, the best-known shot in the film – that of a soldier falling back from the parapet as an attack begins – was actually the only shot of the whole film which is known to have been faked.[29]

But it was after the war, as cinema matured commercially, that film's real mediation of the war took place. The anti-war classics are well known: *Westfront* and *All Quiet on the Western Front*. Just as numerous, on the other hand, were the films that made only a passing stab at criticising the waste and then concentrated on the heroics: *The Big Parade*, *Hearts of the World*, *Four Horsemen of the Apocalypse* (which made a star of Rudolf Valentino) or *Hell's Angels*, to name a few. British films about the war were much less surefooted until very much later. Anthony Asquith's screen adaptation of the Ernest Raymond novel *Tell England* changed significantly the implications of the story. Where the original novel had decidedly heroicised the young officers and their sense of duty, the film was much more ambivalently poised about the value of the sacrifice. It was an arty film that spoke in arty, modernist terms about the war, and the public-school accents of the actors must have been quite impenetrable to many working-class audiences. *Journey's End*, transferred to the screen by Gainsborough Pictures in 1930, was described by the documentary film-maker Basil Wright as 'almost painfully English'.[30]

A problem here was that British sound cinema unmasked the arty middle-class accent, hitherto restricted to live theatre, to a lower-middle-class and working-class audience, no doubt confirming deep suspicions among these audiences about the relationship between art, social class and questionable values. American cinema had developed the commercial base during the war to expand into a world industry, but Hollywood had also developed a populist vocabulary to which Britain for one could not respond. Small wonder, then, that in the inter-war years the new cultural mandarins – the Leavises for instance – should rail against the way in which American popular culture, most obviously in cinema, had effectively invaded Britain.[31] It was another example of the increasing alienation between high culture and popular culture that the Great War had hastened. At the same time, modernism was also turning British experimental culture into something cosmopolitan and international. What remained, then, of a culture that could be described as specifically British?

Conclusion: The Invention of Tradition

In fact, culture was simply adapting, as it always does. Certainly, the pace of change had accelerated greatly because of the tensions caused by the war.

[29] S. D. Badsey, 1983: Battle of the Somme. *Historical Journal of Film, Radio and Television* 3, 99–115.
[30] L. Halliwell, 1977: *Film Guide*, 4th edition. London: Paladin, 753.
[31] Miles and Smith, *Cinema, Literature and Society*, op. cit. (note 19), part 2, ch. 1.

Nobody in Britain could realistically hope that the process which was turning the world into a global village could be stopped. Yet many of the changes themselves soon became part of British national identity, peculiar and unique. It was soldiers of the First World War who first established egg and chips as one of Britain's contributions to fast food. Over the past few years, pub licensing hours seem to have managed to survive the abolition of the legislation that created them in the First World War, in most parts of Britain at least, so deeply ingrained have opening hours become in cultural practice. Much that may have seemed strange and new in the immediate postwar period was to become 'traditional', something to be fought for between 1939 and 1945. 'Above all, it is your civilisation, it is you,' wrote George Orwell in 1942, 'the suet puddings and the red pillar boxes have entered your soul.'[32] How could this have been written in 1916, say, and taken seriously? The First World War marked a fundamental cultural disjuncture in British history, the beginning of a period that we can all recognise as being modern, as part of us rather than part of history. The monumentalisation of the war in the inter-war period helped to democratise its cultural legacy: its villains were to be the Kitcheners, the Haigs and the Old Men, while its heroes were to be the Unknown Soldiers, the lions who had been led by the donkeys. In art forms and in artists' political and social interests, the war both eased the path for modernism and called into question the strict masculine codes of the élite that had made the catastrophe possible. But modernism only expanded the gulf between 'high' and 'popular' culture, confirming a loss of cultural authority among the new generation the old élite had bred. New forms of internationalised popular culture, moreover, suggested that the previously sharp edges of British national identity might become fuzzy and blurred by transatlantic influences.

How ravishing, however, are those glimpses back into the prelapsarian world. The material shell both of Merrie England and of Imperial Britain still exists. The buildings are also still there in Moscow and Berlin, of course, but the Kremlin speaks of Stalin and the Reichstag speaks of Hitler. The Foreign Office and the Admiralty Arch speak of pre-1914, not pre-1939. The Cenotaph, as you walk up Whitehall, still speaks of three-quarters of a million smiling faces in brown photographs who died for an identity that has survived. And this identity is still sold successfully as heritage, because for most visitors from abroad London, Oxford, Cambridge and Stratford make Britain the one country in which you can still apparently see traditional culture unadulterated by the twentieth century. This is an image sedulously cultivated by Anglophiles: witness the extraordinary success of the Merchant–Ivory team, the Laura Ashley school of film-making, in reconstructing the world of E. M. Forster. The use of tobacco-shaded lenses and actors with names like Bonham Carter and Day Lewis suggest a British cultural tradition that no wars could ever truly break.

[32] G. Orwell: The lion and the unicorn. In Orwell and Angus, *Collected Journals*, op. cit. (note 17), vol. 2, 76.

8

The Armed Services

John Gooch

The Great War tested Britain's military institutions to a degree hitherto unparalleled. Total war involved the mass mobilisation of British society and resulted in the formation of field armies eventually numbering over 5 million men. The technological developments of the later nineteenth century produced new weapons such as the submarine, the tank and the aeroplane, completely transforming the nature of combat. Weapons and men had to be brought together to defeat the defensive strength of German trenches and machine-guns in the land war and the offensive power of U-boats in the war at sea. This necessitated the evolution of new tactical and operational methods. The war thus made great demands on the armed services and wrought great changes in them.

The central questions at issue here, therefore, are twofold. How well did each of the armed services respond to the challenges it faced? And what, if any, were the long-term effects of the experience of total war upon those services? These questions will be addressed by examining such issues as the size, composition, strategic purposes, equipment, training and leadership of the three services. Any assessment of the impact of the war necessarily entails some comparison between the pre-war and postwar situations of the armed forces and also some consideration of the trajectory of change in the pre-1914 world, before the military were faced with new, immediate and insistent pressures to which they had to respond.

The Pre-War Situation

The Victorian army had been designed to fight the 'brush-fire' wars of the Empire at as little cost as possible. It was more or less continuously in action throughout the nineteenth century, but only against opponents who were less well armed and less well organised. At the end of the century, however, the army gained a limited but invaluable insight into some of the characteristics of modern war. The Boer War (1899–1902) shocked it out of its comfortable complacency. In South Africa, Britain faced 'the longest, bloodiest and most expensive war fought by the late Victorian army'.[1]

In some respects the army responded well to the test: the mobilisation and dispatch of the first expeditionary corps of 30 000 went like clockwork, and although thereafter it became increasingly difficult to raise fresh drafts of men, the forces in the field (which eventually amounted to 448 435 men) were kept adequately supplied with ammunition, food, clothing and the like. However, severe deficiencies became apparent. The army was entirely unprepared for the 'invisible battlefield' created by smokeless powder and long-range rifles. 'I never saw a Boer', wrote Lord Methuen of his experience at the battle of Modder River (28 November 1899), 'but even at 2,000 yards when I rode a horse I had a hail of bullets round me.'[2] Modern quick-firing guns and ammunition of all sorts were initially in short supply, infantry fire was inaccurate and tactics were outdated. The casualties that resulted from trying to master the new battlefield using old ways were relatively heavy – 5774 men were killed and 16 168 died of wounds or disease during the war – but they were a pale shadow indeed compared to what was to come during the Great War.

The Russo-Japanese war, which followed almost immediately, confirmed all the features of modern warfare that had become apparent on the South African veldt, adding impetus to a movement to reform the army. The framework of reform was shaped both by external and by internal constraints. The external pressures of finance demanded that the army cost no more than £28 000 000 a year, and those of purpose that it be ready to fight almost anywhere. Aware that Continental-style military conscription was politically impossible, R. B. Haldane created a uniquely British 'nation in arms'.[3] The regular army was formed into six large divisions totalling 160 000 men. Behind the British Expeditionary Force (and a small Special Reserve) stood the Territorial Force, a voluntary army numbering a quarter of a million designed primarily for home defence. This structure was a distinct improvement on what had preceded it; but, only six years after its creation, the Great War overwhelmed it.

Internal constraints dictated that structural reform did not bring with it new tactical and operational doctrines which took adequate account of the defensive power of modern rifles and machine-guns. A combination of the traditional amateur approach and the values of the public schools, it has been argued, resulted in a reluctance to introduce basic changes. Behind

[1] Edward M. Spiers, 1992: *The Late Victorian Army, 1868–1902*. Manchester: Manchester University Press, 328.

[2] Thomas Pakenham, 1979: *The Boer War*. London: Weidenfeld & Nicolson, 195.

[3] For Haldane's military reforms, *see* John Gooch, 1981: *The Prospect of War: Studies in British Defence Policy 1847–1942*. London: Frank Cass, 92–115; John Gooch, 1981: Haldane and the 'national army'. In Ian Beckett and John Gooch (eds), *Politicians and Defence*. Manchester: Manchester University Press, 69–86; Edward M. Spiers, 1980: *Haldane: An Army Reformer*. Edinburgh: Edinburgh University Press; Edward M. Spiers, 1980; *The Army and Society, 1815–1914*. London: Longman, 265–87.

this lay 'a simple desire [among many officers] to perpetuate the privileges and attractions of the late Victorian and Edwardian army, with its pleasant life, social networks and amateur ideals.'[4] Likewise, notions that character and social background were the proper qualifications for a commission determined that the reserve of officers would be sought in the public schools and universities. The Officers' Training Corps, founded in 1908, provided over 2000 officers for the Territorial Force and the Special Reserves; in the Great War it was to do literally invaluable service, producing approximately 100 000 of the 230 000 officer candidates who were found to lead Britain's soldiers in battle.[5]

Although Haldane's army had not been designed with the single purpose in mind of fighting on the Continent against Germany and alongside France, this became the commanding scenario by 1910. Clear-cut plans to ship the British Expeditionary Force to France and bring it into line alongside the French were triggered by the German invasion of Belgium, whose integrity Britain was bound by treaty and by national interest to defend, on 4 August 1914.[6] The pre-war reorganisation had been tailored to a short war and a limited British commitment; when the war came, both these presumptions were quickly shattered.

Like the army, the Edwardian navy went through a period of reform before 1914. Although not based directly on the experience of war, naval reforms resembled military reform in one respect: major structural changes in the organisation of the fleet were introduced. In another respect they differed, for there was also a revolutionary reform in *matériel*.

In 1904, Sir John Fisher became First Sea Lord. Fisher's twin tasks were to reform and to economise, and he did both with boundless energy. Purpose shaped Fisher's reforms more directly than Haldane's, for the Royal Navy began to focus on Germany as Britain's most likely enemy in the year of Fisher's appointment. In the space of a very few years, the fleet was reorganised and relocated. Ships were pulled back from the China, North American and Caribbean stations and redistributed among the Channel, Atlantic and Mediterranean fleets. Old or unwanted ships were ruthlessly scrapped. This produced notable economies: naval estimates shrank from almost £37 millions in 1904–5 to under £32 millions in 1906–7 before rising again as the naval race with Germany heated up. The most eye-catching of Fisher's reforms

[4] Tim Travers, 1982: The hidden army: Structural problems in the British officer corps, 1900–1918. *Journal of Contemporary History* 17. (3), 538.
[5] Ian Worthington, 1982: Antecedent education and officer recruitment: An analysis of the public school–army nexus 1849–1908, Ph.D. thesis. University of Lancaster, 242–82.
[6] The best survey of British (and French) military planning is Samuel R. Williamson, Jr, 1969: *The Politics of Grand Strategy: Britain and France Prepare for War, 1904–1914*. Cambridge, Mass.: Harvard University Press. For the army's flirtation with Belgium, *see* William J. Philpott, 1989: The strategic ideas of Sir John French. *Journal of Strategic Studies* 12 (4), 458–78; and Keith Wilson, 1985: *The Policy of the Entente: Essays on the Determinants of British Foreign Policy, 1904–1914*. Cambridge: Cambridge University Press, 121–34.

was the introduction in 1905 of a new type of all big-gun, fast battleship: the *Dreadnought.*[7]

By contrast, Admiralty plans for a future war were for many years confused and unsettled. Fisher declared that the fleet should seek out the enemy, bring him to battle and fight for 'what is the only really decisive factor – the command of the sea'.[8] Increasingly aware that this vision was no substitute for a considered strategy, the Admiralty devised plans in the years before the war to land troops in the Netherlands or Denmark and to blockade the Elbe and bottle up the German High Seas Fleet. Neither scheme was particularly well thought out, chiefly because the navy yearned to fight a cataclysmic naval battle that would decide who commanded the seas.

Allowing for the constraints which acted upon them, both the army and the navy were in some respects well prepared for war in 1914. The technological base had equipped the navy with the world's largest modern fleet. If the army lacked howitzers and heavy guns, that was as much a reflection of its position as the junior service as of its expectations of a fast, mobile war. Nothing more could have been done to increase its size. The late development of high-level staffs – in the army in 1904 and in the navy only in 1911 – marked a distinct deficiency as compared to Continental practice, and reflected a tradition of pragmatism that was to prove a drawback in coming to terms with a war which rapidly took on a shape no one had expected.

The War and the Army

In 1914, Great Britain entered the war with a small regular army, reserves and territorials amounting in all to some quarter of a million men. All the other major participants at once mobilised conscript armies hundreds of thousands strong. The Liberal Government would not contemplate replicating them. It began the war on the basis of 'business as usual', refusing to abandon its attempts to stick as closely as possible to peacetime models of bureaucracy, *laissez-faire* and economic good housekeeping until the pressures of war forced it to change tack in May 1915.

The armed forces could not and did not attempt to follow suit. The army was forced not merely by the immediate circumstances of the war but also by contemplation of its likely future shape and extent not just to adapt but to undertake revolutionary change. Although pre-war plans had tended to assume a war lasting six months to a year, Kitchener had scarcely been Secretary of State for War for a week before he suggested that the conflict

[7] The Fisher reforms are best followed in R. F. Mackay, 1973: *Fisher of Kilverstone*. Oxford: Clarendon Press; Jon Sumida, 1989: *In Defence of Naval Supremacy: Finance, Technology, and British Naval Policy 1889–1914*. London: Unwin Hyman; and A. J. Marder, 1961: *From the Dreadnought to Scapa Flow*. Vol. I, *The Road to War*. Oxford: Oxford University Press.

[8] Quoted by Paul Haggie, 1979: The Royal Navy and war planning in the Fisher era. In Paul M. Kennedy (ed.), *The War Plans of the Great Powers 1880–191ʹ*. London: George Allen & Unwin, 121.

might last three years and talked of expanding the army from six to thirty divisions.[9] Eventually, in April 1916, the target settled at sixty-seven divisions. The process of expansion began long before any comprehensive national manpower policy was even considered, and continued throughout the war.[10] By November 1918, a pre-war army numbering less than 250 000 had swollen to absorb 5 704 416 men.

'Business as usual' meant, among other things, no conscription and so, on 7 August 1914, Kitchener called for 100 000 volunteers to man the first of his New Armies. The response was overwhelming, and there was a rush to the colours in August and September 1914: 30 000 enlisted in one day in September, more than had enlisted in the pre-war regular army in a year. At the end of the year the army had 1 186 357 new recruits.[11]

The social base of the pre-war rank and file had been a narrow one: the regular army had been in essence English, working-class and – at least professedly – Anglican. The social origins of the army now changed markedly. The rank and file of the New Armies came predominantly from the worlds of finance and commerce, the professions and entertainment; industrial, transport and agricultural workers were least strongly represented. Within industry, the lowest response came from textile and clothing workers.[12] There were equally wide regional variations in volunteering. Wales and Scotland produced more recruits in proportion to the size of their populations than did England; and in England the lowest enlistments were registered in the East Midlands and Yorkshire.[13]

One of the most striking features of this 'people's army' – which would have sad consequences when it was blooded on the Somme in July 1916 – was the extent to which it was locally recruited. A total of 115 'Pals' battalions were raised: Lancashire and Cheshire produced 24, Yorkshire and the North-East 15 each and 23 were found in London.[14] As these figures suggest, the untapped reserves of manpower lay in London and the industrial Midlands; the industrial North would raise almost one-third of the total number of service battalions.

The New Armies were a complete departure from tradition. However, existing military institutions were skilfully blended into the new nation-in-arms to

[9] David French, 1982: *British Economic and Strategic Planning, 1905–1915*. London: Allen & Unwin, 125.
[10] For an excellent account of the creation of Britain's first mass army, *see* Peter Simkins, 1988: *Kitchener's Army: The Raising of the New Armies, 1914–1916*. Manchester: Manchester University Press.
[11] Ian Beckett, 1985: The nation in arms, 1914–18. In Ian F. W. Beckett and Keith Simpson (eds), *A Nation in Arms: A Social Study of the British Army in the First World War*. Manchester: Manchester University Press, 7–9.
[12] *See* the table in J. M. Winter, 1977: Britain's lost generation of the First World War. *Population Studies* 31 (3), 454.
[13] Beckett, The nation in arms, op. cit. (note 11), 10.
[14] Clive Hughes, 1985: The new armies. In Beckett and Simpson, *A Nation in Arms: A Social Study of the British Army in the First World War*, op. cit. (note 11), 106.

fill the manpower gap until they could take the field. On 9 August 1914, Kitchener accepted for service overseas any Territorial unit volunteering *en bloc*, and in just over two weeks more than seventy battalions did so. By 1918, a total of 619 territorial battalions had been created, forming twenty-nine infantry and five mounted divisions, whereas the New Armies raised 557 battalions and formed thirty infantry divisions.[15] Thus the Haldane reforms contributed much to Britain's ability to sustain a war of unexpected dimensions until the new mass voluntary and conscript armies appeared.

Although the Asquith government had initially set its face against conscription, events during 1915 inexorably forced it towards a decision that many Liberals found unpalatable, smacking as it did of the very kind of militarist government against which Britain was fighting. The rate of volunteering began significantly to ebb, while the failure of the Dardanelles expedition and the generals' decision, taken in December 1915, to launch attacks on the Western Front with maximum force in 1916 and to wear down the Germans increased the military demand for manpower. Politically, too, the climate changed. Asquith's coalition Government of May 1915 included conscriptionists; and the activities of the compulsory service lobby, which included among its forces Lord Milner and the Beaverbrook press, increased.[16]

A survey carried out in August 1915 revealed that 2 179 231 single men of military age (18 to 40) were not yet in the armed forces. A scheme to persuade bachelors to register for future military service when needed failed to produce enough men, and on 5 January 1916 Asquith was forced to introduce conscription. Initially, it applied only to unmarried men and childless widowers aged between 18 and 41, but liberal exemptions, calls for genuine equality of sacrifice and demands for more soldiers forced Asquith to relinquish the last shreds of the voluntary tradition. On 25 May 1916, a new Military Service Act under which all men aged 18 to 41 were liable to serve received the royal assent.[17] This break with centuries of tradition did not unlock large supplies of military manpower, however, because of the large numbers of exemptions granted for other war work.

In August 1914, the regular and reserve officer corps amounted to 18 497 men. The vast expansion in the size of the army necessitated a proportionate increase in its numbers. High officer casualties increased this demand: in the

[15] Peter Simkins, 1981: 'Kitchener and the expansion of the army'. In Ian Beckett and John Gooch (eds), *Politicians and Defence*. Manchester: Manchester University Press, 98–9; Ian Beckett, 1985; The territorial force. In Beckett and Simpson, *A Nation in Arms: A Social Study of the British Army in the First World War*, op. cit. (note 11), 132.

[16] Asquith's domestic political dilemmas during this period are well analysed in John Turner, 1992: *British Politics and the Great War: Coalition and Conflict 1915–1918*. New Haven, Conn.: Yale University Press, 55–111.

[17] There were four grounds of exemption from conscription, of which conscience was one. The number of conscientious objectors to military service has been estimated as approximately 16 500, or 0.33 per cent of the total recruited voluntarily or by compulsion. *See* John Rae, 1970: *Conscience and Politics: The British Government and the Conscientious Objector to Military Service 1916–1919*. Oxford: Oxford University Press.

first three months of the war more than a quarter of the entire pre-war officer corps became casualties, and during the war as a whole an officer had a one in six chance of being killed and a one in three chance of being wounded. To meet the new requirements, the army tapped a recently established source in the shape of the Officers' Training Corps and, since demand still greatly outstripped supply, it was forced to the novel course of delving into the ranks of non-commissioned officers. As a result, a perceptible change had occurred in the class background of the officer corps as a whole by 1917. The lower-middle-class component was much larger, and whereas only 2 per cent of commissions had gone to rankers before the war, between 1914 and 1918 41 per cent did so.[18] In all, 229 316 combatant commissions were granted during the course of the war.

The trench warfare that characterised the Western Front between 1915 and 1918 was wholly unexpected and posed many problems for the army. The fact that the army had lost sight of some of the most important lessons of the South African war made them all the more difficult to solve. By 1910, pre-war reformers who had campaigned for the encouragement of initiative by subordinate officers, more flexible tactics and decentralised control of artillery had lost the battle to traditionalists who favoured restrictive controls and timetabled tactics.[19] On the eve of the Great War senior officers declared that the Boer War, with its impassable zones of fire, was not typical of modern war and that the Manchurian campaign had shown that bayonet fighting should not be relegated to the military dust-heap.[20] When, by Christmas 1914, the open war of movement which the generals had expected and for which they had planned had disappeared, they reverted to using dense formations of attacking troops and accepted that casualties would be heavy. In the latter respect at least they were correct.

Initially, the high command tried to break through the German lines by using established technology. Sir John French believed that, with enough ammunition, he could blast a way through, but the battles of Neuve Chapelle (10–13 March 1915), Second Ypres (22 April 1915) and Festubert (9 May 1915) showed that the task was beyond the capacities of his artillery. French's problems were partly due to the lack of appropriate weapons: his army had few heavy howitzers and mortars. This reflected inadequacies in the domestic industrial base: not until 1918 did the British Army have sufficient amounts of high-explosive ammunition and enough heavy guns and howitzers to break the German lines. The figures for British heavy guns and howitzers on the Western Front were as follows: in 1915, 3500; in 1916, 4500; in 1917, 6500; and in 1918, 10 700.

[18] Keith Simpson, 1981: The officers. In Beckett and Simpson, *A Nation in Arms: A Social Study of the British Army in the First World War*, op. cit. (note 11), 63–98.
[19] Martin Samuels, 1992: Command or control? Command, training and tactics in the German and British armies, 1864–1918. Ph.D. thesis, University of Manchester.
[20] Tim Travers, 1987: *The Killing Ground: The British Army, the Western Front and the Emergence of Modern Warfare, 1900–1918*. London: Allen & Unwin, 44–5.

Gradually, new technology and equipment came to play an increasingly important role in the war on the Western Front. Gas was first used by the British at Loos (25 September 1915), but was never a decisive weapon. Chemical manufacturing capacity was limited in every country except Germany, and problems in transporting and then using gas were compounded by the development of protective techniques.[21] By the summer of 1916 tanks had appeared on the Western Front, but they were few in number, vulnerable and capricious. Since infantry was still regarded as the queen of the battlefield, and artillery seen as her consort, tanks were used as auxiliary weapons. With the benefit of surprise, tanks made an important contribution during the first day of the battle of Cambrai (20 November 1917), but their losses were heavy and within a week the Germans recaptured all the ground they had lost and more. Unlike aeroplanes, whose technological characteristics changed rapidly during the war, tanks never developed sufficiently to play a truly major role in combat.

Deficiencies in the home manufacturing base were one of the most important brakes on the development and use of both old and new military technology. Volume manufacture of munitions posed problems that were not overcome until the last years of the war: thus a basic weapon of trench warfare, the no. 5 Mills bomb, although accepted into service in May 1915, was not universally available on the Western Front until well into 1917. Quality control, too, was a skill British industry took a long time to master: 30 per cent of the British shells fired during the battle of the Somme were duds.

The slow pace of development of new operational methods meant that new technological wine was often poured into old tactical bottles. Pre-war concepts of training, which concentrated on drill and physical training rather than preparing men to achieve specified objectives in battle, were not broken down until the last year of the war. Forms of training had been a matter for individual divisions to decide, and there was no common approach to the problem until Sir Ivor Maxse was appointed Inspector-General of Training in July 1918. Pre-war mechanisms for learning and innovation were limited and inappropriate, but no new ones replaced them. Until the last year or so of the war the army continued to think in the way it had done before 1914.

Command was no less important than technology and operational methods in shaping the effectiveness of Britain's citizen armies – and determining their fate. Sir Douglas Haig, commander-in-chief of the British armies in France from 1915 to 1918, was guided in all his planning by a rigid strategical design. His paradigm of the three-stage 'structured battle' – engage the enemy, wear him down, then launch the decisive attack – was one he had learned at the Staff College in 1896–7 and he clung tenaciously to it ever afterwards.[22] His operational method involved attacking on a wide front (perhaps 25 or 30 miles), using a mass of guns and lots of troops to wear down the enemy before

[21] Edward M. Spiers, 1986: *Chemical Warfare*. London: Macmillan, 13–33.
[22] Travers, *The Killing Ground*, op. cit. (note 20), 86–7.

sending in the reserves wherever weaknesses appeared.[23] Neither Haig nor his generals doubted that the exercise would be costly. A month before he launched the battle of the Somme, Haig warned that 'the nation must be prepared to see heavy casualty lists for what may appear to the uninitiated to be insufficient object and . . . unimportant results.'[24]

The Somme campaign was followed in 1917 by the equally horrific battle of Passchendaele. Together they probably cost the British armies a million casualties. They were Haig's battles, and they both expressed his strategic thinking and reflected his style of command. Rigid, determined, authoritarian and inflexible, the commander-in-chief would brook no strategic contradiction and heed no advice.[25] Haig's views were by no means shared by all his generals: Sir Henry Rawlinson, for example, favoured a less ambitious 'bite and hold' approach to the Somme battles, but was overruled by his commander-in-chief. Until September 1916, Haig personally appointed all senior commanders and thereafter he continued to exercise a dominating influence. His generals were made in his mould, not merely in appearance but also in outlook.[26]

In the last year of war, British operational methods changed. The shortage of manpower that was evident by January 1918 led Winston Churchill and others to argue that the weight of combat should be taken by the new technology. Haig was not convinced: 'Without sufficient and efficient infantry', he wrote in November 1917, 'machinery can neither win victory in offence, nor save us from defeat in defence.'[27] However, during the spring, key individuals, among them Rawlinson and Maxse, were converted to the primacy of 'mechanical means'. No less importantly, innovative junior commanders such as Maxse and Sir John Monash were training their men in flexible tactics and devolved command to build functionally effective forces.

In July 1918, after the German spring offensive finally ran down, Haig could take the offensive. Guns and high-explosive ammunition were now available in adequate supplies, as were tanks and aircraft. In July and August 1918, carefully prepared and co-ordinated infantry and tank attacks began to break up the German positions; then, between September and November, Haig reverted to traditional set-piece attacks with a heavy reliance on artillery – now much more sophisticated in its use of such techniques as sound-ranging and counter-battery fire. In new circumstances Haig became a flexible com-

[23] G. J. De Groot, 1988: *Douglas Haig 1861–1928*. London: Unwin Hyman, 201–2.
[24] Quoted ibid., p. 242.
[25] On this topic, in addition to the studies of Travers and De Groot (notes 20 and 23), *see* Gerard J. De Groot, 1986: Educated soldier or cavalry officer? Contradictions in the pre-1914 career of Douglas Haig. *War and Society* 4 (2), 51–69; Tim Travers, 1987: A particular style of command: Haig and GHQ, 1916–18. *Journal of Strategic Studies* 10 (3), 363–76.
[26] For a perceptive examination not merely of its subject but also of the weaknesses of the British style of command, *see* Robin Prior and Trevor Wilson, 1992: *Command on the Western Front: The Military Career of Sir Henry Rawlinson, 1914–1918*. Oxford: Blackwell.
[27] Tim Travers, 1992: *How the War was Won: Command and Technology in the British Army on the Western Front 1917–18*. London: Routledge, 37.

mander, accepting more readily the ideas of his senior generals; however, since he had always adopted the traditional 'hands off' view that army commanders should be left to run their own battles once strategy had been decided, this was a less revolutionary stance than it might appear.

The War and the Navy

Whereas the army's size and shape changed dramatically with the onset of war, and its pre-war conceptions of the nature of battle quickly unravelled, neither was the case with the senior service. No new weapons or platforms were introduced at sea to rival the tank and the aeroplane, although the challenge of the submarine had to be mastered, and naval dreams of battle were frustrated rather than destroyed.

The basic facts of strategic geography suggested that, if it were to break the distant blockade which was instituted as soon as war began, the German High Seas Fleet had no other choice but to challenge Britain's Grand Fleet. Only then could Germany break out into the world's sea lanes. Here the outcome of the pre-war naval arms race between the two powers appeared to give Great Britain a crucial advantage: in August 1914 Britain possessed twenty-four modern capital ships to Germany's sixteen.

The Royal Navy hoped and expected to settle the issue in a cataclysmic and decisive battle at sea in which battleships would play the starring role. Indeed, the commander of the Grand Fleet, Sir John Jellicoe, had been groomed by Fisher to play the latter-day Nelson. (In 1912, Fisher had written: 'If war comes before 1914 then Jellicoe will be Nelson at the Battle of St Vincent. If it comes in 1915 he will be Nelson at Trafalgar.')[28] The dominant desire for battle, which was deeply entrenched in the naval mind, was the product of a combination of factors. Captain A. T. Mahan's seminal book *The Influence of Sea Power upon History, 1660–1783*, published in 1890, had demonstrated that battle was the central act of naval war which conferred upon one side or the other the ability to command the sea. The battle of Tsushima in 1905 had witnessed the annihilation of the Russian fleet at the hands of the Japanese. And behind history and literature stood triumphal national experience in the shape of Nelson and Trafalgar. Everything seemed to point to a consummation for which every naval officer wished – and some, doubtless, prayed.

Although the navy's position relative to its opponent appeared to be a favourable one, and although in public it exuded calm and unruffled confidence, its supremacy was in certain important respects a fiction. British battleships and battle cruisers were less heavily armoured than their German opposite numbers and therefore more vulnerable. The Grand Fleet's mines, mine nets and mine-sweeping techniques were all deficient. Its torpedoes were

---

[28] Quoted by Correlli Barnett, 1975: *The Swordbearers: Supreme Command in the First World War.* Bloomington: Indiana University Press, 102.

weak and erratic. British naval boilers were larger, heavier and less efficient
than their German equivalents, and broke down with alarming frequency.
These technological and design deficiencies were the result, it has been
claimed, of the decline in British manufacturing industry which had already
begun.[29]

For a few months, surface warfare at sea resembled pre-war conceptions.
After defeating a weak British squadron at the battle of Coronel, von Spee's
squadron was destroyed at the battle of the Falkland Islands (8 December
1914). However, after three costly 'tip and run' raids on the North Sea coast,
designed to tempt out and destroy portions of the Grand Fleet, the German
navy took to its anchorages in January 1915 and did not venture forth again
until the spring of 1916, when a new commander, Admiral Scheer, began to lay
traps for the British fleet. The only major surface engagement of the war, the
battle of Jutland (30 May 1916), developed out of one such trap.

Arithmetically, the outcome of Jutland, during which the weaknesses of
British ship design and gunnery were vividly exposed, favoured the enemy: the
High Seas Fleet sank 111 980 tons of British shipping and inflicted 6945 casualties, and in exchange lost 62 233 tons of shipping and suffered 2921 casualties. Strategically, however, the battle confirmed that the larger British fleet
truly commanded the sea (or at least commanded its surface); conscious of its
numerical inferiority, the High Seas Fleet never again put to sea to challenge
its rival. The Grand Fleet spent the rest of the war waiting for the great battle
it had no means of bringing about.

While the navy could not revise, or even properly test, its operational and
tactical schemes for surface warfare, it proved reasonably adept at technological innovation. This should scarcely come as a surprise, for the naval environment had been one of continuous innovation since the 1840s.[30] Wireless
telegraphy had been introduced at the turn of the century, as much because
of the work of Admiral Sir Henry Jackson as of the better-publicised activities
of Marconi, and by 1914 the navy had developed significant capabilities in
wireless direction-finding and cryptanalysis of ciphered signals.[31] Within four
months of the outbreak of the war, the Admiralty had in its hands copies of all
three principal German wireless telegraphy codes and ciphers. They soon provided advance warnings of when the German fleet was putting to sea – though
not of where it was going – and of its last known location when it signalled at
sea. From January 1915, the last known daily positions of German U-boats
were also available; their actual positions could not be pinpointed, but daily
broadcasts transmitted during the first 200–300 miles of a cruise gave information on each boat's course and speed. The full fruits of this advantage were

[29] Ibid., 182–5.
[30] Karl Lautenschlager, 1983: Technology and the evolution of naval warfare. *International Security*
8 (2), 3–51.
[31] Nicholas Hiley, 1987: The strategic origins of Room 40. *Intelligence and National Security* 2 (2),
245–73; John Ferris, 1989: Before 'Room 40': The British Empire and signals intelligence,
1898–1914. *Journal of Strategic Studies* 12 (4), 431–57.

denied to the fleet at sea, however, by incompetent central direction in the shape of a lack of co-ordination within the Admiralty and between Whitehall and the fleet commander. At Jutland, a catalogue of errors denied Jellicoe crucial signals information that might have changed the outcome of the battle to his advantage.[32]

Technological innovation played a significant but secondary role in the navy's responses to the two German U-boat campaigns of 1915 and 1917–18. The submarine was scarcely 30 years old when the Great War began, and the Royal Navy had begun to include submarines in its naval exercises only a decade earlier. At that time it was assumed that they would take part in main fleet engagements, not that they would act independently against merchant shipping. The first German submarine campaign, unleashed on 4 February 1915, thus came as an unpleasant surprise but, fortunately for Great Britain, stiff neutral reaction forced Germany to drop the campaign in the summer of 1915. However, German submarines continued to operate against British shipping and, despite the code-breaking activities of Room 40, the Admiralty seemed able to do little to stop them. The conventionally aggressive operational concept of hunting down U-boats was an almost unredeemed failure: in one week in September 1916, three U-boats operating in the Channel sank thirty merchantmen while the area was being patrolled by 572 ships and a considerable number of aircraft.[33]

The second U-boat campaign began on 1 February 1917. The navy had no new weapon to counteract it, although technological innovation had produced the hydrophone in 1915: by 1917, eleven different types of directional and non-directional hydrophones had been developed and from March that year systematic training for specialist personnel made it an important component of the anti-submarine war. The 1915 campaign had also awoken the navy to the need for a new class of fast, small specialised craft for anti-submarine work, resulting in the construction of 'Flower'-class sloops. However, as with the land war, the solution lay not in developing a technological panacea but in devising new and more appropriate operational and tactical methods.

As part of an organisational shake-up of the Admiralty in December 1916, a new Anti-Submarine Division was established under Rear-Admiral A. L. Duff. Recognition of a special new problem in this way went a long step towards solving it – something the War Office never managed to achieve. After 17 April 1917, losses of merchant shipping mounted so rapidly that the navy faced a simple choice: attack the German submarines, an action which offered little hope of success, or defend the merchantmen. Convoying merchant shipping, a technique that went back to Tudor times, seemed an impossible option until analysis of the 2500 sailings a week from British ports revealed that only 120–140 involved ocean-going ships. With a threat thus converted into an

[32] *See* Patrick Beesly, 1984: *Room 40: British Naval Intelligence 1914–1918.* Oxford: Oxford University Press.
[33] Paul M. Kennedy, 1988: Britain in the First World War. In Allan R. Millett and Williamson Murray (eds), *Military Effectiveness,* vol. 1. Boston and London: Allen & Unwin, 58.

opportunity, the Admiralty showed its fundamental flexibility: an experimental convoy sailed from Gibraltar on 10 May 1917, lost no ships, and demonstrated to sceptical naval officers that merchant skippers could keep their ships in station. Although the turning-point in the submarine war did not technically come until July 1918, when the tonnage of new shipping exceeded that sunk, and although much work remained to be done in developing such techniques as air–sea collaboration, the outcome of the war at sea was no longer in doubt.[34]

From August 1914 to November 1918, the everyday naval war against Germany involved enforcing the blockade. By November 1914 it was in place, and between March 1915 and November 1916 the Northern Patrol intercepted on average 286 vessels every month.[35] To tighten the pressure on Germany, Britain first redefined 'absolute' and 'conditional' contraband and then, in 1915, effectively dissolved the distinction between them. By the end of 1916, Britain was rationing imports into neutral countries to prevent their possibly making their way to the enemy. At this stage, and much to the Admiralty's annoyance, the blockade could not be fully enforced for fear of adversely affecting American neutrality. After April 1917, however, supplies of foodstuffs, oil and metals to neutral countries were cut, with some knock-on effects on the German war effort.

Blockade was acknowledged to be a slow-acting weapon, although before the war many had claimed that its effects might be decisive. Its real contribution to the war was both indirect and ancillary. Until 1917, indirect trade and direct supply from neutral countries provided Germany with foodstuffs, metals and raw materials; and the collapse of Romania in 1916 gave Germany oil and grain. Cuts in exports released products to the domestic market, and throughout the war German industrial ingenuity in the shape of *ersatz* (substitute) products and intensive exploitation of available resources helped keep up supplies to both the home and the fighting fronts. Germany's economic decline between 1914 and 1918 was caused not by the blockade but by the excessive demands placed upon the economy by the war as a whole.[36] In four years Germany was drained of food, manpower and industrial resources by a combination of its own and its opponents' military actions. 'Blockade alone was not sufficient to defeat her.'[37]

Neither Jellicoe nor Beatty imposed a style of command and a strategic conception on the navy to rival that of Haig. This was partly a matter of structure: with different commands responsible for different facets of the sea war, and the Admiralty functioning as a provider of resources rather than the central executive authority, no one directed all operations at sea in quite the same

[34] John Terraine, 1989: *Business in Great Waters: The U-boat Wars 1916–1945*. London: Leo Cooper, 40–150; Stephen Roskill, 1970: *Hankey: Man of Secrets*, vol. 1. London: Collins, 355–8, 381.

[35] Arthur J. Marder, 1966: *From the Dreadnought to Scapa Flow*, vol. II. Oxford: Oxford University Press, 373.

[36] Gerd Hardach, 1977: *The First World War*. London: Allen Lane, 34.

[37] Avner Offer, 1989: *The First World War: An Agrarian Interpretation*. Oxford: Clarendon Press, 76.

way. Partly, too, it reflected the naval tradition that the captain commanded his ship and the admiral commanded his station. In other words, the flexibility inherent in the navy as an organisation enabled it to adapt to new circumstances more easily than could the army.

War and the Air Force

The First World War saw the birth of a new arm which grew from infancy to maturity in the space of only four years. Powered flight in England was only four years old when the Royal Flying Corps was established in 1912.[38] In August 1914, Britain's air forces, which included the Royal Naval Air Service as well as the Royal Flying Corps (RFC), possessed 113 first-line aircraft and fewer than 250 officers; by November 1918, the Royal Air Force comprised 3330 first-line aircraft and over 30 000 officers.[39] With no pre-war doctrines or plans to confine it, the air force was in a position to experiment more freely and respond more readily to the military environment it faced. On the other hand, its performance was more directly constrained by industrial factors than was that of either of the other two services.

In August 1914, the RFC sent forty-eight aeroplanes to France. Their initial task was reconnaissance, but they soon also found themselves acting as observers spotting enemy batteries for British artillery. The German air force in its turn began to engage in reconnaissance and bombing missions, and the result was the appearance of aerial combat for the first time early in 1915. Thus, in little less than a year, the fledgling arm had adopted three different but related operational roles. Unlike the army and the navy, however, it had no independent strategic purpose and would not begin to develop one until the last months of the war. These two facts made the air force both flexible and adaptive, while also making it politically vulnerable until it could free itself from the embrace of the older services.

Because aeroplanes were at the start of their cycle of development, their characteristics – and therefore their combat capabilities – changed rapidly during the Great War. Thus a service which was the product of technological innovation developed under the Darwinian stimulus of evolution or destruction. At first both sides used rifles and revolvers in air combat, but in July 1915 a machine-gun was mounted on the top wing of a biplane. In October 1915, Fokker produced a fighter with a synchronised machine-gun that fired through the blades of the propeller, and for the next nine months the tactical

[38] For the prehistory of Britain's war in the air, *see* Alfred Gollin, 1989: *The Impact of Air Power on the British People and Their Government, 1909–14*. London: Macmillan; D. E. H. Edgerton, 1991: *England and the Aeroplane: An Essay on a Militant and Technological Nation*. London: Macmillan; Michael Paris, 1992: *Winged Warfare: The Literature and Theory of Aerial Warfare in Britain 1859–1917*. Manchester: Manchester University Press.

[39] Walter Raleigh, 1922: *The War in the Air*, vol. I. Oxford: Clarendon Press, 5; J. C. King, 1972: *The First World War*. London: Macmillan, 182.

advantage in the air lay with the Germans. Then, in the summer of 1916, the appearance of faster and more manoeuvrable planes such as the De Havilland DH2 and the Sopwith Camel shifted air superiority back to Britain and France. Between September 1916 and May 1917 the aerial balance swung back to the Germans, partly as a result of the introduction of new aircraft types, especially the two-gun Albatross D. As late as August 1918, when Allied production meant that they were numerically overwhelmed, the Germans were still able to inflict heavy losses on the RAF because of the virtues of their new Fokker D VII fighter.

As these facts suggest, the air force was more heavily dependent on the strengths of the home industrial base for success or failure in carrying out its missions than either of the older services. Several features combined to retard its technological development. One was the fact that industrial advantage lay with the Germans, who had a better-developed aero-engine industry and had enjoyed a near monopoly on the manufacture of magnetos before the war. As a result, and for most of the war, German planes were more highly powered than British machines. Up to 1916, Britain depended on French production for aeroplanes; after that its own aero industry expanded, although not at the rate the government had estimated. British aircraft production figures were as follows: for 1915, 2500; for 1916, 6600; for 1917, 14 800; and for 1918, 30 000 planes. Another problem was the lack of vital materials, particularly high-grade steel and ball-bearings. A third was that it took over two years to resolve the conflict as to who should be responsible for aircraft production: in December 1916 the Ministry of Munitions got the job, and thereafter aeroplanes were in competition with the tank programme.

As in every other area of its existence, the air force had to develop its tactics as it went along. Between November 1915 and June 1916, the RFC lost an average of one plane a day while carrying out observation and reconnaissance duties. This led it to develop escorts for reconnaissance flights and close-formation flying as means of protection.[40] Under Sir Hugh Trenchard's direction, it then adopted an aggressive new operational tactic of deep patrols into enemy air space rather than close protection. This was a costly venture, but the local air superiority it provided gave direct help to the troops on the ground as well as instilling a sense of defencelessness into the German infantry.[41] In 1917 and 1918, new techniques of close support and counter-battery work were developed, but again the human costs were high: low-level attacks on German ground forces during the battle of Cambrai (November 1917) resulted in 30 per cent losses a day. The most striking tactical innovation of the

[40] For a good description of these developments, *see* Lee Kennett, 1991: *The First Air War.* New York: The Free Press. The high command and air policy are examined by Malcolm Cooper, 1986: *The Birth of Independent Air Power.* London: Allen & Unwin.
[41] H. A. Jones, 1928: *The War in the Air,* vol. II. Oxford: Clarendon Press, 235, 251. The direct help provided included aerial photography, reporting on the condition of barbed wire and trenches and co-operating with artillery.

air war – the 'circus', in which mobile groups of air aces fought together rather than operating as lone killers – came from the Germans.

Pilots and publicists combined to present the air war as glamorous and chivalric, but in reality it was a war of attrition just like the war on the ground. In proportion to the numbers involved, the rates of loss were in fact higher. Trenchard's deep patrolling was costly – 141 pilots were killed or went missing during the battle of the Somme, four times the German rate of loss – and close-support and counter-battery work cost the RFC some 200 pilots a month between June and November 1917. Loss rates mounted until the end of the war: the heaviest monthly toll came in September 1918 (235 aircraft lost). Training was even more lethal than combat: between 1914 and 1918 some 8000 pilots died in training, while 6166 were killed in action. On occasion these rates outpaced the training schools' capacity to produce replacements. Nevertheless, unlike the French and Germans, the British insisted that all pilots must be officers – a reflection of social constraints on change which the army had no choice but to relax.

Although the fighting on the Western Front dominated the air war, the first steps towards strategic bombing were taken during the Great War. In the winter and spring of 1914–15, units of the Royal Naval Air Service and the RFC bombed Zeppelin sheds and German fleet anchorages. Technological limitations meant that these early forays did little damage: bombs were small (20 lb. in 1914 and 250 lb. in 1917–18), partly because aeroplanes were small, and a sophisticated bomb-sight did not become available until 1916.[42] Four raids on English cities by German Gotha bombers between 27 May and 7 July 1917 gave the first clear indication of the potentialities of strategic air power.[43] The consequence of this glimpse into an unpleasant but seemingly inescapable future was the creation of the Independent Air Force in May 1918. Its task was to carry out strategic bombing of Germany, but it had little to boast about when the war ended: it had dropped only 543 tons of bombs at a cost of 109 bombers missing and 243 wrecked. Its commandant, Trenchard (who, ironically, became the high priest of strategic bombing between the wars), viewed it at the time as a 'gigantic waste of effort and personnel'.[44]

Officers who rise to the highest levels of command are commonly forceful and frequently opinionated. The traditions of the service through which they climb, and the school of thought which predominates within it, erode many idiosyncrasies to produce a commonality of attitude and outlook. Coming from the other two services, air force officers had nothing much in common except their interest in aviation – indeed, they were not even members of a separate service until the Royal Air Force came into being on 1 April 1918. Thus, they disagreed as frequently with one another as with outsiders.

[42] Neville Jones, 1973: *The Origins of Strategic Bombing: A Study of the Development of British Air Strategic Thought and Practice up to 1918.* London: William Kimber.
[43] John Sweetman, 1981: The Smuts Report of 1917: Merely political window dressing? *Journal of Strategic Studies* 4 (2), 164–5.
[44] Cooper, *The Birth of Independent Air Power*, op. cit. (note 40), 136.

Throughout the war, deep tensions existed between operational commanders at the front and the high command in London, as each party fought for authority, and between the high command and its civilian ministers, who were disinclined to pay the airmen's views the attention they thought was warranted. Personality clashes inside the service were deep and long-lasting.[45] It is difficult to assess the exact effect of such volatility on the overall performance of the air force – it may perhaps have encouraged flexibility and adaptiveness – but the perturbations among the leadership of the army and the navy were certainly less marked.

Postwar Developments and Conclusions

The war ceased on 11 November 1918, when the terms of the Allied armistice came into force. Conscription was maintained until 30 April 1920 in order to meet the many demands on the services, and particularly upon the army, in the immediate postwar period. In November 1918 the army numbered 3 779 825 and twelve months later its strength was 888 952 (of whom 126 693 had been recruited during 1919).[46] Thereafter it soon reverted to its pre-war size: by 1922, it numbered 231 062 men.

The immediate function of the army was to provide occupation forces in Germany and Turkey, to suppress insurgencies in Ireland, Mesopotamia, Iraq and Persia, and to fight against the Bolsheviks on behalf of the White Russians. It also faced the prospect of domestic violence: for some months, intelligence agencies covertly observed the activities of the ex-servicemen's organisations which were springing into existence as likely hotbeds of revolution.[47] No signs of the bacillus were discovered, but the authorities remained wary of unrest: in January 1920, the Chief of the Imperial General Staff was working on a scheme 'in the event of Soviet Government at Liverpool'.[48] The creation of the British Legion in 1921 neutralised the veterans' movements, by which time most of the other immediate military obligations had been liquidated in various ways. Thereafter the army reverted to its pre-1900 role as an imperial police force, believing that war with Germany was 'unique' and that India would be the scene of future fighting. Not until 1932 was a committee set up to study the findings of the army's official history of the Great War, volumes of which were appearing slowly.[49]

[45] Malcolm Cooper, 1980: A house divided: Policy, rivalry and administration in Britain's military air command, 1914–1918. *Journal of Strategic Studies* 3 (2), 178–201.

[46] Keith Jeffrey, 1985: The post-war army. In Beckett and Simpson, *A Nation in Arms: A Social Study of the British Army in the First World War*, op. cit. (note 11), 212–14.

[47] Stephen R. Ward, 1973: Intelligence surveillance of British ex-servicemen, 1918–1920. *Historical Journal* 16 (1), 179–88.

[48] Keith Jeffrey, 1984: *The British Army and the Crisis of Empire, 1918–1922.* Manchester: Manchester University Press, 27–8.

[49] The army of the 1920s is expertly depicted by Brian Bond, 1980: *British Military Policy between the Two World Wars.* Oxford: Clarendon Press, 35–71.

In terms of recruitment, too, the inter-war army soon resembled its pre-1914 predecessor. The geographical composition of the rank and file changed in one respect when Irish recruiting was suspended in December 1921; otherwise it looked much as it had before the war. The difficulty of attracting men with technical or mechanical qualifications seems likewise to have been just as great after the war as before it, as shown by Table 8.1.[50] The officer corps, discarding its 'temporary gentlemen', was composed largely of wartime regulars who had perforce to lose several steps in rank; in 1920 the future Field Marshal Lord Wavell was demoted to major from brigadier-general, a rank it took him ten years to regain. The wartime generation dominated the higher reaches of the army throughout the 1920s and well into the 1930s, with the result that a generation was kept waiting, probably to the general detriment of the service.

The manner in which the battles of 1918 had been won meant that, in terms of equipment, the army stagnated. Artillery had apparently proved its claim to be the primary support of the infantry, and tanks had not played a major role in defeating the German Army. Nor would they be of much value in India. Large stocks of wartime guns (some of which were gratefully retrieved from store in 1939) obviated the need to spend money on fresh equipment. The apostles of mechanised war remained an embattled minority during the inter-war years as the cavalry resumed its rightful place: on horseback.

The army was propelled backwards to an Edwardian shape and a Victorian function by a combination of external and internal constraints. From without, the stiff pressure to cut public expenditure joined forces with a diplomatic retreat from Europe – the League of Nations and Locarno notwithstanding.

Table 8.1   Composition of the Brigade of Guards, November 1920

Occupation	Number
Unskilled labour	1787
Agriculture	261
Engineering	459
Crafts	391
Building trades	181
Food trades	180
Labourers, carters, porters	53
Commercial	214
Servants	95
Miners	304
Various	1500

[50] Combat monograph of Great Britain, 17 March 1921. RG 165 Box 636/2017-428. National Archives, Washington, DC. Analysis based on nine of the ten battalions.

Public opinion became increasingly opposed to war in general and the army in particular as some writers and poets developed the proposition that the Great War had been nothing but a huge and purposeless blood-letting.[51]

The navy, unlike the army, confronted strong international competition after the war just as it had done before 1914 (although the German fleet was now removed from the lists). Faced with much enlarged American, French and Japanese fleets, and claiming the historic need to maintain supremacy over any likely combination of rivals, it sought in 1919 to retain thirty-three battleships, sixty-eight cruisers and 352 destroyers.[52] In taking this position, the navy was regressing to the position it had occupied before Anglo-German naval rivalry concentrated its attentions in one direction, although the basic principle was much the same.

As far as *matériel* was concerned, wartime experience suggested that both the aeroplane and the submarine had raised question marks over the supremacy of the battleship. In the immediate post-war years, construction policy and naval doctrine were reviewed in the light of experience, but the navy harked back to tradition. Although it recommended the construction of two types of aircraft carrier, the Admiralty did not believe that aircraft showed any signs of rendering the capital ship obsolete; it held firmly to the view that the development of the aeroplane had not altered the fundamental principles of naval strategy, since ship-borne and land-based aircraft alike had only a short range and could therefore have little effect on capital ships.[53] Indeed, the navy wanted to build larger battleships of 43 000 tons armed with fifteen-inch guns.

In the event, while internal factors determined the shape of the Royal Navy, external constraints determined its size. Treasury pressure halved the naval budget in 1919–20 (from £334 millions to £157 millions), and halved it again the following year (to £84 millions).[54] No less important were international pressures to control any post-war naval arms race, in which Britain faced the challenge of the United States. At the Washington Conference (1921–2), Britain accepted a relationship in capital ship tonnage with the United States and Japan of 5:5:3, a maximum size limit of 35 000 tons and a ten-year building 'holiday', along with upper limits on cruisers of 10 000 tons and eight-inch guns.[55] In all the excitement over battleships, convoying was forgotten; it had to be rediscovered in 1939.

After the war ended, it seemed briefly as though the Royal Air Force might go out of existence as an independent arm. Its future role was far from clear, and it had to fight with the two other services for a share of a peacetime

[51] *See* Paul Fussell, 1975: *The Great War and Modern Memory*, Oxford: Oxford University Press; Samuel Hynes, 1990: *A War Imagined: The First World War and English Culture*. London: The Bodley Head; Modris Eksteins, 1990: *Rites of Spring: The Great War and the Birth of the Modern Age*. London: Black Swan.

[52] Stephen Roskill, 1968: *Naval Policy between the Wars*, vol. 1. London: Collins, 104.

[53] Lecture by Captain C. J. C. Little, Naval bases and sea Power, 18 October 1928. RG 165 Box 925/2124-101/1. National Archives, Washington, DC.

[54] Christopher Hall, 1987: *Britain, America and Arms Control 1921–37*. London: Macmillan, 21–2.

[55] Roskill, *Naval Policy*, op. cit. (note 52), 300–30.

budget which the Treasury determined should be no greater than that of 1914, with allowance for inflation. Three could not live as cheaply as two, and in the early 1920s a bitter struggle went on, chiefly between Beatty and Trenchard, in which the stake was the RAF's very being. Several factors determined the outcome – though none had very much directly to do with the war that had just been fought.

Trenchard proved a shrewd, skilful and sometimes brutal political in-fighter. He was able to take advantage of a situation in which spiralling defence costs had to be drastically cut, while at the same time a troublesome Empire had to be policed. In 1919, the RAF ran down the 'Mad Mullah of Somaliland', who had been evading capture since before 1914, in three weeks; and in 1921 it took over responsibility for subduing the rebellion in Iraq, cutting costs in the process from £32 000 000 in 1920–1 to only £1 648 000 by 1927–8.[56] Almost immediately, the threat apparently presented by the French air force allowed Trenchard to devise and develop the notion of a bomber deterrent as the cheapest and most effective military agent of Britain's European diplomacy.[57]

Unlike the other two services, the RAF could take advantage of the external constraints that restrained both its rivals. Embracing the restrictive financial environment, it could offer cheaper defence than they could. The aeroplane could meet the needs both of a revived (indeed, expanded) imperial commitment and of defence against threats from Europe. And as an instrument of deterrence, the bomber met the wishes of all those whose heartfelt cry was 'Never again'. At the same time, the RAF was free from the powerful internal constraint of *idées fixes* which did so much to shape the outlook of the other services. Thus, while the army forgot the Great War and the navy ignored those aspects of it which did not fit its innermost convictions, the air force alone looked forward and built a strategic doctrine of strategic bombing based upon the slenderest of wartime experiences. It is not easy to say which service deluded itself the most.

[56] David Killingray, 1984: 'A swift agent of colonial government': air power in British colonial Africa, 1916–1939. *Journal of African History* 25 (4), 429–44; Jaffna L. Cox, 1985: A splendid training ground: The importance to the Royal Air Force of its role in Iraq, 1919–1932. *Journal of Imperial and Commonwealth History* 13 (2), 157–84; David E. Omissi, 1990: *Air power and Colonial Control: The Royal Air Force, 1919–1939*. Manchester: Manchester University Press.

[57] John Ferris, 1987: The theory of a 'French air menace', Anglo-French relations and the British home defence air force programmes of 1921–1925. *Journal of Strategic Studies* 10 (1), 62–83.

9

Foreign Policy

Ruth Henig

The aim of this chapter is to assess the impact of the First World War both on the main objectives of British foreign policy and on the means by which it was conducted. As is true of other areas of British policy, the overall impact of the Great War is difficult to measure because of its wide-ranging and often contradictory effects. In some areas, the war accelerated trends that were already emerging before 1914, such as the growing financial, commercial and naval challenges to Britain of the United States of America and Japan. Yet at the same time the war removed other dangerous threats to the British Empire, through the defeat of Germany and the destruction, for the time being, of its naval power, and the collapse of the Russian Empire. The later stages of the war saw the rise of new challenges to Britain and its Empire, in the shape of Bolshevism and of Wilsonian diplomacy with its emphasis on self-determination, anticolonialism and a League of Nations. Yet at the same time, as the final chapter will show, there was the prospect after the war of closer imperial ties and a more systematic exploitation of the resources of the great British Empire.[1]

The chapter will start by looking at the aims of British foreign policy before 1914 and at the British Government's increasing difficulties in achieving them. As we shall see, mounting challenges to Britain's position as the world's leading industrial and imperial power, and to its naval supremacy, brought about a significant change in the direction of British foreign policy and contributed to the outbreak of war in 1914. The chapter will seek to assess the extent to which involvement in the First World War posed new challenges to British foreign policy, through the conclusion of secret agreements and treaties, the entry into the war of the United States, and the Bolshevik revolution in Russia. The economic cost of waging the war – a staggering £7 million per day by 1917 – also had repercussions for foreign policy. Since most of the

---

[1] For different perspectives on the impact of the First World War on Britain's position as a world power, *see* D. Reynolds, 1991: *Britannia Overruled: British Policy and World Power in the Twentieth Century*. London: Longman; P. Kennedy, 1976: *The Rise and Fall of British Naval Mastery*. London: Allen Lane: C. Barnett, 1972: *The Collapse of British Power*. London: Eyre Methuen.

money came in the shape of loans from American East Coast bankers, Britain owed the United States some £850 million plus accumulated interest by the end of the war.[2] The need to secure vital war supplies and finance from the United States was a crucial element in shaping British foreign policy during the war, and the repayment of war debts in the 1920s became a contentious issue in postwar Anglo-American relations.[3]

Just as British policy makers were preparing for the most complex peace conference the world had ever seen, they faced a variety of foreign policy dilemmas at a time when the country's capacity to deal with them had been weakened by a range of economic, political and psychological factors. The final section of the chapter will look at the ways in which successive governments sought to deal with the problems bequeathed by the war, and at the extent to which prewar policy aims continued to be pursued after 1919. It will also attempt to assess the strength and impact of popular pressures both on the shaping of foreign policy objectives and on the means through which they were carried out.

There is no doubt that popular pressures had an important influence on foreign policy in the inter-war period. Indeed, it could be argued that the most significant effect of the war on Britain was its psychological impact, both in terms of the enormous numbers of combatants killed and wounded, and as a result of new weapons of war, such as the aeroplane and the submarine, which could unleash direct attacks on a defenceless civilian population.[4] The passing of the 1918 Representation of the People Act gave the British public a strong electoral voice that could not be ignored by politicians. The resolve that fathers, husbands and sons should not have died in vain, that the Great War should be the 'war to end all wars', and that disarmament and the new League diplomacy must be vigorously pursued to prevent such a calamity from occurring again had a very considerable impact on British foreign policy in the years after 1919.[5]

Britain as a World Power before 1914

In the later nineteenth century, Britain was unquestionably the world's greatest power: the dominant sea power, the leading colonial power and the

---

[2] Kennedy, *The Rise and Fall of British Naval Mastery*, op. cit. (note 1), 308; A. J. P. Taylor, 1965: *English History, 1914–45*. London: Oxford University Press, 123.

[3] K. Burk, 1985: *Britain, America and the Sinews of War, 1914–18*. London: Allen & Unwin; S. Tillman, 1961: *Anglo-American Relations at the Peace Conference*. Princeton, NJ: Princeton University Press. *See also* W. N. Medlicott, D. Dakin and M. E. Lambert (eds), 1968: *Documents on British Foreign Policy 1919–39*, series Ia, vol. II. London: HMSO.

[4] It is estimated that over 6 per cent of Britain's male population between the ages of 15 and 49 were killed, or, on another calculation, 9 per cent of all males under 45. In addition, 1.6 million men were injured, many of them permanently disabled. *See* Reynolds. *Britannia Overruled*, op. cit. (note 1), 105 and Kennedy, *The Rise and Fall of British Naval Mastery*, op. cit. (note 1), 307.

[5] *See*, for example, R. B. McCallum, 1944: *Public Opinion and the Last Peace*. Oxford: Oxford University Press; M. Ceadel, 1980: *Pacifism in Britain, 1914–45: The Defining of a Faith*. Oxford: Oxford University Press; P. Kyba, 1983: *Covenants without the Sword: Public Opinion and British Defence Policy, 1931–5*. Waterloo, Ontario: Wilfred Laurier University Press.

world's industrial giant. In the 1860s, Britain, with 2 per cent of the world's population, 'was generating about one fifth of Europe's gross national product, producing half the world's iron and steel, and accounting for 40% of world trade in manufacturing goods.'[6] In the last thirty years of the nineteenth century, the British Empire increased in size by nearly 5 million square miles and in population by some 88 millions. In 1900, it covered one-fifth of the globe and governed some 400 million subjects. In 1883, the Royal Navy possessed thirty-eight battleships and the rest of the world forty.[7]

Inevitably, having established a position of such emphatic global supremacy, British governments sought to protect it. Foreign policy aims were therefore defensive: to preserve naval supremacy, to seek to resolve conflicts and potential challenges to British power through peaceful means, to promote and to extend free trade across the globe and to protect British shores through the exercise of diplomacy geared to ensuring that no single power built up a position of military dominance in western or central Europe.

But the last two decades of the nineteenth century brought a growing number of challenges to Britain's pre-eminence. The spread of the industrial revolution and particularly of the railway enabled other countries to modernise and to begin to compete industrially with Britain. A second revolution, this time scientific and technological, was harnessed much more effectively in the United States and in Germany than it was in Britain, though in some fields, such as cable technology, Britain retained its dominance until after the First World War.[8] However, in steel production, Britain was overtaken first by the United States and then by Germany. By 1913, Britain was producing only a quarter of the steel output of the United States and barely half that of Germany, and was now only the world's third biggest producer of manufactured goods behind these two competitors.[9] Despite the mounting cost of military technology, an increasing number of powers aspired to build up modern armaments, including battle fleets. By 1897, the Royal Navy's sixty-two battleships were being challenged by a combined Franco-Russian total of fifty-four, and had also to take into account the naval expansion of Germany, Japan, the United States and Italy. Britain's traditional naval measure of security, the 'two-power standard', whereby the Royal Navy should be at least as strong as the size of the next two largest fleets combined, was coming under serious threat.[10]

The full extent of Britain's world-wide interests was increasingly difficult to protect, in the face of such growing competition. From the turn of the century,

---

[6] Reynolds, *Britannia Overruled*, op. cit. (note 1), 9.
[7] R. Hyam, 1976: *Britain's Imperial Century, 1815–1914*. London: Batsford; Kennedy, *The Rise and Fall of British Naval Mastery*, op. cit. (note 1), 247.
[8] For a detailed examination of the evolution of cable technology, *see* D. Headrick, 1991. *The Invisible Weapon: Telecommunications and International Politics, 1851–1945*. Oxford: Oxford University Press.
[9] Reynolds, *Britannia Overruled*, op. cit. (note 1), 82–3: Barnett, *The Collapse of British Power*, op. cit. (note 1), 84.
[10] Kennedy, *The Rise and Fall of British Naval Power*, op. cit. (note 1), 247.

Britain faced the prospect of an increasingly vulnerable world empire, scattered as it was across the globe, and the mounting cost of protecting vital sea communications, supply bases and trade routes. By 1902, Joseph Chamberlain was not exaggerating too greatly when he gave his famous description of the British Empire as a 'weary Titan staggering under the too vast orb of his own fate'. Jan Smuts, later to become South Africa's Defence Minister and a leading member of Lloyd George's Imperial War Cabinet, described the British Empire at this time as a 'ramshackle structure' containing

> *great countries largely inhabited by antagonistic peoples, without any adequate military organisation designed to keep the peace in case of disturbance or attack. The domination that the British Empire exercises over the many tribes and peoples within its jurisdiction rests more upon prestige and moral intimidation than upon true military strength.*[11]

The full implications for the future of the British Empire of Smuts' perceptive analysis would only be revealed after the first great European 'civil war' which so gravely undermined European prestige and powers of moral intimidation in the wider world. As early as the 1880s, a German observer had warned that the British Empire was 'an artificial world power' as its territorial base was 'just a European country'. Its far-flung colonies lacked a natural unity and were held to Britain only 'through the threads of the fleet, and these could all be broken or cut'.[12]

The Boer War, which revealed Britain's diplomatic isolation and resulted in more than 20 000 British casualties, starkly exposed the vulnerability of the British Empire and the need to plan more effectively for its protection. And growing Russian strength, both naval and military, threatened British interests in the Middle East, in Persia and, above all, in India. Prime Minister Balfour told his Foreign Secretary in 1902, 'A quarrel with Russia anywhere, about anything, means the invasion of India.' To protect this jewel in the imperial crown, a large part of the British army, almost 75 000 troops, was stationed there alongside an Indian force twice as strong, since the loss of this valuable Asian colony could not be contemplated. As Lord Curzon wrote in 1901, when serving as Viceroy of India, 'as long as we rule India, we are the greatest power in the world. If we lose it we shall drop straight away to a third-rate power.'[13]

At the turn of the century, therefore, British statesmen urgently sought through diplomatic means to reach agreements with other powers which would hopefully reduce threats to the security of the Empire, and at the same time lighten the load of world-wide responsibilities. Britain had stayed aloof from European entanglements for over a hundred years, as it reached the zenith of its world power. It is ironic to reflect that in the first decade of the

---

[11] The 'weary Titan' description is from Julian Amery, 1951: *The Life of Joseph Chamberlain*, vol. 4. London: Rupert Hart-Davis. Quoted in M. Howard, 1972: *The Continental Commitment: The Dilemma of British Defence Policy in the Era of Two World Wars.* London: Temple Smith, 11.
[12] Reynolds, *Britannia Overruled*, op. cit. (note 1), 25–6.
[13] Quoted in Howard, *The Continental Commitment*, op. cit. (note 11), 14.

twentieth century tentative steps towards limited agreements designed to safe-guard the periphery of the Empire and the existing status quo were to lead inexorably to massive military involvement on the European mainland itself.

The first reductions of British naval power came in the straits around Constantinople and in the western hemisphere. Even before 1900, Britain had decided to withdraw from Constantinople and base the defence of the route to India upon Cairo and the Suez Canal.[14] In 1901, the conclusion of the Hay–Pauncefote treaty with the United States signalled British willingness to retreat from American waters. Britain's naval bases at Halifax and Esquimault were abandoned, the Jamaica dockyards were closed, and the West Indian and North American naval squadrons abolished.[15] Britain also gave up its treaty right to claim a half share in the construction of any Isthmian canal and, in 1903, agreed to a settlement of the Alaskan boundary dispute which went in favour of United States claims.[16] Henceforth, the security of Canada and British possessions and trade in the West Indies and Central America were left in the care of the United States government.

To counter what were seen as growing Russian threats to the security of India and the integrity of the Chinese empire, Britain sought through diplo-matic means to enlist the help of Germany. Though some limited agreements were concluded between the two powers between 1898 and 1900 over the divi-sion of the Portuguese colonies, Samoa and the Chinese 'open door', Germany proved a difficult suitor. It demanded a high price for a more gen-eral agreement and was, perhaps understandably, not as anxious as Britain was to check Russian Far Eastern expansion. Instead, therefore, Britain concluded what was seen at the time as a rather surprising alliance with Japan, which was also alarmed at growing Russian power in the Far East. This primarily naval agreement was designed to counter the challenge of the combined Russian and French naval forces in the North Pacific, and to enable Britain to strengthen its home fleet. But it also involved Britain in an obligation to go to war if France joined Russia in a conflict against Japan, and was therefore 'the first step along the road to external military commitment'.[17]

As Japan and Russia edged closer to conflict over rights in Manchuria and Korea, their respective allies, Britain and France, became concerned to minimize the possibility of being dragged into a war in the region. Both pow-ers also welcomed the chance to demarcate conflicting colonial interests in Egypt and Morocco. The result was the Anglo-French *entente* of 1904, which was not, at the outset, directed against Germany. However, growing German naval strength, based on the ambitious German navy bills of 1898 and 1900, and clumsy German attempts to split the newly formed *entente* over Morocco in 1905, and again in 1911, transformed the nature of the agreement. This change of emphasis was also assisted by Japan's unexpected defeat of Russia in

[14] Z. Steiner, 1977: *Britain and the Origins of the First World War*. London: Macmillan, 22.
[15] Howard, *The Continental Commitment*, op. cit. (note 11), 30.
[16] Kennedy, *The Rise and Fall of British Naval Power*, op. cit., (note 1), 250–1.
[17] Steiner, *Britain and the Origins of the First World War*, op. cit. (note 14), 28.

1905, which dealt at least a temporary blow to Russia's Asiatic ambitions. From the first Moroccan crisis of 1905 onwards, Germany rather than Russia was seen by Britain as the greatest danger to the British Empire, particularly as it posed a challenge both to British naval supremacy and to the European status quo.

In January 1906 the British Foreign Secretary in the new Liberal Government, Sir Edward Grey, authorised military conversations with France, and preliminary plans were sketched for sending an expeditionary force of six divisions to France in the event of German aggression against that country. This dramatic change in the strategic priorities of the British army – from the defence of the Indian north-west frontier to a supporting role on the European mainland – was confirmed after the second Moroccan crisis of 1911, which brought Britain, France and Germany to the brink of war. Much more concrete military arrangements were now entered into by the British and French military establishments, which involved the landing of 150 000 British troops in France, with their own separate though complementary sphere of operations. These agreements were sanctioned by the Committee of Imperial Defence in August 1911.[18]

By this date, British advisers and substantial sections of the Cabinet were convinced that they faced a serious and growing dual German challenge: to British naval supremacy and to the balance of power on the European mainland which had provided security for Britain for over a century. The containment of aggressive German ambitions was now Britain's most pressing concern, and the *entente* with France was seen as an essential element in this operation. Fear of growing German strength contributed, in 1907, to the conclusion of an agreement with the British Empire's former leading antagonist, the Russian Empire. (As with the earlier *entente* with France, a mutual desire to disentangle imperial rivalries, in this case in Persia and central Asia, also played an important part.) Again, however, the European dimensions of the new *entente* became more prominent, as Britain feared a possible Russo-German *rapprochement* and sought ways to maintain Russian friendship.

By 1912 it was clear that Britain had won the naval race initiated by von Tirpitz in Germany some twelve years earlier. Britain remained a great world power with the economic resources and the will to respond positively and effectively to the German naval challenge. By 1914, Britain had twenty Dreadnoughts to Germany's thirteen, nine battle cruisers to Germany's six, twenty-six pre-Dreadnought battleships to Germany's twelve, and double the number of German cruisers.[19] But the cost of victory was a further naval retreat, this time from the important imperial artery of the Mediterranean Sea. In 1912, a one-power standard was adopted for the Mediterranean battle fleet, excluding France, and this was followed by a French move to concentrate the French Navy at the Toulon naval base in the Mediterranean. At the same time, Britain

[18] Ibid., 198.
[19] Ibid., 98.

consolidated its naval strength in home waters, and by April 1913 had agreed with France that, in the event of a war in which Britain decided to participate, Britain would assume the defence of the Straits of Dover and the western Channel.

However, Britain gained little respite from the successful containment of Germany's naval challenge, because this served only to strengthen a German bid for mastery in Europe, and it was this threat that finally brought Britain into war in Europe in 1914. As Grey had already explained to Empire leaders in 1911,

> *If a European conflict, not of our making, arose in which it was quite clear that the struggle was one for supremacy in Europe, . . . our concern in seeing that there did not arise a supremacy in Europe which entailed a combination that would deprive us of the command of the sea would be such that we might have to take part in that European war. That is why the naval position underlies our European policy . . .*[20]

Though Britain's political leaders had taken great care not to conclude formal binding alliances with France or Russia, which would automatically involve Britain in war if they were attacked, they could not stand by and watch Germany invade Belgium and France. British security was too directly menaced, and it was in acknowledgement of the danger posed to Britain by German military victory in western Europe that Britain entered the First World War.

Thus British foreign policy had failed to secure one of the country's most important interests: peace. Diplomacy geared to securing world-wide British objectives with the minimum of conflict had led instead to involvement in a Continental war. A range of foreign policy approaches, which included a network of treaty agreements and *ententes*, policies of deterrence and finally a Continental commitment, had had the cumulative effect of enmeshing Britain firmly into the European diplomatic network that erupted so explosively in August 1914. Not surprisingly, the tremendous cost of the failure of these approaches had a great impact on the formulation and conduct of foreign policy after 1919. The elements of what came to be regarded in the 1920s as traditional and secret pre-war diplomacy – as opposed to the 'open' diplomacy of the postwar period – were widely distrusted as being dangerous and likely to result in another conflict. Thus while the overall aims of British foreign policy were to remain very similar after 1919, the means by which they were pursued were to change considerably in a conscious bid to avoid a repetition of the pre-1914 situation.

War and Peace

Having failed to avert a war, British efforts were now aimed at waging it successfully and ending it quickly. However, advances in military technology

[20] Quoted in ibid., 211.

transformed the 'bright and jolly war'[21] into a lengthy and exhausting stalemate, which the British Government then sought to break by means of secret agreements and colonial bargaining. As the conflict widened, the cost escalated, and Britain was driven to more desperate agreements with partners and potential allies, and to the crucial courting of the United States for financial and then military support. The United States' entry into the war was finally secured, but on terms that only served to emphasise growing American power and predominance. The main elements of Woodrow Wilson's peace programme came into an embarrassing collision with earlier Allied wartime diplomacy, resulting in a whole range of problems that had to be resolved at the end of the war. Woodrow Wilson's bid to dictate the terms of the peace settlement was one of the major factors that by 1919 were severely constraining Britain's ability to protect its world-wide interests, preserve its naval supremacy and conclude a peace that would safeguard its shores.

At the outset of the war, British strategists believed that the most effective way of waging war against a Continental enemy would be by utilising Britain's naval supremacy and instituting a naval blockade around the coasts of the enemy. However, technological advances had both lessened the effectiveness of the weapon of blockade and made Britain itself more vulnerable to attack. The invention of the mine, the torpedo, the submarine and the long-range coastal ordnance rendered a close blockade of the enemy's coast extremely dangerous. Britain could still keep Germany bottled up in Europe by a long-range blockade that would render the north and south exits to the Atlantic Ocean impassable. But this strategy exaggerated the extent of German reliance on overseas trade, and underestimated the degree to which Germany could make up losses from elsewhere in Europe, or manufacture substitute products.[21] It was Britain that was more vulnerable to attack on its overseas trade routes. By the eve of the First World War, Britain was importing seven-eighths of its raw materials, including all its cotton, four-fifths of its wool, most of its non-phosphoric iron ore and almost all of its non-ferrous metals. Britain was the world's largest importer of iron and steel, with Germany one of its most prolific suppliers. Even more crucially, Britain imported over half its food supplies, including 55 per cent of its grain and 40 per cent of its meat. As Admiral Fisher remarked, 'It's not *invasion* we have to fear if our Navy's beaten, it's *starvation.*'[22]

While millions of pounds had been spent on the British navy before 1914, it was, ironically, the army that was to bear the brunt of the fighting in the war, and this again was a development which had not been foreseen. Britain, along with the other great European powers, anticipated a short war. British leaders confidently predicted that the expeditionary force would be home by Christmas 1914; the Germans hoped that the war in the West would be over before the British Expeditionary Force was able to arrive in France and take

---

[21] Kennedy, *The Rise and Fall of British Naval Power*, op. cit. (note 1), 235–7.
[22] Quoted in ibid., 237: *see also* Barnett, *The Collapse of British Power*, op. cit. (note 1), 90.

part in the proceedings. Again, however, throughout Europe the impact of advances in military technology had not been fully appreciated. The defensive power of the machine-gun and of barbed wire was lost on all but the most prescient observers. But Bloch's claim, ignored at the time, that future wars would be drawn-out tests of endurance, and that 'the spade would be as indispensable to a soldier as his rifle', turned out to be all too horribly true.[23] Britain's carefully limited Continental commitment turned into the nightmare of the mass battles of the Somme and Passchaendale. Twentieth-century warfare proved to be very different from that of the nineteenth century, and it tested Britain's capacity as a great world power much more searchingly than the conflicts and challenges of the earlier period.

Economically, Britain proved able to sustain a long and costly war, contrary again to popular expectations before 1914. But, in the process, the country was driven to bargain with its partners, to woo potential allies and increasingly to court the United States. The resulting wartime diplomacy, and growing American involvement in Europe, were to shape in crucial ways the postwar settlement and Britain's ability to continue to play a leading world role.

The secret treaty of London, concluded in April 1915 between Britain, France, Russia and Italy, was designed to keep Russia in the war after disastrous defeats at the hands of the German Army on the Eastern Front, and to bring Italy into it on the Allied side. Britain and France agreed in principle to the acquisition by Russia of Constantinople and the Bosporus provided the war was fought by all three to a victorious conclusion; only the collapse of Tsarist Russia in 1917 and the subsequent Bolshevik repudiation of secret wartime agreements saved Britain from the consequences of what would have been a dramatic increase in Russian power in the eastern Mediterranean.

The inducements offered to Italy in return for its entry into the war were more wide-ranging. In addition to somewhat vague assurances that Italy would receive a 'just share' in any partition of the Ottoman Empire, and further territory if Britain and France annexed any German colonies, Italy was promised sovereignty over the Dodecanese islands, which it was already occupying, and major territorial gains at the expense of the Habsburg Empire. To the north, Italy was to absorb the German-speaking Alpine regions of the Trentino and South Tyrol, and across the Adriatic Sea it was to acquire Istria and part of Dalmatia, both regions populated principally by Slavs. If these specific promises materialised, almost a quarter of a million German-speaking Austrians and well over half a million Slavs and Turks would find themselves in Italy after the war. No wonder Lloyd George, British Prime Minister after 1916, remarked ruefully that 'war plays havoc with the refinements of conscience'.[24]

[23] Kennedy, *The Rise and Fall of British Naval Power*, op. cit. (note 1), 237.
[24] For details of wartime Allied diplomacy, *see* J. A. S. Grenville, 1974: *The Major International Treaties, 1914–73*. London: Methuen, 15–37; F. Northedge, 1966: *The Troubled Giant: Britain among the Great Powers, 1916–39*. London: London School of Economics/Bell, 1–16; for Lloyd George's views, *see* D. Lloyd George, 1938: *War Memoirs*. London: Odhams, and D. Lloyd George, 1938: *The Truth about the Peace Treaties*, vol. 1. London: Gollancz, 27–9.

Italy's national aspirations were strongly encouraged by these and subsequent wartime agreements, and the feeling after 1919 that Italy had been betrayed by its erstwhile wartime allies was to contribute substantially to the rise of Italian fascism with its in-built challenge to the postwar territorial settlement.

Whereas Italian manpower was desperately needed in Europe to try to break the military stalemate there, Britain also endeavoured to work towards victory by hitting at the territories held by Germany and its allies outside Europe. In an attempt to encourage an Arab rising against the Turkish Empire, Britain's High Commissioner in Egypt, Sir Henry McMahon, corresponded with the Sherif of Mecca in 1915 and early 1916. He promised that Britain would recognise and support the independence of the Arabs in all regions demanded by the Sherif, save for the coastal strip west of the line Damascus–Hama–Homs–Aleppo, and save for areas where Britain was not free to act without detriment to French interests. No specific mention was made of Palestine.

The partition of the Ottoman Empire was spelt out in more detail in an exchange of notes between Britain, France and Russia in 1916, referred to subsequently as the Sykes–Picot agreement. French and British spheres of influence were mapped out, and Palestine was designated as an international sphere of influence. However, in 1917 the celebrated Balfour Declaration, issued by the British Foreign Secretary, promised a national home in Palestine for the Jewish people. The motives behind what was to be seen in future years as the most contentious of promises were mixed, but included both the hope that the establishment of a largely Jewish Palestine would help to consolidate Britain's position in the Middle East, and the prospect of increasing support for the Allied cause from Zionists in Russia and eastern Europe and in the United States.[25] In a further agreement, drawn up at St Jean de Maurienne in April 1917, Britain and France agreed to the establishment of an Italian sphere of influence in the region of Adalia and Smyrna; Greece subsequently entered the war on the Allied side and also entertained extensive ambitions in the eastern Mediterranean, which were to lead to military conflict with Turkey, and considerable complications for Britain in the Near East between 1920 and 1922.[26]

By the end of the war, therefore, Britain was enmeshed in a web of conflicting promises relating to the Ottoman Empire. The commander-in-chief of the Egyptian Expeditionary Force, Sir Edmund (later Lord) Allenby, who had led his troops to victories in Palestine in 1917 and 1918, predicted all too accurately in November 1918 that

> *Politics in Palestine and Syria are not going to be too easy in the future. Jews, Arabs, French, Italians, English and other nations, all think they have special interests and special claims and rights; and every known religion asserts itself and adds knots to the tangle.*

[25] M. Beloff, 1987: *Britain's Liberal Empire, 1897–1921*, 2nd edition. London: Macmillan, 261–4.
[26] Grenville, *The Major International Treaties*, op. cit. (note 24), 20–2; for more details about the Near Eastern situation which led to the Chanak crisis, *see* D. Walder, 1969: *The Chanak Affair*. London: Hutchinson.

Chief of the Imperial General Staff, Sir Henry Wilson, commented gloomily to Allenby, in June 1919, 'We have made so many promises to everybody in a contradictory sense that I cannot for the life of me see how we can get out of our present mess without breaking our word to somebody.'[27] Britain's attempts to mediate between Arab and Zionist aspirations in Palestine after 1919 necessitated armed interventions on an escalating scale: by 1936, eighteen battalions were engaged in Palestine on peace-keeping operations.[28]

In the Far East, too, wartime agreements had serious repercussions on Britain's power and influence after 1919. Japan entered the war as an ally of Britain in August 1914, in a conscious bid to expand its overseas empire and economic interests in China and Manchuria. Japan lost no time in seizing German concessions in China and colonies in the North Pacific such as the Caroline and Marianne Islands, and asserting its influence over China through the infamous 'twenty-one demands' of 1915.[29] In a secret agreement of 1917, concluded at a moment when the British Admiralty was desperate for Japanese naval assistance in the Mediterranean, Japan was given an assurance of British support for Japanese claims to keep the ex-German possessions it had captured, while Japan in turn promised to back British or Dominion claims to German colonies seized in the Pacific south of the equator. The strong position in east Asia that Japan was able to establish for itself by the end of the war laid the foundations for the country's expansionist policies of the 1930s. Japan had exploited the preoccupation of the European powers with the conflict in Europe to strengthen what was already a significant challenge to European power in east Asia before 1914. By the late 1920s, only the combined naval power of Britain and the United States could hope to check Japanese ambitions in the Pacific and on the Chinese mainland.

The repercussions of secret wartime diplomacy were bound to cause serious problems for British foreign policy at the end of the war. They were also to cause mounting embarrassment, as the agreements reached were in many ways in violent conflict with the new tenets of Wilsonian dipomacy. The emergence during the First World War of the United States as a leading world power was to throw up new challenges to Britain's global position. Well before its entry into the war in April 1917, the United States was providing finance to the Allies, which by 1918 amounted to some $2000 million. With such economic power came naval aspirations, attempts to mediate in the war and to further American interests, and growing political ambitions to shape a peace settlement for Europe. By October 1916, Chancellor of the Exchequer Reginald McKenna was warning that 'by next June or earlier, the President of

[27] Quoted in K. Jeffrey, 1984: *The British Army and the Crisis of Empire, 1918–22*. Manchester: Manchester University Press.

[28] Howard, *The Continental Commitment*, op. cit. (note 11), 117.

[29] Grenville, *The Major International Treaties*, op. cit. (note 26), 20–2. For the impact of the twenty-one demands on China, *see* R. Pelissier, 1967: *The Awakening of China, 1793–1949*. London: Secker & Warburg, 265–7.

the American republic will be in a position, if he wishes, to dictate his own terms to us.'[30]

The opportunities to be gained from this pivotal diplomatic position were not lost on the crusading President Wilson. He confided to his close adviser, Colonel House in 1917, 'England and France have not the same views with regard to peace that we have by any means. When the war is over we can force them to our way of thinking because by that time they will ... be financially in our hands.'[31] Wilson's 'way of thinking' was extremely moralistic and very idealistic. Yet at the same time, this 'unrepentant Gladstonian liberal' was most concerned to safeguard and to promote American values and interests, particularly in the economic field. His animosity towards the exercise of British belligerent rights at sea and vigorous propounding of the doctrine of the 'freedom of the seas' were bound to arouse fierce British opposition and cause concern for the future. His belief in the virtues of self-determination and the satisfying of 'well-defined national aspirations' could be supported in Europe, but was deemed as being not applicable to more backward colonial subjects in the British Empire. Alarmingly, however, President Wilson made it clear that his peace programme, based on 'new diplomacy' and a League of Nations under American leadership, was aimed not just at Europe but at the entire world. And Wilson was not blind to the opportunities that this new era could offer for American commercial and economic expansion.[32]

After the entry of the United States into the war, as a carefully demarcated 'associated power' and not as an ally, the Prime Minister of Australia, Hughes, warned the Imperial War Cabinet, 'You are going to have endless trouble from Wilson in the conduct of the war and with the terms of peace.' 'Yes – in the peace', replied Austen Chamberlain, 'but you cannot change the President.'[33] The British Imperial War Cabinet could only watch uneasily as Wilson took the initiative in laying the foundations for a peace settlement. It was on the basis of his Fourteen Points, delivered as part of a speech to Congress on 5 January 1918, that the astute German high command sued for peace.[34] The Allied governments had never been asked to approve the points as a framework for peace. While the British Foreign Secretary, Balfour, found them 'admirable but rather abstract', Clemenceau's response was rather more typical of the feelings of allied leaders: '[Wilson] exasperates me with his Fourteen Commandments when the good God had only ten!'[35]

[30] P. Kennedy, 1981: *The Realities Behind Diplomacy*. London: Fontana, 162.

[31] Tillman, *Anglo-American Relations*, op. cit. (note 3), 16, quoting from R. S. Baker, *Wilson: Life and Letters*, vol. 7, p. 43, no. 3. Wilson to House, 21 July 1917.

[32] *See* C. Seymour, 1928: *The Intimate Papers of Colonel House*, vol. 3. London: Ernest Benn; and A. Sharp, 1991: *The Versailles Settlement: Peacemaking in Paris, 1919*. London: Macmillan, 14. For the impact of Wilson's diplomacy in China, *see* Pelissier, *The Awakening*, op. cit. (note 29), 261–78.

[33] T. Jones, 1969: *Whitehall Diary*, vol. 1. Oxford: Oxford University Press, 66.

[34] For the full text of the Fourteen Points speech, *see* Lloyd George, *The Truth about the Peace Treaties*, vol. 1, op. cit. (note 24), 70–3.

[35] Quoted in H. Elcock, 1972: *Portrait of a Decision: The Council of Four and the Treaty of Versailles*. London: Eyre Methuen, 33.

With little prior consultation, Britain and France found themselves endorsing a Wilsonian peace programme in late October 1918. The British Government made it clear that it would not accept point 2 relating to the freedom of the seas, which Lloyd George claimed would prevent Britain in future from imposing a blockade of the kind enforced against Germany throughout the war.[36] Clarification was also sought on point 7 about the precise meaning of 'restoration' of invaded territories, and about what compensation was to be paid by Germany for its 'aggression . . . by land, by sea and from the air'. But Colonel House's threat that the United States might consider concluding a separate peace with Germany if the Allies raised too many objections at this stage had the desired effect of limiting Allied protests to just the two noted above.[37]

In fact, there was no serious conflict of interest between Britain and the United States as far as peace aims in Europe were concerned. Both powers wanted to see the eradication of Prussian militarism, though not necessarily a major reduction of German power in Europe, since both were becoming increasingly concerned about the growing threat of Bolshevism. By the closing stages of the war, British leaders had committed themselves to the principle of self-determination for the peoples of the Habsburg and Ottoman Empires, having realised the extent to which encouragement of national and cultural aspirations would precipitate the break-up of these two allies of Germany. In western Europe, there was agreement on the return to France of Alsace and Lorraine, and Britain was prepared to support the establishment of a League of Nations. The main conflicts were likely to come in the Mediterranean and the Near East, over the secret war agreements to which President Wilson had not been a party, and over the British Empire's colonial gains at the expense of Germany and expansionist aims in the Middle East. Naval rivalries were also likely to cause serious friction.

At the Paris peace conference, British delegates worked closely with their American counterparts on many issues, though there was no formal agreement between the two nations.[38] But given the length and severity of fighting in the First World War, and the destruction of large parts of northern France and Belgium, peacemaking was bound to be a complex process, and one that could not satisfactorily be tailored to the Fourteen Points peace programme and the Wilsonian moral and political philosophy. Endless procedural wrangles, conflicting claims on the part of successor states, and disputes on a wide range of economic and political issues both within and between delegations caused delay, despondency and extreme fatigue. Paris became yet another battlefield on which Lloyd George, Clemenceau, Wilson and the Italian leader Orlando struggled to evade or reinterpret the Fourteen Points so as to further their respective national interests in the peacemaking process. The British

---

[36] Lloyd George, *The Truth about the Peace Treaties*, vol. 1, op. cit. (note 24), 77–9.
[37] Elcock, *Portrait of a Decision*, op. cit. (note 35), 33.
[38] *See* Tillman, *Anglo-American Relations*, op. cit. (note 3).

Treasury's representative at Paris, J. M. Keynes, described the process some months later as one in which Wilson's 'peace programme' was systematically and successfully subverted by Clemenceau's 'Carthaginian' peace terms, but this assessment is too simplistic.[39] The peace settlement was inevitably a compromise, and one with which no party was completely happy. The French Government and military advisers castigated the treaty as too lenient, and Marshall Foch warned, 'This is not Peace. It is an Armistice for twenty years.'[40] Lloyd George, though reasonably satisfied, feared that the treaty was too punitive. Italian leaders walked out of the conference in protest at the way in which their territorial claims were being challenged, and Italy became fatally alienated from the whole peace process. The new democratic German Government, meanwhile, sought to strengthen its rather shaky position domestically by contrasting the 'Versailles diktat' with Woodrow Wilson's original Fourteen Points.[41]

But the most serious opposition of all to the original Wilsonian peace programme and to the subsequent Paris peace settlement came from the United States. In the mid-term Congressional elections of November 1918, the Republican Party made sweeping gains in both houses, despite Wilson's appeal to American voters to support him and thus strengthen his position in the forthcoming peace negotiations. The scale of the Republican victory meant that United States' ratification of any peace treaties agreed at Paris would henceforth depend on Republican support. Republican leaders, however, left their European counterparts in no doubt that they were bitterly hostile to Wilson's Fourteen Point peace programme.[42] None the less, the allies had to negotiate at Paris on the basis of Wilson's proposals, though they were painfully aware that the resulting treaties might well be repudiated in the United States. In the autumn of 1919, and again in March 1920, the United States Senate refused to ratify the Treaty of Versailles and signed a separate peace with Germany instead. Thus Wilsonian diplomacy, having challenged and to some extent replaced secret wartime agreements and Allied peace aims, was itself repudiated in the United States. Europe's leading powers were left to implement a compromise peace, with which no party was very happy, without the political and economic support of the United States, in a war-torn, impoverished and highly unstable continent. This outcome would inevitably pose enormous problems for postwar British foreign policy.

[39] J. M. Keynes, 1919: *The Economic Consequences of the Peace.* London: Macmillan, ch. 3 and 4.
[40] Quoted in Sharp, *The Versailles Settlement,* op. cit. (note 32), 189.
[41] For detailed accounts of peacemaking at Paris, *see* Sharp, *The Versailles Settlement,* op. cit. (note 32); Elcock, *Portrait of a Decision,* op. cit. (note 35); Tillman, *Anglo-American Relations,* op. cit. (note 3); H. Temperley, 1920–4: *A History of the Peace Conference of Paris.* London: Frowde, under the auspices of the Institute for International Affairs, 6 vols; and M. Dockrill and J. D. Goold, 1981: *Peace Without Promise: Britain and the Paris Peace Conferences, 1919–23.* London: Batsford.
[42] A. J. Mayer, 1968: *Politics and Diplomacy of Peacemaking.* London: Weidenfeld & Nicolson, 29.

The Postwar Period

Superficially, Britain's position in the summer of 1919 seemed stronger and more secure than before the war. Victory in the war had brought about an expansion of the British Empire to its greatest extent ever. At its peak, in 1933, the Empire covered nearly one-quarter of the earth's land surface and embraced about a quarter of its population – over 500 million people. In addition, Britain still retained extensive trading concessions and economic influence in China, in the Persian Gulf and Arabia, and in Latin America.

It seemed that Britain had strongly and successfully met the German challenge, and had negotiated a peace which secured Britain's main interests. Prime Minister Lloyd George could be forgiven for boasting to his good friend, the press baron Lord Riddell,

> *We have got most of the things we set out to get . . . the German Navy has been handed over, the German mercantile shipping has been handed over; and the German colonies have been given up. One of our chief trade competitors has been most seriously crippled and our Allies are about to become her biggest creditors. . . . In addition, we have destroyed the menace to our Indian possessions.*[43]

At the end of the war, therefore, Britain was clearly a satisfied power, concerned only to maintain its strength. As the First Sea Lord, Admiral Chatfield, expressed it very frankly, in 1934; 'we have got most of the world already, or the best parts of it, and we only want to keep what we have got and prevent others from taking it from us.'[44]

It was sentiments such as these that were so strongly to shape British foreign policy after 1919. Britain's overriding objectives remained, as before the war, to preserve and to protect the British Empire and its vital world-wide communications network and trade routes, and, nearer to home, to secure a balanced and stable Europe. 'To seek peace and ensure it' was the guiding British maxim in the inter-war period, a policy designed not just to preserve the status quo but to stimulate a recovery of world trade and therefore of British economic strength. But how could such desirable goals best be achieved? What sort of diplomacy would most effectively calm postwar anxieties, reconcile former enemies and promote political and economic stability?

The establishment of world-wide peace proved even more difficult to secure after 1919 than it had been before 1914. The war itself, while failing to solve most of the problems that had brought it about, speeded up the challenges of emerging great powers such as the United States and Japan, as we have seen. It also stimulated the development of new military technology, and saw the spread both of strong nationalist movements across the British Empire and of the Bolshevik challenge. The Empire proved to be even more vulnerable in the postwar world than it had been before 1914, and Europe after 1919, far

[43] Lord Riddell, 1933: *Intimate Diary of the Peace Conference and After.* London: Gollancz, 42.
[44] Quoted in Reynolds, *Britannia Overruled*, op. cit. (note 1), 60–1.

from shaking down into a period of stability, remained highly unsettled and difficult to pacify.

To add to this catalogue of difficulties, the sentiments of the British electorate, stimulated by the unprecedented experiences of the war, had to be taken into account. Successive inter-war British governments went out of their way to show that they had learned the lessons of the pre-1914 situation, that they would turn their backs on entangling alliances and secret diplomatic and military agreements, and that they would give full support to the new League of Nations and its open, multilateral approach to international relations. Hardly surprisingly, therefore, British foreign policy after 1919 was defensive, seeking to limit postwar commitments and to resolve conflicts with other powers through negotiation and diplomacy. But this policy of appeasement failed to remove growing challenges to the Empire and deep-seated animosities in Europe.

The problems facing the British Empire were especially acute between 1918 and 1922. At the close of the war, British troops were operating over a huge territorial expanse that stretched from Africa through the Middle East to India, and extended northwards into the Caucasus and Transcaspia. But while there were strong political and economic pressures for rapid demobilisation, British rule came under increasing challenge in Egypt, India and Mesopotamia, not to mention southern Ireland, and, as the final chapter will show, the challenges seemed strongest in areas where imperial strategic needs demanded the maintenance of close imperial control.[45] The Secretary to the Cabinet, Sir Maurice Hankey, in his personal diary, pinned all the blame for the unrest on 'President Wilson and his fourteen points, and his impossible doctrine of self-determination. The adoption of this principle at the peace conference has struck at the very roots of the British Empire all over the world from Ireland to Hong Kong, and has got us into a hideous mess.'[46]

How could a volunteer army, which was rapidly shrinking back to its pre-war strength, cope with all the demands now being placed on it? Never before in peacetime had the British army been stretched so thinly, upholding so many world-wide commitments. A General Staff appreciation of the military liabilities of the Empire, in July 1920, concluded wearily that 'Our liabilities are so vast, and at the same time so indeterminate, that to assess them must be largely a matter of conjecture.'[47] A diary entry by Sir Henry Wilson echoed the same gloomy message: 'our army is much too scattered . . . in no single theatre are we strong enough – not in Ireland, nor England, nor on the Rhine, nor in Constantinople, nor Batoum, nor Egypt, nor Palestine, nor Mesopotamia, nor Persia, nor India.'[48] Wilson's solution was to concentrate forces on 'our four storm centres' of Ireland, Egypt, Mesopotamia and India, but this would not

[45] *See* Jeffrey, *The British Army and the Crisis of Empire*, op. cit. (note 27).
[46] Hankey, diary entry for 3 January 1921, quoted in ibid., 161.
[47] Quoted in Howard, *The Continental Commitment*, op. cit. (note 11), 76–7.
[48] Quoted in Kennedy, *The Realities Behind Diplomacy*, op. cit. (note 30), 250.

solve the basic problem of Britain's postwar 'classic and gigantic ... strategic over-extension'.[49]

After 1922, the wave of postwar violence and agitation subsided, but the basic problem for the British Empire remained. A volunteer army of around 200 000 men could police individual Empire trouble-spots, but could not hold back the rising tide of nationalist feeling in Egypt, in the Middle East and in India. At the same time, because of growing challenges within the Empire, troops could not be spared for use in Europe, which limited Britain's capacity to deal with crises in Europe.

At the close of the war, the British Government had hoped that the United States might be persuaded to shoulder some international responsibilities, and take on commitments in the Near East or in the Middle East, as well as in Europe. As we have seen, such hopes were dashed, but at the same time the United States announced its intention of launching a post-war bid for parity with the Royal Navy. This challenge, though emanating from a country more friendly to Britain than imperial Germany had been, was equally dangerous to the long-term security of Britain and its Empire. Britain could not hope to match the great resources of the United States, and if the United States chose to build up a strong fleet, and to use it to enforce the doctrine of the freedom of the seas, Britain would be hard pressed to resist. A period of naval supremacy spanning two centuries was about to come to an end, as the British Government sought to appease the United States and to contain the American naval challenge. In the process, a series of naval agreements were reached between Britain, the United States and Japan at the Washington naval conference in 1922, the results of which have been described by one historian as 'one of the major catastrophes of English history', though a more recent assessment believes the outcome enabled Britain to safeguard vital global and naval interests.[50]

There is no doubt that American pressure on Britain at Washington to agree to parity with the United States in battleships and heavy battle cruisers, and to a ten-year naval 'holiday', to terminate the Anglo-Japanese alliance, to agree instead to a four-power pact with America, Japan and France, and to develop a naval base at Singapore had grave consequences for Britain's strategic, commercial and economic position in the Far East. Unremitting American efforts to persuade Britain to accept futher naval reductions led to a cruiser limitation agreement at London in 1930 that further impaired Britain's ability to protect its position in the Far East in the face of a strong Japan. The First World War had transformed Japan into a confident, expan-

[49] Quoted in Jeffrey, *The British Army and the Crisis of Empire*, op. cit. (note 27), 20; Barnett, *The Collapse of British Power*, op. cit. (note 1), 80.
[50] Barnett, *The Collapse of British Power*, op. cit. (note 1), 272: B. J. C. McKercher, 1991. *Anglo-American Relations in the 1920s: The Struggle for Supremacy*. London: Macmillan. For a full account of Anglo-American naval rivalry in the 1920s, *see* S. Roskill, 1968: *Naval Policy between the Wars*. Vol. 1, *The Period of Anglo-American Antagonism, 1919–29*. London: Collins, and C. Hall, 1987: *Britain, America and Arms Control, 1921–37*. London: Macmillan.

sionist nation seeking markets and trading concessions on the Chinese mainland and throughout Asia. By the early 1930s, Britain was no longer able to
contain Japan's expansion into Manchuria; in 1937, Japan's ambitions
widened to include the occupation of the Chinese mainland, and Britain was
powerless to prevent Japanese aggression without American co-operation in
economic or military sanctions or a naval blockade. Such co-ordination of policy or even a strategy of close co-operation was never achieved and, by 1941,
Britain's whole empire in the Far East was under threat.[51]

The British Isles themselves became dangerously vulnerable in the inter-war
period as new military and naval technology, pioneered in the decades before
1914, came to maturity in the Great War. Submarines, aircraft, tanks and a
range of explosive devices changed the nature of warfare and posed frightening new threats to Britain and to its Empire on land, at sea and from the air.
Britain's traditional sea defences had finally and most emphatically been
breached.[52] By 1918, the war had demonstrated that the aeroplane and the
submarine had the capacity to inflict destruction on a massive scale both on
land and at sea.

Britain's foreign and defence policies after 1919 were heavily influenced by
these new and frightening developments. Attempts were made, unsuccess-
fully, to abolish the submarine at a succession of inter-war disarmament conferences. Air power was a more difficult matter, since its civilian uses were
increasingly obvious in the postwar world. Britain's leaders tried to limit military aircraft through air pacts and arms limitation conventions, but again their
efforts were unsuccessful. They felt themselves to be helpless in the face of the
bomber, which, in Stanley Baldwin's famous words of 1932, would 'always get
through'.[53] Until the late 1930s, the only deterrent against the bomber was
considered to be massive retaliation in kind, and thus Britain spent considerable sums of money in the inter-war period assembling and maintaining an air
force of bombers. French air strength in the early 1920s and German air rearmament in the 1930s provoked a spirited British response but at the same time
emphasised to British leaders just how vulnerable British cities were to air
bombardment, with all the political and social disorder that this would bring.[54]

The advent of air power had the important effect of shifting Britain's strategic frontiers to western Europe. The Chief of the Imperial General Staff, Lord
Cavan, told the Cabinet in 1925 that henceforth 'The true strategic position of

[51] For accounts of Britain's strategy in the Far East, and of the growth of Japanese imperialism, *see*
W. R. Louis, 1971: *British Strategy in the Far East.* Oxford: Oxford University Press; I. Nish (ed.),
1982: *Anglo-Japanese Alienation.* Cambridge: Cambridge University Press; B. Lee, 1973: *Britain and
the Sino-Japanese War.* Stanford, Calif.: Stanford University Press; and P. Lowe, 1977: *Great Britain
and the Origins of the Pacific War.* Oxford: Oxford University Press. More general works include W.
G. Beasley, 1987: *Japanese Imperialism 1894–1945.* Oxford: Oxford University Press, and A. Iriye,
1987: *The Origins of the Second World War in Asia and the Pacific.* London: Longman.
[52] Kennedy, *The Rise and Fall of British Naval Mastery,* op. cit. (note 1), 295; Taylor, *English History,*
op. cit. (note 2), 43–4.
[53] Baldwin, House of Commons, 16 November 1932.
[54] Howard, *The Continental Commitment,* op. cit. (note 11), 82–5.

Great Britain is on the Rhine.' Stanley Baldwin rephrased the situation in 1934: 'When you think of the defence of England you no longer think of the chalk cliffs of Dover. You think of the Rhine. That is where our frontier lies today.'[55] This new development reinforced the traditional concern of British leaders that the Low Countries and western Europe should not fall under the control of a great military power, and that they should seek to promote a balance of power on the European mainland. Unfortunately, four years of warfare had left Europe highly unstable and unbalanced. While in the short term this had the effect of increasing Britain's security, in the long term it considerably hampered attempts to restore the continent and to seek a more even distribution of power.

Appeasement policies, designed to heal the wounds of war, reconcile former antagonists and promote economic and political recovery on the European mainland, failed to restore Europe to a state of peaceful equilibrium. Arguably, only a close alliance with France would have served to uphold the Paris peace settlements, to enforce them on a defiant Germany and subsequently to bring about their orderly revision. However, this was never a realistic political option in postwar Britain, at a time when pre-war *entente* diplomacy, and its accompanying military agreements, were being blamed for bringing about the 'encirclement' of Germany and the involvement of Britain in war. The memory of the pre-war 'Continental commitment' was too painful to too many people; rather than preventing conflict, it had precipitated mass slaughter. Instead, many British statesmen after 1919 saw French ambitions as an obstacle to their pursuit of appeasement policies in Europe.

Only France appeared capable of establishing military hegemony over Europe in the 1920s, and British concerns about French air strength and about a possible revival of Napoleonic ambitions help to explain growing Anglo-French antagonism after the war. As early as 1918 Curzon noted: 'I am seriously afraid that the great Power from whom we may have most to fear in the future is France. . . . She is powerful in almost all parts of the world, even around India.'[56] British governments wished to leave the policing of the European settlement to the Continental powers themselves, so that British energies could be concentrated further afield on the protection of the increasingly restless Empire. However, intransigent French policies, such as the demand for military sanctions and the invasion of German territory to punish breaches of the disarmament or reparations clauses of the peace settlement, had the effect of inflaming German grievances and pinning down British forces in Europe. In response, British leaders pushed forward the gradual rehabilitation of Germany, in an effort to create that elusive European 'balance' which would safeguard Britain's own security and enable Britain to disengage from Europe.

---

[55] Cavan is quoted in Howard, ibid., p. 94. Baldwin is quoted in G. M. Young, 1952: *Baldwin.* London: Rupert Hart-Davis, 80.
[56] Quoted in Kennedy, *The Realities Behind Diplomacy,* op. cit. (note 30).

But what many British politicians perceived as overweening French strength was in reality a cover for profound French weakness, a fact acutely perceived by some officials in the Foreign Office.[57] France had only accepted the Treaty of Versailles, and given up its demand for a Franco-German frontier running along the Rhine, in return for an Anglo-American guarantee of military assistance in the event of German aggression against France. This was rejected out of hand by the American Senate, and the British Government proved unwilling to honour the commitment alone, or to agree to military talks or to a substitute arrangement. Acutely aware of the disparity in population and in industrial capacity between itself and Germany, France sought alliances in eastern Europe with Poland, Czechoslovakia, Romania and Yugoslavia which increased British hostility towards France. Successive British governments viewed eastern Europe as a highly unstable area, full of excitable people and unresolved nationalist tensions, and an area, moreover, in which substantial German minorities had been cut off from the new German republic. Effective appeasement policies would require substantial territorial revisions in eastern Europe, in Germany's favour, to be brought about by patient negotiation and concession. The attempt by France to build up an alliance system with east European countries, reminiscent of the pre-war period, would prevent such a revisionist policy from being successfully pursued.

The conclusion of the Locarno agreements in 1925 was seen in Britain as a victory for the policy of appeasement. France, Belgium and Germany guaranteed their common frontiers, the demilitarisation of the Rhineland was reaffirmed, and Germany was to be welcomed into the League of Nations. Britain committed itself to act against any violation of the status quo in western Europe, but, as the General Staff pointed out in 1926, there were only two skeletal divisions available for service in Europe, and then only 'when the requirements of Imperial Defence so permit'.[58] However, the British Foreign Secretary, Sir Austen Chamberlain, placed the emphasis firmly on the reconciliation and arbitration side of the agreements, and entertained the hope that the Locarno treaties would serve as a model for other troubled parts of Europe.

But it did not prove possible to extend the 'Locarno spirit' to eastern Europe. Indeed, the conclusion of the Locarno treaties made it less likely that agreements could be reached in the east. Germany would not agree to the same guarantees of its eastern frontiers as it had consented to in the west, and German–Polish friction persisted over the Polish corridor and Upper Silesian settlements. As one historian has observed, Locarno was 'widely interpreted as a green light for Germany in the east'.[59] Further south, tensions remained

[57] *See*, for example, minutes by Sir Eyre Crowe, Permanent Under-Secretary in the Foreign Office, 1920–5, in Foreign Office files, Western department (Public Record Office, FO 371 series), and memorandum by H. Nicolson, British policy considered in relation to the European situation, Foreign Office, 20 Feb. 1925, FO 371/11664.

[58] Quoted in Howard, *The Continental Commitment*, op. cit. (note 11), 95.

[59] S. Marks, 1976: *The Illusion of Peace: International Relations in Europe, 1918–33*. London: Macmillan.

between Hungary and its neighbours, and between Italy, Yugoslavia and Albania. And over to the east remained the problem of unfulfilled Russian aspirations.

Territorially, Russia was cut off from the rest of Europe by the creation in 1919 of an independent Poland. The British Foreign Secretary, Balfour, viewed this development with dismay, because he foresaw that the separation of Germany and Russia by the establishment of Poland as a buffer state between them would free them both for future expansion. The reconstitution of Poland would mean that 'France would be at the mercy of Germany in the next war, for this reason, that Russia could not come to her aid without violating the neutrality of Poland.'[60] As he wrote in 1917, 'Personally, from the selfish western point of view, I would rather that Poland was autonomous under the Russians, because if you make an absolutely independent Poland, you cut off Russia altogether from the West.'[61]

Balfour's hopes that a durable post-war east European settlement could be based on a strong Russia balancing Germany were dashed by the two Russian revolutions of 1917. After the seizure of power by the Bolsheviks in November, there were many people in Britain who fervently hoped that Russia could indeed henceforth be cut off from the West in every possible aspect. For in giving birth to a revolutionary regime with a deliberately destabilising ideology, the Great War had made perhaps its most significant contribution to postwar instability. From Moscow and Petrograd, Lenin and Trotsky utilised new communications technology to broadcast across Europe and Asia demands for an immediate end to the war, for a peace with no indemnities and annexations, and for the workers of the world to rise up against their economic and political oppressors. The Bolsheviks, declared Lenin, were 'fighting against the capitalism of all countries, against world capitalism, for the freedom of all workers' in a struggle that was bound ultimately to be successful. 'No force on earth', he declared, 'could hold back the progress of the world communist revolution and the world Soviet republic.'[62]

Such messages struck a responsive chord in war-weary Europe, and even in Britain secret reports of militancy in the South Wales coalfields and on Clydeside, and the appearance of the red flag over Glasgow Town Hall, greatly alarmed the government. Sir Henry Wilson noted in his diary on the day before the armistice was signed, 'Our real danger now is not the Boches but Bolshevism.'[63] But Bolshevik propaganda was not aimed only at workers in advanced industrial nations. Increasingly, it was targeted at less developed peoples who were perceived to be the victims of imperialism, the highest stage of capitalism. And in this propaganda war, the British Empire stood in the

[60] R. Butler, 1968: The peace settlement at Versailles. In *The New Cambridge Modern History*, 2nd edition. Vol. 12, *The Shifting Balance of World Forces*. Cambridge: Cambridge University Press, 227.

[61] Quoted in H. Nelson, 1971: *Land and Power: Britain and Allied Policy on Germany's Frontiers, 1916–19*, 2nd edition. Newton Abbot: David & Charles, 18.

[62] S. White, 1979: *Britain and the Bolshevik Revolution*. London: Macmillan, 114.

[63] Quoted in Jeffrey, *The British Army and the Crisis of Empire*, op. cit. (note 27), 24.

front line of capitalist–imperialist enemies to be attacked. 'The very fact of the existence of Soviet Russia places a question mark over the centuries-old possessions of the British bourgeoisie, over all the British colonial empire', proclaimed a Bolshevik pamphlet; 'the establishment of the power of the Soviets in Russia will give a powerful impetus to the liberation of the peoples of the East.' One leading Bolshevik saw the regime's 'main and most dangerous enemy' as 'the most powerful imperialist power of today – Britain, always seeing in a strong and united Russia a threat to the hegemony of Great Britain in Persia, Afghanistan and especially in India.'[64] When Zinoviev called for a 'holy war . . . against British Imperialism' in September 1920, Curzon thundered, 'The Russian menace in the East is incomparably greater than anything else that has happened in my lifetime to the British Empire.'[65]

The twin threat of Bolshevism, aimed at the subversion of the social and economic order within Britain and at the liberation of colonial peoples throughout the Empire, greatly preoccupied British leaders and their advisers after 1919. It added to the difficulties both of European pacification and of Empire policing. The fear that the only gainers from future conflicts would be the Bolsheviks and their supporters obsessed many conservative politicians. A strong loathing of communist leaders and of their subversive doctrines and activities strongly influenced British foreign policy in the inter-war years. It reinforced Britain's desire in the 1920s to re-establish a strong Germany which could act as a bulwark against the expansion of Bolshevism into central and western Europe, and it largely explains Britain's reluctance to collaborate with Russia in the later 1930s to stem Nazi expansionism.[66]

One way in which Britain sought to combat the ideological challenges of Bolshevism, contain Russian power and help to maintain a stable world order was through the League of Nations. This most enduring of Woodrow Wilson's legacies was intended by him to usher in the 'new diplomacy' that would 'conquer the international anarchy which had brought on the war'.[67] It would preside over disarmament, ensure the peaceful settlement of future conflicts, and enforce collective agreements. While the new international body drew its inspiration from many sources, there is no doubt that without Wilson's insistence it would never have been established as an integral part of the peace settlement.[68]

However, the very existence of the League created enormous complications

---

[64] Quoted in White, *Britain and the Bolshevik Revolution*, op. cit. (note 62), 111.

[65] Quoted in Jeffrey, *The British Army and the Crisis of Empire*, op. cit. (note 27), 48.

[66] *See*, for example, M. Gilbert, 1966: *The Roots of Appeasement*. London: Weidenfeld & Nicolson; and W. R. Rock, 1977: *British Appeasement in the 1930s*. London: Edward Arnold, 50–1.

[67] G. Egerton, Ideology, diplomacy and international organisation: Wilsonism and the League of Nations in Anglo-American relations, 1918–20. In McKercher, *Anglo-American Relations*, op. cit. (note 50), 21–2. *See also* R. Henig (ed.), 1973: *The League of Nations*. Edinburgh: Oliver & Boyd, 5.

[68] *See* letter from Eustace Percy to Harold Temperley, enclosing his draft of the League of Nations chapter for Temperley's *History of the Peace Conference*, 10 Nov. 1920. 'I find it specially difficult to explain "Why the League happened at all". As a matter of cold historical fact it happened because Cecil and Wilson wanted it – and for no other reason!' Temperley Papers, Box 16/2a, Royal Institute of International Affairs.

for the conduct of post-war British foreign policy. It attracted massive public support, as it was seen as one of the few tangible gains of the war, the body that really would ensure that the last war would be 'the war to end all wars'. The League of Nations Union became one of the largest pressure groups in Britain in the 1920s, boasting 60 000 members by the end of 1920, and ten times that number by the end of 1926.[69] British governments of the 1920s vied with each other to demonstrate their support for the League, and to appoint Cabinet ministers with specialist League portfolios. But could a League which did not at the outset include the United States, Russia or Germany amongst its members offer Britain a realistic alternative means of securing world-wide peace and European stability? Might it not instead impose a considerable extra burden of world-wide policing on Britain's hard-pressed military and naval forces without bringing any tangible benefits?

As a founder member of the League, Britain accepted a number of unspecified and potentially onerous obligations, including the employment, in certain defined circumstances, of economic and military sanctions. With the United States at least temporarily out of the League, any dispute involving a South American member or requiring the imposition of economic or naval sanctions would immediately bring Britain into potential conflict with the United States over the exercise of belligerent rights at sea, an issue unresolved at Paris. It might also necessitate a considerable naval force, which only Britain, as the world's leading naval power, was in a position to supply. It was hardly surprising, therefore, that while British governments after 1919 loudly professed their support for the League, in practice they bent their efforts to minimising Britain's League responsibilities, in particular aiming to restrict any naval burdens that might be placed on Britain's shoulders. They also supported League-sponsored disarmament initiatives, while stressing the unique role of the Royal Navy, which would require special consideration in any draft disarmament convention to enable it to continue to protect the British Empire. This special pleading greatly annoyed France and its east European allies, whose immediate concern was to promote schemes that would strengthen the League's machinery and thereby guarantee additional security for League members against unprovoked attack. Given the widely conflicting aims and interests of member states, progress towards a disarmament convention was extremely slow, and the negotiations merely served to highlight fundamental differences and unresolved tensions, particularly among the major European participants.

A major political problem throughout the 1920s was the disparity in armaments between Germany and its neighbours. Germany's League delegates used their platform at Geneva after 1926 to demand the speedy conclusion of a disarmament convention which would reduce the forces of other European powers to their own modest levels and would prohibit weapons of war denied to Germany under the Treaty of Versailles. The inclusion of Russian delegates

---

[69] D. Birn, 1981: *The League of Nations Union.* Oxford: Oxford University Press, 24.

on the League's Preparatory Commission for Disarmament, which sat at Geneva from 1926 to 1930, ensured support for German demands, and indeed added sweeping proposals for general and universal disarmament to the agenda. When the Disarmament Conference itself finally met in Geneva in 1932, under the chairmanship of Arthur Henderson, the former Foreign Secretary in the second Labour administration of 1929–31, it failed to resolve the welter of political, military and technical problems identified by the Preparatory Commission, and, in particular, German demands for equality. The conference for all practical purposes ended after the dramatic walk-out of the German delegation under Hitler in October 1933. Its conspicuous lack of success in concluding a disarmament convention caused fervent League supporters in Britain to castigate the Government for not displaying enough commitment and determination to bring disarmament about. While the problems facing the British Government in the field of disarmament were undoubtedly complex, a recent assessment that British policy throughout the conference was one of 'vacillation: hoping for the best, anticipating the worst, avoiding blame' suggests that contemporary public criticisms had some substance. What Britain was really hoping to achieve at the Disarmament Conference, it is alleged, was to 'legitimise British rearmament' while paying 'lip-service to international disarmament for internal political reasons'.[70]

If the pursuit of disarmament proved to be a potential minefield, disputes involving major League powers were equally difficult to resolve through the elaborate League machinery designed to prevent or to localise conflict. Italy successfully evaded censure in the Corfu crisis of 1923, with the connivance of France, and Japan was able to ignore League recommendations in 1931 and again in 1932 to withdraw its troops after invading and occupying the remote Chinese province of Manchuria. After the publication of the Lytton Commission's report in 1933 proposing a number of recommendations aimed at resolving the dispute, Japan announced that it intended to remain in occupation of the renamed Manchukuo, and that it would henceforth leave the League.[71] By the mid-1930s, a renascent Germany under its new Chancellor, Adolf Hitler, having, as we have seen, also left the League, was able to exploit the international crisis caused by Italy's invasion of Abyssinia and the League's attempt to enforce sanctions against the invader. Far from proving effective as a peace-keeping body, the League was weakened by the conflicting interests of its members, and its inability in most crises to promote a unity of purpose and common approach. Instead of serving as a useful body through which Britain

---

[70] D. Richardson and C. Kitching, 1993: Britain and the World Disarmament Conference. In P. Catterall (ed.), *Britain and the Threat to Stability in Europe, 1918–45*. London: Leicester University Press.

[71] For an account of the Corfu crisis, see J. Barros, 1965: *The Corfu Incident of 1923: Mussolini and the League of Nations*. Princeton, NJ: Princeton University Press. The Manchurian crisis is fully documented in C. Thorne, 1972: *The Limits of Foreign Policy: The League, the West and the Far Eastern Crisis of 1931–3*. London: Macmillan; and in D. Dutton, 1992: *Sir John Simon*. London: Anderson Publications.

could promote its diplomacy of conciliation and peaceful revision, it brought the threat of increased commitments and costs. British membership of the League, therefore, only served to exacerbate the problems already facing Britain in Europe and throughout the world.

At the same time, membership encouraged the British electorate to believe that it represented a most effective, and ethical, approach to the prevention of future conflict.[72] British governments were therefore caught in a dilemma in the inter-war period as they attempted to achieve foreign policy goals through a mixture of traditional diplomatic means and the new League machinery. By the early 1930s, leading policy-makers were acutely aware of the League's limitations as a peace-keeping body, but politicians feared the electoral consequences of spelling them out to the British public. Therefore, as late as 1935, strong support for League of Nations action against Italy was a central plank in Baldwin's general election campaign, with no hint of the difficulties that might arise from the implementation of this firm pledge. Thus the framing of British foreign policy was significantly affected in the inter-war period by the pressures exerted by the British electorate.

All the evidence suggests that a majority of the British public after 1919 strongly supported disarmament and the League of Nations. Furthermore, they wanted their taxes to be spent on housing and welfare schemes, and not on wasteful and costly armaments. In the new era of universal suffrage for all over 21, which finally arrived in 1928, such strong electoral pressures could not be ignored by any democratically elected government. Government spending on social services, which had accounted for a third of public expenditure in 1913, rose to 46.6 per cent in 1933. Conversely, defence-related expenditure fell in the same period from nearly 30 per cent to 10.5 per cent.[73]

Undoubtedly two of the most important legacies of the First World War in Britain were a determination among those on the left of the political spectrum to press ahead as rapidly as possible with a socialist transformation of society, and a fervent wish on all sides to avoid another Great War. Any policies that might have the effect of involving Britain in conflict – arms races, secret diplomacy, alliances, imperial ventures – were inevitably going to arouse strong criticism. Therefore successive foreign secretaries, considering their responses to various crises or League initiatives, brooded above all on what the public reaction might be. Popular pressures, whether articulated by the popular press or by the churches or the League of Nations Union, were an ever-present influence on British foreign policy after 1919, steering it firmly and insistently in the direction of appeasement.[74]

Of course, as we have seen, the exposed position of the British Empire, the

[72] Henig, *League of Nations*, op. cit. (note 67); Kyba, *Covenants without the Sword*, op. cit. (note 5); M. Cowling, 1975: *The Impact of Hitler*. Cambridge: Cambridge University Press.
[73] Kennedy, *The Realities Behind Diplomacy*, op. cit. (note 30), 240.
[74] *See*, for example, Birn, *The League of Nations Union*, op. cit. (note 69); Kyba, *Covenants without the Sword*, op. cit. (note 5); and Ceadel, *Pacifism in Britain*, op. cit. (note 5).

urgent need to promote commercial and financial recovery, and the need to heal war wounds both at home and abroad all pointed in the same direction. In particular, the elevenfold rise in the national debt between 1914 and 1918 forced postwar governments to cut back on public spending as much as possible, and the armed forces were obvious targets for savings. Spending on the armed forces fell from £766 million in 1919–20 to £189 million in 1921–2, and £102 million in 1932, as a consequence of each service being asked to frame its estimates on the assumption that the British Empire would not be engaged in any great war during the following ten years, and that no expeditionary force would be required.[75] While, as we have seen, the Government tried to promote international arms limitation agreements that would bring about similar reductions of the forces of rival powers, its efforts had the unfortunate effect of raising expectations for more disarmament among the British electorate, while doing nothing to reduce the scope of American and Japanese naval ambitions or to relieve the anxieties of Continental nations such as France, Poland and Czechoslovakia. Thus serious tensions in Europe remained unresolved, while Britain's capacity to protect its world-wide interests declined.

Conclusions

There can be no doubt at all that the First World War did have a considerable impact on Britain's pre-war position of world leadership. Not only did it weaken Britain financially and bring about a radical change in public attitudes, but it also accelerated pre-war economic and political challenges and introduced new ones of a technological and ideological nature.

Some historians have questioned the extent to which the war affected Britain's global and economic power, and have argued that Britain's leaders after 1919 did not make the most of the opportunities available to them to safeguard world-wide interests. It is said that they failed to restore influence and recapture lost markets, that they followed public opinion rather than leading and educating it to the changed postwar realities, and that they failed to identify the major threats facing Britain, especially in the 1930s.[76]

But the wealth of sources now available for the inter-war period reveal very clearly that Britain after 1919 was a power in decline, a power struggling to protect its world-wide Empire and economic interests in the face of mounting

---

[75] The celebrated 'Ten Year Rule' was not rescinded until 1932. *See* Howard, *The Continental Commitment*, op. cit. (note 11), 78; and Kennedy, *The Realities behind Diplomacy*, op. cit. (note 30), 240. For a detailed examination of the formulation of British strategic policy in the 1920s, *see* J. R. Ferris, 1989: *The Evolution of British Strategic Policy*. London: Macmillan.

[76] *See*, for example, Barnett, *The Collapse of British Power*, op. cit. (note 1); Reynolds, *Britannia Overruled*, op. cit. (note 1); A. J. P. Taylor, 1961: *The Origins of the Second World War*. London; Hamish Hamilton; S. Aster, 1989: Guilty men: The case of Neville Chamberlain. In R. Bryce and E. Robertson (eds), *Paths to War*. London: Macmillan; and R. A. C. Parker, 1993; *Chamberlain and Appeasement*. London: Macmillan.

commercial, economic, political and military challenges. While the causes of the decline and the rise of new competitive forces can be traced back into the previous century, the war unquestionably weakened Britain's capacity to deal effectively with the problems already facing the country, while at the same time adding a new array of challenges. By the 1930s, Britain did not possess the resources to meet the simultaneous threats of a strong Japanese challenge in the Far East, opportunistic Italian naval expansion in the Mediterranean, and a remorseless German rearmament programme geared in its first stages to eastward expansion and European domination.

Neither old nor new diplomatic means were able to resolve the conflicts or to reduce the threats. Ironically, it has been strongly argued that only policies aimed at deterrence would have been successful against Hitler and Mussolini in the 1930s.[77] Given the outcome of such policies before 1914, a majority of politicians and of the public were strongly and understandably opposed to the use of threats of confrontation until the late 1930s. The fervent hope was that the pursuit of appeasement policies would satisfy legitimate grievances and therefore avoid another war. While it is possible to argue that Britain's inter-war leaders should have done more to face up to, and to educate the public to, the range of international problems facing Britain after 1919, their ability to resolve them was in fact very limited. There can be no doubt that the war had been responsible for both speeding up and introducing extensive change both in Europe and in the wider world, and at the same time it weakened Britain's resolve and limited its means to respond effectively.

[77] W. Wark, 1985: *The Ultimate Enemy: British Intelligence and Nazi Germany, 1933–39.* London: I. B. Tauris.

10

Britain and the International Economy

Mary B. Rose

The impact of the First World War on the position of Britain in the international economy is the principal focus of this chapter. Whether attention is directed to the Victorian era or to the 1920s, the barometer of British economic health was external prosperity and stability. It was, moreover, upon the strength of the country's economy that Britain's global status depended. Despite the enormity of this exogenous shock, the war should not, however, be seen solely as a watershed in Britain's international economic relations. Rather it exaggerated existing trends, as well as creating new ones. The identification of continuity, as well as change, makes a relatively long historical perspective important. In this context the study of Britain's late nineteenth-century experience is as relevant as that between 1914 and 1918 and during the 1920s.

To show the extent of continuity and change surrounding the First World War the chapter explores several interrelated themes. The notion of the war as an exogenous shock to the British economy and to world economic relations is subjected to critical scrutiny. The analysis of pre-war patterns of trade, overseas investment and international monetary and free trade policy allows an appreciation of the foundations of Britain's nineteenth-century prosperity. It also highlights the seeds of vulnerability that lay within it. Similarly, focus on the pre-war position of Britain in the world economic system emphasises the delicacy of the balance in the international economy. There follows an examination of the immediate impact of hostilities on Britain's trade, debt patterns and external government policies. The purpose of this is to establish the nature of any changes in direction and the extent to which they proved durable. So it is of equal importance to establish what factors influenced British government policy responses to any changes in the functioning of the international economy. In this context both historical continuities and the impact of changes outside Britain will be examined.

This chapter also explores the impact which the First World War had upon British international economic hegemony and the extent to which the origins of declining power, especially *vis-à-vis* the United States, lay between 1914 and 1918. An analysis of the effects of the war on the American economy places Britain's wartime and postwar experience in its appropriate international context. Equally, only when the influences of the war on the international standing of the United States are explored is it possible to appreciate fully the results for British external economic policy. By pointing to the limitations of the United States' pre-war international economic and indeed political position, the chapter will demonstrate how greatly the First World War benefited the United States' economy. It will also show that while the final eclipse of Britain's international economic standing may have lain in the years after 1945, that standing was significantly dented after 1918.

Pre-War Exports

In spite of popular conceptions, the overwhelming dominance of British manufactured exports in world markets was extremely short-lived and was already in relative decline long before the outbreak of the First World War. In the 1820s and 1830s many British manufacturers were so confident of the superiority of their products that they were convinced that they would be the beneficiaries of any move towards free trade. Growing foreign demand for British capital goods in the wake of the repeal of the Corn Laws in 1846 seemed ample proof of British prowess. Yet even as early as the Great Exhibition of 1851, cracks in the façade were already apparent. The display of the McCormick reaper at the Crystal Palace was a mere foretaste of the 'American system of manufacture', which was to undermine Britain's competitive advantage in some world markets even before the First World War.[1] Although sceptical of the extent to which Britain's lacklustre twentieth-century performance could be explained by the failures of the nineteenth century, Pollard has pointed to a growing unease as foreign competition gathered strength after 1880. Thus he observed that: 'To a nation accustomed to look upon itself as the world's leading economic power and the undisputed economic success story, the last three decades of the nineteenth century brought unwelcome and ominous signs of change.'[2]

For twenty years after 1873 primary and industrial overcapacity, combined with a series of serious downswings, afflicted the international economy. In Britain, heavy reliance on the staple industries, which were especially seriously affected, has led the period to be referred to as the Great Depression. In these decades, moreover, the industrialisation of Germany and the United States altered the international competitive environment. Inevitably such economic development reduced Britain's share of the world's manufacturing output from nearly 20 per cent in 1860 to 14 per cent on the eve of the First World

---

[1] Nathan Rosenberg (ed.), 1969: *The American System of Manufactures.* Edinburgh: Edinburgh University Press, 7–8.
[2] Sidney Pollard, 1989: *Britain's Prime and Britain's Decline.* London: Edward Arnold.

War.[3] More alarming, for an economy heavily reliant upon exports, was the even sharper decline in Britain's share of world trade in manufactures. While Britain was still the world's pre-eminent industrial trading nation, its share had already fallen substantially before the outbreak of war from 41.4 per cent in 1880 to 29.9 per cent in 1913. Table 10.1 shows, however, the extent to which the world's manufactured exports were produced in Europe before the First World War. Labour productivity in American industry may have overhauled that in Europe by the 1890s,[4] but Britain's closest trade rival before the outbreak of war remained Germany.

The significance of Britain's declining share of world exports before 1914 should not, however, be exaggerated. In a world where the international transfer of expertise, capital and technology was not seriously inhibited, it would have been extraordinary had Britain retained its dominance of world trade. Moreover, a relative diminution in Britain's lead should not be mistaken for absolute decline. Between 1873 and 1899, the rate of growth in the volume of Britain's manufactured exports may have dipped from its mid-Victorian peak, but none the less remained positive. Indeed, the early twentieth century showed an extremely healthy annual rate of growth of 2.72 per cent in the volume of manufactured exports.[5]

Far more worrying than the decline in Britain's lead in world trade was the narrowness of its export base and the increasing reliance upon Empire markets. Long before the First World War rocked and dislocated the international economy, British prosperity was vulnerable because Britain's exports were dangerously concentrated on a narrow range of staple industries. Despite some widening in range, coal, iron and steel, machinery, vehicles, ships and textiles made up two-thirds of Britain's exports in 1911–13, with textiles, especially cotton goods, predominating (Table 10.2).

Despite a combination of foreign competition and tariffs, Lancashire's pre-war position seemed unassailable: 'With 40% of the world's spinning and doubling spindles and one-third of its power looms, Britain's exports of cotton piece goods averaged 6,665m yards p.a in the period 1910–13, or three times

Table 10.1   World Exports of Manufactures

	1880	1890	1899	1913
United Kingdom	41.4	40.7	32.5	29.9
United States	2.8	4.6	11.2	12.6
Germany	19.3	20.1	22.2	26.5

Figures are percentages of world exports.
Source: S. B. Saul, 1965: The export economy, 1870–1914. *Yorkshire Bulletin of Economic and Social Research* 17, (Table 5) 12.

[3] F. Capie, 1983: Tariff protection and economic performance in international trade. In J. Black and L. A. Winters (eds), *Policy and Performance in International Trade*. London: Macmillan, 5.
[4] W. Lazonick, 1991: *Business Organization and the Myth of the Market Economy*. Cambridge: Cambridge University Press, 14.
[5] W. A. Lewis, 1978: *Growth and Fluctuations, 1870–1913*. London: George Allen & Unwin, 122.

Table 10.2   United Kingdom Exports by Category (Current Prices), 1870–1919

	Textiles	Cottons	Iron and steel	Machinery	Coal	Vehicles
1870–9	55	33	16	4	4	–
1880–9	49	32	15	5	5	–
1890–9	44	28	14	7	7	–
1900–9	38	26	14	7	10	3
1910–19	40	25	12	5	10	2

Figures are percentages of UK exports.
Source: B. Mitchell and P. Deane, 1962: *British Historical Statistics*. Cambridge: Cambridge University Press, 303–6.

the combined exports of the next 6 largest exporters – Italy, France, the USA, Germany, Belgium and Japan.'[6] Yet the cotton industry was extraordinarily vulnerable to changes in the international economy. More than any of Britain's staple industries it was reliant on foreign markets. Indeed, in 1913, 85 per cent of British cotton cloth was exported.[7] However, the relative simplicity of textile technology made international diffusion straightforward and foreign competition likely. In addition, in the late nineteenth century rising tariff protection began to close off once lucrative European markets for yarns. It was, however, Lancashire's disproportionate reliance on the Indian market which made the prosperity brought by the trade especially precarious. From the 1880s onwards around 40 per cent of cotton piece goods were destined for the Subcontinent.[8]

The narrowing compass of the export markets served by the cotton industry after the 1880s was reflected in less extreme form in other industries. Between 1870 and 1914 the proportion of British exports destined for Empire markets rose from 23 per cent to 35 per cent.[9] The rapid growth in the size of the Empire, rising protectionism and growing foreign competition meant it would have been surprising had this not been the case. Nevertheless, growing export narrowness with an increased reliance on predominantly Empire primary producers meant that even without the First World War, a significant proportion of British industry would have been in a precarious position in the event of either an exogenous shock or the continued international process of industrialisation.

Pre-War Competitiveness and National Efficiency

Largely unaware of and certainly unconcerned about the long-term dangers of an increasingly restricted export base, politicians, industrialists, the media

[6] Alex J. Robertson, 1990: Lancashire and the rise of Japan, 1910–1937. *Business History* 32, 88.
[7] S. Pollard, 1983: *The Development of the British Economy, 1914–1980*. London: Edward Arnold, 36.
[8] R. Tyson, 1968: The cotton industry. In D. H. Aldcroft (ed.), *The Development of British Industry and Foreign Competition*. London: George Allen & Unwin, 111.
[9] F. Capie, 1983: *Depression and Protectionism: Britain between the Wars*. London: George Allen & Unwin, 13.

and contemporary commentators were, nonetheless, of the belief that in the 1880s and 1890s all was not well in the British economy. Alert to the link between economic strength and power in the international arena, politicians were not blind to the dangers of a relative decline in Britain's economic position. The Great Depression helped to focus public and government attention on the industrial sector. Similarly, the humiliation of the Boer War caused serious alarm, not only over Britain's position as a great power, but also on the industrial and commercial leadership which underpinned Britain's previous standing. Moreover, for some there were invidious comparisons to be drawn between the competitive performance of German and British industry.

Not surprisingly, economic liberalism became for a while a questionable source of economic well-being. The strictures of the Great Depression and the reverses of the Boer War saw some stirrings of protectionism as a way of bolstering Britain's position in the international economy. Moreover, these difficulties coincided with rising tariff levels among Britain's principal competitors. In 1879, for example, Germany had introduced tariffs, which were to be further strengthened in 1903. Similarly, the Americans imposed the McKinley tariff in 1890, followed by the Dingley tariff of 1897.[10] Born, therefore, of the difficulties of the 1880s, Chamberlain's tariff reform movement was revitalised in the aftermath of the Boer War. Shifts in the international balance of economic and political power led Chamberlain to conclude in 1903 that 'Britain would have to adapt if it was to survive as a great power in a world of competing empires.'[11] This adaptation, he believed, involved a shift from liberalism to protectionism. Yet tariff reform proved electorally unpalatable, and, despite brief flirtations in time of crisis, British governments remained committed to free trade before 1914. Thereafter, the pressures of the First World War and its aftermath placed protection firmly on the agenda.[12] Before the war, however, trade liberalism represented both a policy orthodoxy derived from the experience of the nineteenth century and a critical cornerstone to the growing standing of the City of London's institutions at the hub of the world's financial markets. Equally, growing invisible earnings from shipping and insurance were dependent on the continuation of free trade.[13]

Another response to the crisis of confidence at the turn of the century was the cross-party National Efficiency movement. Primarily concerned with politics and government, the disciples of National Efficiency realised the importance of industrial prowess if Britain's international prestige was to be maintained, and recommended government intervention, especially in education, to achieve this end. Of particular relevance here was the critical link that was made between international standing, naval power and industry. It

---

[10] Ibid., 26.
[11] Scott Newton and Dilwyn Porter, 1988: *Modernization Frustrated: The Politics of Industrial Decline in Britain since 1900*. London: Unwin Hyman, 15–16.
[12] Capie, *Depression and Protectionism*, op. cit. (note 9), 63.
[13] Newton and Porter, *Modernization Frustrated*, op. cit. (note 11), 9.

was recognised that naval warfare, by the turn of the nineteenth century, had become highly mechanised and that the strength of the fleet was a reflection of a country's industrial efficiency. This perception was critical at a time when Anglo-German naval rivalry was increasing. Previously, Britain's industrial and technological lead had ensured British naval supremacy. This lead was probably retained until 1909, when the extension of the German shipyards at Kiel and the expansion of the Krupp armament works signalled an intensification of the arms race between the two countries. The National Efficiency movement was, however, singularly unsuccessful in convincing governments of the need to tackle the long-term problems of British industry, even in the face of Germany's growing industrial superiority.

That is not to say that governments ignored the problem of international competitiveness in British industry in the late ninteenth century. Concerned by growing levels of unemployment, unrest and bankruptcy in regions reliant on the staple industries in the 1880s, the Government set up a Royal Commission to examine the experience of the depression. The *Report on the Depression of Trade and Industry* of 1886 examined the problems being felt by Britain's staple industries. The commissioners did make recommendations regarding the need for a technically skilled work-force, languages and quality, while further commissions were established to investigate the state of technical education. In an effort to explain the difficulties of British industry the sources of enhanced performance elsewhere were explored. Attention was predominantly directed towards the German competitive threat, although the United States did not escape scrutiny. Thus in 1902, the Moseley Commission examined the structure and organisation of American industry in comparison to British. Nevertheless, the conclusion was drawn that industry was beleaguered by short rather than long-term difficulties. Similarly, there was apparent confidence that there was little fundamentally wrong with the competitiveness, still less the sectoral mix, of British industry, a view that seemed vindicated by the subsequent recovery and boom of 1904–13.

Pre-war Overseas Investments and Invisible Earnings

The origins of Britain's international standing in the nineteenth century were undoubtedly industrial and commercial. Yet, even at the peak of Britain's preeminence, growing food and raw material imports left a visible trade deficit, which grew substantially before 1914.[14] Especially after 1870, Britain's ability to maintain a current account surplus was dependent upon invisible as opposed to visible trade. This meant, as Table 10.3 shows, that deficits in trade in goods were counterbalanced by earnings from services and, especially after 1890, from rising earnings from overseas lending. Indeed, a recent estimate has suggested that Britain's overseas assets represented 30 per cent of national wealth

[14] F. Crouzet, 1982: *The Victorian Economy*. London: Methuen, 357.

Table 10.3   British Annual Average Balance of
Payments 1870–1909 (£m)

	Visible trade	Invisible trade	Overseas investment earnings
1870–9	−84.9	+88.5	+50.9
1880–9	−97.1	+94.0	+70.8
1890–9	−133.4	+94.4	+96.1
1900–9	−159.7	+121.7	+125.5

Source: Mitchell and Deane (*see* Table 10.2), 334–5

on the eve of the First World War.[15] Of this, much was portfolio investment in transport and infrastructure development, with countries of recent settlement such as North America and Australasia taking the lion's share, though Latin America received 17 per cent of new issues.[16] Foreign direct investment by British firms before 1914 was not, however, negligible and accounted for around 35 per cent of total capital exports by 1914.[17]

There has been lively and yet inconclusive debate concerning the impact of high levels of foreign investment on the British economy. Some historians believe that British industry was starved of finance as a result of the international interests of the City of London. On the other hand, it has been suggested that the foreign orientation of merchant banks was merely a reflection of their origins and spheres of influence, and that industrial finance was in any event available, within industrial communities, from the commercial banking sector.[18] Irrespective of their influence on the British economy, however, the direction of capital flows and their relationship to trade patterns turned out to be beneficial to the international economy. Before 1890 the counter-cyclical nature of British foreign investment, by dampening down recessionary tendencies, contributed to the relative stability of the international economy, even during the Great Depression.[19] It was, however, between 1890 and 1914 that British foreign lending, combined with the country's free trade policy, was especially significant in maintaining what was, in reality, an extremely fragile balance in

[15] M. Edelstein, 1982: *Overseas Investment in the Age of High Imperialism: The United Kingdom, 1850–1914*. London: Methuen, 3.

[16] Ibid., 39–40.

[17] J. H. Dunning, 1983: Changes in the level and structure of international production: the last one hundred years. In M. Casson (ed.), *The Growth of International Business*. London: George Allen & Unwin, 87.

[18] W. P. Kennedy, 1974: Foreign investment, trade and growth in the UK, 1870–1913. *Explorations in Economic History* 11, 436–9; W. P. Kennedy, 1987: *Industrial Structure, Capital Markets and the Origins of British Economic Decline*. Cambridge: Cambridge University Press; D. N. McCloskey, 1970: Did Victorian Britain fail? *Economic History Review*, 2nd series, 23, 446–59; N. F. R. Crafts, 1979: Victorian Britain did fail. *Economic History Review*, 2nd series, 32, 533–7; D. N. McCloskey, 1979: No it did not, a reply to Crafts. *Economic History Review*, 2nd series, 32, 538–41.

[19] S. B. Saul, 1960: *Studies in British Overseas Trade, 1870–1914*. Liverpool: Liverpool University Press, 45–56.

the international economy. The *Pax Britannica* was thus based on Britain acting as the world's major creditor at the heart of a complex web of multilateral settlements during the heyday of the gold standard. Moreover, by 1900 it was clear that 'Britain could only dominate the world economy and act as a successful imperial power as long as other nations chose to use the City of London as the contact point for their bilateral and multilateral arrangements.'[20]

The international spread of industrialisation fundamentally changed the pattern of world economic relations after 1890. From being a collection of largely independent trading areas, each nourished separately by flows of British finance, there emerged a complex, world-wide system of multilateral settlements. Industrialisation meant that there was a growing demand for primary produce from Europe, the United States and latterly from Japan which was directed primarily towards the countries of the British Empire. As a result the industrialised world, apart from Britain, amassed deficits, especially with India and Australia. These were, however, counterbalanced by visible surpluses with Britain. Britain's own visible deficits, especially with the United States and Europe, were, on the other hand, offset against impressive surpluses with several parts of the Empire, but particularly with India. Britain thus occupied a critical position in the world trading and settlements system. At the same time, the high levels of British overseas investment, by promoting the development of primary production, facilitated the expansion of international commerce, while world trade was principally financed by British credit.[21] The international transactions involved in such a settlement system were, on the other hand, underpinned by the operation of the gold standard.

Faith in the power of the international gold standard, as an automatic mechanism of adjustment responsible for such relative stability, was strong. The gold standard was a system of fixed exchange rates that pegged currencies of trading nations to the value of gold and hence to each other. This, in theory, created a kind of world currency for balance of payments settlements. The domestic money supplies of participating nations were freely convertible into gold and their size tied to inward and outward movements of the precious metal. It was believed that this system ensured automatic international balance of payments adjustment, as internal prices and interest rates responded to the gold flows created by disequilibria. The result, it was argued, was the restoration of internal and external equilibrium.[22]

[20] B. R. Tomlinson, 1982: The contraction of England: National decline and the loss of Empire. *Journal of Imperial and Commonwealth History* 11, 65.
[21] Saul, *Studies in British Overseas Trade*, op. cit. (note 19), 107, 109, 114–15, 117, 120–1, 129–31; M. W. Kirby, 1981: *The Decline of British Economic Power since 1870*. London: George Allen & Unwin, 16–17.
[22] This is not the place for a detailed discussion of the theory of the international gold standard. Excellent analyses can be found in A. G. Kenwood and A. L. Lougheed, 1981: *The Growth of the International Economy, 1820–1980*. London: Unwin Hyman; Ian M. Drummond, 1987: *The Gold Standard and the International Monetary System, 1900–1939*. London: Macmillan, 9–26; Barry Eichengreen (ed.), 1985: *The Gold Standard in Theory and History*. New York: Oxford University Press; James Foreman-Peck, 1983: *A History of the World Economy: International Economic Relations since 1850*. Brighton: Wheatsheaf, 160–82.

With hindsight, it is clear that the international economy was precariously balanced and heavily dependent upon British patterns of trade and investment. Moreover, the whole system was centralised in London, the world's clearing-house, and co-ordinated by the City's institutions.[23] With London as the nerve centre of this system, the Bank of England represented its heart, making small changes to bank rate in response to any fluctuations in reserves. Yet it was the very configuration of British balance of payments *vis-à-vis* the rest of the world, and the role of sterling as a reserve currency, that meant that the gold standard operated with minimum disruption to the internal economies of the participants. In reality, residual gold flows were minimal and the amount of British control and management consequently slight. Instead, Britain's 'export of capital and the adverse balance of trade on the one hand and the invisible income from shipping, insurance and interest on the other, more or less matched each other . . .'.[24]

At the same time, as has already been shown, within the multilateral system that had emerged there were few outstanding imbalances in visible trade, provided Britain remained committed to free trade. Nevertheless, a misplaced faith in the powers of the pre-war gold standard was to have lasting consequences for monetary policy and the health of the international economy in the aftermath of the First World War. Then the desire to reconstruct the pre-war international economic order showed little appreciation that the world economy had been precariously balanced even before 1914. There was still less realisation that the conditions that had allowed for a smooth operation of the gold standard had been swept away.

Britain's trade patterns made its economy vulnerable to war. In the first place, while Britain derived a significant proportion of food and raw materials from the Empire, 16 per cent of British imports came from France and Germany. These imports, which included a range of manufactured goods as well as industrial raw materials, were inevitably susceptible to disruption in the event of a European war. Second, the dangerous reliance of the British cotton industry on the Indian market has already been commented on. In the event of a major war that disrupted both shipping and Britain's domestic production patterns, the possibility of import substitution in the Subcontinent increased.

Also, the health of the British economy was not dependent only upon overseas trade. It has been demonstrated that the maintenance of a favourable external balance relied upon a combination of invisible trade and overseas investment. Conversely, the prosperity of the City of London, which derived from its position at the centre of the international monetary system, was dependent upon economic and political stability. It also relied upon the maintenance of substantial flows of overseas investment. A major war, by creating

[23] Kenwood and Lougheed, *The Growth of the International Economy*, op. cit. (note 22), 197–8; B. Eichengreen, 1992: *Golden Fetters: The Gold Standard and the Great Depression, 1919–39*. Oxford: Oxford University Press, 42.
[24] G. Hardach, 1987: *The First World War: 1914–18*. Harmondsworth: Penguin Books, 2.

uncertainty, would only serve to disrupt the operation of the international monetary system, while its attendant financial burdens could only alter debt patterns.

Impact of War on British Overseas Trade

Of the changes that occurred in the international economy during the First World War, the alteration in the pattern of international trade was substantial and its consequences, for Britain at least, lasting.[25] Economic warfare was pursued with increasing vigour by both the Allies and the Central Powers. The effectiveness of the early Allied blockade of Germany has been questioned. It has been shown that, at least in 1914 and 1915, goods were often channelled to the enemy, ironically via London, through neutral ports, especially in the Netherlands and Scandinavia.[26] Germany, on the other hand, encircled by an ever tighter blockade after 1915, used U-boats to wage a commercial war against British shipping. There can, however, be little doubt that Allied responses to the U-boat campaign helped to alter world trading and industrial patterns in ways that were not all reversed by peace.

Those changes had profound implications for Britain's position in the international economy.[27] In the first place, trade was reorganised along the shortest possible routes, the prime focus being the North Atlantic. As a result, the United States, neutral until 1917, became the principal supplier of food, raw materials and subsequently armaments and merchant ships for Britain and the Allies. This development had important and worrying repercussions for Britain's shipbuilding industry. A modern, rationalised American shipbuilding industry, using assembly line techniques, became the world's largest producer of merchant ships, overtaking Britain in 1918.[28] Before 1914 Britain's merchant fleet had dominated the world's carrying trade.[29] Since such pre-eminence underpinned Britain's high level of pre-war invisible earnings and indeed London's importance, loss of leadership to the United States offered a worrying prospect for the future.

Britain's trade with Australia, the Far East and South America, so important before 1914, diminished considerably.[30] As the war dragged on, such trade dwindled still further. This was because the increasing need to reserve shipping space for essential imports led to the introduction of import quotas on such commodities as raw cotton. These controls help to explain why there was a decline in Britain's traditional exports, with any shortfall in visible trade

[25] Eichengreen, *Golden Fetters*, op. cit. (note 23), 88.
[26] M. Siney, 1957: *The Allied Blockade of Germany, 1914–1916*. Ann Arbor: University of Michigan Press, 261; Hardach, *The First World War*, op. cit. (note 24), 13–19.
[27] Hardach, *The First World War*, op. cit. (note 24), 27–52.
[28] Ibid., 45–6; J. A. Salter, 1921: *Allied Shipping Control: An Experiment in International Administration*, Oxford: Clarendon Press, 361.
[29] Newton and Porter, *Modernization Frustrated*, op. cit. (note 11), 7.
[30] Hardach, *The First World War*, op. cit. (note 24), 49.

being financed by predominantly American credit. The First World War in general and the U-boat campaign in particular, therefore, resulted in a reordering of Britain's trade priorities and contributed directly and indirectly to the United States' increasing economic prowess. American exports to Britain, which had not been negligible even before 1914, grew substantially, while the Allied demand for war materials stimulated import substitution and continued organisational change in the United States' manufacturing and shipbuilding industries.

The most serious market losses for Britain came in the Far East, especially India and China, and in Latin America. A combination of wartime import substitution and import penetration by Japan and the United States transformed the postwar export prospects of British producers. In the Far East, wartime interruption of the trade in Lancashire piece goods hastened the development of the Indian cotton industry. In addition, the need to raise revenue to cover war outlays led the Indian government to increase tariff levels. Expansion continued after the war as rising Indian nationalism fuelled further protectionism.[31] Yet of the 53 per cent decline in Britain's cotton cloth exports between 1913 and 1923, it has been shown that only a quarter was due to the development of the Bombay cotton industry.[32] Of far greater long-term significance, had Lancashire's mill owners but realised it, was the continued expansion of the Japanese cotton industry and its ability to penetrate the Indian, Chinese and even the Australian market. Between 1913 and 1918 Japanese cotton cloth production grew by 55 per cent while piece goods exports quadrupled. In the same period Japan's share of India's imports rose from 1 per cent to 21 per cent.[33] This growth trajectory was to continue, with only minor interruptions, into the 1930s, when Japan became the world's leading exporter of cotton textiles, its industry performing consistently better than Britain's in a range of markets.[34] It was, however, the First World War which, the British Consul in Osaka affirmed,

> *accorded to the industry its great opportunity. . . . Not only did Japanese manufacturers find themselves freed from competition in their main market – China – but owing to the incapacity of England and other regular suppliers . . . they were able to build up a great trade in substitute goods with markets . . . to which they had not previously found entry.*[35]

Given the disproportionate reliance of Lancashire on Far Eastern markets, the long-term implications of this expansion were substantial. Indeed, it has been

[31] Ian M. Drummond, 1972. *British Economic Policy and Empire, 1919–1939*. London: George Allen & Unwin, 123.

[32] A. Milward, 1970: *The Economic Effects of the World Wars on Britain*. London: Macmillan, 50.

[33] Hardach, *The First World War*, op. cit. (note 24), 279.

[34] Robertson, Lancashire and the rise of Japan, op. cit. (note 6), 88–90; William Mass and William Lazonick, 1990: The British cotton industry and international competitive advantage: The state of the debates. *Business History* 32, 9–65.

[35] W. B. Cunningham, 1927: *Report on the Cotton Spinning and Weaving Industry in Japan*. London: HMSO, 17, quoted in Robertson, Lancashire and the rise of Japan, op. cit. (note 6), 88.

calculated that the resultant loss in trade volume between 1913 and 1925 amounted to around one-third of England's cotton-weaving capacity, with the greatest decline being felt in the Indian market.[36] Nor was Japanese wartime industrial development confined to cotton textiles. Like the United States, Japan benefited generally from the war. Enhanced export opportunities combined with Allied armament demand meant there was also a spectacular level of growth in engineering, shipbuilding, chemicals and iron and steel.[37]

A similar, though less acute, trend was to be found in Latin American markets, which had also previously been dominated by British exporters. Between 1914 and 1918 there was comparatively modest growth in domestic manufacturing output in Argentina and Brazil. Yet, as in the Far East, there was also substantial import penetration. This time it was from the United States, whose exports to Latin America grew by 75 per cent in 1916 alone.[38] Such market pressures, combined with a continuing trend of protectionism in the United States and Europe during the 1920s, contributed to the continued deterioration in Britain's visible trade balance, and to an increased reliance upon Empire markets generally.

It is true that there was some general restoration of pre-war trade patterns in the 1920s, but for Britain the First World War shook the very basis of prosperity of the export-oriented staple industries, greatly accentuating the problem of overcommitment.[39] For the cotton industry, for example, with its disproportionate pre-war reliance on Far Eastern markets, the future was bleak indeed.

The changes in trading patterns were not confined to industrial goods, or to effects on Britain. The First World War and its aftermath altered world patterns of primary production and contributed to the problem of chronic overcapacity in the 1920s. The war seriously disrupted European grain production, and the resultant shortfall stimulated expansion elsewhere. While the United States emerged as the principal supplier of food and raw materials for the Allied war effort, the growth in agricultural production was not exclusively American. Canadian wheat acreage, for example, increased by 80 per cent between 1914 and 1918, with meat production also growing.[40] Disruption of agricultural production in continental Europe was not, however, confined to the war period, so that the expansion of grain production outside Europe continued into the 1920s. Similarly the war and the postwar boom of 1919–21 stimulated plantation investment in such commodities as rubber, tea and coffee in Latin America and many of the countries of the British Empire. As a result, raw material production grew by 4.7 per cent per annum between 1913 and 1925.[41] Given the relative inelasticity of supply of agricultural goods, stem-

[36] Robertson, Lancashire and the rise of Japan, op. cit. (note 6), 91.
[37] Hardach, *The First World War*, op. cit. (note 24), 259; Paul Kennedy, 1988: *The Rise and Fall of the Great Powers: Economic Change and Military Conflict from 1500 to 2000*. London: Fontana, 385–6.
[38] Eichengreen, *Golden Fetters*, op. cit. (note 23), 88–9.
[39] Kenwood and Lougheed, *The Growth of the International Economy*, op. cit. (note 22), 175.
[40] Eichengreen, *Golden Fetters*, op. cit. (note 23), 91–2.
[41] C. H. Lee, 1969: The effects of depression on primary producing countries. *Journal of Contemporary History* 4, 141.

ming from long maturation periods of plantation crops and difficulties in altering land use, the future well-being of primary producers was dependent upon the maintenance of price and demand patterns. Yet the eventual recovery of European agricultural production by 1925 seriously undermined world prices. This jeopardised the position of such substantial wheat producers as Canada or meat producers such as New Zealand, not to mention the United States. Equally, the suppliers of raw materials also faced overcapacity.

All this occurred well before the world slump in industrial production, which began as early as 1928. For Britain, increasingly reliant upon the Empire primary producers for export markets, there were serious repercussions. Collapsing primary product prices, by eroding the export earnings of countries such as Canada, Australia and New Zealand, reduced their propensity to import British manufactured goods and thus created further problems for Britain's staple industries.[42]

The Impact of the War on Economic Liberalism

Chamberlain's flirtations with tariff reform aside, the true origins of Britain's inter-war protectionist zeal lay in the First World War, which rendered commitment to free trade increasingly difficult. As Capie has observed:

> *War and depression have proved to be two common sources of protection and it was the First World War that proved the catalyst for Britain. Some protective duties were introduced then, but more importantly a great clamouring for protection developed, with the various claimants pointing to the pivotal nature of their industry and their contributions to national security.*[43]

Introduced in 1915, the McKenna duties, placed on a range of luxury goods, served the dual purpose of raising revenue and saving valuable shipping space.[44] Yet although these survived the war, they represented a comparatively minor and almost inevitable departure from pre-war trade liberalism. It was the combination of the embarrassing vulnerability of Britain with respect to certain strategic industries and a fear of postwar dumping, especially by an undefeated Germany, which most contributed to wartime plans for protectionism.[45] Early fears that Germany would be sufficiently powerful, even after military defeat, to wage a commercial war undoubtedly altered the predominantly free trade perspectives of both businessmen and the government. Even the Manchester Chamber of Commerce, that Victorian bastion of trade liberalism, voted in 1916 against the reaffirmation of free trade principles with

[42] Capie, *Depression and Protectionism*, op. cit. (note 12), 20.
[43] Ibid., 63.
[44] Ibid., 40–1.
[45] Peter Cline, 1982: Winding down the war economy: British plans for peacetime recovery, 1916–19. In Kathleen Burk (ed.), *War and the State: The Transformation of British Government, 1914–1919*. London: George Allen & Unwin, 162–5.

respect to Germany. Similarly, the signing of the Paris Resolutions, also in 1916, removed any possibility of continued government reluctance to intervene on trade, and the Balfour of Burleigh Committee on Industry and Trade was established. The Final Report demonstrated an overwhelming concern with the economic security of British industry and commerce with respect to Germany.[46]

While peace and a defeated Germany saw a renewed commitment to classical free trade principles,[47] the belief that Britain's economic security could no longer be entirely guaranteed by economic liberalism remained. Protection of the vulnerable industries identified during the war began with the Dyestuffs Act of 1920, while the Safeguarding of Industries Act of 1921 afforded protection for selected goods of strategic importance. At the same time, a measure of protection was extended to certain 'key industries' deemed to be especially susceptible to dumping.[48] This legislation should not be taken to reflect the general abandonment of *laissez-faire*; it was after all very modest in comparison with the continued moves towards economic nationalism in the United States and Europe. In addition, Conservative defeat in 1923, on a manifesto combining protection with imperial preference, is proof that such sentiments lacked electoral appeal in the 1920s. Nevertheless, the legacy of the First World War was a rising tide of protectionist pressure from industrial groups, such as iron and steel, claiming special industry status.[49] This undoubtedly made it psychologically easier to abandon free trade principles in 1932, as world depression removed the last shreds of prosperity from British industry. That such a move was bolstered in 1932 by a system of 'imperial preference' can also in part be traced to the First World War, which if nothing else highlighted the potential dangers faced by a nation that was heavily reliant on imported foodstuffs and raw materials. More pertinent, however, to the move towards imperial preference was the rising tide of political and economic nationalism that surfaced within the British Empire in the aftermath of the First World War.[50]

It can be seen, therefore, that while the ultimate abandonment of economic liberalism by Britain was delayed until the 1930s, many of the origins of the shift to protectionism lay in the war. It has been shown that Britain's adherence to free trade had been essential to the smooth running of the pre-war international economy and to Britain's central position within it. Its abandonment was thus both a symptom and a cause of the inter-war difficulties of the international economy.

---

[46] Ibid., 163.
[47] P. Clarke, 1989: *The Keynesian Revolution*. Oxford: Clarendon Press, 29.
[48] Capie, *Depression and Protectionism*, op. cit. (note 12), 40–4.
[49] Ibid., 63–6.
[50] *See* Drummond, *British Economic Policy and Empire*, op. cit. (note 31), 25–88 for discussion of this issue; *see also* Chapter 11 in this volume.

The Impact of the War on International Finance

One of the most striking influences of the First World War was upon the pattern of international debt. The phenomenal financial burden of total war was reflected in the growing national debt of the belligerents, while the demands of war transformed the structure of international finance.[51] Even more than in the sphere of overseas trade, the effects of these changes continued from war to peace. Between August 1914 and April 1917, Britain assumed economic leadership in the struggle with Germany and acted as the principal banker and loan-raiser for the Allies. This involved raising finance for Britain's own war requirements, while underwriting borrowing by Russia, Italy and France. In order to meet these requirements it was necessary for the Government to abandon its *laissez-faire* attitude to foreign investment by placing restrictions on external capital flows.[52] By the spring of 1917, the British Government, through a combination of tax increases and the sale of government bonds, had covered 88 per cent of the $4.3 billion inter-allied credit, while at the end of the war Britain's net credit stood at some $7 billion. Even in this earlier period, however, the Allies in general and Britain in particular were becoming increasingly indebted to the United States. The rising tide of munitions and raw materials imported from the United States led to a growth of borrowing on American money markets.[53] Yet this was nothing compared to the latter part of the war when, following the United States' entry into hostilities, the United States Treasury took responsibility for financing Allied war supplies. As a result, more than $9.5 billion was put at the disposal of European governments.[54] After April 1917 the United States became crucial to the British war effort,[55] and ultimately the Government 'borrowed from the American government to pay for the "absolute necessaries of life and warfare" not far short of [$4000 million]'.[56] Thus around two-thirds of Europe's debt to America was owed by Britain.[57] The changing transatlantic financial links were not, however, confined to war debts, for there was also a rise of American business activity in Europe. Between 1914 and 1919 foreign direct investment by American firms rose from $2.7 billion to $3.9 billion, and reached $8 billion by 1930.[58]

[51] Eichengreen, *Golden Fetters*, op. cit. (note 23), 67.
[52] J. Atkin, 1970: Official regulation of British overseas investment, 1914–31. *Economic History Review*, 23, 324.
[53] Kennedy, *The Rise and Fall of the Great Powers*, op. cit. (note 37), 346; Hardach, *The First World War*, op. cit. (note 24), 145.
[54] W. Woodruff, *America's Impact on the World: A Study of the Role of the United States in the World Economy, 1750–1970.* London: Macmillan, 75.
[55] K. Burk, 1985: *Britain, America and the Sinews of War, 1914–1918.* London: George Allen & Unwin, 10.
[56] Milward, *The Economic Effects of the World Wars*, op. cit. (note 32), 46.
[57] Woodruff, *America's Impact*, op. cit. (note 54), 76; Hardach, *The First World War*, op. cit. (note 24), 145; F. Costigliola, 1977: Anglo-American financial rivalry in the 1920s. *Journal of Economic History* 37, 914.
[58] Woodruff, *America's Impact*, op. cit. (note 54), 235.

The scale and pattern of inter-allied debt inevitably affected the monetary policies of belligerent nations. Monetary expansion to finance war activities, combined with restrictions on capital flows, rendered the gold standard inoperable even if, as in Britain, it was retained in name.[59] Britain's position in Europe, combined with increasing reliance on the United States for supplies and finance, had direct bearing on wartime monetary arrangements. There was no longer a system of fixed exchange rates based on gold. Instead, as a result of Britain's position as Europe's banker, most currencies floated with sterling, and were thereby pegged to the dollar.

Such a transformation of the pattern of international indebtedness and investment had consequences which went far beyond mere financial considerations. For Britain the legacy was an unprecedented national debt and severe inflation, even though Britain remained a net creditor to Europe. For a Government convinced, by the Treasury and the Bank of England, that the pillars of sound policy were the pre-war triumvirate of balanced budgets, gold standard and free trade, this inheritance vastly complicated postwar policy.[60] Monetary expansion to finance borrowing from the United States Treasury contributed to higher rates of inflation in Britain. As a result, pre-war parity could only be achieved through deflationary government policy, which was damaging to Britain's internal economy.[61]

It was, however, the impact of changed Anglo-American relations on the timing and manner in which the gold standard was restored that is of particular relevance here. To all intents and purposes the gold standard had been inoperable for the duration of the war. Britain did not, however, formally abandon it until gold exports were banned in 1919. Almost immediately the Cunliffe Committee, convinced that it had been the basis of pre-war prosperity, argued for its eventual reconstruction, while in the early 1920s the Chamberlain Bradbury Committee was unequivocal in its support for a restored gold standard.[62] Similarly Montagu Norman, the Governor of the Bank of England, argued that 'The Gold Standard is the best "Governor" that can be devised for a world that is still human, rather than divine.'[63] Nevertheless, when Churchill, 'deafened by the clamorous voices of conventional finance', restored the gold standard at pre-war parity, he was, according to Keynes, guilty of great folly.[64]

The desire to revert to monetary orthodoxy at the 1914 pound–dollar parity of \$4.86 was undoubtedly, in part, a reflection of a desire to 'return to normalcy' and to the bygone prosperity of Britain's Edwardian heyday. Yet the return to gold in April 1925 was far more complex than a misplaced faith in

[59] Drummond, *The Gold Standard*, op. cit. (note 22), 29; Hardach, *The First World War*, op. cit. (note 24), 139–40.
[60] Clarke, *The Keynesian Revolution*, op. cit. (note 47), 29.
[61] Ibid., 31; Hardach, *The First World War*, op. cit. (note 24), 171–2.
[62] W. B. Reddaway, 1970: Was \$4.86 inevitable in 1925? *Lloyds Bank Review* 96, 17 and 24.
[63] Quoted in Clarke, *The Keynesian Revolution*, op. cit. (note 47), 36.
[64] J. M. Keynes, 1925: *The Economic Consequences of Mr Churchill.* London: Hogarth.

the institutions of a bygone age. It has, for example, been suggested that in the absence of powerful advice to the contrary, Churchill had little option but to return to gold.[65] Yet the decision can only be fully understood in the context of the changed patterns of debt and economic power which were the result of four years of war. In the first place, the transformed financial relationship between Britain and the United States left the latter in a position to influence international monetary arrangements in ways which favoured American interests.[66] Secondly, for the Bank of England, that organ of City interests, a restored gold standard was essential to the re-establishment of London's pre-war financial hegemony.

From a position of strength, as the world's major creditor, the United States Government was keen to ensure that the postwar order proved favourable to American interests. There was agreement between Britain and America that a stable postwar order was crucially dependent on the settling of war debts, balanced budgets and a form of gold standard. Yet differing wartime experience and national objectives meant that interpretation varied, and the gold-wealthy United States favoured the restoration of a full gold standard. Britain, on the other hand, preferred a gold exchange standard based on sterling and the dollar, to be co-odinated through central bank co-operation under the leadership of the Bank of England. The British expectation was that the international popularity of sterling would reap for Britain the dual benefits of bolstering depleted gold reserves and restoring the City of London to a position of international financial pre-eminence. That the United States was able to veto this proposal at the Genoa Conference highlighted the strength of the American bargaining position in the international economy.[67]

More important, however, in influencing the timing of the restored gold standard, was Britain's subsequent failure to create a trading bloc. By 1925 it was clear that unilateral British attempts to create a sterling trading bloc, alongside the US gold standard, had foundered. Few major economies chose to join, while, even more ominously, the dominions were threatening to join the gold bloc. This prospect undoubtedly hastened the return to gold by Britain in April 1925. At a time of growing Empire nationalism and when the United States was already penetrating Empire markets, such a defection would have been extremely damaging to Britain's economic outlook. Returning to the gold standard, on the other hand, offered the prospect of reuniting the Empire, which was critical if Britain was to have any hope of regaining its pole position in the international economy.[68]

As Churchill observed, if Britain had not restored the gold standard,

> *Australia would have trade with South Africa and all the Dominions would have trade with the United States on a gold basis . . . with the pound left out. . . . It*

[65] Reddaway, Was $4.86 inevitable?, op. cit. (note 62), 15–27.
[66] Costigliola, Anglo-American financial rivalry, op. cit. (note 57), 912–26.
[67] Ibid., 912–18.
[68] Ibid., 920–3.

would have been gold on the basis of the dollar and not the pound. That would have been disastrous.[69]

The United States' status as the leading creditor nation during the First World War thus had implications for postwar international relations. It had also seriously dented the interests of the City institutions. Eichengreen doubts the absolute leadership of the Bank of England in the operation of even the pre-war gold standard.[70] Yet from the perspective of the leaders of London's banking community, the meteoric rise of New York as a world financial centre was a major psychological shock. The return to gold at $4.86 was thus seen to be of great symbolic if not material significance. No matter that the position of Britain's manufacturing industry, already increasingly uncompetitive, was damaged as a result. Without parity, London's ability to compete with New York on relatively equal terms would have been seriously impaired.[71]

The conventional view that the problems of the postwar gold standard were the result of a decentralised system,[72] rather than one in which London was the pivot, has recently been challenged.[73] It may be that the failings of the recon-structed international monetary mechanism stemmed from the relative in-experience of New York financiers and the Federal Reserve. Alternatively, it is possible that a breakdown of pre-war co-operation, however tacit, and the decline in credibility of the gold standard made it inoperable in the postwar world. Against the background of altered trade and financial arrangements, international political instability, a fragmented Europe, complicated by repa-rations it comes as no surprise that the restored gold standard brought few of the hoped-for rewards, either for Britain or the international economy. It proved to be a façade of maladjusted exchange rates which could function only if there was no major dislocation or withdrawal of credit, by either the United States or Great Britain. In addition, it was incapable of removing grow-ing imbalance in the international economy. As Drummond bluntly puts it, the slump of 1929–32 meant that 'Humpty Dumpty fell from his perch and could not be reassembled.' This legacy of postwar reconstruction was swept away by 1931.[74]

Conclusions

The assassination, in Sarajevo, of Archduke Franz Ferdinand on 28 June 1914 shattered European political stability and created an international financial crisis even before the outbreak of hostilities in August. The war itself irre-

[69] Quoted in ibid., p. 926.
[70] Eichengreen, *Golden Fetters*, op. cit. (note 23), 5.
[71] Newton and Porter, *Modernization Frustrated*, op. cit. (note 11), 58–9.
[72] Charles P. Kindleberger, 1973: *The World in Depression, 1929–39.* Berkeley: University of California Press.
[73] Eichengreen, *Golden Fetters*, op. cit. (note 23), 5–11.
[74] Drummond, *The Gold Standard*, op. cit. (note 22), 43–4.

versibly changed the face of the international economy and Britain's position within it. It has become clear that the First World War

> *unleashed forces that continued to shape international economic relations for decades. The war destroyed and distorted industrial capacity across Europe while stimulating manufacturing on other continents. In its aftermath national borders were re-drawn, altering the structure of national industries and the pattern of trade.*[75]

Thus, whatever the lasting effects of the First World War on the internal economic, social and political relations of the belligerents, its impact on the functioning of the international economy was considerable.

The international balance of economic power was irreversibly tilted away from Europe by the First World War. From the Eurocentric world of the pre-war era there emerged a bipolar order as the economic strength of the United States, bolstered by the war, increased that country's international standing. The dramatic expansion of American manufacturing industry began in the nineteenth century, but it was the First World War that translated that strength into world economic and indeed political power. Between 1914 and 1918, therefore, the United States did not just become the Allies' principal source of foodstuffs, raw materials and manufactures, it also became a major source of finance. Alone of the Western pre-war industrial nations, then, the United States emerged from the First World War economically stronger than in 1914, with both visible and invisible trade in surplus. Moreover, the war induced alterations in patterns of international trade and debt, and these, by undermining the pivotal position of Britain, began the process, which was completed in the Second World War, whereby hegemony in the international economy moved across the Atlantic to the United States.

Britain, while still fulfilling an important role in the international economy, had been seriously weakened by four years of war. This was not from industrial devastation, as in Belgium and northern France, or from defeat and crippling reparations, as in Germany and central Europe. Instead it stemmed in part, though not exclusively, from the loss of markets, which were hard to recapture. That said, it should not be concluded that all the problems faced by the British economy in the inter-war period had their origins in the First World War. It has been shown that signs of economic vulnerability could be detected in the late nineteenth century. Rather, it can be argued, as Keynes did, that 'the most serious problems for [Britain were] brought to a head by the War, but are in their origins more fundamental',[76] and lay in reliance upon an organisational and institutional structure that a changing world had rendered outmoded.

In the sphere of international finance the impact of the war on Britain and its position in the international economy was none the less striking. If the late

---

[75] Eichengreen, *Golden Fetters*, op. cit. (note 23), 67.
[76] J. M. Keynes, 1919: *The Economic Consequences of the Peace*. London: Macmillan, 238.

Victorian period was marked by a relative decline in the visible economy, the stature of Britain's financiers and of the City of London, at the hub of the international economy, was undented before 1914. London's powerful position as the world's creditor was the key to its pivotal role within the international monetary system and the multilateral payments which the gold standard facilitated. It was, moreover, the invisible earnings from shipping, financial services and interest on foreign investment which ensured that Britain's balance of payments remained healthily in surplus.

It would be wrong to exaggerate London's loss of importance in international finance after 1914. Nevertheless, all the signs were that American, rather than British, institutions dominated world financial markets. Similarly, it was New York rather than London that was the prime mover in the reconstructed gold standard. The emergence of the United States as a major international creditor and a sharp rise in American wartime and postwar gold reserves both contributed to the disappearance of London's lead in the international economy. In the postwar world, the enhanced economic and financial strength of the United States gave that country the initiative in moulding the international monetary system. At the same time, the stability of the European economy and the reconstructed gold standard depended upon American flows of finance as never before.

The extent to which the First World War altered relations between Britain and the United States was captured by Burk when she argued:

> *Between 1895 and 1918, Anglo-American relations were transformed. The transformation was as much a function of British weakness as of American strength: its roots lay in Britain's relative economic decline and the changing power relations in Europe and Asia. But the weakening of Britain's international position may well have been more gradual had it not been for the First World War, which while a military victory for Britain and her allies was an economic catastrophe.*[77]

The result was a heightened tension and rivalry between the United States and Britain.[78] As the British Ambassador to the United States sourly observed:

> *The central ambition of this realist school of American politicians is to win for America the position of the leading nation in the world and also of the leader among English speaking nations. To do this they intend to have the strongest navy and the largest mercantile marine. They also intend to prevent us from paying our debt by sending goods to America and they look for the opportunity to treat us as a vassal State so long as the debt remains unpaid.*[79]

The United States had been a diplomatic nonentity in the late nineteenth century, but the First World War vastly enhanced American economic and

---

[77] Burk, *Britain, America and the Sinews of War*, op. cit. (note 55), 1.
[78] F. Costigliola, 1988: *Awkward Dominion: American Political, Economic and Cultural Relations with Europe, 1919–33*. Ithaca, NY: Cornell University Press.
[79] Costigliola, Anglo-American financial rivalry, op. cit. (note 57), 912.

financial status and thus the United States' international political responsibilities. Although the Americans were desirous of remaining aloof from European politics, the substantial debts owing to the United States, which they were determined should be paid, made isolationism unworkable. When a combination of debt reparations and inflation threatened to plunge Europe into chaos in 1923–4, the American government could not stand aside. After all, American economic well-being was dependent on European prosperity. The resultant Dawes plan, attempting to link reparations to reconstruction, was designed to work in the United States' interests. Like the gold standard, it was yet another reflection of the United States' enhanced bargaining position.[80]

It is ironic, given the impact of the First World War on the operation of the international economy, that so little had changed within Britain, and that its external policies showed such continuity with those of the pre-war era. As was seen in Chapter 3, while the war spawned new industries, it represented a lost opportunity, in terms of the transformation of the organisation and competitiveness of Britain's staple industries. Despite some expansion of new industrial sectors during the First World War, the export-oriented staple industries, on which nineteenth-century prosperity had depended, continued to be important in the 1920s. Given the wartime market losses faced by British manufacturing industry, as a result of import substitution and penetration in key markets, this was especially unfortunate. In terms of Britain's external relations it is, however, clear that the pressures to reconstruct the gold standard were far more complex than had once been thought, and were themselves intimately related to Britain's changed relationship with the United States.

[80] F. C. Costigliola, 1976: The United States and the reconstruction of Germany. *Business History Review* 50, 477–502.

11

Britain and the Empire

Stephen Constantine

At 11.00 p.m. on 4 August 1914, King George V on the advice of his ministers formally declared war on Germany. He did so on behalf of the entire British Empire.[1] This action assumed the loyalty and co-operation of the king's imperial subjects. The decision also confirmed that combat would take place between the overseas territories of the British Empire and the non-European possessions and assets of Germany (and of its future ally, Turkey), and thereby helped transform a European war into a world war. Moreover, the declaration implied that the human and material resources of the British Empire might be drawn upon not just to fight localised extra-European campaigns but to service the military needs of British forces soon to be dispatched across the English Channel for a war of uncertain duration. It may also have assumed a consciousness and approval in Britain of the self-proclaimed status of the nation as the centre of a wider imperial entity, sustained by a larger imperial patriotism: the coins of George V in the pockets and purses of the British people identified him not just as king but as emperor.[2]

British wartime claims upon the loyalty and resources of the overseas possessions of the crown inescapably tested the relationship between the metropolis and the Empire. A war fought ostensibly in the defence of Belgium, recognisably in the defence of Britain's national security and world role, and plausibly in the defence of British liberal principles was to be in part paid for with the lives and resources of peoples who did not necessarily share the same concerns or values. Moreover, the imperial assumptions of the British people might be unsettled by the effort to sustain Britain's imperial status.

Given the human and material price exacted by the war, its impact upon the British Empire might therefore seriously affect Britain's future international

---

[1] A. J. P. Taylor, 1965: *English History 1914–1945.* Oxford: Clarendon Press, 2.
[2] The title of Emperor of India descended from that granted to Victoria by the Royal Titles Act 1876; 'IND IMP' ('Indiae Imperator') appears on the coins illustrated in S. Mitchell and B. Reeds (eds), 1994: *Coins of England and the United Kingdom,* 29th edition. London: Searby, 312–22.

aspirations, capacity and authority. If the war really did impose such a 'test' upon Empire loyalties, resources and values, in Britain and in the Empire, did relationships 'dissolve' under examination, were they 'transformed' by the experience, and, if they shifted, in which direction did they travel?[3] On the one hand, the war might appear as an unprecedented demonstration of imperial unity and to have initiated a greater awareness in Britain of the merits of the Empire plus practical programmes for developing greater intimacy between its parts. On the other hand, it could be that the arrogant assumptions reflected in King George's declaration of war and the way in which British and Empire governments subsequently managed the war provoked challenges to imperial pretensions by formerly subordinated polities and peoples. Did the First World War mark both the high noon of the Empire and the dip into its long goodnight?[4]

The Empire before the War

Answering such a question is made more complex by the very nature of the Empire as it had evolved by 1914. The territories of which it was formally composed varied enormously in their cultures, their economic resources, their strategic importance and, furthermore, the degree of political independence from Britain they enjoyed.

The white settler societies of Canada, Newfoundland, Australia, New Zealand and South Africa enjoyed virtual autonomy in running their internal affairs. Most British North American colonies had had internal self-government since 1848 (becoming the unified Dominion of Canada in 1867), Newfoundland since 1854, most Australian colonies since 1855 (becoming the federated Commonwealth of Australia in 1901), New Zealand since 1856, Cape Colony since 1872, Natal since 1893, and the Union of South Africa (incorporating the former Boer republics of the Transvaal and Orange Free State) since 1910. In contrast, British rule in India and the Colonial Empire was undoubtedly more authoritarian: viceroys and governors were appointed by the British government, and local participation in policy-making was slight. However, only a handful of Europeans exercised British rule in these huge territories, therefore government necessarily also depended on the negotiated co-operation of indigenous local élites such as princes, chiefs, landowners and the urban middle classes – though punitive policing and military actions could also be sanctioned. Ireland, as ever, was a special case, entirely incorporated into the United Kingdom since the Act of Union in 1800 and with MPs at Westminster, but with no more autonomy than any other region of the

[3] The terms are those employed by Arthur Marwick, 1970: *Britain in the Century of Total War.* Harmondsworth: Penguin Books.
[4] For a short assessment of these issues, *see* A. J. Stockwell, 1988: The war and the British Empire. In John Turner (ed.), *Britain and the First World War.* London: Unwin Hyman, 36–52.

metropolis. Elsewhere, however, the authority of the British government over the globally dispersed peoples of the Empire was in practice always constrained even before 1914. Moreover, the pace and direction of change in these pre-war decades also varied, and some assessment of this is needed if we are to judge properly the impact of the First World War.

It is possible to interpret this period as a time when the formal Empire became of increasing importance in the satisfying or protection of British interests and when greater co-operation between its constituent parts was proposed and even achieved. In part these instincts were encouraged by the flows of British external trade, by the destinations of British capital investments overseas, and by the movement of British emigrants, which suggested a bias towards Empire. British-funded and British-engineered railway lines, British domination of international shipping and cable routes, and even the construction in British territories of newfangled wireless stations appeared to bind together this global empire.

However, other observers were less impressed by current statistics and more disturbed by growing foreign economic competition in Britain's domestic and overseas markets. In response, they insisted that Britain's long-term economic future lay in firming up relationships with the developing but dependent economies of the overseas Empire, especially through tariffs and imperial preferences. A natural harmony did or should exist between on the one hand Britain, whose large and largely urban population crucially needed overseas supplies of food and other primary products, and on the other hand the Empire, made up, it seemed, mainly of rural producers, whose needs for manufactured goods, capital supplies and services it was reckoned Britain was uniquely able to provide. Moreover, in a wider world more crowded with rivals (Russia, France, the United States and Japan as well as Germany), economic consolidation was also often seen as a way of gaining greater political and military security for Britain by strengthening ties with kith and kin in the self-governing parts of the Empire. Such arguments were variously expressed by, for example, the Royal Colonial Institute (first formed as the Colonial Society in 1868), the Imperial Federation League (1884), the United Empire Trade League (1891), the Tariff Reform League (1903) and the Round Table Movement (1909).[5]

Even British governments before the war sometimes seemed attracted by notions of imperial consolidation. As Secretary of State for the Colonies from 1895 to 1903, Joseph Chamberlain had endeavoured to unlock through scientific investigation and public investment in colonial infrastructures the resources of what he called the 'undeveloped estates' of the tropical empire.[6]

[5] Trevor R. Reese, 1968: *The History of the Royal Commonwealth Society 1868–1968*. London: Oxford University Press, 64–79; Peter Cain, 1979: Political economy in Edwardian England: the tariff-reform controversy. In Alan O'Day (ed.), *The Edwardian Age: Conflict and Stability 1900–1914*. London: Macmillan, 34–59.

Conservative and Liberal administrations also began to confer regularly with the prime ministers of the self-governing colonies at a sequence of Colonial and Imperial Conferences, beginning in 1887.[7] Imperial defence was high on their agendas. Traditionally, the Imperial government had provided for the security of the whole Empire against external threat, though also drawing on the manpower resources of British India. However, in a more challenging world, when the cost of weapons (especially of navies) was soaring, British governments were looking for assistance. They could not demand payments for defence from these territories, endowed as they were with traditions of self-taxation, but consultations and explanations might persuade them to contribute.[8]

The chances of co-operation had increased because those same self-governing societies were looking towards Britain for support. Partly this was for defence purposes. European colonies on the frontiers in the wider world had traditionally expected imperial protection. While the threat from Iroquois, Maori or Zulu had subsided, concerns had grown about expansionist Russia and then of Germany. Moreover, white settler communities in Australia, New Zealand and on the Pacific coast of Canada trembled before the perceived 'yellow peril' of Japan. They were therefore susceptible to British requests for contributions to an imperial defence system which would benefit themselves. In 1909, for example, New Zealand chose to donate the cost of a battle-cruiser to Britain, and Australia decided to launch a navy of its own which the British Admiralty might command in the event of major war.[9] Moreover, these societies still needed British economic resources – capital, labour and skills – for their internal development. Even in Canada the prevailing fear of absorption economically by the United States kept Canadians alert to the British connection. It was, indeed, first Canada and then Australia that pressed upon British ministers at Imperial Conferences the need for a system of imperial preferences (entailing British tariffs on Britain's non-Empire imports) to improve their sales in the all-important British market.

However, this movement towards imperial centralisation was even then outweighed by centrifugal developments. It is true that primary resistance in the

---

[6] Robert V. Kubicek, 1969: *The Administration of Imperialism: Joseph Chamberlain at the Colonial Office.* Durham, NC: Duke University Press; Michael Havinden and David Meredith, 1993: *Colonialism and Development: Britain and its Tropical Colonies, 1850–1960.* London: Routledge, 70–114.

[7] J. E. Tyler, 1967: The development of the Imperial Conference, 1887–1914. In *Cambridge History of the British Empire*, vol. 3 [henceforth *CHBE*]. Cambridge: Cambridge University Press, 406–37. Later conferences were held in 1894, 1897, 1902, 1907 and 1911, and a defence conference met in 1909.

[8] Max Beloff, 1969: *Imperial Sunset: Britain's Liberal Empire 1897–1921.* London: Methuen, 83; W. C. B. Tunstall, 1967: Imperial defence, 1897–1914. In *CHBE*, 563–604; *see also* Aaron L. Friedberg, 1988: *The Weary Titan: Britain and the Experience of Relative Decline, 1895–1905.* Princeton, NJ: Princeton University Press.

[9] Michael Howard, 1974: *The Continental Commitment.* Harmondsworth: Penguin Books, 24–6; Tunstall, Imperial defence, op. cit. (note 8); Ian McGibbon, 1991: *The Path to Gallipoli: Defending New Zealand 1840–1915.* Wellington: GP Books, 171–80.

colonial Empire had been largely suppressed, and as yet there were very few signs of new nationalist movements. On the other hand, the Indian National Congress, formed in 1885, and the Muslim League, formed in 1906, although lacking consistent mass support, were a sufficient presence to prompt in 1909 the so-called Morley–Minto reforms, which increased the political participation of Indians, especially in provincial legislatures.[10]

Emerging national consciousness in the self-governing white settler societies was still more immediately potent, and the Imperial government was more willingly responsive. Their status was enhanced in 1907 when the title 'dominions' was adopted to distinguish them from India and the dependent colonies and protectorates, and their relationship with the Imperial government was also reformed by the creation within the Colonial Office of a separate Dominions Department to handle their affairs. They were also allowed to appoint High Commissioners in London to represent their interests.[11] Culturally, the dominions were changing, not least because demographically they had all become mature societies with immigrants forming a smaller proportion of their populations than the native-born.[12] Economically, too, they were more developed, less satisfied solely with British markets for their products and less content to remain merely primary producers dependent on imported manufactured goods from Britain. In Canada the change was particularly advanced, with farmers and foresters not only looking to their southern neighbour for markets but with industrialists gaining increased tariff protection even against British imports. Symptomatically, the Canadian government insisted on negotiating its own commercial treaties with countries outside the Empire. The dominions also generated their own sub-imperialist goals, New Zealand eventually annexing the Cook Islands in 1901 and Australia taking control of Papua in 1906.[13] Even the experience of dominion volunteers waging war alongside (and often in front of) British troops in the Boer War of 1899–1902 had increased national pride, while it is claimed that the rugby tour of Britain by the 1905 All Blacks stimulated remarkable New

[10] Judith Brown, 1985: *Modern India: The Origins of an Asian Democracy*. Oxford: Oxford University Press, 142–4, 175–85.

[11] A. F. Madden, 1967: Changing attitudes and widening opportunities. In *CHBE*, 397–405; John Eddy and Deryck Schreuder (eds), 1988: *The Rise of Colonial Nationalism*. Sydney: Allen & Unwin; J. A. Cross, 1967: *Whitehall and the Commonwealth*. London: Routledge, 5–37.

[12] Seventy per cent of the Australian population were native-born by 1881, 80 per cent by 1901, and the number of native-born white New Zealanders exceeded the number of immigrants by 1886: Eddy and Schreuder, *The Rise of Colonial Nationalism*, op. cit. (note 11), 118, 144; James Jupp, 1991: *Immigration*. Sydney: Sydney University Press, 125, 127.

[13] O. Mary Hill, 1977: *Canada's Salesman to the World: The Department of Trade and Commerce, 1892–1939*. Montreal: McGill-Queen's University Press, 71–95, 148–66; Angus Ross, 1964: *New Zealand Aspirations in the Pacific in the Nineteenth Century*. Oxford: Clarendon Press; Stuart Macintyre, 1986: *The Oxford History of Australia*. Vol. 4, *1901–1942 The Succeeding Age*. Melbourne: Oxford University Press, 122–41: claims by Queensland had driven the British government to establish a protectorate over Papua as early as 1884.

Zealand self-esteem.[14] Expressions of imperial devotion in the dominions were often accompanied by demands for enhanced national status, certainly within the Empire but as equal partners with the mother country and no longer as deferential daughters.[15]

Dominion politicians were also aware of the pluralistic make-up of their societies. They had to be careful not to alienate powerful interest groups at home by provocative commitments to Britain. Organised labour in Australia and to a lesser extent in New Zealand was affected by the anti-British sentiments of Irish components and even by some nodding allegiance to international socialism. The Union of South Africa contained a large and disaffected minority of Afrikaner nationalists unreconciled to military defeat in the Boer War and to the incorporation of their former republics into a unitary state within the British Empire. Even a hundred and fifty years of British control and settlement in Canada had not dissipated French-Canadian consciousness, particularly in the province of Quebec. And in Ireland, nationalism was strong enough to persuade the Liberal Government in 1912 to push a (third) Irish Home Rule Bill through the Commons, though the modest devolution of power proposed and the apparent willingness of the Irish Nationalist Party to compromise with the British left unsatisfied a growing body of nationalist militants, including Sinn Fein (founded 1908).[16] The imperial connection was therefore not unquestioned in these societies even before 1914.

It must also be conceded that British governments before the First World War were not prepared to allow dominion governments a share in imperial policy-making. The Colonial Office might pass on information on international matters from the Foreign Office, dominion representatives might be briefed at Imperial Conferences, but the crucial decisions affecting the security of the Empire and of the United Kingdom were taken by the British government alone. Moreover, in the pre-war decade several decisions appeared to the dominions more like British disengagement from the wider world than enhanced commitment to it. Alliance with Japan allowed a withdrawal to British home waters for purposes of domestic defence of much of the British battle fleet, which heretofore had seemed to guarantee Australasian security. Similarly, in the Caribbean, British policy-makers unilaterally conceded local supremacy to the United States. British naval bases on Canada's Pacific and Atlantic coasts were also vacated in these years. And Britain's naval presence in the Mediterranean was reduced and primary responsibility devolved upon France. Evidently, once the principal danger to British interests was identified

[14] Essays by Sinclair and Eddy in Eddy and Schreuder, *The Rise of Colonial Nationalism*, op. cit. (note 11); Keith Sinclair, 1986: *A Destiny Apart: New Zealand's Search for National Identity*. Wellington: Allen & Unwin, 125–55; Jock Phillips, 1987: *A Man's Country?: The Image of the Pakeha Male – a History*. Auckland: Penguin Books, 108–22, 137–52.
[15] Carl Berger, 1970: *The Sense of Power: Studies in the Ideas of Canadian Imperialism 1867–1914*. Toronto: University of Toronto Press.
[16] Eddy and Schreuder, *The Rise of Colonial Nationalism*, op. cit. (note 11); F. S. L. Lyons, 1973: *Ireland since the Famine*. Glasgow: Fontana, esp. 256–328.

as Germany in Western Europe and in the North Sea (instead of, as formerly, Russia in the wider world), then British governments unilaterally decided upon appropriate diplomatic relations with other powers and the consolidation of armed forces closer to home.[17]

It had also been impressed upon the dominions that there was no immediate prospect of a restructuring of the British economy upon obsessively Empire lines. Proposals for British government-funded large-scale schemes of colonial economic development, or for state-funded emigration to the Empire or, most spectacularly, for tariff reform and imperial preferences were all frustrated – the last at the 1906 general election, which unequivocally revealed a popular commitment to free trade and the limits to imperial patriotism in Britain. In any case, as analysis of sectoral support for free trade suggests and as the distribution of British overseas earnings confirms, many British industrialists and the world of finance and services were committed to international and not merely to imperial customers. British external economic interests contained an Empire but were not constrained by it.[18]

In brief, on the eve of war, Britain and the scattered portions of its overseas Empire were indeed closely though variably connected by ties of sentiment, of kinship, of authority and of self-interest. But British external interests and policies were governed by British national perceptions. They were neither coterminous with Empire nor were they defined collectively through Empire consultation. Moreover, the adherence of Empire peoples to the Empire connection was not unchallenged, unconditional or unchanging. Only minority political groups within the Empire as yet advocated a total rejection of the British link. However, political pressure for change was growing in India and was rampant in Ireland, and colonial nationalism in the dominions was already leading to a demand for either equal partnership or autonomy within the Empire. Tension and change may already be discerned, even before the outbreak of war.

War and Imperial Unity

Early indications suggested that King George's presumption about the loyalty of the Empire was not misplaced. While all territories were automatically drawn into the conflict by the British decision – neutrality was not an option – imperial enthusiasts in Britain were gratified by the apparent warmth of response, which seemed to endorse their vision of a co-operative and even centralised Empire. There seemed at least a congruence between British interests and objectives and those of Empire peoples.

[17] Paul Kennedy, 1983: *The Rise and Fall of British Naval Mastery*. Basingstoke: Macmillan, 205–37; *see also* Keith Robbins, 1973: Sir Edward Grey and the British Empire. *Journal of Imperial and Commonwealth History* [henceforth *JICH*] 1, 213–21.

[18] Cain, Political economy in Victorian England, op. cit. (note 5); A. J. Marrison, 1983: Businessmen, industries and tariff reform 1903–1930. *Business History* 25, 148–78.

Immediate declarations of support echoed round the Colonial Empire, among 'all sections of the peoples of India',[19] and in the dominions, where enthusiasm for the Empire's cause was widely reported. In Canada, for example, the loyal response of Sir Robert Borden's Conservative Government was endorsed not only by Sir Wilfrid Laurier for the Liberal Opposition but initially even by Henri Bourassa, the outspoken advocate of French-Canadian nationalism.[20] The outbreak of war also united the (predominantly Afrikaner) South African Party and the (basically British) Unionist Party. Even the South African Native National Congress (forerunner of the African National Congress) and the African Political Organisation (representing the coloured communities) formally expressed their loyalty to the British Empire.[21] Just as remarkable, John Redmond, the leader of the Irish Nationalist Party, pledged Ireland's support for the Allied cause.[22]

Rhetoric was swiftly followed by practical help. Empire assistance was widely publicised in Britain. For example, serialised contemporary histories such as the *Manchester Guardian*'s weekly magazine and John Buchan's multi-volume history of the war published by Nelson devoted distinctive space to the activities of imperial troops. On 6 August 1914 the British Cabinet authorised six campaigns against Germany's overseas colonies,[23] and in enthusiastic response New Zealand forces at once occupied German Samoa while Australian troops took over German New Guinea and Nauru. Imperial soldiers also invaded German Togoland and the Cameroons in West Africa, the South Africans crossed into German South West Africa, and an imperial war in microcosm broke out in German East Africa, involving British-officered King's African Rifles from Uganda and the East Africa Protectorate, reinforcements from other British African colonies, infantry brigades from India, and a strong force from South Africa. Imperial troops ensured that after the war these former German colonies were incorporated into the British Empire as League of Nations mandated territories.

Imperial forces were also engaged against the Ottoman Empire. The Indian Army was committed to an initially disastrous but ultimately successful advance through the oilfields of the Persian Gulf into Mesopotamia, concluded by the occupation of Baghdad in March 1917. Australian and New

[19] Hugh Tinker, 1968: India in the First World War and after. *Journal of Contemporary History* 3, 89.

[20] R. G. Moyles and Doug Owram, 1988: *Imperial Dreams and Colonial Realities: British Views of Canada 1880–1914*. Toronto: University of Toronto Press, 235; *see also* reports in *The Times*, 4–6 August 1914.

[21] T. R. H. Davenport, 1987: *South Africa: A Modern History*, 3rd edition. London: Macmillan, 273; N. G. Garson, 1979: South Africa and World War I. *JICH* 8, 74.

[22] Lyons, *Ireland*, op. cit. (note 16), 310–11, 329; Stephen Hartley, 1987: *The Irish Question as a Problem in British Foreign Policy, 1914–18*. London: Macmillan, 18–19.

[23] John S. Galbraith, 1984: British war aims in World War I: A commentary on 'Statesmanship'. *JICH* 13, 23–45. For accounts of the colonial military campaigns, *see* C. E. Carrington, 1967: The Empire at war, 1914–1918. In *CHBE*, 607–22; W. Roger Louis, 1967: *Great Britain and Germany's Lost Colonies 1914–1919*. Oxford: Clarendon Press; and Byron Farwell, 1986: *The Great War in Africa 1914–1918*. New York: Norton.

Zealand troops were an important element in the forces first blooded wastefully at Gallipoli from 25 April 1915 to 8 January 1916 but then used more effectively (with some South African contingents) in extending the formal British Empire in the Middle East. Indian and dominion troops therefore helped ensure that in the eventual peace settlement Britain secured mandated control of Palestine, Trans-Jordan and Iraq (Mesopotamia).

Dominion (and some Indian) forces were also committed to war on the Western Front, as distinctive divisions, brigades or battalions, but seemingly welded into the British Army. British observers praised their actions. Examples include Canadian troops at Ypres in 1915 and Vimy Ridge in 1917, and the Newfoundland Regiment on the first day of the Battle of the Somme in 1916 (when it was virtually annihilated). Similarly effective were the South Africans, especially at Delville Wood, and Australian and New Zealand forces also at the Somme and later, with the Canadians, in the mud of Passchendaele in 1917. Noticeable too were men from the dominions in the Royal Flying Corps, 12 000 from Canada alone: several of the leading 'aces' were Canadians, including Bishop (with 72 'kills').[24]

The demographic resources of the Empire were copiously drawn upon in these campaigns, initially usually from volunteers, later, in places, by compulsion. Official statistics record that during the war 458 218 Canadians served overseas, of whom 56 639 were killed. Similarly, 331 814 Australians went abroad to war and 59 330 died. The New Zealanders going overseas totalled 112 223, and 16 711 did not come back. Even some Maori tribes had insisted on their involvement, and Maori contingents totalled 2227. From South Africa, scene of recent internal war between Boer and Briton, 76 184 troops from both communities fought abroad, and 7121 were killed. Even tiny Newfoundland contributed 2000 men to the Royal Navy plus 6173 as soldiers, of whom 1204 died.[25]

More remarkable perhaps were the contributions from Britain's autocratically run Empire. Indian princes with martial traditions immediately offered their personal services and those of their troops. Altogether 1 440 437 additional recruits were gathered into the Indian Army, notionally on a voluntary basis, and 943 344 had been sent abroad by the end of October 1918. The white officers thought necessary to command these forces were also expanded by drawing in India upon the British community formerly engaged in civil administration or commerce: only 2586 British officers had made up the pre-war establishment in the Indian Army, but 23 040 British officers served abroad before the end of the war. There was an equivalent expansion of medical, transport and other support services. At the final roll

[24] Carrington, The Empire at war, op. cit. (note 23); Denis Winter, 1982: *The First of the Few.* London: Allen Lane, 20–3.

[25] Carrington, The Empire at war, op. cit. (note 23), 641–2; P. O'Connor, 1967: The recruitment of Maori soldiers, 1914–18. *Political Science* 19, 65.

call, in all theatres, 62 056 members of the Indian Army had died in the Empire's cause.[26]

The Colonial Empire also made its military contributions. Even the tiny West Indian colonies produced enthusiastic volunteers, not just the 90 men of the all-white Bermuda Volunteer Rifle Corps but also from the West Indian black and coloured communities, who pressed reluctant British authorities to allow them to serve overseas in Britain's 'white man's war'. Eleven battalions were eventually allowed, made up of 397 officers and 15 204 other ranks (185 were killed and a dispiriting 1071 died of sickness). About 34 000 troops were also raised in British East Africa, of whom 2000 were killed, and another 25 000 were enlisted in British West Africa, of whom about 850 were killed. Troubled Ireland also produced volunteers for the British Army, from both Protestant and Catholic communities, adding nearly 135 000 to the 50 000 Irishmen already serving in the regular Army and suffering 35 000 dead by the end of the war.[27] Such blood sacrifices seemed to many British observers inspiring evidence of imperial loyalties.

But it was not just combatants that this war needed. Battle required the support of non-combatant labour. The campaigns in tropical Africa – where mechanised mobility was restricted by limited road, rail and river communications and where even animal transport was confined by tsetse fly – were highly dependent upon largely conscripted carrier and labour forces. Nearly a million men were recruited in East Africa alone; maltreatment and horrendous conditions caused over 90 000 deaths among these non-combatants. Industrialised warfare on the Western Front had its own peculiar appetites, to build base camps and rail and road links to the Front, to heave up weapons, ammunition and other supplies, to cart away and cope with the casualties. In September 1916, in response to an Imperial government request for help, the South African government attracted some and coerced other black Africans into the South African Native Labour Contingent. By January 1918, when the contingent was disbanded, some 21 000 had laboured in France. It is reckoned that in November 1918 labour units from Empire sources who were serving outside their own countries included 82 000 Egyptians, 20 000 Indians, 8000 West Indians, 1200 Cape Coloureds, 1000 Mauritians and even 100 Fijians; there were also some 92 000 Chinese labourers.[28] Such military participation

[26] Carrington, The Empire at war, op. cit. (note 23), 642; L. F. R. Williams, 1932: India and the war. In *Cambridge History of India*, vol. 6. Cambridge: Cambridge University Press, 477, 481–2; Gregory Martin, 1986: The influence of racial attitudes on British policy towards India during the First World War. *JICH* 14, 91–113; Jeffrey Greenhut, 1983: The imperial reserve: The Indian Corps on the Western Front, 1914–15, *JICH* 12, 54–73.

[27] C. L. Joseph, 1971: The British West Indies Regiment 1914–1918. *Journal of Caribbean History* 2, 94–124; Carrington, The Empire at war, op. cit. (note 23), 642; Terence Denman, 1992: *Ireland's Unknown Soldiers*. Blackrock, Co. Dublin: Irish Academic Press.

[28] Albert Grundlingh, 1985: Black men in a white man's war: The impact of the First World War on South African blacks. *War and Society* 3, 56–7; Geoffrey Hodges, 1986. *The Carrier Corps: Military Labor in the East African Campaign 1914–1918*. Westport, Conn.: Greenwood, esp. pp. 110–11; Carrington, The Empire at war, op. cit. (note 23), 642.

by Empire peoples – often alongside British troops, always under white if not necessarily under immediate British command, and broadly under British strategic direction – was inevitably interpreted in British sources as literally vital proof of the integrity of the Empire.

Financial contributions from the Empire to Britain's war effort were also much needed and often generously given, though sometimes more forcefully obtained. The Raj government presented £100 million (more than a full year's revenue) to the British Treasury on behalf of the unconsulted Indian people. In addition, the cost of supporting Indian troops overseas, running at £20 to £30 million a year, which would normally have been a charge upon the British government, was assumed by the Indian government and therefore Indian taxpayer. Colonial Empire governments that had sent men to help the Empire at war similarly found themselves saddled with many of the financial costs of their support. More valuable to Britain financially, the governments of the dominions, with the approval of their parliaments, funded most of the financial cost of their own armies overseas as well as other war-induced public investment. While much of this dominion expenditure depended on loans from Britain (and thereby competed with the British government's own domestic borrowing), internal dominion resources and some external funds were also drawn upon. Canada, for example, increased its national debt from £67 million to £317 million, by borrowing about £48 million in Britain and the rest locally or from the United States. The story for Australia and New Zealand is similar, whereas South Africa, prospering on demand for its gold and farm produce and benefiting financially from the increased use of the Cape by shipping, had to borrow much less. At the other extreme, dear to imperial sentimentalists, were the tiny tributes from the Empire's poor, such as the £200 from the Galla tribe in the East Africa Protectorate.[29]

Raw materials and other supplies were also given, purchased or taken for the Empire's cause. The treasure house of Empire was unlocked as never before. Foodstuffs, palm oil, rubber, cotton and minerals such as tin and copper were sometimes forcibly obtained from colonial sources or at prices fixed below market rates by colonial administrations. India's cotton, jute, and iron and steel industries were cranked up; output of manganese, saltpetre, rubber, petroleum, tea, wheat and other products increased; and the tungsten mines of Burma hastily developed. The Indian Munitions Board, set up in 1917, helped equip the Indian Army and thus ease the demands on British output. Similarly, the New Zealand government's choicely named Department of Imperial Government Supplies was established early in 1915, and monopolised for the British market at agreed prices all New Zealand's exports of frozen meat, wool, butter, cheese and hides. Both Australia and Canada also contributed to the war effort not just by increasing primary production but by

[29] Carrington, The Empire at war, op. cit. (note 23), 642–3; Williams, India and the war, op. cit. (note 26), 483–4; Joseph, The British West Indies Regiment, op. cit. (note 27), 108–9; Macintyre, *The Oxford History of Australia 1901–42*, op. cit. (note 13), 154; Robert Bothwell, Ian Drummond and John English, 1987: *Canada 1900–1945*. Toronto: University of Toronto Press, 179–80; Michael Crowder, 1984: The impact of two world wars on Africa. *History Today* 34, 13.

manufacturing munitions. Irish output of foods and textiles similarly grew. The Marakei people in the Gilbert Islands offered a supply of coconuts. 'That coco-nut spirit of contributing your utmost was characteristic of the whole Empire', claimed Lloyd George. All this seemed encouraging evidence to British observers that the Empire was indeed a rich and loyal asset in wartime, whatever pre-war family tensions might have agitated the air.[30]

However, the war also showed that not all the manpower, financial or economic needs of wartime Britain were being met from existing British and imperial resources. Pre-war supplies from continental Europe were cut off and much had to be derived from the United States. Shortages exasperated especially those who before the war had been lobbying for imperial economic development and closer imperial economic ties. The resources of the huge British Empire cried out for state-activated development, for reasons of military security as well as economic prosperity. This thesis was promoted in specialist and popular periodicals and by various pressure groups, and was largely endorsed by official inquiries. Moreover, government acceptance of new economic strategies that often contained an imperial dimension seemed to be creeping in, especially with the passage of Imperial War Conference resolutions favouring imperial preferences in 1917 and Empire migration in 1918.[31]

Such a reorientation of British policy away from a broad commitment to international economic interests towards a more concentrated attention on Empire components seemed to be matched by political consolidation. Dominion prime ministers, especially Borden from Canada and Hughes from Australia, coupled their dispatch of troops and supplies to Britain's war with a more insistent demand for consultation in their usage, and those requests appeared to be granted. Information flows increased. Borden in July 1915 and Hughes in March 1916 actually attended routine British Cabinet meetings. Representatives of Australia and Canada attended the Paris Economic Conference of the Allies in June 1916. More strikingly, Lloyd George invited dominion prime ministers to fourteen meetings of a specially convened Imperial War Cabinet from March to May 1917, held in parallel with sessions of an Imperial War Conference. As another symbol of imperial unity, for the first time this also included two Indians – the Maharajah of Bikaner and

[30] Crowder, The impact of two world wars on Africa, op. cit. (note 29), 13; Williams, India and the war, op. cit. (note 26), 480, 483; M. F. Lloyd Prichard, 1970: *An Economic History of New Zealand to 1939*. Auckland: Collins, 236–7; Macintyre, *The Oxford History of Australia 1901–42*, op. cit. (note 13), 155; Bothwell *et al.*, *Canada 1900–45*, op. cit. (note 29), 169–76; Lyons, *Ireland*, op. cit. (note 16), 359–60; Garson, South Africa and World War I, op. cit. (note 21), 77–8; David Lloyd George, 1938: *War memoirs*, vol. 2. London: Odhams, 2005.

[31] Stephen Constantine, 1984: *The Making of British Colonial Development Policy 1914–1940*. London: Cass, 32–9; David Killingray, 1982: The Empire Resources Development Committee and West Africa 1916–20. *JICH* 10, 194–210; Reese, *The History of the Royal Commonwealth Society*, op. cit. (note 5), 116–19; Kent Fedorowich, 1990: The assisted emigration of British ex-servicemen to the dominions, 1914–1922. In Stephen Constantine (ed.), 1990: *Emigrants and Empire: British Settlement in the Dominions between the Wars*. Manchester: Manchester University Press, 45–71; Suzann Buckley, 1974: The Colonial Office and the establishment of an Imperial Development Board: The impact of World War I. *JICH* 2, 308–17.

Sir S. P. Sinha – among the three representatives of the Indian government. This exercise in consultation was repeated during the summer of 1918 when another Imperial War Conference was summoned and further meetings of an Imperial War Cabinet were held. However, perhaps Lloyd George's boldest imperial gesture was the appointment of General Smuts, already a member of Botha's South African Government, to his own War Cabinet in June 1917. It was not long since Smuts had been leading Afrikaner troops against the British Army in the Boer War. Imperial unity had its brightest image.[32]

War and Imperial Tensions

But the impression of imperial consolidation was misleading. Pre-war tensions within and between the constituent parts of the Empire and the pre-war trajectories of development in intra-imperial relations were neither eased nor reversed by the experience of waging an imperial war. In many respects the war served to exacerbate and to accelerate. While the predominant and official response across the Empire was to endorse the war as an imperial commitment, that reaction was not universally welcomed. Moreover, efforts to extract material and especially human resources from each territory to fight this unexpectedly long war often deepened pre-existing divisions. Those components of the population already critical of the dominant culture were most likely to remain at least aloof from the war effort and sometimes became even more antagonistic towards official policy, with implications for the Empire's integrity.

It is true that in most parts of the Colonial Empire wartime challenges to British imperial rule were only local and limited. Passive and occasionally active resistance to the recruiting of non-combatant labourers and desertion during the campaigns in West and East Africa show that loyalties were less deep than imperial enthusiasts were prepared to admit. Unrest was also sparked by wartime rises in prices and restrictions on imports. In Egypt such problems were exacerbated when, with the outbreak of war against Turkey, the fiction that Egypt was part of the Ottoman Empire was shredded, and a British protectorate was declared over this strategically vital territory. But at least active political resistance, such as the rebellion led by John Chilembwe in Nyasaland in 1915, was rare, and was vigorously repressed.[33]

The war accelerated the pace of political change in India. Comparatively

[32] Carrington, The Empire at war, op. cit. (note 23), 631–2; Nicholas Mansergh, 1969: *The Commonwealth Experience*. London: Weidenfeld & Nicolson, 170–5; Lloyd George, *War memoirs*, op. cit. (note 30), vol. 1, pp. 1023–57.

[33] *See* essays in the special issue of *Journal of African History* 19 (1978) and in Melvin E. Page (ed.), 1987: *Africa and the First World War*. London: Macmillan; Michael Crowder, 1985: The First World War and its consequences. In A. Adu Boahen (ed.), *Unesco General History of Africa* Vol. 7, *Africa under Colonial Domination, 1880–1935*. London: Heinemann, 283–311; Akinjide Osuntokun, 1979: *Nigeria in the First World War*. London: Longman, ix–xi; Joseph, The British West Indies Regiment, op. cit. (note 27), 119–21; S. E. Katzenellenbogen, 1973: Southern Africa and the war of 1914–18. In M. R. D. Foot (ed.), *War and Society*. London: Elek, 117–20; R. von Albertini, 1969: The impact of two world wars on the decline of colonialism. *Journal of Contemporary History* 4, 20 and 23; John Darwin, 1981: *Britain, Egypt and the Middle East: Imperial Policy in the Aftermath of War 1918–22*. London: Macmillan, 47–79.

few of India's huge population of 315 million found themselves in imperial armies, and there was never any serious suggestion of introducing conscription, but popular toleration of the Empire's war was disturbed as elsewhere by the rapid rise in prices and other economic dislocations. Also, many Indian Muslims were uneasy when the King-Emperor went to war against the Sultan of Turkey, the titular head of the Islamic faith. Indeed, such was the British sense of insecurity in India that Territorial Army units were brought in from Britain to sweat out the war as an imperial police force.[34] Violent political dissent, like the ill-supported revolutionary Ghadr movement, was limited and easily if brutally suppressed. But the Indian National Congress and the Muslim League worked more closely together and employed the democratic rhetoric of the war for their own purposes. The British authorities responded by trying to satisfy moderate nationalists by pre-emptive conciliatory gestures. In August 1917 the Secretary of State for India, Edwin Montagu, committed the British government to 'the progressive realisation of responsible government in India as an integral part of the British Empire'. This was the first official acknowledgement that India might become a 'brown' dominion. After consulting nationalist leaders (Tilak and Jinnah) and the viceroy (Lord Chelmsford), Montagu finally produced in 1918 a blueprint for postwar constitutional reform. Such promises raised nationalist expectations.[35]

More urgent were problems closer to home in Ireland. Not surprisingly, the decision of John Redmond and the Irish Nationalist Party in 1914 to support Britain's war was unacceptable to Sinn Fein and other extreme nationalists. Less expected, however, was the Easter Rising in Dublin in 1916, when an Irish republic was proclaimed. The immediate military danger to the Empire was easily suppressed, though over 450 people died in the fighting. However, the gesture and the subsequent insensitivity of the British authorities, with their courts martial and executions, radicalised Irish opinion. Public feeling was additionally disturbed when the needs of war induced the Imperial government in April 1918 to revive plans to impose on Ireland the system of military conscription operating in Britain since 1916. Rates of volunteering in Ireland (especially outside Ulster) had always been much below British averages,[36] but a forced levy would be especially provocative. In the postwar general election in December 1918, support for the moderate Irish Nationalist Party, with its modest programme of Home Rule, collapsed. Sinn Fein, determined on republican independence, won seventy-three seats and promptly challenged

[34] For a biographical account, *see* C. P. Mills, 1988: *A Strange War: Burma, India and Afghanistan 1914–1919*. Gloucester: Alan Sutton.
[35] Judith Brown, 1973: War and the colonial relationship: Britain, India and the war of 1914–18. In Foot, *War and Society*, op. cit. (note 33), 85–106; Brown, *Modern India*, op. cit. (note 10), 187–98; Sumit Sarkar, 1989: *Modern India 1885–1947*, 2nd edition. London: Macmillan, 147–53, 165–78; S. R. Mehrotra, 1965: *India and the Commonwealth 1885–1929*. London: Allen & Unwin.
[36] Comparable figures for enlistments during the war are 26.9 per cent of males aged 15–49 in Scotland, 24.2 per cent in England and Wales and 10.7 per cent in Ireland: J. M. Winter, 1985: *The Great War and the British People*. London: Macmillan, 28.

the authority of the Imperial government by refusing to attend Parliament in Westminster, by declaring again an Irish republic, and by launching Ireland into a war for independence. Ireland had been poised on the brink of civil war before August 1914, but, clearly, events during the First World War had given credibility to nationalist extremists and shaken the imperial connection.[37]

In South Africa, similarly, the decision to endorse the British war polarised opinion, although again on predictable lines. Louis Botha's Government and his South African Party were challenged by Afrikaners unreconciled to British imperial control. His decision to commit South African forces to the attack on German South West Africa even provoked uprisings, and this rebellion distracted from South Africa's war effort until its final suppression in February 1915. Not surprisingly, discontent remained and put limits to the degree of South African commitment to the war. For example, only 11.12 per cent of the white male population were recruited into the South African armed services, distinctly fewer than the proportion from other dominions (the comparable United Kingdom figure was 22.11 per cent), yet the government shrank from proposals to introduce conscription. The general election of 1915 showed that already Botha was losing Afrikaner support, and he was driven awkwardly to rely on the British loyalists of the Unionist Party. Hertzog and his National Party adopted the radical goal of republican independence, and after the first postwar election in 1920 became the largest single party in Parliament. The Government survived only with the support of Unionists and Independents. The domestic impact of the First World War had therefore left the South African Party even more in danger of being outflanked by militant Afrikaner nationalists hostile to the British connection. The effect on official relations with the Imperial government was to be discernible after the war.[38]

Even in Canada, wholehearted popular and political commitment to the imperial war effort proved impossible to sustain. Economic mobilisation had opened up a clash of interests between employers (frequently waxing wealthy on war-induced orders) and workers (chasing rising prices). But it was the effort to meet the war's manpower needs that was especially divisive. Volunteering for active service was in general sluggish among all Canadian-born men. Canadian troops sent overseas rose no higher than 13.48 per cent of the male population. Only 51 per cent of the total Canadian Expeditionary Force were born in Canada, and British-born immigrants formed nearly 65 per cent of the first contingent. But it seemed to British Canadians that it was the French Canadians who were particularly reluctant to enlist. French-Canadian commitment was not encouraged by official unwillingness to form French-speaking regiments or to employ more French-speaking officers. But detachment boiled over into anger when the Conservative Prime Minister,

[37] Lyons, *Ireland*, op. cit. (note 16), 330–408; Hartley, *The Irish Question*, op. cit. (note 22).
[38] T. R. H. Davenport, 1963: The South African rebellion. *English Historical Review* 78, 73–94; Davenport, *South Africa*, op. cit. (note 21), 271–4; Katzenellenbogen, Southern Africa and the war, op. cit. (note 33), 107–21; Garson, South Africa and World War I, op. cit. (note 21).

Robert Borden, pushed through in August 1917 the Military Service Act. Conscription was interpreted in Quebec as a hostile attack upon French Canadians by the British majority. Most British Canadians, including many Liberals, rallied behind the Government, and this allowed Borden to form a so-called Union Government later in 1917. French Canadians remained an excluded and self-consciously embattled minority. Divisions were confirmed by the general election of December 1917. Anti-conscription riots broke out in Quebec at Easter 1918, five protestors were killed, and the Quebec provincial legislature debated secession. The Liberal Party faced particular problems: it had been badly split and in Quebec risked being outflanked by embittered and assertive French-Canadian nationalists (as had happened to Redmond in Ireland and faced Botha in South Africa). Mackenzie King, who became the new Liberal Party leader in August 1919, was conscious of the consequences for Canada and for the Liberals of the dominion's too ready response to imperial demands.[39]

In Australia, also, the effort to mobilise resources for war eventually exposed social divisions. By the summer of 1916, the Labor Prime Minister, William Hughes, concluded, like Borden in Canada, that the rising casualty figures and the needs of Britain's war required the introduction of military conscription. Hughes put the matter to a referendum in October 1916, and lost. In the process he split the Labor Party. He survived by creating a National Coalition with the Liberals in January 1917 and won a general election in May, but in a second referendum in December 1917 a (small) majority again rejected conscription. While the volume of voluntary recruitment indicates extensive support for Australia's participation in the Empire's war, the resistance to conscription reveals the limits of tolerance. Recruitment levelled out at 13.43 per cent of the white male population. Opposition was only partially a defence of civil liberties. Rather it reflected the hostility of many trade unionists, who resented government's failure to control prices and maintain wages; of many farmers who feared a shortage of labour; of many Irish Australians (20 per cent of the population) whose anti-British feelings had not been sweetened by British behaviour in Ireland after Easter 1916; and of much of the Roman Catholic hierarchy led by Archbishop Mannix, who voiced cultural and political objections to state authoritarianism and to British imperialism. Hughes managed to win the federal election of 1919, but he governed a divided country, aware of the cost of supporting Britain's war and awaiting compensatory rewards for Australia.[40]

[39] Bothwell *et al.*, *Canada 1900–45*, op. cit. (note 29), 119–37; J. L. Granatstein and J. M. Hitsman, 1977: *Broken Promises: A History of Conscription in Canada*. Toronto: Oxford University Press, 22–104; R. MacGregor Dawson, 1958: *William Lyon Mackenzie King: A Political Biography 1874–1923*. London: Methuen, 296–9, 319, 329.
[40] Macintyre, *The Oxford History of Australia 1901–42*, op. cit. (note 13), 142–91; Ian Turner, 1974: *1914–19*. In F. K. Crowley (ed.), *A New History of Australia*. Melbourne: Heinemann, 312–56; Ernest Scott, 1936: *Official History of Australia in the War of 1914–1918*. Vol. 9, *Australia during the War*. Sydney: Angus & Robertson, esp. pp. 286–480; E. M. Andrews, 1993: *The Anzac Illusion: Anglo-Australian Relations during World War I*. Cambridge: Cambridge University Press, 120–8.

It is true that when military volunteering began to fall in New Zealand, especially after Gallipoli, opposition to conscription was more muted. A Military Service Act was passed on 1 August 1916, undoubtedly with majority popular support. Altogether a remarkable 19.35 per cent of white males eventually served overseas. Only a few registered their dissent on grounds of conscience, and only a tiny number were prepared to carry their resistance to the limits. Nevertheless, conscription had aroused the opposition of socialists and some trade unionists, already antagonised as in Australia by official failures to control prices and profits. From the splinters of the pre-war labour movement was formed the New Zealand Labour Party in July 1916. Moreover, many among the Irish community resented the official commitment to the Empire's cause and especially conscription. They were further distressed by the bigotry of the Protestant Political Association, formed in July 1917 and endorsed, they feared, by the Prime Minister, William Massey, an Ulster Presbyterian by birth. It is revealing of social wounds that after the war the Roman Catholic hierarchy was not invited to join Anzac Day services until late in the 1930s. Strikingly, too, in spite of volunteer enlistment by some Maori, the state backed away from plans to impose conscription upon all Maori peoples, fearing especially rejection by those tribes in central North Island still smarting from comparatively recent land confiscations. Massey's authority was never seriously challenged in the war, but no more in New Zealand than elsewhere had waging war closed social gaps.[41]

Even the allegiances of those from the dominions most committed to the imperial cause were often altered by battlefield experiences. Dominion soldiers were commonly irritated by the ill-concealed social prejudice of many British regular army officers against non-professional and invariably non-deferential soldiers from 'the colonies'. British military values jarred with dominion concepts of 'mateship' and social equality. Dominion resentment was exacerbated when the competence of British commanders was also called into question. The alleged wasteful sacrifice by British 'brass hats' of 'good blokes' from the dominions fired up the sense of difference.[42] Moreover, the very achievements of dominion forces in spite of (rarely because of) such leadership fuelled a national pride. Those who got out of Gallipoli or survived the Western Front regarded themselves as national heroes. That self-esteem was amplified during the war by public responses at home, among family and friends, by the press and politicians.[43] War experiences seem to have induced

[41] Paul Baker, 1988: *King and Country Call: New Zealanders, Conscription and the Great War.* Auckland: Auckland University Press; P. S. O'Connor, 1974: The awkward ones: Dealing with conscience, 1916–1918. *New Zealand Journal of History* 8, 118–36; O'Connor, The recruitment of Maori soldiers, op. cit. (note 25), 62–83; Maureen Sharpe, 1981: Anzac Day in New Zealand. *New Zealand Journal of History* 15, 105; Phillips, *A Man's Country?*, op. cit. (note 14), 159–63.

[42] Denis Winter, 1969: *Death's Men: Soldiers of the Great War.* Harmondsworth: Penguin Books, 46–9; Phillips, *A Man's Country?*, op. cit. (note 14), 172–6, 179–81; Turner, 1914–1919, op. cit. (note 40), 323, 347; Macintyre, *The Oxford History of Australia 1901–42*, op. cit. (note 13), 180–1; Andrews, *The Anzac Illusion*, op. cit. (note 40), 165–89.

[43] Phillips, *A Man's Country?*, op. cit. (note 14), 163–4; Turner, 1914–1919, op. cit. (note 40), 324, 349; Macintyre, *The Oxford History of Australia 1901–42*, op. cit. (note 13), 151; K. S. Inglis, 1965: The Anzac tradition. *Meanjin Quarterly* 24, 25–44.

if not the birth of new nations at least their accelerated coming of age. At the popular level, then, even willing participation in Britain's war did not leave unaffected the speed with which intra-imperial relationships were developing.

As such these shifts paralleled developments at the level of high politics. Dominion politicians like Borden, who before 1914 had sought to assert national status by bidding for a more collective approach to imperial policy-making, became seriously disillusioned by the actual experience of working with the British during the war. They felt that the volume of dominion resources – men and materials – contributed to the war effort entitled them to a greater say in London in their usage, but they were discouraged by the partial attention they were granted. Neither the flows of intergovernmental information nor the consultative show of the Imperial War Conferences were adequate, and the Imperial War Cabinets were of little practical value when Lloyd George ran the war in largely presidential style. Indeed, the traditions of pre-war British policy-making were generally preserved. Dominion prime ministers learnt that even in war the Empire was the entity to which things happened rather than the co-operative venture to which at least some of them had aspired. Although constitutional relationships were not formally altered during the war, every opportunity was henceforth taken to assert dominion claims to higher status and greater autonomy. This was patently revealed at the conclusion of the war when the dominion prime ministers insisted on being present at the Versailles peace conference, on adding their signatures to the peace treaty, on placing their representatives in the consequent League of Nations, and on retaining their controls over the former German colonies they had conquered (under the thin disguise of League of Nations mandated territories). From the British perspective, these developments were giving a further spin to the Empire's centrifugal tendencies.[44]

There were other shifts too which by the end of the war blunted the optimism of imperial enthusiasts. The economic merits of grandiose empire development plans seemed more doubtful in Britain around the time of the armistice when financial costs and probable returns were further considered. The war was leaving British manufacturers keen to re-enter world and not just limited Empire markets. Financiers were likewise attracted by global opportunities. Above all, the Treasury, backed by taxpayers, was determined to cut public expenditure. In such a climate and subjected to such political pressure for 'a return to normalcy', the 'economics of siege' commitments were challenged from the end of 1918 by a revival of enthusiasm for deflation, lower

[44] Mansergh, *The Commonwealth Experience*, op. cit. (note 32), 170–80; Beloff, *Imperial Sunset*, op. cit. (note 8), 218–24; K. C. Wheare, 1967: The Empire and the peace treaties, 1918–21. In *CHBE*, 645–66; P. Wigley, 1977: *Canada and the Transition to Commonwealth: British–Canadian Relations 1917–1926*. Cambridge: Cambridge University Press, 20–95; R. C. Brown, 1970: Sir Robert Borden, the Great War and Anglo-Canadian Relations. In J. S. Moir (ed.), *Character and Circumstance*. Toronto: Macmillan, 201–24; G. L. Cook, 1971: Sir Robert Borden, Lloyd George and British military policy, 1917–1918. *Historical Journal* 14, 371–95; Macintyre, *The Oxford History of Australia 1901–42*, op. cit. (note 13), 178–82; Louis, *Great Britain and Germany's Lost Colonies*, op. cit. (note 23), 117–55.

taxes, limited public sector borrowing and free trade. The more ambitious war-induced schemes for tariff reform and for state-funded colonial develop-ment, assisted migration and imperial science collided with a remarkable resurgence of faith in pre-war orthodoxies.[45]

In sum, the war created an illusion of imperial unity and raised for the dura-tion high expectations of postwar imperial consolidation and development. But in reality waging war could not close pre-existing fault lines, reverse pre-war centrifugal trajectories or obscure Britain's need to sustain its interna-tional as well as imperial interests. Rather, divisions within Empire societies, which even before the war had a bearing on imperial loyalties, were exacer-bated by the conflict. The self-governing dominions especially had become still more conscious of their nationhood and assertive of their status and autonomy. The Imperial government may have steered the Empire to victory (with help from its allies and the Americans), but imperial rule and intra-imperial relations would evidently need renegotiation and further adaptation after the war.

The Empire after the War: Change and Continuity

Containing demands for change might seem to be no easy task. After all, the American president, Woodrow Wilson, had attempted to redefine the war as a crusade for democracy and national self-determination, and the Allies them-selves had adopted the destruction of the German, Austro-Hungarian and Turkish Empires as war aims. It might be difficult to confine such zeal to enemy empires, especially if the League of Nations, another Wilsonian ideal, was realised to trumpet the cause of nation states. It was just conceivable too that the professed anti-imperialism of the new Soviet Union might encourage dissidents within the dependent Empire to challenge British rule. Moreover, a Britain manifestly damaged by the economic and financial strains of war and by the physical casualties of battle might have lost both the capacity and the appetite for imperial grandeur. It was also unlikely that the nationalist aspira-tions nourished, if not created, by the war would diminish and allow British imperial presumption to go unchallenged.

It is true that in the Colonial Empire most demobilised soldiers and labour-ers were reintegrated quite easily into their communities – more experienced, sometimes wealthier, perhaps less overawed by white rulers. But their political contribution to subsequent nationalist movements appears to have been mod-est.[46] In East and West Africa, for example, the 1920s were characterised more by the laying down of infrastructures for permanent colonial rule than by com-bating colonial nationalism. However, the promised crisis in Egypt erupted in

---

[45] Constantine, *The making of British Colonial Development Policy*, op. cit. (note 31), 39–56. *See also* Chapter 3 of this book.

[46] To judge by the balance of the essays in *Journal of African History* 19 (1978) and Page, *Africa and the First World War*, op. cit. (note 33).

1919 and seriously threatened British security astride the key imperial route through the Middle East, while efforts to impose British rule in Palestine, Trans-Jordan and Iraq also proved unpopular. Arab nationalism had been harnessed during the war to assault the Turks, but it was a problem to contain it within the imperial system in the 1920s and 1930s.[47]

Political nationalism was also more assertive in postwar India. Nationalist leaders were not satisfied by the Government of India Act in 1919, which increased the political responsibilities of Indian ministers in provincial governments but only partially honoured Montagu's wartime declaration. Dominion status had been promised, and many aspired to full independence. Political dissent also drew upon much discontent with prices and living standards and also on the indignation raised by punitive actions against nationalist demonstrators (as at Amritsar in 1919, when 379 were killed and some 1200 wounded). Gandhi (not without setbacks) helped create and sustain into the 1940s a more geographically extensive, socially deep and religiously united nationalist movement, and a serious challenge to British authority.[48]

In response to Irish nationalism, Lloyd George's postwar Coalition Government was at least ready to introduce Home Rule, and this was eventually imposed on the Unionist majority in six counties of Ulster by the Government of Ireland Act in 1920. But most Irish nationalists demanded republican independence and had been waging war since January 1919 against British army garrisons and the Royal Irish Constabulary. It is true that in December 1921 Lloyd George persuaded most Irish leaders to make peace and accept a compromise that endowed Ireland (minus the six counties of Ulster) with the status and powers of a dominion within the Empire. But this settlement left unsatisfied those still insisting upon an independent republic. In the ensuing civil war of 1922–3, the Irish Free State Government successfully defended the treaty and the new constitution, but it remained electorally vulnerable to its republican opponents. One argument in favour of accepting the 1921 treaty was that dominion status was not constitutionally fixed and that demonstrably it had evolved and seemed capable of further evolution. Inevitably, then, not least to protect themselves from republican critics, Irish representatives of this new dominion aimed, especially at Imperial Conferences, to escape the remaining authority claimed by Britain over the dominions and to assert Ireland's independent international status.[49]

The Union of South Africa, containing a similar irreconcilable nationalist component, paralleled most closely Ireland's trajectory of change. Botha died in 1919, but his strategy and his problems were inherited by Smuts. His aim

[47] Kenneth Robinson, 1965: *The Dilemmas of Trusteeship*. London: Oxford University Press; Darwin, *Britain, Egypt and the Middle East*, op. cit. (note 33); Beloff, *Imperial Sunset*, op. cit. (note 8), 297–306; Keith Jeffery, 1984: *The British Army and the Crisis of Empire 1918–22*. Manchester: Manchester University Press, 110–54.

[48] Brown, *Modern India*, op. cit. (note 10), 196–276.

[49] Lyons, *Ireland*, op. cit. (note 16), 411–72, 495–7, 504–19; D. W. Harkness, 1969: *The Restless Dominion: The Irish Free State and the British Commonwealth of Nations 1921–31*. London: Macmillan; Mansergh, *The Commonwealth experience*, op. cit. (note 32), esp. 200–11.

was to renegotiate the relationship with the Imperial government so as to retain the perceived advantages of the imperial connection while gaining greater autonomy in the running of South Africa's internal and external affairs. This was needed, not least and as always, in order to fend off the more extreme Afrikaner nationalist challenge, and Smuts pressed hard for greater dominion autonomy at Imperial Conferences in 1921 and 1923. But he was still ousted from power by the National Party in the election of 1924. It therefore fell to Hertzog to represent South Africa at the next Imperial Conference in 1926. Postwar efforts to accommodate South Africa within the Empire became increasingly problematical.[50]

The First World War had also heightened awareness in Canada of the price in personal and material terms of the imperial connection. An instinct for political isolationism grew up in the 1920s, similar to the sentiment expressed simultaneously in the United States, which aimed to dissociate North America from any future British war in Europe. Moreover, the industrialisation accelerated by the war obliged national politicians to take still more account of Canada's mixed economy when defining and advancing national interests. Canadian ministers became yet more cautious in their response to schemes for imperial economic co-operation.[51] But the fundamental political problem of Canadian politicians had been left unchanged by the war, namely how to sustain the unity of a dominion composed of such huge and disparate provinces and containing a substantial community of French Canadians. True, resistance to the blandishments of the United States had traditionally been a helpful technique for generating national unity; but putting political space between Canada and Great Britain had also been an attractive option, particularly to Liberals. Mackenzie King restored his party's integrity, enhanced its electoral appeal to British and French Canadians and secured his personal popularity as prime minister by maintaining a balance, on the one hand professing a loyalty to the crown and to the principles of a British Empire, while on the other denouncing centralised imperial policy-making and claiming greater national autonomy for Canada.[52]

It is true that British ministers generally found the postwar governments of Australia and New Zealand less pressing for revision of the constitutional relationship between Britain and the dominions. At the Imperial Conferences of the 1920s they distrusted the Irish, South African and Canadian proposals as unnecessary legalisms and preferred a pragmatic realisation of dominion powers. But, as before the war, both countries tempered expressions of loyalty with a practical assertion of national self-interest whenever obliged to respond to

[50] Davenport, *South Africa*, op. cit. (note 21), 273–308; Katzenellenbogen, Southern Africa and the war, op. cit. (note 33), 112–13.
[51] Ian M. Drummond, 1974: *Imperial Economic Policy 1917–1939*. London: Allen & Unwin, esp. 219–89; Stephen Constantine, 1993: Anglo-Canadian relations, the Empire Marketing Board and Canadian national autonomy between the wars. *JICH* 21, 357–84.
[52] Wigley, *Canada and the Transition to Commonwealth*, op. cit. (note 44), 96–281; Bothwell *et al.*, *Canada 1900–45*, op. cit. (note 29), 199–244.

imperial initiatives or anxious to promote their own perceived national needs. For example, even a publicly committed Empire loyalist like Massey kept New Zealand's labour needs uppermost in responding to Britain's postwar assisted emigration schemes.[53] Moreover, at a popular level, recollections of the war served to enhance national pride in both these dominions. While for some the war might remain a satisfying demonstration of their supranational loyalty to crown and Empire, probably for most people in Australia and New Zealand in the 1920s and 1930s the annual Anzac Day ceremonies, the erection of war memorials in virtually all settlements, the lobbying by the various associations of ex-servicemen, the official dominion histories of the war, and perhaps above all the memories of combatants and their families largely sustained national rather than imperial mythologies.[54]

The First World War had therefore affected this variegated Empire to different degrees. There were, however, immediate postwar crises in Egypt, India and Ireland, difficulties in the Middle East and a more demanding nationalism in the self-governing dominions. It is true that these aspirations were largely derived from pre-war circumstances, though possibly enhanced and extended by the experience of imperial war. But by either assessment it did not follow that the British government or the British people would merely abandon their imperial traditions and jettison imperial interests. The entire history of the British Empire had been measured by adaptation to challenge as well as by response to opportunity. There was no reason for policy-makers or public to assume that the Empire had lost its value or that the options for adaptation and response had run out.

Certainly, it would be incorrect to assume that the trauma of war had somehow expunged from the British people a commitment to Empire and ushered in strong waves of anti-imperialism. Critics of Empire remained few in number, even in the Labour movement, and more intent on the reform of Empire than its urgent destruction.[55] Indeed, in the postwar years, imperial ideals probably achieved a deeper cultural penetration of British society than ever before. Victory in the war was often interpreted as an achievement of Empire. Moreover, the legitimacy of Empire was reformulated, to enhance its status as a force for international peace, to proclaim its virtues as a Commonwealth of kith and kin, to legitimise its rule as a preparation for eventual Indian self-government, or to uphold the principles of protective trusteeship and good

[53] Mansergh, *The Commonwealth Experience*, op. cit. (note 32), 212–42; Ian M. Drummond, 1972: *British Economic Policy and the Empire 1919–1939*. London: Allen & Unwin, 36–88; Macintyre, *The Oxford History of Australia 1901–42*, op. cit. (note 13), 203–6; R. M. Burdon, 1965: *The New Dominion: a Social and Political History of New Zealand 1918–39*. Wellington: Reed, 183–9; Stephen Constantine, 1990: Immigration and the making of New Zealand 1919–39. In Constantine, *Emigrants and Empire: British Settlement in the Dominions between the Wars*. op. cit. (note 31), 135–8.

[54] Inglis, The Anzac tradition, op. cit. (note 43); K. S. Inglis, 1985: A sacred place: the making of the Australian war memorial. *War and Society* 3, 99–126; Sharpe, Anzac day, op. cit. (note 41).

[55] Stephen Howe, 1993: *Anticolonialism in British Politics: The Left and the End of Empire 1918–1964*. Oxford: Oxford University Press, 27–81; Partha Sarathi Gupta, 1975: *Imperialism and the British Labour Movement 1914–1964*. London: Macmillan, 1–274.

government (instead of self-government) over 'backward' colonial peoples. Such messages, necessarily as varied as the Empire itself, were relayed on to the general public officially and unofficially via school textbooks and school lessons, through newspapers and magazines, over the radio and in film, by the British Empire Exhibitions and the Empire Marketing Board. Britain's great-power status and moral standing were still derived, it seemed, from being the centre of a benign and beneficent Empire-Commonwealth whose focal point remained loyalty to the British king-emperor.[56]

Moreover, the economic value of the formal Empire to Britain increased in the 1920s and 1930s. True, British business, like British ministers, remained keen after the war on the restoration of European markets and of zones of informal empire in South America and the Far East.[57] It was also true that British exporters of manufactured goods had to cope with fresh tariff barriers erected within the Empire, including hurdles put up by India as well as by the dominions.[58] Nevertheless, the prospects for British commerce appeared greater inside many Empire markets than outside when overseas trade slumped late in 1920 and persistently high levels of domestic unemployment set in. In response, during the 1920s and 1930s, far more than before or during the war, the Imperial government promoted Empire economic development and closer imperial economic ties. Funds were found for assisting emigration to Empire destinations, for capital projects in the colonies and for scientific research to help Empire production. Faltering steps towards preferential tariff arrangements with the dominions were also taken, coming to a conclusion at the Imperial Economic Conference at Ottawa in 1932. Such official initiatives hardly suggest a Britain detached from its Empire by the war. Nor do the statistics, which show British trade with Empire partners rising as a percentage of total external commerce.[59]

Britain's commitment to the military defence of the Empire also revived

[56] John M. MacKenzie, 1984: *Propaganda and Empire: The Manipulation of British Public Opinion 1880–1960*. Manchester: Manchester University Press; John M. MacKenzie (ed.), 1986: *Imperialism and Popular Culture*. Manchester: Manchester University Press, especially essays by Richards, MacKenzie and Constantine; Stephen Constantine, 1986: *Buy and Build: The Advertising Posters of the Empire Marketing Board*. London: HMSO.

[57] P. J. Cain and A. G. Hopkins, 1993: *British Imperialism: Crisis and Deconstruction 1914–1990*. London: Longman, esp. 146–70, 235–62.

[58] The Indian government faced a financial crisis after the war and in response in 1919 the Imperial government conceded fiscal autonomy. Tariffs were imposed even on British imports, partly to protect local industries, largely to raise government revenues: *see* especially B. R. Tomlinson, 1975: India and the British Empire, 1880–1935. *Indian Economic and Social History Review* 12, 337–80, and Drummond, *British Economic Policy and the Empire*, op. cit. (note 53), 121–40.

[59] Drummond, *British Economic Policy and the Empire*, op. cit. (note 53); Constantine: *Emigrants and Empire: British Settlement in the Dominions between the Wars*, op. cit. (note 31); Constantine, *The Making of British Colonial Development Policy*, op. cit. (note 31); Basudev Chatterji, 1992: *Trade, Tariffs and Empire: Lancashire and British Policy in India 1919–1939*. Delhi: Oxford University Press; Havinden and Meredith, *Colonialism and Development*, op. cit. (note 6), 115–205.

after the war. Indeed, those withdrawals from the wider world which had alarmed the dominions in the run-up to war in Europe were substantially reversed. Following the destruction of Germany's North Sea battle fleet, the Royal Navy resumed its global imperial role. Overseas bases were restocked, and the commitment to expand facilities at Singapore realised bit by bit. These naval priorities ensured that Japan became the Imperial government's principal naval concern, a challenge, self-evidently, not to national security as Germany had been in 1914 but to imperial frontiers and sea routes. Similarly, after the war, the Army got back to 'real soldiering'. Its forces, though scaled down, were redeployed to old imperial bases in India and Egypt and to new ones in Palestine and Iraq. As for the Royal Air Force, it preserved its independence, its aircrews and its aircraft by adopting with some success the role of imperial police force in trouble spots in Somaliland, the Middle East and northern India. There was, it is true, a sense of overstretch in the immediate postwar world, and imperial defence became increasingly problematical in the later 1930s. But while the game became harder to play and to win, there is no sign that the First World War had induced an unwillingness to compete.[60]

What was certainly required in addition was a strategy of political concession to preserve as much as possible of the content of control, perhaps at the expense of form. So, for example, the dissent engendered by Britain's formal protectorate over Egypt was largely contained by its official termination in 1922. Britain relied instead upon the ostensibly independent yet in practice generally compliant King Fu'ad, who was charged with keeping his dissatisfied nationalist subjects in order. This arrangement reserved to Britain the use of military bases, confirmed by a treaty in 1936. Likewise, in the face of Arab nationalism, Britain abandoned most of its formal rule over Iraq in 1922, but secured the use of military bases plus commercial access to Middle Eastern oil. This arrangement was preserved even after Britain's mandate was formally ended in 1932. Indian aspirations for independence were similarly contained within the Raj for another generation, not least by allowing Indians a limited share of power under the Government of India Act of 1919 and by its more radical extension in 1935. And in much the same way and for similar duration, Ireland was contained within the Empire by the enforced compromise of the 1921 treaty and by a more grudging tolerance of Ireland's revised constitution of 1937.

The British desire to conserve by concession was also more generally apparent in official responses to dominion (including Irish) demands for greater autonomy. Once the dominions had secured their own representatives at the Versailles peace conference and their own seats at the subsequent League of Nations, it was obvious that their changed constitutional relationship with the

[60] Anthony Clayton, 1986: *The British Empire as a Superpower 1919–39*. London: Macmillan; David E. Omissi, 1990: *Air Power and Colonial Control: The Royal Air Force, 1919–1939*. Manchester: Manchester University Press; Jeffery, *The British Army and the Crisis of Empire*, op. cit. (note 47). *See also* Chapter 8 of this book.

Imperial government would have to be formally recognised. This was the burden of postwar Imperial Conferences and especially that of 1926, when the self-governing portions of the Empire, including the United Kingdom, were redefined: they were 'autonomous communities within the British Empire, equal in status, in no way subordinate one to another in any aspect of their domestic or external affairs, though united by a common allegiance to the Crown, and freely associated as members of the British Commonwealth of Nations.'

This was the concept subsequently embodied by the British Government in the Statute of Westminster in 1931. The dominions acquired control at last over their own foreign policies, including therefore the right to decide in future whether or not to go to war. Yet such a redefinition and such concessions largely recognised the realities of British–dominion relations as they had been evolving even before the war. Moreover, as British ministers intended, the new egalitarian relationship was compatible with dominion consultation on imperial defence and economic issues and dominion participation in a variety of imperial scientific and cultural organisations. This preserved for Britain the concept and many of the rewards of Empire–Commonwealth unity. Concessions also conserved residual loyalties to the monarchy and indeed to Britain in a manner which an authoritarian assertion of power would have destroyed.[61]

Furthermore, postwar Imperial governments preserved Britain's imperial interests without sacrificing the tradition of independent British decision-making. Contrary to some dominion and especially Canadian suspicions, there was no more desire in Britain after the war than there had been before it to introduce collective imperial policy-making. Imperial Conferences, imperial committees and High Commissioners were there for consultation, but no attempts were made to transform their meetings into imperial councils whose recommendations would be automatically binding on all participants, not least on Britain. Circumstances surrounding, for example, the Chanak crisis of 1922, the Treaty of Locarno in 1925 and the Polish guarantee of 1939 all show that British prime ministers from Lloyd George to Neville Chamberlain continued to make critical decisions with often limited regard for the dominions.[62]

Finally, whatever stimulus the First World War may have given to nationalist movements in the Empire, the postwar world exposed their limitations. Crucially, the imperial authorities retained their powers of patronage and influence, including the opportunities to negotiate and distribute to subordinate clients such rewards as economic opportunity, social prestige and local

[61] John Darwin, 1980: Imperialism in decline? Tendencies in British imperial policy between the wars. *Historical Journal* 23, 657–79; Max Beloff, 1989: *Dream of Commonwealth 1921–42*. London: Macmillan; Mansergh, *The Commonwealth Experience*, op. cit. (note 32), 212–42.

[62] Wigley, *Canada and the Transition to Commonwealth*, op. cit. (note 44); D. C. Watt, 1965: *Personalities and Policies*. London: Longman, 139–74; Mansergh, *The Commonwealth Experience*, op. cit. (note 32), 269–94; Beloff, *Dream of Commonwealth*, op. cit. (note 61), 270–306; Ritchie Ovendale, 1975: *'Appeasement' and the English Speaking World*. Cardiff: University of Wales Press; R. F. Holland, 1981: *Britain and the Commonwealth Alliance 1918–1939*. London: Macmillan.

power. Rarely in the dependencies and not even in India did British rulers after the war fail to find favours to grant or clients to recruit.

Moreover, this was manifestly true even in Britain's relations with the dominions. Nationalist extremists (some French Canadians, some Afrikaners, some Irish republicans) might aspire to complete independence. But for the most part even vigorous pretenders to dominion autonomy opted to retain a place within the Empire-Commonwealth, not least for what Britain provided. Great Britain, after all, still accepted principal responsibility for imperial defence, and Australia and New Zealand, after the war as before, were nervous of Japan and relied largely on the Royal Navy. Economically, too, even the mixed and more mature economies of the dominions continued to need Britain. Canada might draw more upon the dollars of its neighbour but still relied upon Britain for most of its postwar migrants, some of its capital, large proportions of its imports and many consumers of its primary products. To different degrees this was true also of South Africa, Australia and especially of New Zealand, and nor could the Irish Free State be indifferent to the huge British market for foodstuffs on its doorstep. The First World War may have damaged Britain's international standing as an economic power and as a source of finance, as was shown in Chapter 10, but most countries of the British Empire, including the dominions, still found themselves relatively privileged in the British market and consequently unwilling or even unable to abandon the ties of self-interest as well as sentiment that had been so sedulously threaded before 1914.

Conclusions

It seems then that changes did occur within some Empire countries during and even as a result of the First World War and that relations between Britain and the Empire were affected. But nevertheless continuities predominated. True, the war had accelerated the drive towards Irish independence and dominion autonomy, but essentially the shifts were on lines entirely predictable from pre-war trajectories. Moreover, those changes were still contained within an imperial structure on the whole bound by common values and mutual economic and political self-interest. Likewise, the war may have had stimulating effects upon the political aspirations of subject peoples in India, but the direction of change followed pre-war signposts and the pace of change remained under constraint. As yet, too, the vast terrain of Britain's Colonial Empire seemed in general untroubled politically by the experience of global war, and its long-term future was still expected to lie within an ostensibly benign imperial system. And neither the impact of the war on Britain nor its effects upon the British Empire disabused the British people of their imperial mythologies and instincts.

The limited degree of change effected by the First World War was perhaps signified when in September 1939 another British king and emperor, George

VI, again declared war on Germany. Once more he did so on behalf of the United Kingdom and also of his global possessions. These still included the colonies and protectorates, from where once again resources were extracted to fight another world war, and also India, where nationalist protests were again, albeit temporarily, ignored. True, the dominions this time exercised their newly obtained powers of autonomous review and made their own decisions about peace or war. But only Ireland opted for neutrality. Within a week of King George's declaration, South Africa, Australia, New Zealand and Canada had joined Britain in what was again to be an imperial as well as a European war.[63]

---

[63] John W. Wheeler-Bennett, 1958: *King George VI*. London: Macmillan, 404–14.

Index